Ancient China

Ancient China: A History surveys the East Asian Heartland Region—the geographical area that eventually became known as China—from the Neolithic period through the Bronze Age, to the early imperial era of Qin and Han, up to the threshold of the medieval period in the third century CE. For most of that long span of time there was no such place as "China"; the vast and varied territory of the Heartland Region was home to many diverse cultures that only slowly coalesced, culturally, linguistically, and politically, to form the first recognizably Chinese empires.

The field of Early China Studies is being revolutionized in our time by a wealth of archaeologically recovered texts and artefacts. Major and Cook draw on this exciting new evidence and a rich harvest of contemporary scholarship to present a leading-edge account of ancient China and its antecedents.

With handy pedagogical features such as maps and illustrations, as well as an extensive list of recommendations for further reading, *Ancient China: A History* is an important resource for undergraduate and postgraduate courses on Chinese History, and those studying Chinese Culture and Society more generally.

John S. Major taught East Asian History at Dartmouth College, US, from 1971 to 1984. Thereafter he has been an independent scholar based in New York City, US.

Constance A. Cook is Professor of Modern Languages and Literature at Lehigh University, US.

Ancient China
A history

John S. Major and Constance A. Cook

An East Gate Book

Routledge
Taylor & Francis Group

NEW YORK AND LONDON

First published 2017
by Routledge
2 Park Square, Milton Park, Abingdon, Oxon OX14 4RN

and by Routledge
711 Third Avenue, New York, NY 10017

Routledge is an imprint of the Taylor & Francis Group, an informa business

© 2017 John S. Major and Constance A. Cook

British Library Cataloguing in Publication Data
A catalogue record for this book is available from the British Library

Library of Congress Cataloging in Publication Data
A catalog record for this book has been requested

ISBN: 978-0-7656-1599-2 (hbk)
ISBN: 978-0-7656-1600-5 (pbk)
ISBN: 978-1-315-71532-2 (ebk)

Typeset in Times New Roman
by Sunrise Setting Ltd, Brixham, UK

Contents

Figures

Maps

Tables

Illustration credits

8.8   *Chu wenwu zhanlan tulu* (Beijing: Wenwu Press, 1954)
8.9   *Suixian Zeng Hou Yi mu* (Beijing: Wenwu Press, 1980)
9.1   JSM photo
9.2   CAC photo
10.1 *Jiangling Mashan yihao Chu mu* (Beijing: Wenwu Press, 1985)
10.2 *Changsha Mawangdui yihao Han mu* (Beijing: Wenwu Press, 1973)
10.3 *Zhongguo gudai tianwen wenwu tuji* (Beijing: Wenwu Press, 1980)
10.4 *Historical Relics Unearthed in New China* (Beijing: Foreign Languages Press, 1973
10.5 *Historical Relics Unearthed in New China* (Beijing: Foreign Languages Press, 1973)
10.6 Drawing by Sandra Smith-Garcès © JSM
11.1 Courtesy of the American Numismatic Society
11.2 *Wenhua da geming qijian chutu wenwu* (Beijing: Wenwu Press, 1972)
11.3 Courtesy of the Museum of Far Eastern Antiquities, Stockholm
12.1 *Hebei bowuguan* (Beijing: Wenwu Press, 1983)
12.2 *Wenhua da geming qijian chutu wenwu* (Beijing: Wenwu Press, 1972)
12.3 *Yinan gu huaxiang shimu fajue baogao* (Beijing: Wenwu Press, 1956)
12.4 JSM photo of original rubbing in private collection
12.5 *Zhongguo shiku: Yongjing Binglingsi* (Beijing: Wenwu Press, 1989)

All maps by Ji'en Zhang, with data from China Historical Geographic Information Service (CHGIS), Center for Geographic Analysis, 1737 Cambridge Street, Cambridge, Massachusetts 02138.

The quotation in Chapter 6 from Bernard Karlgren, *The Book of Documents* (*Bulletin of the Museum of Far Eastern Antiquities* 22; Stockholm, 1950), pp. 55–6 (modified JSM), is used courtesy of the Museum of Far Eastern Antiquities, Stockholm.

About the authors

John S. Major taught East Asian history at Dartmouth College from 1971 to 1984. Thereafter he has been an independent scholar based in New York City. An authority on the intellectual history of the Han dynasty, he is the co-translator (with Sarah A. Queen, Andrew Seth Meyer, and Harold D. Roth) of *The Huainanzi* (2010), co-translator (with Sarah A. Queen) of the *Chunqiu fanlu* (*Luxuriant Gems of the Spring and Autumn*), and co-author and co-editor, with Constance A. Cook, of *Defining Chu: Image and Reality in Ancient China* (1999). In addition to his scholarly works on early China, he has published widely in other fields, including books for young readers, local and family history, and the pleasures of reading.

Constance A. Cook is Professor of Modern Languages and Literature at Lehigh University. She specializes in the study of excavated texts from ancient China. She is co-author and co-editor, with John S. Major, of *Defining Chu: Image and Reality in Ancient China* (1999), author of *Death in Ancient China: The Tale of One Man's Journey* (2006), and author of *Ancestors, Kings, and the Dao* (2017). In these and other publications she focuses on the examination of excavated texts in the context of material culture and what they can tell us about belief systems and local social practices.

1 Introduction to Ancient China

Introduction

There was no such place as China for most of the time period covered by this book. Long before China arose as a concept, a place-name, and a political reality, a variety of cultures, polities, and states occupied parts of the physical landscape that we now know as China (Map 1.1). Some of the first manifestations of such cultures could be called "proto-Chinese" or "Sinitic"—that is, showing characteristics that would later be identified with China—while others clearly stood apart from the Chinese ethno-cultural world. The name China itself apparently comes from the state of Qin (pronounced "chin"), which in 221 BCE completed the forcible unification of the various states that occupied the Yellow River Plain and the Yangzi River Valley, imposed central rule upon them, and created the first authentic imperial Chinese state. But a succession of proto-states and kingdoms had existed in parts of that territory for some 2,000 years before "Qin" gave rise to "China," and Neolithic cultures had existed there for thousands of years earlier. Indeed, human existence in various places in East Asia can be documented back over 50,000 years. How, then, is one to refer to China before "China"? And why does it matter?

It matters because the use of such terms as "North China" for the territory of the Shang kingdom (c. 1555–1046 BCE), or "Far Western China" for the Tarim Basin (the home of what seems to have been the easternmost outpost of the ancient people who would later be known as the Celts), tends to homogenize ancient history and obscure the diversity of the ancient East Asian world. It falsely suggests the existence of "China" as a political entity in very ancient times. And it obscures the reality that what is known as Chinese culture today has diverse regional and cultural roots.

Ancient China, as historians commonly use that term, refers to the period from the beginning of the Neolithic era, about 10,000 years ago, to the fall of the Eastern Han dynasty in 220 CE. "Early China," in common usage, is a more restrictive term, used for the period from the Early Bronze Age to the end of the Eastern Han. The Three Kingdoms Period, 220–265 CE, marks the transition from Early China to Medieval China. In this book, we will generally avoid using the word China to refer to the period before 221 BCE. Instead we will refer to sociopolitical entities as they existed at any given time (for example, "the Shang kingdom" or "the state of Lu"), and locate them by using terms that refer to specific geographical features ("the Yellow River Plain," "the South-Central Coastal Region") rather than by such terms as "east-central China" or "the North China Plain." Fortunately many Chinese place-names are geographically specific (such as the province names Shandong, "east of the mountain," and Hunan, "south of the lake"), allowing us to use them freely within our frame of reference.

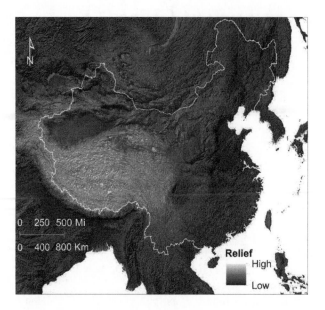

Map 1.1 Relief map of East Asia, with the present borders of China. Political boundaries change drastically over time; physical features are relatively much more stable.

Our basic focal area will be the East Asian Heartland Region and, surrounding it, the Extended East Asian Heartland Region. The first refers to the grain-growing regions roughly comprising the basins of the eastward-flowing Yellow and Yangzi River Valleys and the Sichuan Basin. The second, the Extended Heartland, encompasses the forests, grasslands, arid lands, mountains, high plateaus, and subtropical jungles that surround the Heartland Region. We will define these terms more precisely in Chapter 2; here we simply posit them as the landscape within which, over a long period of time, Sinitic culture and the Chinese nation gradually came into being.

Diversity and continuity in ancient China

To study the history of early China requires constantly navigating a course between two poles: change within continuity and continuity within change. In the long history of human societies in the East Asian Heartland we find both important structural commonalities and a wide range of cultural responses to widely differing environmental circumstances. Neolithic cultures worldwide are in some senses similar in their general characteristics (agriculture, villages, ceramics, stone tools), but highly diverse in the specific manifestations of those characteristics. The cultures of the Yellow River Plain, the Yangzi River Valley, and the south-eastern coast, to name just three key regions, exhibit differences even today; the roots of those differences are unmistakably visible in the archaeological record over a period of 8,000 years or more and clearly reflect different ecologies and agricultural economies. For example, the people in the Yangzi River Valley mainly grew rice, while those in the Wei River Valley and the Yellow River Plain, to the north, grew several varieties of millet as well as barley and wheat. Coastal peoples in the south consumed large amounts of seafood and had access to abundant fruits and vegetables, both cultivated and gathered in the wild. Within some cultures hunting evolved from a daily pursuit to an elaborate and ceremonial elite activity, while elsewhere small populations of hunting and gathering tribal peoples continued to exist well into the era of dynastic states and great cities. Even when, over a period of many centuries, some northern and southern cultures in the two great river valleys began to amalgamate and coalesce into the root culture we call Chinese, many areas, large and small, remained unassimilated. During China's first imperial period, the Qin–Han era lasting from 221 BCE to 220 CE, the empire struggled to define its relationship with the many non-Sinitic peoples within and along its borders. Substantial populations of ethnically non-Chinese people remain in the southern, western, and northern highlands to this day. In the early twenty-first century at least fifty-five languages are still spoken within the borders of the People's Republic of China. It is reasonable to assume that in ancient times there was far greater ethnolinguistic diversity within the Heartland Region.

On the other hand it is equally true that a strong thread of cultural continuity runs though the Heartland Region's tangle of cultural diversity. To that extent the oft-repeated claim that China has "the world's oldest continuous civilization" can be taken as valid. The mask-like décor found on jade ritual objects of the Liangzhu Culture that flourished in the Yangzi River delta in the late fourth and early- to mid-third millennia BCE are clearly ancestral (with several intermediate steps) to the mask-like décor of bronze ritual objects of the Shang dynasty, 2,000 years later. Many shapes of ceramic vessels of the late Longshan Culture (c. 2600–2000 BCE) were directly copied in bronze during the Early Bronze Age Erlitou Culture and the subsequent Shang dynasty. Neolithic cultures in many parts of the Heartland, and their Jade Age and Bronze Age successors, exhibit a shared enthusiasm for the building of pounded-earth walls (village walls, city walls, eventually state-boundary walls), as well as a post-and-beam architectural style for large buildings, usually sited on pounded-earth platforms. The earliest known written language in the East Asian Heartland, found on animal bones and turtle shells used for divination during the late Shang Period, is unmistakably an early form of Chinese, and the subsequent written record shows the inexorable spread of Chinese as the region's common language, leaving other languages to survive only in scattered pockets. Many other examples of long-term continuity will be adduced in this book's pages, and because of that continuity we will often write in terms of "proto-Sinitic," "Sinitic," and (from the Qin–Han period onwards), "Chinese" culture.

Nevertheless, to say that there were fundamental continuities in the ancient East Asian Heartland is not to say that the region's societies, whether in the emerging mainstream of Sinitic culture or on its fringes, remained static throughout time. Societies may change in response to internal evolutionary developments or external pressures, or both. They might even be swept away and replaced. For example, the Liangzhu Culture (c. 3200–2300 BCE) seems to have simply disappeared (possibly as result of a period of persistent flooding in the Liangzhu homeland in the Yangzi delta). Some attributes of Liangzhu Culture reappear in the Longshan Culture, which arose in western Shandong c. 2600 BCE and gradually spread widely across the Yellow River Plain; were those cultural attributes introduced by Liangzhu refugees who moved northward into Longshan territory? Or were they simply the result of long-term cultural contact? Did Longshan overlords conquer what remained of Liangzhu near the end of its cultural existence? And, in turn, did the final stage of the Longshan Culture lead directly into the beginning of the East Asian Bronze Age? Clear answers await further archaeological work.

New archaeological discoveries and new studies continue to redefine drastically our understanding of the cultural diversity of the ancient Heartland Region, and of the evolution there of political powers and of competing civilizations. It has revealed many early complex societies that were not recorded in the traditional histories but which must be taken into account to achieve a full and reliable picture of how China became China.

Eras, cultures, nations, states, and dynasties

Chinese history is conventionally divided into "dynasties," defined as rule over all, or at least a substantial portion, of China's territory from a politically symbolic center by a single lineage of kings or emperors over time. Thus it is commonplace to speak of the Han dynasty, the Tang dynasty, the Ming dynasty, and so forth, and these terms are both familiar and well understood. For the ancient period, however, the concept of a "dynasty" is much less clear, and the old convention of referring to early Chinese history as a sequence of dynasties (the Xia, Shang, and Zhou) tends to imply a much greater degree of territorial control and political centralization than appears in fact to have been the case. It is important, therefore, to be clear about the various kinds of social and political entities that existed in the Heartland Region, and the terms used to describe them, over time.

"Era" and "age" are usefully flexible terms that usually denote fairly long expanses of time, often distinguished by major political change or by technological advances. Often the two go hand-in-hand. For example, the "Bronze Age" applies to a time when a great deal of social energy was devoted to the production of metal artifacts, mostly of bronze. In the East Asian Heartland the Bronze Age began some 4,000 years ago (though pre-metallurgical working of native copper was found many centuries before that in several Heartland Neolithic cultures), coinciding with the development of early proto-states and states. The Bronze Age continued through the Shang and Zhou Periods. It began to wane during the Warring States Period (481–221 BCE) when other materials, especially iron, eclipsed the importance of bronze; it ended with the advent of China's imperial era: that is, with the Qin and Han dynasties. (Of course, the production of bronze artifacts continued during the imperial era, but bronze had ceased by then to be the defining characteristic of the age.)

The Bronze Age itself grew out of the "stone" or "lithic" eras. The Paleolithic era was the "old stone" age, during which a fairly limited range of tools and weapons made of chipped stone were used in hunting and gathering. The Neolithic era was the "new stone" age, in which stone tools were more finely crafted and diverse in form and function, and were employed in hunting, agriculture, warfare, and as decorative or religious artifacts. The final phase of the Neolithic era in the East Asian Heartland is often known as the Jade Age, because cultures in several parts of the Heartland devoted significant human and material resources to the production of precisely crafted objects of jade, objects that seem to have served symbolic (as opposed to utilitarian) purposes.

Artifacts, whether of stone, jade, bronze, ceramic, or other materials, are sometimes recovered from ancient sites by archaeologists, who assign them to cultures on the basis of analytical investigations of their characteristics. "Culture" in this sense refers to a complex of characteristics including livelihood, settlement patterns, a suite of material objects of distinctive shape and ornamentation, and (to the extent that these things can be known), language, beliefs, and traditions. Cultures can, but do not always, evolve through stages of complexity and can, under some circumstances, give rise to civilizations (complex urban cultures) and to nations and states. We follow the common practice of anthropologists in describing four cultural steps toward civilization:

1   Simple villages, engaging in agricultural production and simple craft production, with little differentiation of social status and craft specialization, little organized warfare, little external trade, and limited contact with neighboring villages.

2   Simple chieftainships, a network of one or more towns with surrounding villages, engaged in agricultural production and some specialized craft production, with some distinctions of social rank and occupational specialization. Rudimentary government is led by non-hereditary chiefs, often claiming special military or religious authority, with the consent of a council of elders or some similar social organ. There is some organized warfare, wall-building for military defense, and some long-distance trade.

3   Complex chieftainships (nations or proto-states), encompassing a city and, often, its associated ceremonial center, several towns, and numerous villages. Agricultural production may include extensive irrigation works. Agricultural producers owe a portion of their crops to members of the ruling elite. Craft production is highly specialized. Rule, sometimes informally hereditary for several generations in succession, is monopolized by a military elite with the support of a religious elite. Warfare is common; defensive walls are massive. Residential and ceremonial buildings used by elites are large and elaborate. Ceremonials, including elite funerals, involve rare and expensive materials such as jade and metal. Trade is active and can include both specialized craft products and important raw materials. Complex chieftainships sometimes constitute nations, meaning a group of people (often united by common language, shared beliefs and traditions including supposed common descent from a founding ancestor, shared material culture, and territorial contiguity) who are conscious of themselves as a people distinct from others.

4   Highly stratified societies (civilizations, states), controlling an extensive territory with a capital city, other cities sited for strategic, ritual, or economic reasons, and numerous towns and villages. Society is complex and highly stratified, with social ranks ranging from a royal family through aristocrats, priests, craft specialists, traders, farmers, and slaves, among others. There is frequent, large-scale offensive and defensive warfare, including military action to take and hold territory. A wide range of finely produced goods is available for elite use; there is highly developed craft specialization and extensive external trade. Agricultural production is controlled by elites, and agricultural workers are in effect serfs. Rule is likely to be hereditary within a royal clan, and the term "dynasty" begins to be appropriate as a description of the political regime. A system of writing is adopted or invented.

In this book we will encounter cultures of all four stages in various parts of the East Asian Heartland Region.

Dynastic rule in the ancient East Asian Heartland Region

The mass production of bronze vessels and weapons occurred at the same time as nations or proto-states evolved into full-fledged states in the central Yellow River Valley during the late third and early second millennia BCE. According to traditional histories handed down through time for over 2,000 years, these polities were the states of Xia, Shang, and Zhou. They were ruled by "kings" (*wang*) who followed one another in orderly dynastic succession, frequently father-to-son but sometimes also brother-to-brother or uncle-to-nephew. These states, then, are known as dynasties for their characteristic system of hereditary monarchy within a single royal house or clan. Sometimes the Xia, Shang, and Zhou are referred to both in early texts and in modern historical writing as the "Three Dynasties" to reflect the idea of a continuous "Chinese" civilization and to emphasize the centrality and dominance of the Xia, Shang, and Zhou kingdoms within the East Asian Heartland Region. But the old idea of the Three Dynasties as isolated beacons of civilization surrounded by the territories of uncouth "barbarians" has been drastically revised by modern historical and archaeological studies, and the concept of a dynasty itself requires some qualification with respect to the Xia, Shang, and Zhou. Some scholars are reluctant (because of the absence of definitive evidence) to accept the existence of a Xia dynasty at all. The Shang dynasty undoubtedly did exist, but the extent of its territorial control is still unclear, as is the nature of its relations with its neighbors. And it is open to question whether the Zhou dynasty (conventionally dated 1045–256 BCE) can be said to have continued to exist in any meaningful way during the Spring and Autumn (722–479) and Warring States (479–221) Periods, when China became divided into a large number of quasi-independent states that at best acknowledged only the symbolic and ritual or religious authority of the Zhou kings.

The history of the state of Qin illustrates both the complexities of state formation in early China and why the term "dynasty" is problematical for the Zhou era. The Zhou kings, having replaced the Shang dynasty, established direct rule over a large territory and also extended their authority by establishing a number of aristocratic states that owed ritual fealty and military service to them. The Qin people, perhaps descendants of Qiang sheep-herding nomads (identified by some historians as "proto-Tibetan") of the arid northwest, had organized themselves into a state within this Zhou multi-state system. This new state of Qin lay to the northwest of the Zhou royal domain in the Wei River Valley, an area that had served as the core region of the early Zhou rulers since the eleventh century BCE. Accepted as one of the many states allied with the Zhou through networks of kinship and aristocratic obligations, the Qin then began to assimilate the Zhou-style agricultural way of life, adapting to (and contributing to) Zhou-style methods of territorial administration.

In the eighth century BCE the Qin state expanded into the Wei River Valley, which had lately been overrun by another northern nomadic group, the Rong. This Rong invasion forced the Zhou kings to move their capital eastward to the Yellow River Plain in 771 BCE. In the Wei River Valley, meanwhile, the expanding Qin state evicted the Rong and reclaimed for themselves the area "within the passes" (just west of the bend in the Yellow River Valley where, after flowing southward through the Loess Highlands, it encounters the Qinling Mountains and turns east). There, making the most of the region's important geopolitical advantages, they established a thoroughly Sinitic capital city. The Qin rulers then pursued a policy of expansion eastward and southward from their Wei River Valley stronghold, in the process becoming one of the most powerful of all the Zhou-era states, while the royal Zhou domain itself diminished to relative insignificance. At this point, the notion of a Zhou "dynasty" becomes problematical.

Eventually Qin came to dominate the entire East Asian Heartland in the late third century BCE, when they established China's first, short-lived, imperial state (221–206 BCE). To emphasize the importance of their unification of the Heartland Region, they discarded the ancient term for the supreme ruler, *wang* (conventionally translated as "king"), and coined a new term, *Huangdi* ("emperor," literally "brilliant lord"), a term that was adopted by all succeeding rulers until the system of imperial dynasties itself collapsed in 1911 CE.

The Qin rulers were able to unite China but did not succeed in establishing a durable dynasty. When the Qin imperial venture collapsed, however, the powerful Western (or Former) Han dynasty (206 BCE–7 CE) that followed built on the Qin model of dynastic rule and even established its imperial capital in the same place. The founders of the Han dynasty had more in common culturally with Yangzi Valley peoples than with the Qin northwesterners, yet the Han too occupied the old Zhou/Qin capital "within the passes" for strategic reasons. Long after the fall of the Han, the capital of China would return again and again to the same location at Chang'an, in the Wei River Valley, for another 1,000 years (through the Tang dynasty, 618–907 CE). The continuity is evident; perhaps less so, but no less important, was the change. During the 2,000 years spanning the fully developed Sinitic culture of the Zhou, the robust Chinese culture of the Han, and the cosmopolitan empire of the Tang there were enormous changes in land tenure, government administration, military technology and the conduct of warfare, intellectual life, and religious belief and practices; yet all of those changes took place in the context of a unifying cultural trajectory.

Two historical myths: "isolated China" and "unchanging China"

The myth of "isolated China," found in book after book in Europe and America throughout the nineteenth and well into the twentieth century, drew some support from the fact that, for the last few centuries of the imperial era (c. 1450–1900 CE), China's rulers were conspicuously uncurious about, and uninterested in engaging with, the world beyond China's immediate neighborhood. But even a small amount of historical investigation would have sufficed to show that China did not evolve in isolation, nor was any particular set of political boundaries permanent. For example, the Silk Road—actually a network of caravan trails linking northwestern China to India, Persia, and the eastern Mediterranean—was a potent carrier of both goods and ideas in both directions for many centuries, beginning during the Han dynasty. Roman glass has been found in China, and Chinese silk in Rome. Buddhism came from India to China along the Silk Road, with enormous consequences for Chinese religion and philosophy. During the Tang dynasty (618–907 CE), China was unusually open to influences from Turkish and Persian cultures in Central Asia, with lasting effects in fields as diverse as music, furniture, and sports. Such examples could be multiplied indefinitely, as China went through long-term cycles of relatively more or less openness to outside influence. What is less well known is that contact and influence between the East Asian Heartland Region and areas outside the region precede the opening of the Silk Road by many thousands of years.

During the late Paleolithic period the retreat of the Ice Age glaciers reshaped the landscape of much of the Eurasian continent, producing widespread and drastic changes in terrain, climate, and ecology. These changes invited, or sometimes forced, large-scale population movements throughout the continent. No political boundaries existed at that time, and throughout the Extended East Asian Heartland Region—today's modern nation of China and its immediate periphery—peoples migrated freely and sometimes en masse, spreading languages and cultures into new territories. Genetic and linguistic studies are just beginning to sort out some of the details of these ancient migrations. In the late prehistoric and early historic periods, traders, raiders, envoys, and even missionaries crossed the mountains, deserts, and unsettled areas that surrounded the Heartland, spreading new goods and ideas. Although archaeological details are still lacking, many scholars now believe that the idea of making bronze—a very useful alloy of copper and tin (and sometimes arsenic and lead)—most likely entered the East Asian Heartland from Mesopotamia via Central Asian or steppeland intermediaries some time during the third millennium BCE. (This instance of technology transfer involved adaptation as well as adoption, however; the Early Bronze Age peoples of the Heartland developed an indigenous technology of bronze casting that was distinctively different from that used in western Asia.) It is certain that the military chariot (and a whole complex technology of horsemanship to go with it) entered the Heartland from western Asia during the mid-Shang dynasty. The cultivation of wheat also was borrowed from western Asia during the Shang Period or perhaps somewhat earlier. These and other imported technologies and crops had enormous consequences for the future of Sinitic culture. (It had long been believed that domesticated sheep also arrived in the Heartland from western Asia at around the time of the Shang dynasty, but the discovery of sheep bones in some Heartland Neolithic sites complicates that picture.) Yes, the distances were great and the dangers were many; but historians of the ancient world now realize that overland distances could not stop the slow but steady migrations of peoples and the faster spread of ideas and techniques from one culture to another. The idea that the ancient East Asian Heartland was somehow walled off against external influence is untenable.

So too is the idea of an "unchanging China," which confuses continuity with stasis. We have already commented at length about the interplay of continuity and change in Chinese history. Here it will suffice to elaborate on a single example. The Shang dynasty and the Han dynasty demonstrate cultural continuity in many important aspects, such as the written Chinese language, an ancestor-centered religion, hereditary monarchy, and the high cultural value placed on jade and bronze (although by the Han bronze was becoming a material employed simply for the production of luxury goods rather than for the manufacture of religiously potent ritual objects). On the other hand, if a member of the late Shang elite could have been magically transported a thousand years ahead in time to the court of Emperor Wu of the Han he would have found his new world unrecognizable in virtually every way. New ways of thinking, arguing, and writing; new styles in art, architecture, and music; new weapons and military tactics; new qualifications for government service—new phenomena of every kind would have been bewildering to the visitor from the Shang. Exactly the same argument can be made for a hypothetical high official of the Han magically transported to the capital of the Ming dynasty (1368–1644 CE). Given enough time, our visitors from the past would no doubt have been relieved and reassured to identify many familiar basic cultural continuities, but they probably would never have lost their sense of amazement at how much had changed.

In this book virtually every important point that we make about the Chinese past will involve, explicitly or implicitly, the interplay of continuity and change.

Why study ancient China?

Ancient China is unquestionably remote from the present day, perhaps so much as to prompt the question: Why study ancient China at all? We offer several reasons.

The first is that ancient Chinese history is intrinsically interesting, and getting more so all the time. Barely a century ago the Shang dynasty was almost totally unknown except for written accounts of very dubious reliability in texts recorded many centuries after the fact. The discovery of Shang "oracle bones" and the excavation of the Shang royal tombs near Anyang have given us a surprisingly detailed and vivid picture of the Shang state. We are able now to visualize the Shang kings almost obsessively cracking oracle bones to seek the advice of their ancestors on everything from illness to military expeditions, and to place that image in context as one of the building-blocks of Sinitic culture. Again, four decades ago no one even suspected the existence of the astonishing and unique Bronze Age culture now known from excavations at Sanxingdui, near Chengdu, Sichuan. The discovery of that culture radically revised the entire picture of Bronze Age civilization in the early Heartland Region and illuminated more than 1,000 years' worth of local history in Sichuan. The process of discovery continues today, as new excavations—some planned, and some accidentally uncovered in the course of road-building or well-digging—turn up, year after year, new finds of bronze vessels, ancient texts, cities and walls, and sometimes even whole new cultures. Studying ancient China offers the genuine thrill of a field in which much is known and much more is still to be learned.

A second reason is that, with the sweeping away of the dusty myths of "isolated China" and "unchanging China," China, both ancient and modern, emerges as a full-fledged part of world history. The more we know about ancient China, the better we understand the historical forces at work in other centers of ancient civilization, from Mesopotamia and Egypt to the Indus Valley and the Yucatan—and vice versa. The civilizations of the ancient world are always comparable and were sometimes (even to an astonishing degree) interconnected. The study of ancient China illuminates the study of the ancient world.

Finally, despite the truly earth-shaking changes that have taken place in modern China—despite the manufacturing juggernaut and the hypermodern mega-cities, despite Internet-savvy, globe-trotting Chinese youth, despite expanding superhighways and shocking CO_2 emissions—China's claim to have the world's oldest continuous civilization deserves to be taken seriously. Despite an unprecedented burst of change and modernization, it is impossible to understand the Chinese present without understanding the Chinese past. Issues of citizenship and ethnic identity among Tibetans, Uighurs, and others in today's Extended East Asian Heartland Region hark back to issues of diversity and interconnectedness, identity and assimilation, that originated thousands of years ago. In today's China, Buddhism—introduced along the Silk Road 2,000 years ago, and recently thought virtually extinct under the reign of Chairman Mao—is once again thriving. Elaborate funerals, of a kind praised by Confucius as respectful and condemned by the philosopher Mozi as wasteful, are a common sight in many Chinese communities (though less so in today's mainland China, where costly funerals are restricted by law). Paper BMWs and airplanes have replaced ceramic figurines as funerary offerings; is this tradition, or modernity, or both? A spirit of Chinese nationalism argues for the literal reality of such mythical "ancient rulers" as the Yellow Emperor and Lord Millet, and modern Chinese leaders draw strength from the legends of these ancient sage-kings. Confucius, once condemned as a symbol of "old" China, is now revered once again. To evaluate the modern manipulation of these old symbols we must first understand their original contexts. To understand China today, we must look to China's past.

2   Geography, climate, and the physical setting of Chinese history

Introduction

The history described in these pages was played out on the stage of the East Asian Heartland Region, comprising the great drainage basins of the Yellow River (Huanghe) and the Yangzi River (Changjiang) and nearby plains suitable for agriculture. That history also involved considerable and continuous interaction with the Extended East Asian Heartland Region, a term denoting the forests, grasslands, deserts, and mountains surrounding the Heartland itself. The East Asian Heartland Region is large and geographically diverse, ranging from semi-arid highlands in the north to semi-tropical mountains and valleys in the south. It is quite mountainous, except for the broad flood plains of the great rivers, and only a small fraction of its area is suitable for agriculture as delimited by topography, soil quality, and availability of water. The Heartland Region is bounded on the east by the Pacific Ocean. Throughout the land area, the general tendency is for mountain ranges to increase in height from east to west; the region's major rivers therefore run roughly from west to east, and are fed by tributaries that flow northward or southward to join them. The geographic diversity of the Heartland Region was echoed in the diversity of its Neolithic cultures, which all, broadly speaking, in various ways became part of the roots of Chinese civilization. The fertility and breadth of the Yellow River's flood plain contributed to the eventual emergence there of a relatively advanced proto-Sinitic culture that spread outward to interact with cultures in other parts of the Heartland. This process was part of the transition from the Neolithic era to the Bronze Age.

The East Asian Heartland Region can meaningfully be divided into northern and southern zones, corresponding to differences in terrain, soil, climate, crops, and other factors that have shaped the lives of the people who live in those zones (Map 2.1). The line dividing north from south first follows the upper reaches of the Han River where it flows roughly from west to east (before making a sharp bend southward to join the Yangzi River). The imaginary dividing line then leaps eastward overland and picks up the course of the Huai River, which flows from west to east across Anhui and Jiangxi Provinces and into the Yellow Sea. The Qinling Mountains, a range of rugged peaks running west to east along a line south of and parallel to the Wei River Valley (and thus north of and parallel to the upper reaches of the Han River), play a crucial role in dividing the northern and southern zones of the Heartland Region into two distinctively different climatic spheres.

The Northern Heartland Region

The Northern Heartland Region is bounded on the east by two shallow extensions of the Pacific Ocean, namely the Gulf of Bohai (nearly enclosed by the Liaodong and Shandong

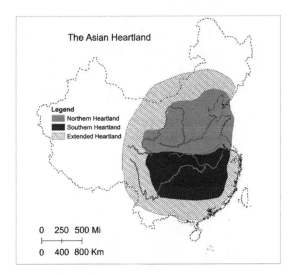

The Asian Heartland

Legend
Northern Heartland
Southern Heartland
Extended Heartland

0   250   500 Mi

0   400   800 Km

Map 2.1 The East Asian Heartland Region and the Extended East Asian Heartland Region. Many different cultures flourished here before China became China.

Peninsulas) and the Yellow Sea (between Shandong and Korea) (Map 2.2). The northern and western margins of the region are not clearly delineated, but rather are formed by a series of mountain ranges, grasslands, deserts, and highlands that mark a shifting and uncertain frontier between where agriculture is feasible and where it is not. The key geographical features of the Northern Heartland Region are the Loess Highlands, the Yellow River, the Yellow River Plain, and two nearly contiguous rocky peninsulas, Liaodong and Shandong. The interactions among these geographical features determine the principal characteristics of the region.

The Loess Highlands dominate the western part of the Northern Heartland Region (see Focus: Loess), forming a huge highland region within and around the great bend of the Yellow River. Loess is a type of soil, the accumulated result of thousands of years of windblown dust. Soft and crumbly, it is easily eroded by wind and water. This has turned the Loess Highlands into a region of cliffs and steep valleys, in which flat land is scarce and flood plains are narrow (Figure 2.1). The Yellow River itself cuts a deep channel around and through the Loess Highlands, transporting water past the surrounding area rather than bringing water to it. The same is true of the Fen River, an important tributary of the Yellow River, which flows from north to south through the eastern zone of the Loess Highlands. Because of a semi-arid climate with low rainfall, the Loess Highlands as a whole are chronically short of water, despite the mighty rivers flowing nearby.

Immediately to the south of the Loess Highlands is the Wei River Valley, formed by a tributary of the Yellow River running from west to east at the southern edge of the Loess Highlands and bordered on the south by the Qinling Mountains (see Focus: The Qinling Mountains); its flat and hospitable terrain was the home to some of China's earliest Neolithic cultures. The Wei River joins the Yellow River at a set of narrow gorges (The "Three Gates Gorges," *Sanmenxia*), where the Yellow River descends from the highlands and makes an abrupt eastward turn to flow into and through its extensive flood plain. That gorge gives rise to the name that has long been applied to the Wei River Valley: "the land within the passes"

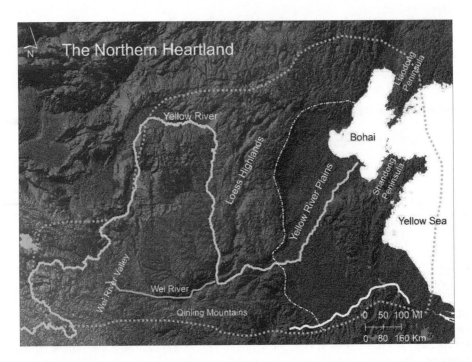

Map 2.2 Important features of the East Asian Heartland Region: North.

Figure 2.1 The landscape of the Loess Highlands in the northwestern Heartland Region is characterized by windblown soil that is fertile but easily eroded.

(*guanzhong*). Its easily defended terrain helped make the Wei River Valley a stronghold of powerful states at various times in Chinese history.

The Yellow River is the world's ninth longest river, stretching some 3,400 miles (5,500 kilometers) from its source in the Bayankala Mountains (part of the Qinghai Plateau). It is also one of the world's largest by volume of water carried, and it is without rival as the muddiest large river in the world. It takes its name from the huge amount of light tan eroded loess soil that it carries as silt—approximately 1.4 billion tons per year at the point where the river emerges from the Loess Highlands. At peak flood season the amount of silt carried by the river can exceed 20 percent of the total volume of water. This makes the Yellow River what hydrologists call a depositing river. As the river emerges from the highlands and is deflected eastward by the Qinling Mountains to enter the Yellow River Plain, its water slows down and thus becomes less able to move a high volume of silt. The silt therefore settles out of the water and is deposited as mud in the channel of the river. This mud is eventually, through periodic floods, spread as soil over large areas of countryside. When the floodwaters recede, the river does not return to its silted-up old channel, but rather has to find a new course to the sea. The river's course has thus shifted many times since the end of the last Ice Age, and these shifts have meant that the mouth of the river sometimes winds up north of the Shandong Peninsula (emptying into the Gulf of Bohai), and sometimes south of it (emptying into the Yellow Sea). As economic exploitation in recent centuries stripped the Loess Highlands of much of what remained of its protective cover of vegetation, the flooding of the Yellow River, and consequent cutting of new channels, has increased dramatically in frequency. Over the millennia, the river itself, by silt deposition and flooding, has created thousands of square miles of alluvial land.

The Yellow River Plain is the dominant feature of the Northern Heartland Region east of the great bend of the Yellow River. During the Ice Age the plain was much more extensive; because a much larger fraction of the world's water was locked up in ice sheets, the sea level was much lower than it is at present. The Gulf of Bohai and parts of the Yellow Sea were then dry land. With the melting of the ice sheets, a process that lasted from about 18,000 to 12,000 BP (Before the Present), the level of the ocean rose steadily and fairly rapidly, turning much of what is now the Yellow River Plain into a shallow sea (of which the Gulf of Bohai is the modern remnant), and isolating what is now the Shandong Peninsula as an island. Silt deposited by the Yellow River then began the ongoing process of filling in the shallow sea again, shrinking the western margins of the Gulf of Bohai and the Yellow Sea. The Yellow River Plain today encompasses the area east of the Loess Highlands and north of the Huai River, wrapping around the Shandong Peninsula and extending northward to the mountains north of the present-day city of Beijing. The Yellow River Plain (also known as the North China Plain, and anciently as the *Zhongyuan* or Central Plain) forms an extensive area of good soil and fairly level terrain, highly suitable for the growing of grain; it was one of the cradles of civilization in eastern Asia for that reason (see Focus: Millet). Generally speaking, the Yellow River Plain merges imperceptibly with the sea in dull vistas of tidal mudflats, shallow waters, and what in ancient times apparently were extensive marshes dominated by tall reeds (now almost entirely cleared to create cultivated land). With few elevated beaches, navigable channels, or sheltered harbors, this was a coastal terrain ill-suited to habitation or navigation. The ancient cultures of the Yellow River Plain seem to have been oriented inward and in effect land-locked, despite the proximity of the sea.

The Liaodong Peninsula is the most conspicuous feature of the region we call the Near Northeast, which also includes the Liao River Valley and the narrow coastal plain along the northwestern shore of the Gulf of Bohai. This was the homeland of an important Jade Age people, the Hongshan Culture. The Near Northeast seems to have formed a shifting frontier between peoples who would eventually be absorbed into the expanding Sinitic culture of the East Asian Heartland, and the ancestors of the Koreans (and, at least in part, of the Japanese).

The Liaodong and Shandong Peninsulas are a pair of "arms" that nearly meet to enclose the Gulf of Bohai; Shandong separates the Gulf of Bohai from the Yellow Sea. Liaodong ("east of the Liao," i.e. the Liao River) and Shandong ("east of the mountain," i.e. the tall, isolated peak of Mt. Tai) form two refuges of hills, forests, rocky coastlines, and sheltered harbors on what is otherwise the flat and featureless coast of the Northern Heartland Region. The isolation of the two peninsulas led to their being inhabited, well into historical times, by peoples who were culturally, and almost certainly ethno-linguistically, different from the peoples of the plains.

The Southern Heartland Region

The geography of the southern zone of the East Asian Heartland Region is much more complicated than that of the north, but it too is dominated by a single feature, the vast drainage basin of the Yangzi River (Map 2.3). The Yangzi, the world's fourth longest river (about 3,700 miles/6,000 kilometers), has its origin in the eastern part of the Tibetan Plateau, not far south of the headwaters of the Yellow River. In Chinese it is usually known as the Changjiang ("Long River"); in its initial passage across the Tibetan Plateau it is called the Jinsha ("Golden Sand") River. It is one of a series of rivers arising close together in eastern Tibet (others include the Red River, the Mekong, the Salween, the Irrawaddy, and the Brahmaputra) that fan out to distribute glacial water in a vast arc from the East Asian Heartland across southeast Asia to northeastern India.

For the ancient period of Chinese history, the East Asian Heartland Region extends southward only as far as the great drainage basin of the Yangzi River. For the people of the Bronze Age, and

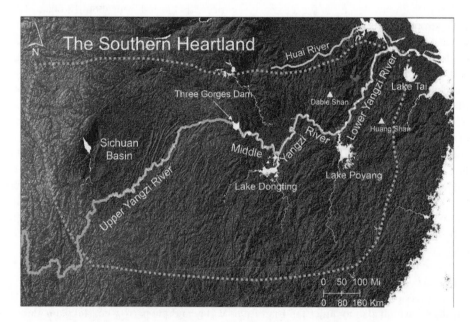

Map 2.3 Important features of the East Asian Heartland Region: South.

into early imperial times, the Yangzi Valley (which today we would call "Central China") *was* the south; whatever lay even further south was largely *terra incognita*. If one were referring to later imperial dynasties it would be appropriate to consider some more southerly areas to be part of the Heartland as well, as they were gradually absorbed into the Chinese realm.

Within the Heartland Region (that is, excluding its long course across the Tibetan Plateau before it descends to the Sichuan Basin) the Yangzi River can be divided conceptually into three sections: Lower, Middle, and Upper. The Lower Yangzi Valley is a flood plain, somewhat like that of the Yellow River and contiguous with the Yellow River Plain south of Shandong (the Huai River conventionally marks the boundary between the two). But the Yangzi River Plain is wetter than the Yellow River Plain; it meets the sea in a complicated network of estuaries and is strewn everywhere with tributary rivers and lakes, including Lake Tai, one of the largest lakes anywhere in the Heartland Region. From prehistoric times and well into the historic era much of this flood plain consisted of marshy wetlands. Yet humans, adaptable as always to diverse habitats, have lived along the Lower Yangzi since Paleolithic times; early Neolithic villagers domesticated rice there (see Focus: Rice). The Yangzi Delta was the home of the important Liangzhu Culture, a Jade Age culture that endured from about 3200 to about 2300 BCE.

Between the Lower and Middle reaches of the Yangzi its valley narrows for some distance, compressed between two mountain ranges, the Dabie Shan and Huang Shan. In the Middle Yangzi the valley opens up again in a wide, watery land of lakes, from Poyang Lake in the east to Dongting Lake in the west. The land along the river and surrounding the lakes is low-lying and, in ancient times, was swampy; today the land has mostly been drained to make way for agriculture. Laced by secondary rivers and canals, it is now one of China's principal rice bowls. It also historically supported an important fishing industry, now damaged by the environmental effects of the Three Gorges Dam and contemporary over-fishing. An important tributary of the Yangzi, the Xiang River, rises in the Nan Ling ("Southern Peaks") Mountains to the south and flows northward to Poyang Lake, eventually draining into the Yangzi. The Xiang River Valley provided an ancient route from the Middle Yangzi to the lands further south.

The Upper Yangzi flows through the celebrated Three Gorges, a series of narrow canyons (the Qutang, Wu, and Xiling Gorges) that extend for a total of about 120 miles (200 kilometers). At the beginning of the twenty-first century the river within the gorges was transformed into a huge lake by the Three Gorges Dam; but, until that event, the river's passage through the gorges was turbulent and dangerous for boats and afforded little room for humans on foot. The gorges were therefore a potent barrier, though not an insurmountable one, to the travel of goods and ideas between the Middle and the Upper Yangzi regions. The Upper Yangzi also includes the southern rim of the Sichuan ("Four Rivers") Basin, where important tributary rivers water the Chengdu Plain before merging with the mighty Yangzi.

Sichuan is a high basin (average altitude over 2,000 feet/650 meters) bounded on the southwest, west, and northwest by the foothills of the Tibetan Plateau and on the north, east, and south by a series of small mountain ranges. It is blessed with a temperate climate, ample rainfall, and good soil, and is one of the most productive agricultural areas of the Heartland Region. As we will see, Sichuan has its own Neolithic, Jade Age, and Bronze Age history, with cultures that were in contact with, but for many centuries also notably distinct from, the proto-Sinitic and Sinitic cultures to the east.

The Extended East Asian Heartland Region: The northeast and north

North and east of the Heartland's Near Northeast region is an extensive zone of forests and grasslands, once known as Manchuria and now called in Chinese simply Dongbei, "the

Northeast." Politically the territory is now shared by China, Russia, and the two Koreas, but geographically and historically it can be considered a single region, bounded on the west by the Xing'gan Mountains, on the north by the Amur (Heilongjiang) River, and on the east by the Sea of Japan; the Korean peninsula marks its southern extension.

The terrain of the Northeast is largely mountainous, with a large central valley and with swampy lowlands in the lower reaches of the Amur. Its vegetation ranges from mixed forest in the southern regions to evergreen forest in the north, with broad areas of grasslands where local rainfall is insufficient to support woodlands. There is evidence of some ancient trade between the region and the expanding sphere of Bronze Age Sinitic influence in the Heartland—for example, of furs from the northeast in exchange for silk and bronze from the Heartland—but most of the northeast remained remote from Chinese affairs until well into the imperial era. Korea is an exception to this; the peoples of the Korean Peninsula were in contact with the Heartland, via the Near Northeast, since the Bronze Age, while nevertheless retaining their linguistic and cultural distinctiveness and eventual political autonomy.

West of the Xing'gan Mountains, and extending in a vast sweep across the northern reaches of the Heartland from the Yellow River Plain to the Loess Highlands and beyond, is a zone of grasslands and deserts that is unsuitable for agriculture over most of its area and that therefore marked the limit of the expansion of Sinitic culture. Virtually the entire area consists of highlands, with few elevations below 3,200 feet (1,000 meters) and mountain ranges that are much higher. The areas of lowest elevation tend to be the most arid, forming the several linked basins of the Gobi Desert. Much of the Northern Region consists of grasslands, known by the Russian word *steppe* (what would be called prairie in North America). In its northernmost zone the steppe merges gradually with the evergreen and birch forests of Siberia.

The steppelands proper have long been sparsely inhabited by horse-riding tribal peoples who herd animals such as horses, sheep, and goats in a highly specialized way of life known as pastoral nomadism (pastoral, for herding animals; nomadism, for moving around among seasonally variable sources of grass and water). Like the peoples of the Northeast, the northern pastoral nomads were in regular but distant trading contact with the Heartland. Groups of pastoral nomads often raided the Heartland's northern frontier. Occasionally, confederations of pastoral nomadic tribes would grow strong enough to invade, or even, at several times during the imperial era, to conquer and rule, the northern reaches of the Heartland itself. From the late third to the late sixth centuries CE much of northern China was ruled by tribal peoples from the north.

In ancient times the steppe extended not only across the territory north of the East Asian Heartland Region but all the way across Eurasia from the Xing'gan Mountains to the plains of Ukraine and Hungary. (In recent times much of the western reaches of the steppelands, like much of the American prairie, have been plowed and converted to agriculture, interrupting what had been the trans-Asian steppe belt.) This was of great historical importance, because it made it possible to walk, or ride a horse, or drive an oxcart, completely across Asia. Of course, few people—maybe no one at all—made the entire journey; but trade to and from one intermediary after another (so-called "down-the-line trade") made it possible for goods and ideas to travel much further than individual humans. It appears very likely that the basic idea of bronze metallurgy reached the East Asian Heartland from further west along the steppe route, and virtually certain that such Western Asian innovations as the chariot (and the horsemanship to go with it) and the cultivation of wheat entered the Heartland via the steppelands in the mid-second millennium BCE. The steppe belt was also a highway for large-scale migrations of peoples, in both directions, in ancient times. It remained the principal route for long-distance travel and trade until innovations in caravan technology, and the extension of Chinese military power into Central Asia, opened the Northwestern Corridor and the Silk Road in China's early imperial era.

The Extended East Asian Heartland Region: The northwest and west

Leading northwestward from the Wei River Valley and extending beyond the Heartland Region's Loess Highlands is the Northwestern Corridor, a narrow valley, well watered with glacial meltwater from the Tibetan Plateau, that gradually rises on its way to the deserts, mountains, and oases of Central Asia. Much of the terrain of Central Asia, such as the arid Tarim Basin and the dangerous Taklamakan Desert, was too difficult for travelers on foot or on horseback to traverse safely; travel along the routes leading westward from the Northwestern Corridor (a network of trails that much later came to be known as the Silk Road) became feasible only with the domestication of the Bactrian (two-humped) camel, perhaps around the ninth century BCE. Regular caravan trade along the Silk Route did not begin until early imperial times. Much earlier than that, however, the Northwestern Corridor provided a route of access to the Heartland Region for groups of raiding or invading pastoral nomads; states (such as Zhou and Qin) that were established in the Wei River Valley therefore had to deal with the necessity of protecting their northwestern frontier.

The Northwestern Corridor was temporarily brought under Chinese military control during the first century BCE, under the Han dynasty. Twice during the imperial era—during the first half of the Tang dynasty (618–750 CE) and again under the Qing dynasty (1644–1911 CE)—all of Central Asia westward from the Northwestern Corridor to the foothills of the Pamir Mountains was incorporated into the Chinese empire. The present western borders of the People's Republic of China largely preserve the territorial conquests of the Qing dynasty.

The western limits of the East Asian Heartland Region are entirely bounded by the foothills and high table-lands of the Tibetan Plateau. The plateau covers a much larger area than the present political boundaries of Tibet under Chinese administration. Geographically it also includes the territories of Qinghai and Amdo, as well as the high mountainous areas of western Sichuan and Yunnan. In ancient times there appears to have been little interaction between the East Asian Heartland Region and the sparsely populated Tibetan Plateau, though in later imperial times relations between China and Tibet did develop to some extent.

The Extended East Asian Heartland Region: The south

The southern zone of the Extended Heartland Region is a confused and confusing mixture of mountains, plateaus, river valleys, and coastal lowlands (Figure 2.2). Major geographic features include the Southeastern Highlands and the Southeastern Coast; the Southern Coastal Zone (also known as Lingnan); the South-Central Plateau; and the Southwestern Mountains. These areas are conventionally counted as part of the East Asian Heartland Region for China's imperial era, and by late imperial times they were firmly under Chinese administration. In ancient times, however, they were largely isolated from the proto-Sinitic and Sinitic cultures that were gradually achieving a position of dominance further north. Even nominal Chinese suzerainty over much of the southernmost region was not achieved until the early imperial era, and local cultures remained strong. Still today, many parts of southern China are inhabited by non-Chinese minority ethnic groups. In ancient times there was certainly a steady but small-scale flow of trade between the southernmost region and the expanding zone

Figure 2.2 Much of the terrain of the southern Heartland Region is mountainous, with steep valleys and abundant water. Over a period of many centuries, hillsides have been terraced to create paddy fields.

of Sinitic culture, but the spread of Sinitic influence into the far south was slow and halting. During the Zhou era the northern part of the South-Central Plateau was incorporated into the state of Yue, regarded by the so-called Central States of the Yellow River Plain as being ethnically non-Sinitic but nevertheless a major player in the warfare and inter-state political maneuvering of the late pre-imperial period. The people of Yue were regarded by the people of the Sinitic states as culturally "other," being renowned, for example, for their skill at handling boats. (It is not that there are no rivers, and no boats, in the Yellow River Plain; but travel in the north was typically by road whereas, in the south, water transport predominated.)

The Southeastern Highlands includes the part of today's Zhejiang Province that lies south of Hangzhou Bay, and all of today's Fujian Province. It is a land of high mountain ranges and steep valleys, bisected by the Min River; the highland region south of that river is often known as Min'nan, "south of the Min." The region's narrow coastal lowlands meet the sea in a broken landscape of cliffs, beaches, and rock-bound harbors. Genetic and linguistic evidence suggests that this coastal region was the ancestral homeland of the Austronesian (also called Malayo-Polynesian) peoples, great seafarers who spread out to inhabit Taiwan, the Philippines, Borneo, and other points east and west. The island of Taiwan, where distinctive Neolithic cultural remains have been investigated archaeologically, was inhabited solely by Austronesian peoples until early modern times and played no role in the ancient history of the East Asian Heartland Region.

The Southern Coastal Zone stretches in a long arc across the southern boundary of the Heartland Region, from the modern city of Shantou in the east to the city of Nanning in the west, and encompassing in its central area the modern Pearl River Delta cities of Guangzhou (Canton), Shenzhen, Hong Kong, and Macao. The large tropical island of Hainan, near the present border between China and Vietnam, could be regarded as an extension of the Southern Coastal Zone, but there was little ethnic Chinese settlement in Hainan until early modern times. The mainland portion of the zone has traditionally been known as Lingnan ("South of the Peaks"), an apt description of its geographical position south of the South-Central Plateau and of the Nan Ling Mountains in particular. Much of the zone is hilly and broken by narrow valleys. With abundant water but relatively poor soil, it has become an important rice-growing region through extensive terracing of paddy fields and the use of natural and artificial fertilizers. It has a subtropical climate, with steamy summer temperatures and a strong summer monsoon; northwestern winds bring the region a short but surprisingly damp and chilly winter. The Southern Coastal Zone is notable for its many harbors, and archaeological finds of well-preserved ancient ships, both large and small, give strong evidence of a seafaring culture and maritime trade since at least late Neolithic times. More than other far southern regions, the Southern Coastal Zone was in contact with the Sinitic cultures of the north, and the region was brought under Chinese administration early in the imperial era.

The South-Central Plateau is a large region of limestone mountains and valleys encompassing the inland portion of modern Guangxi Province, western Hunan, and the eastern half of modern Guizhou Province. It includes the spectacular and world-famous limestone karst formations along the Li River near modern Guilin. Agriculture, including rice cultivation in terraced fields, is practiced in the region's many valleys, but much of the land is unsuitable for agriculture and historically was heavily forested (although much of the forest has been clear-cut for timber in recent decades). The area's remoteness and difficult terrain have made it a marginal part of the Heartland Region to the present day, and its population continues to be dominated, at least outside major urban centers, by Zhuang, Miao, and other so-called "national minority" peoples.

The Southwestern Mountains region includes the highlands of western Guizhou Province, southwestern Sichuan, and all of Yunnan Province, and is bounded on the west by the Tibetan Plateau. Almost all of the region lies at an altitude of more than 5,000 feet (1,500 meters), with steep river valleys forming almost impassable barriers between adjacent mountain ranges. The present-day city of Kunming is situated in an upland basin that has long been a center of agriculture; despite its southern latitude, its high altitude gives it a perpetually temperate, spring-like climate. The upper reaches of the Mekong River drain the western portions of the Southwestern Mountains, but its steep valley made trade along the middle reaches of the river difficult. More accessible was the valley of the Red River, flowing past Kunming and on to the modern Vietnamese cities of Hanoi and Haiphong; the Red River acted as the highway of the Heartland's southwest, linking the Bronze Age culture of Yunnan with that of northern Vietnam. But, despite its remoteness, the Southwestern Mountains region was in trade contact with the Sinitic world, shipping cowry shells and metal ingots (from the ancient tin and lead mines of northeastern Yunnan), undoubtedly via intermediaries, as far away as the Shang kingdom in the Yellow River Plain.

The climate of the East Asian Heartland Region

The Earth's climate is generally fairly stable on a scale of decades, but is variable at larger scales—over the course of a millennium the Earth's average temperature can vary by a few degrees Celsius, with proportionate effects on the amount and distribution of precipitation. (The fact of long-term climate fluctuations greatly complicates the assessment of human-generated greenhouse-effect climate change in our own time.) These long-term climate fluctuations had direct effects on the timing and extent of the great Neolithic cultural shift from hunting and gathering to farming, and on agricultural yields, settlement patterns, state formation, and other historical phenomena in the ancient East Asian Heartland Region.

With the retreat of the great Ice Age glaciers (beginning about 18,000 BP and complete by about 12,000 BP), extensive continental fringes that had been dry land for tens of thousands of years were submerged beneath the ocean, while vegetation began to cover the barren land exposed by the vanishing ice. The earth's climate then entered a new cooling phase between about 10500 and 9800 BCE before decisively warming once again. This long-term warming trend culminated in the Mid-Holocene Climatic Optimum, a very warm period lasting from about 6000 to 2500 BCE. (The Holocene is the most recent phase of Earth's geological history, the era in which we are still living.) At its height, the Mid-Holocene Climatic Optimum saw Earth's average temperature rise by several degrees Celsius; rising sea levels inundated broad areas of coastal land everywhere around the globe. In the East Asian Heartland Region, average summer temperatures around 4500 BCE were two degrees Celcius higher than at present, and winter temperatures as much as five degrees Celcius higher. The Yellow River Plain and much of the Loess Highlands region were heavily forested, and wild elephants, rhinoceroses, and water buffalo ranged as far north as the Yellow River itself. Early Neolithic farmers were able to raise rice as well as millet in the southern fringes of the Yellow River Plain. The Yangzi Valley was a land of steaming marshes and semi-tropical jungle, teeming with alligators and crocodiles. Tigers and leopards were found throughout the Heartland Region.

Thereafter the Earth entered a long and gradual cooling phase, but average temperatures did not fall to contemporary levels until the end of the Shang Period, around 1000 BCE. A period of severe and prolonged drought affected all of Eurasia around 2200 BCE, but the specific effects of that drought on East Asian populations are still not well understood. With the end of the Mid-Holocene Climatic Optimum sea levels again fell, exposing coastal land along the Yellow River Plain and the Yangzi Delta. The northern grasslands reclaimed the northern reaches of the Yellow River Plain, forests in much of the core area of the Plain became less widespread and less dense, and semi-tropical animals and plants began slowly to retreat southward. The Loess Highlands region lost some of its forest cover. Nevertheless, these changes took effect slowly, and in the mid-second millennium BCE the East Asian Heartland Region was still relatively warm.

Strong evidence indicates that average temperatures at the beginning of the Shang dynasty (c. 1555–1046 BCE) were still higher than at present by as much as one degree Celcius in summer and as much as three degrees Celcius in winter, and wetter as well. This amount of greater warmth, though mild in comparison with the high point of the Mid-Holocene Climatic Optimum, continued to have significant consequences. The growing season was longer, and the zone of feasible agriculture may have moved significantly to the north of the Yellow River Plain. In combination with greater rainfall, crop yields on average would therefore have been abundant. Greater growth of vegetation in uncultivated lands would have supported more game animals that could be hunted. On the other hand, more rainfall would have produced greater siltation in the Yellow River; both the added water and the added silt would have made devastating floods in the Yellow River Plain more frequent and more severe. Moreover, this general pattern does not mean that shorter-term climate fluctuations ceased to occur. Periodic droughts occurred at irregular intervals, in accordance with normal weather patterns in the northern Heartland, and such droughts had adverse short-term consequences. Evidence from inscriptions on oracle bones (by which the Shang dynasty kings solicited advice and assistance from their deceased ancestors) indicates that both damagingly violent rainstorms and droughts were matters of concern to the Shang rulers. On the whole the warmer climate of the Shang era was probably beneficial, however, and may have contributed (through greater agricultural surplus wealth, for example) to the spread of Shang military power and political control over a wider area than any other East Asian polity had yet achieved, and to the further development of Shang political and administrative institutions.

By the end of the Shang dynasty and the beginning of the Zhou dynasty (1046 BCE), temperatures in the East Asian Heartland Region were approximately like those of the present day. The northern zone of the Heartland region had become cooler and drier, with rainfall more variable and periodic droughts more common. The cooler climate, combined with ongoing human harvesting of timber, removed the native tree cover from much of the Loess Highlands and the Yellow River Plain. Wetlands and rice fields continued to dominate the Yangzi River Valley, but there, too, the cooling effect was felt as tropical conditions gave way to a semi-tropical climate.

Regardless of long-term climate fluctuations, the northern and southern zones of the East Asian Heartland had, and continue to have, dramatically different climates. The north has a continental climate, dominated by the great land-mass of the Eurasian continent. Prevailing winds are from the northwest, from the continent's interior mountains and arid terrain. Rainfall is scarce and irregular, with precipitation occurring mostly during the winter months but with significant variability in timing and amount. Droughts are not uncommon; floods are less common but can be devastating when they do occur. Travel in the ancient period was mainly by road—on foot, in wheeled vehicles from the Shang onwards, on horseback beginning only in the late pre-imperial period. Settlements, whether villages, towns, or cities, were compact, heavily fortified with walls, and surrounded by agricultural lands. Fields tended to be laid out in a regular pattern of long narrow strips worked by hand with hoes, mattocks, and similar tools. The soil in the northern zone, both in the Loess Highlands and the Yellow River Plain, is generally very fertile, but water scarcity is a limiting factor on agriculture. The staple crops of the northern zone are millet, wheat, and soybeans.

The southern zone, in contrast, has an oceanic climate, the main generators of weather being the Pacific Ocean and the South China Sea. The southern zone has a regular summer monsoon of heavy, abundant rainfall. As is true elsewhere in the monsoon belt of South and Southeast Asia, the monsoon can sometimes fail, leading to severe drought and crop failures; the monsoon can also be too extreme, with widespread flooding as a result. Travel in the southern zone since ancient times has been largely by boat. Villages are often strung out along one or both banks of a river or a canal; towns and cities were frequently built at the confluence of rivers, with the rivers themselves serving a defensive function as well as being transportation routes. Fields were often irregular in shape, following the region's hilly terrain, and, since at least the beginning of the imperial era, were often organized into networks of terraces and irrigation channels. In general the southern zone has ample water but poor, stony, leached-out soil that requires large amounts of manure, compost, or other fertilizer. The staple crop of the southern zone is rice. Bamboo grows abundantly and was put to a wide variety of uses, especially before the modern invention of plastics and other synthetic materials.

The human landscape

It is often said, with only slight exaggeration, that there is not a single square inch of Chinese territory that has not been transformed by human agency. While much of that transformation has taken place in modern times, the statement is also true to a remarkable extent for the ancient East Asian Heartland Region. Thousands of years of human occupation, agriculture, construction, irrigation, and other activities had already significantly changed the Heartland's landscape even before the dawn of the imperial era.

The earliest agriculture, consisting of little more than tending stands of wild plants and selectively sowing seeds of improved varieties, had relatively little environmental impact, but the later laying out of fields, and the establishment of boundary walls and pathways among them, began to work a significant rearrangement of the land. In the Loess Highlands the natural tendency of loess to erode to terrace-like formations in river valleys was encouraged by artificial terracing and leveling of fields, and by the establishment of paths to the riverbanks to obtain water for irrigation. In southern regions the earliest efforts to level and terrace rice paddies and to control the flow of water to them probably date back to the mid- to late Neolithic period. By the beginning of the imperial era a sizeable portion of the Yangzi River marshlands had been converted to agricultural use. In the northern border regions attempts to spread agriculture into semi-arid grassland environments very likely resulted in increased rates of soil erosion.

Agriculture means villages, and the establishment of settled populations in the East Asian Heartland wrought many changes in the landscape, including alterations in the biodiversity and abundance of native plants, animals, and birds in nearby areas. Even early Neolithic villages were often surrounded by defensive ditches, and sometimes also low walls made from the excavated soil. As towns and, later, cities grew more common and more sizeable, wall-building continued at an accelerated pace; in fact, wall-building became one of the characteristic features of proto-Sinitic and Sinitic cultures, especially in the northern zone of the Heartland. City walls of pounded earth grew ever higher and more massive, sometimes consisting of millions of cubic feet of earth even in pre-Bronze Age times. Not only did walls delineate the outer boundaries of cities, but they began to be built within cities as well, dividing the urban space into neighborhoods segregated by status and occupation.

Other earthen structures also modified the landscape. All of the known Jade Age cultures of the Heartland built elaborate sacrificial structures of pounded earth near the tombs of their elite classes. Those tombs were themselves earthen structures of considerable magnitude, though not yet topped with the enormous pyramidal mounds that would become the characteristic feature of Chinese tombs from the mid- to late-Zhou era onwards. Large-scale buildings were usually sited on artificial platforms of pounded earth, sometimes tens of feet tall. The construction of all such earthworks required massive amounts of excavated soil as well as thousands of worker-days of labor.

Perhaps the most conspicuous, and the most environmentally damaging, anthropogenic change in the early Chinese landscape was deforestation (see Focus: Ox Mountain). The peoples of the East Asian Heartland Region required wood for several purposes: as fuel for cooking and domestic heating; as timber for the construction of buildings and tombs; and as fuel for energy-intensive industries such as ceramics and bronze. The supply of domestic fuel was potentially large, because small and misshapen pieces of wood can serve the purpose well; but in semi-arid environments even that relatively unselective harvesting of wood can denude an area over time; the demand may seem small, but it is unrelenting. The requirements for construction timber are more stringent; only certain types of wood are strong, straight, and durable enough to be suitable for use in building. The characteristic Sinitic style of building, with tall wooden columns holding up a massive roof (so that walls fill the space between columns but do not bear any of the roof's weight), meant that sufficiently tall and straight trees, suitable for columns, were always in short supply. Probably the greatest demand for wood, however, came from the kiln-firing of ceramics and the smelting of bronze (and, by the mid-Zhou period, iron). Wood used in metallurgy was usually first baked into charcoal, which burns at a higher temperature than raw wood—a process that itself requires fuel. The massive, industrial-scale bronze workshops of the Shang dynasty would have put intense and sustained pressure on the forest resources of the Loess Highlands and the Yellow River Plain. Indeed, some scholars have suggested that the last relocation of the Shang capital, from the banks of the Yellow River to a more northerly location (near present-day Anyang) at the boundary between the Loess Highlands and the Yellow River Plain, was prompted in large part by the need to find new sources of wood.

It is commonplace to observe that geography, topography, and climate can both constrain and facilitate human endeavors. Nowhere is that more emphatically true than in the East Asian Heartland Region, where humankind's early alterations of the physical environment, both deliberate and inadvertent, would reverberate down through the centuries of historical time. The Chinese state rested on a base of intensive agriculture that was able not only to feed millions of people but to generate the wealth required to maintain a highly developed civilization. But the building of that agricultural base had unintended consequences, such as deforestation, erosion, and the destruction of wetlands. Over the long sweep of history China's rulers made efforts—ranging from religious interventions to the maintenance of public granaries to the construction of large-scale dikes, canals, and other public works—to control, or compensate for, droughts, floods, and other natural disasters, some of which were exacerbated by human impacts on the environment. Failure to respond effectively to such disasters could mean widespread suffering and starvation, unrest, and rebellion—even, in extreme cases, dynastic overthrow. The environmental cost of "development" continues to be one of the most pressing policy issues facing the Chinese government in the present day.

Focus: Loess

The German word *loess* (pronounced midway between "loss" and "loose") names a kind of fine, powdery, wind-deposited soil found in a number of different places in the world and which is the dominant physical feature of the Loess Highlands of the Northern East Asian Heartland Region. In some places in the highlands the loess soil is as much as 100 meters (330 feet) deep. Geologists believe that, through successive Ice Ages over the course of hundreds of thousands of years, each time the ice sheets retreated they caused long-enduring patterns of strong winds that blew from northwest to southeast. Passing over what is now the western Gobi Desert, the winds scoured the land, picking up the surface soil in huge annual dust-storms, century after century, and depositing it when the winds got farther away from the glacial margins and slowed down. Today much of the Gobi is a stony or gravelly desert, with its surface soil long since blown away. And today, too, milder dust-storms continue to characterize the winter months in northern China, though major loess deposition has long since ceased.

Fertile, largely free of stones, and easily worked even with rudimentary tools, loess soil was one factor that enabled the early development of agriculture in the Northern Heartland Region. The fine-scale structure of loess soil grains is such that it erodes easily (especially if not protected by surface vegetation) and is vertically stable, the result being that the Loess Highlands are a region of steep cliffs, narrow natural terraces, and deep valleys, a rugged and broken landscape that allows for small-scale settlements but inhibits travel. The soil's vertical stability also means that structurally reliable caves can easily be carved out of cliffsides for use as dwellings or storage pits.

Perhaps the most remarkable feature of loess is that it is highly compactable, a feature that was taken advantage of throughout the loess region (as well as in the "secondary loess" region of alluvial soil in the Yellow River Plain) to make walls and building platforms. Confined within board forms and compacted by prolonged pounding with tamping hammers (a technique known in China as *hangtu*, "pounded earth"), loess can become as hard and stable as soft stone, able to endure for decades or centuries in the semi-arid environment of the Northern Heartland Region. This had a profound effect on the development of Sinitic and Chinese architecture and on the design and defensive fortifications of villages, towns, and cities.

Loess's light tan color and susceptibility to erosion gives the mud-laden Yellow River its name, and is probably responsible for the long-standing identification, in early Chinese cosmology, of the color yellow with the central region of the inhabited world.

Focus: The Qinling Mountains

The Qinling Mountain range spans a distance of about 600 miles (about 950 kilometers) from west to east. Its westernmost peaks arise near the present-day city of Tianshui, Gansu Province; in the east it subsides in a range of modest hills near the present-day city of Luoyang, Henan Province (near the ancient proto-state of Erlitou). For much of its length the mountain range forms the southern flank of the Wei River Valley, and to the east runs south of and parallel to the Yellow River after it emerges from "within the passes." Its highest peak, Taibai Shan, in the west-central portion of the range, rises to over 12,000 feet (over 3,600 meters). The Qinling Mountains play a major role in causing the dramatically different climates of the northern and southern zones of the East Asian Heartland Region by acting as a barrier to two contrary systems of prevailing winds. The major wind systems of the southern zone are part of a monsoon pattern blowing from south to north, bringing moisture picked up from the South China Sea and replenished as the winds move across the lake district of the central Yangzi Valley. When those winds reach the Qinling Mountains their warm, moist air is forced abruptly upwards. Cooling, the air releases its moisture in summer rains that fall steadily on the mountains' southern slopes. The now wrung-out air passes north over the mountains, but has no further moisture to disgorge; the northern slopes of the mountains are dry, in the "rain shadow" of the peaks. In the winter, cold, dry winds out of the northwest blow across the Loess Highlands, seldom carrying enough moisture to bring rain. When those winter winds hit the Qinling Mountains they yield up what little moisture they have to water the Wei River Valley, before being turned aside to blow as westerly winds over the Yellow River Plain.

The dynamic interplay of winds and mountains ensures that the climates of the northern and southern zones are dramatically different, though separated only by the 100-mile (or less) width of the Qinling mountain range. South of the mountains the climate is moist and temperate and the landscape is green; in premodern times the hills and mountains were heavily forested. During the Neolithic and early dynastic eras wild elephants, rhinoceroses, and water buffalo roamed as far north as the Qinling Mountains; later, with increasing human settlement, crops could be grown year-round (a typical combination was rice in the summer and cabbage in the winter).

North of the mountains, on the other hand, the land was dry and dependent on irregular rainfall (supplemented by various methods of irrigation). The Wei River Valley was a partial exception, with more rainfall as well as more favorable terrain than the Loess Highlands further north. But everywhere north of the mountains, cold winters limited agriculture to a single growing season. Ancient northern fauna included wild cattle, mountain sheep, and antelope, and forest cover was limited.

The Qinling Mountains thus were a major contributor to the development of northern and southern "cultural styles" in China that persist to the present day.

Focus: Millet

There are several species of millet, all of them belonging, like most grains, to the grass family. Though there are different varieties of millet, all bear heads of small round edible seeds. Several species of millet grew wild in the Northern Heartland Region and were undoubtedly collected by bands of hunter-gatherers for many millennia. Two species, foxtail millet and panicled millet (also called broomcorn), were among the first plants to be domesticated in that part of the Heartland, beginning probably as soon as gardening began to replace gathering at the beginning of the Neolithic Era (Figure 2.3). Remains of foxtail millet have been recovered from archaeological sites dating back to 6500 BCE. Other millet varieties, including black millet and red millet, are mentioned in early texts. Millet early on became one of the most important staple grains of the Northern Heartland, and remained so well into the imperial era.

Millet was usually prepared as a whole grain dish, boiled or steamed to form a sort of porridge or gruel. It can be ground or milled into flour, and millet flatbread and noodles may have been a part of the Neolithic diet. But moistened millet flour ferments quickly, making it liable to spoilage. On the other hand, its rapid fermentation makes it ideal for the brewing of an alcoholic beverage (*jiu*, usually translated as "wine" but properly speaking a form of ale), the roots of which appear to go back into early Neolithic times as well. Ceramic and, later, bronze vessels specifically designed for the heating and serving of millet ale form an important part of the assemblage of artifacts found in Neolithic, Jade Age, and Bronze Age sites throughout the Heartland Region. The aptness of millet for brewing ale may explain why a divinity named Houji, "Lord Millet," was supposed to have been the first ancestor of the royal house of the Zhou dynasty.

Focus: Rice

Rice—the seeds of the cultivated wetland grasses *Oriza sativa* and *Oriza japonica*—is one of the most important staple food crops in the world; it is the second most widely planted grain crop worldwide (after maize). Controversy surrounds the issue of when and where rice was first domesticated, but archaeological evidence increasingly points to the earliest phases of the Neolithic era as the time and the Lower Yangzi River Valley as the place. There is firm evidence for the harvesting of wild precursors of *O. sativa* and *O. japonica* in that region as

Figure 2.3 A woman threshing millet, using technology nearly unchanged from the Neolithic era.

early as 9500 BCE, and for the cultivation of early domesticated varieties in the same area no later than 6500 BCE. Recent evidence indicates that early rice cultivators in the Yangzi Valley were already employing the technique of sequentially flooding and then draining fields to encourage the growth of rice plants and discourage the infiltration of weeds.

Rice cultivation was widespread in the southern zone of the East Asian Heartland Region by 3000 BCE, and across Southeast Asia and in climatically appropriate areas of India and Pakistan as well. It is still unclear whether domesticated rice spread from a single source in the Lower Yangzi Valley or whether it was domesticated independently a second time somewhere near the northern Bay of Bengal (northeastern India, Myanmar, or perhaps Thailand).

Rice is widely grown in China today, wherever sufficient water and a frost-free growing season will permit its cultivation. In many areas of southern China two crops of rice are harvested each year, with fields left fallow or planted with vegetables in the remaining months of the year. Paddy rice cultivation (the term comes from the Sanskrit word *padi*, meaning "uncooked rice") is extremely labor-intensive. Seedlings are grown in specially prepared seed-beds while the paddy fields are plowed, flooded, and smoothed to create an even surface of mud under several inches of water. Seedlings are transplanted by hand from the seed-beds to the paddy fields and the fields are weeded several times during the growth phase of the plants (Figure 2.4). As the rice plants mature and develop seed heads, the fields are drained. When the seeds are fully ripe they are harvested, often by hand using knives or sickles, threshed, and further processed to enter the food chain. From early times rice cultivators pounded rice in mortars to remove the bran, converting it from "brown rice" to "white rice." This was done not so much for culinary reasons but to retard spoilage: white rice can be stored for much longer than brown rice without beginning to rot. Some phases of the rice cycle, particularly plowing and threshing, have been mechanized in modern times to replace muscle power with mechanical power, but rice cultivation remains laborious.

Figure 2.4 Farmers weeding a recently planted rice field. Rice produces a high yield of calories per area of land, but is very labor-intensive.

Because of the hilly terrain in much of southern China paddy fields are often part of elaborate networks of irrigated terraces extending far up hillsides and far down into valleys. Many of these terrace networks were established in early times—some as far back as the Han dynasty—and maintained and extended over a period of centuries. Rice plants will rot in stagnant water, so the terraced fields are carefully constructed to be very slightly tilted. Water (originating from a stream, spring, or reservoir) flows into each terrace at one uphill corner and exits through the opposite downhill corner, where it flows into the next terrace downhill. Networks of paddy-field terraces have transformed the landscape of much of the East Asian Heartland Region, and have profoundly influenced settlement patterns and social organization wherever they exist.

Focus: Ox Mountain

The Confucian philosopher Mencius (Mengzi; 391–308 BCE) intended his famous account of the deforestation of Ox Mountain as a parable illustrating how people, through depravity or neglect, could lose their innate sense of goodness. But, taken at face value, it is also a vivid account of an environmental disaster, and perhaps represents a cultural memory of the destruction of forests in the northern Heartland zone in ancient times.

> The trees of Ox Mountain were once beautiful. But because it was located near the borders of a large country, people came with axes and hatchets to cut them down. Could the mountain then retain its beauty? Still, with the fresh air day and night, and the moisture of the rain and the dew, some new buds and shoots sprouted again. But then cattle and sheep came to browse on them, so that the mountain became bare and barren. Now, people looking at it cannot conceive that it once was forested. But how can that be termed the nature of the mountain?

Indeed, even by the late pre-imperial period it would have been hard to believe that parts of northern China had once been heavily wooded.

3   The Neolithic Era and the Jade Age

Introduction

The "Neolithic Period" or "new stone age" covers the time period during which small, mobile groups of people with a tribal form of social organization evolved into settled agricultural village societies and, later, into town-based, socially stratified cultures and possibly early kingdoms or proto-states. It was a time when some communities developed a wide range of new technologies and methods affecting everything from cooking, sewing, pottery-making, and farming to hunting and warfare. Religious beliefs and rituals associated with ancestor worship helped to justify a rising elite class, a class rich enough to support an oral tradition of lineage history.

The term "revolution" is sometimes used to describe the Neolithic era. But the fact that this process took place during a period of as much as 10,000 to 15,000 years suggests that it was more an "evolution" than a "revolution." It was basically a slow process, but one that probably also included occasional technological leaps forward, rapid social transformations, and violent setbacks. In some places such discontinuities, such as the sudden displacement of one culture by a neighboring one, are visible in the archaeological record.

Overview

The Neolithic era in Asia, as in other parts of the world, is marked by the rise of organized communities of people who gradually traded a lifestyle based on the harvesting of wild plant and animal resources for one that emphasized living in permanent houses and engaging in agriculture. The transition from hunting and gathering to the cultivation of crops and the raising of domestic animals, from dwelling as nomads in camps or natural shelters such as caves to living in villages, took place in the East Asian Heartland Region wherever increasing population density in the post-Glacial period made more intensive food production necessary and where local resources would support such intensive production.

The transition from earlier ways of life to Neolithic culture thus occurred in some places but not in others, depending on local conditions. Nor did Neolithic societies always necessarily develop along a uniform trajectory from small agricultural villages to full-scale urban civilization. In isolated areas with limited resources and low population density it was possible for groups of people to retain a hunting and gathering way of life or to reach a plateau at one or another stage of the Neolithic. In some grassland environments people made a Neolithic transition not to agriculture but to the comparably advanced set of cultural techniques known as pastoral nomadism—the raising of flocks and herds of domestic animals in a pattern of shifting habitation (with people living in portable tents rather than permanent houses) according to seasonal cycles of water and pasturage. But in environments characterized by good soil, sufficient water, a benign climate, and increasing population density the Neolithic transition was, it seems, inevitable. Inevitable, that is, because no other solution could be found to the problem of how to feed a larger and denser population than hunting and gathering could support. The East Asian Heartland came to be dominated by Neolithic cultures, which in many cases traded and competed with each other and influenced each other in various ways.

Our knowledge of Neolithic cultures is completely reliant upon archaeological excavations of the past 100 years or so. Neolithic societies were preliterate. Written accounts of the earliest stages of Chinese history consist of creation myths and tales of ancient sage-kings recorded thousands of years later than the events that they purport to describe. Such late written accounts are valuable as evidence of Bronze Age beliefs but provide no information about the Neolithic era itself. (Interestingly, these accounts tell not only of the creation of Heaven and Earth by various divinities, but of the invention by the ancient sage-kings of houses, farming, textiles, writing, religious and secular rituals, and other key phenomena diagnostic of early stages of civilization. This seems to indicate that the Chinese of the Bronze Age at least understood that the rise of civilization was a prolonged and gradual process marked by the development of new technologies.) The substitution of verifiable, reliably dated archaeological evidence of early cultures and civilizations for a prehistory understood only in terms of myths and legends was one of the principal tasks of Chinese scholarship in the twentieth century.

Despite a century's worth of excavations and investigations, however, vast sections of the archaeological record are missing in parts of the East Asian Heartland where local geological conditions have not been conducive to the preservation of sites and artifacts. Even where archaeological remains are relatively abundant they are never complete enough to give a comprehensive view of the cultures they represent. The archaeological record is necessarily fragmentary and incomplete, dominated as it is by durable materials such as stone, bone, seashell, and ceramic. Fossilized pollen and seeds can tell researchers about prevalent plants, which in turn allows inferences to be made about climate and agricultural practices; occasional imprints on ceramic vessels give evidence of cord and cloth. But of a probably rich variety of artifacts of rope and string, netting and textiles, as well as clothing and footwear, baskets, bowls, and other objects made of perishable materials such as wood, bamboo, and leather, few traces remain, although those few can be very informative. Intangible cultural manifestations such as language and music, stories and prayers, are irretrievably lost or available to us only as inferences from other evidence.

While historical change during the Neolithic Period was on the whole slow and evolutionary, the intensifying pace of the development of new cultural technologies during this time period was revolutionary in its long-term impact. The East Asian Heartland Region in this way mirrors changes that are clearly evident in the archaeological remains of pre-Bronze Age cultures throughout the world—rising and evolving on different continents at earlier and later time periods. In eastern Asia the most sophisticated societies, distinguished by their use of advanced technology as well as by cultural and social phenomena such as ritual and hierarchy, rose up in the Northern Heartland Region—that is, the middle Yellow River Valley and the Yellow River Plain. Culturally distinct communities began to appear even earlier along the Middle and Lower reaches of the Yangzi River and its tributaries, but those societies remained for the most part less urbanized and stratified than those in the Yellow River region. In addition to the communities along the two major river systems of the Heartland Region, Neolithic cultures developed in many places along the east coast, extending far to the north and to the south of the great river deltas.

The East Asian Heartland Neolithic era is usually divided into three approximate stages: the Early Stage, from 7000 to 3500 BCE, the Middle Stage, from 3500 to 2600 BCE, and the Late Stage, from 2600 to 2000 BCE. To these could be added a Preparatory or Transitional Stage, from c. 16000 to 7000 BCE, characterized by the first signs of a transition away from the Paleolithic way of life and the gradual development of Neolithic characteristics. The Middle and Late stages are often, and usefully, referred to together as the Jade Age. These stages are only approximations, and the transition of any given culture from, for example, "middle" to "late" was usually gradual rather than abrupt. While each local culture advanced at its own pace, some early cultures were also in contact with, and mutually influenced, others in different regions.

The end of the Paleolithic, and the Neolithic transition

For most of the 100+ millennia of the existence of the human species *Homo sapiens* people lived by hunting wild animals and gathering wild plants. Human population densities were low, and people lived in small bands of usually not more than 200 or 300 individuals. People typically would not remain long in any one place, but would travel within a familiar territory using a highly developed knowledge of the location of available resources at different seasons to harvest a sufficient and varied diet throughout the year. If the size of a band increased too much, putting undue pressure on wild resources, some people would migrate away from the band's territory and find a new, uninhabited region in which to establish themselves. It is also likely that competing bands sometimes clashed violently in disputes over control of resources; the losers in such conflicts might flee in search of safer territory. The complex dynamics of conflict, branching, and migration led to the peopling of most of the globe, as groups found, adapted to, and developed new technologies to exploit habitats ranging from boreal forests to tropical islands.

The peopling of the territory that we now know as China appears to have been part of a large-scale series of migrations of peoples at the end of the last Ice Age (a gradual process as the great glaciers receded from south to north between about 18,000 and 12,000 years ago). As the ice receded and gave way to grasslands teeming with game, people throughout Eurasia expanded into areas that had been denied to them by ice and cold. While it was once widely believed (and is still argued by many scholars in China) that the Chinese people were directly descended from "Peking Man" (members of an extinct earlier human species, *Homo erectus*, whose remains, dating to more than 500,000 years ago, have been found in caves near Beijing), and thus have in effect always lived in China, genetic and linguistic evidence now supports the theory that the present-day majority inhabitants of China—the Han people—arrived as part of this extensive wave of migration, perhaps from an ancient homeland near the Caspian Sea, in comparatively recent times. If that is so, then the East Asian Heartland Region participated in, rather than being isolated from, continent-wide processes that were leading inexorably to the Neolithic Revolution.

As long as population densities remained low and the safety valve of migration to unin-habited lands remained available, hunting and gathering provided most of the world's people with a generous and healthy (though at times strenuous and dangerous) way of life. With even a very low rate of population increase over a long period of time, however, empty lands filled up. The abundant game resources of the post-glacial era fueled just such a population increase on a continental scale. Deprived of the safety valve of out-migration, the steadily increasing numbers of people put pressure on wild resources, and on one another. Food and other necessities were no longer freely available in such abundance as to require neither human ownership nor human intervention.

Human manipulation of natural processes was the predictable response, and one unintended long-term result of that was the invention of agriculture. People in migratory bands found that stands of desirable wild plants could be identified, tended, and harvested, year after year. That small degree of human intervention—nurturing particular plant resources—pursued for short-term gain (more, and more reliable, food every year) over a long period of time, was enough to bring about, eventually, the domestication of certain plants. How could that be so? A close look at one of those small interventions will illustrate the process. Grains, as members of the very large family of plants called grasses, have their seeds clustered together in seed-heads or "ears." Typically in wild plants, the individual ears "shatter" when the seeds are ripe, dropping seeds on the ground and in effect sowing the next year's crop of plants. Shattering is very inconvenient for human gatherers, who have to pick up the individual ripe grains from the surface of the ground (where, in addition to being difficult to harvest, they might have become damp or dirty). The natural response would be for people to preferentially harvest ears of grain that adhered a bit longer and more firmly to the stem. Such seed-heads could be carried back to camp and threshed manually, a much more convenient way of collecting the seeds. For a long time, perhaps for many centuries, this had the paradoxical effect of removing anti-shattering genes from the plants' gene-pool, as those seeds were harvested and eaten. This initially worked against the creation of domesticated varieties of grain. But eventually, when people began not only to eat the harvested grain but to plant some of it in selected and specially prepared plots of land, anti-shattering genes (and other desirable genes) would have proliferated rapidly. People then would have quickly noticed that desirable traits could be encouraged by the selection and planting of the best seeds; fully domesticated plants, dependent on human intervention for their propagation, would be the inevitable result. This process of domestication is clearly visible in the archaeological record. Paleobotanists, examining fossilized seeds through microscopes, can readily distinguish between seed-husks (or "spikelets") of wild grain, which have smooth scars where the seeds have dropped naturally from the seed-head, and those of domesticated grain, which have jagged scars where the seeds have been torn from the ears by some process of threshing.

A similar logic explains the domestication of animals. As the gatherers (usually women) of migratory bands were learning to practice gardening, the bands' hunters were learning to "manage" herds of prey animals (usually large herbivores such as horses, cattle, sheep, and goats), defending them against other predators and (by preferentially killing hard-to-handle individuals) encouraging docility and other favored traits. (This kind of proto-domestication can be seen even today in the cultures of the Sami and some other peoples of northern Siberia, who tend and manage herds of wild reindeer.) Paralleling the invention of agriculture, this tending of herds of wild animals led to the invention of animal husbandry. Over time these animals became so adapted to human intervention that they could not only be easily killed for food but also be exploited for milk and employed to carry burdens or pull vehicles.

Other animals, such as wolves, wild swine, and jungle fowl, became domesticated through a sort of voluntary partnership with humans, by becoming scavengers around human encampments and settlements. (Biologists refer to such animals as being "commensal" with humans, literally meaning "eating at the same table.") Aggressive and threatening animals were killed or driven away by villagers, while docile ones were tolerated as sources of security (making noise if strangers approached), useful services (eating the settlement's garbage), and food.

The simple act of selecting for tameness (like the analogous process of selecting and planting seed-heads that would not shatter) had wide-ranging, unintended consequences: the transformation of wolves into dogs, wild swine into pigs, and jungle fowl into chickens.

The Neolithic transition in East Asia

In the East Asian Heartland Region the earliest signs of the transition from the Paleolithic to the Neolithic are found at Yuchanyan, in the lake district of the central Yangzi Valley (present-day Hunan Province). There, pottery has been found in association with organic materials radiocarbon-dated to an astonishing 16,300–15,500 BCE. Recent finds of pottery fragments in other ancient cave-shelters in the same general region and of comparable date confirm that the people of the central Yangzi Valley produced the oldest ceramic wares so far found anywhere in the world. Fossilized grains indicate that the Yuchanyan people were harvesting, and perhaps tending, stands of wild rice, pushing back by several millennia the prehistory of the domestication of rice. The archaeological remains of the Yuchanyan people were found in a cave that evidently was used repeatedly as a shelter; no evidence has been found of huts or houses. Pottery, being too heavy to be carried by hunter-gatherers constantly on the move, has traditionally been seen as diagnostic of Neolithic culture, but the Yuchanyan evidence forces a re-evaluation of that conclusion. Present evidence suggests that the Yuchanyan people were in a pre-Neolithic transitional stage, perhaps having developed a semi-sedentary lifestyle in which tended wild plants (and possibly managed populations of wild animals, though evidence of this is lacking) were beginning to assume increasing importance. Their food-gathering techniques apparently allowed them to maintain control over an important cave site, for occupancy (whether full-time or not) and the storage of durable goods. The shape of some of the Yuchanyan pots indicates that they were used for cooking, suggesting that the East Asian habit of boiling or steaming grain-based food (in contrast to the western Eurasian preference for grinding grain into flour and baking it into bread) has very deep cultural roots.

The early stages of the transition to the Neolithic era occurred slowly and gradually; they must have been nearly imperceptible to the people who actually lived through them. But the evidence in the archaeological record is clear. As the Transitional Stage merged into the Early Stage of the Neolithic, people in several different parts of the East Asian Heartland began to depend increasingly on the management of indigenous plants, leading steadily to actual cultivation of domesticated plant species—that is, agriculture in the full meaning of the word. Settlements grew larger and more permanent, turning into villages as long-term habitation of specific sites became the norm. The hunting of wild game and the gathering of wild plant foods and medicines continued, but the diet of ordinary people became increasingly dependent on a narrow range of foods, principally boiled or steamed grain (millet in the north, rice in the south). Domestic animals were kept as material wealth, as sources of meat, and because they were useful in other ways. With management of food resources came the concept of ownership, on the principle that only those who expended the effort were entitled to reap the rewards; with ownership went the need to defend what was owned. People settled in villages not only for a sense of community but also because village life afforded safety and security.

The sedentary, agrarian lifestyle of village-dwellers allowed them to produce and store surplus grain and to make and accumulate durable goods such as pottery vessels and a variety of specialized, well-crafted stone and bone implements. The accumulation of material goods and food resources led in turn to the need for protection, achieved through the construction of moats or walls around established settlements. (This construction of moats and walls poses a challenge to older, romanticized anthropological theories that viewed Neolithic village life as matriarchal, peaceful, and communal, needing defensive fortifications only to guard against fierce wild animals. More recent trends in anthropology stress the probable prevalence of violence in Neolithic life, with a consequent need to defend against raiding or feuding fellow-humans. In this view, warfare and the emergence of a warrior class was one of the principal drivers of social change in the evolution of civilization.)

The material trail of durable goods that early peoples left behind gives us a glimpse into the richness of their cultures. From the stone and bone tools and weapons for farming, hunting, and fishing we can learn about the growing importance of grain production in addition to the traditional arts of hunting and gathering. Spindlewhorls and loomweights reflect the rise of textile production. From the impressions and charred remains of seeds, we know that millet and barley farming began over 8,000 years ago—that is, before 6000 BCE—in the upper, middle, and lower Yellow River Valley system. Rice varieties were cultivated in the wetlands around the Yangzi River system and regions farther south, perhaps beginning as early as 8000 BCE and with domestic varieties gradually becoming more prevalent between about 5000 and 4000 BCE. Grinding stones with stone rollers and food residues in fired clay pots tell us that the ancient peoples in some places processed their grain in various ways and then cooked it in pots along with meats, vegetables, and other ingredients, and that they produced a number of different dishes. The processing and fermenting of grain to make ale also seems to have begun in the Early Neolithic era. Large pottery vessels and pits dug into the ground were also used for storage.

Wherever the Neolithic transition took hold, with its commitment to farming and a grain-based diet, human populations increased at a faster rate than had been the case during the hunter-gatherer Paleolithic Age. But, although the transition to farming produced more calories per unit of land, it also meant less varied diets for most people, with unfortunate consequences. Skeletal remains of early grain consumers show that they were in fact shorter, less robust, and less physically fit than their hunter-gatherer nomadic ancestors. Their more monotonous, carbohydrate-based diet was poorer in vitamins and protein than the Paleolithic diet of meat and wild vegetables; the sugars in grain promoted tooth decay, while the many hours spent daily by women kneeling to process grains or carry out other tasks led to chronic deformations of the bones of their lower legs and feet. The Neolithic transition, clearly, entailed heavy costs as well as significant benefits; but once a group of people had embarked on that course, there was no turning back.

The Early Neolithic

The Early Neolithic Stage in the East Asian Heartland is clearly visible in the Peiligang Culture (c. 7000–5000 BCE) and is seen in paradigmatic form in the important Yangshao Culture, which lasted from approximately 5000 to 3000 BCE and is attested from many sites in the northern zone of the Heartland (Table 3.1; Map 3.1). During the early Yangshao Period many villages produced their own specially designed kiln-fired pottery, hand-built from coils of clay during the early phases of the period, and later made on a wheel. Already a distinction between fine wares for elite or ceremonial use and ordinary pottery for daily use had become evident.

Village life probably encouraged people to develop long-term commitments to locales and their culture. Durable ties to the land, already promoted by the practice of farming, were strengthened through the development of distinctive burial customs and treatment of

Table 3.1 Neolithic and Jade Age cultures.

	Shaanxi—North-west and Wei River	Inner North-east	Middle Yellow River; Wei River; Central Plains	Shandong and North-east Coast	Middle Yangzi and Han River Valleys	Central East Coast; Huai River Valley	South-east Coastal
10,000–5000 Early Neolithic: Farming; stone tools; burial grounds; pottery; signs; music	Laoguantai 6500–5000	Xinle 7000–5000 Xinglongwa 6500–5000	Cishan-Peiligang 8000–5000 Lijiacun 5500–4500	Houli Beixin 6500–5000	Diaotonghuan 10,000–6000 Yuchanyan 8000 Chengbeixi Pengtoushan 6500–5000	Beiligang Jiahu 6500–5000	
5000–3000 Yangshao: Copper work; pottery wheel; kilns; ritual; settlements; hierarchy	Banpo 5000–4000	Hougang Hongshan		Hougang Dawenkou	Xuejiagang Beiyin Daxi	Qiliangang	Hemudu Majiabang 5000–4500
4000–3500 Mid Yangshao	Xiyin Miaodigou	Xiyin Hongshan	Xiyin	Mid Dawenkou	Late Daxi		Hemudu
3500–3000 Late Yangshao Writing?	Majiayao Banshan	Late Hongshan 3000–2500		Late Dawenkou	Early Qujialing	Early Songze	Early Liangzhu
3000–2600 Longshan	Miaodigou 2 Qijia Kexingzhuang		Miaodigou 2 Longshan Hougang	Longshan	Qujialing		Liangzhu
2600–2000 Late Longshan: Rice/millet cultivation; animal husbandry; fine pottery production kilns; wells; pounded earthen walls and platforms; copper; brick-walled cities; boats	Kexingzhuang 2	Xinjiadian	Hougang 2 Taosi (city 2300 BCE)	Longshan	Shijiahe		Liangzhu

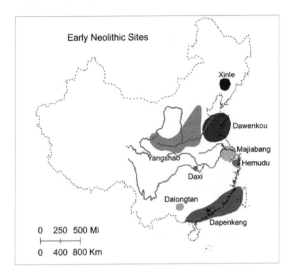

Map 3.1 Important Early Neolithic sites in the Heartland Region.

the dead. Careful study of material remains from burials—which form the major part of all recovered materials—tells us that these early agriculturalists lived in villages of 200 or 300 people by the Early Neolithic Period. Their ceremonies involved music (evidenced by bird-bone flutes and ceramic ocarinas), libations, and local traditions of decorative arts. Trace evidence of perishable goods is sometimes present, both deliberate (in the form of designs made by pressing cord or cloth into the surface of pottery vessels while the clay was still wet) or accidental (patterns preserved in solidified tomb mud). Such goods include finely woven baskets and cloth, felted and leather body coverings, and items made from knotted ropes and yarns.

Networks of economically linked settlements focused on protected centers, which had begun to grow from villages to towns. Linked networks of trade and communication, and possibly of kinship, spanning significant distances, marked the clear evolution of society from scattered and largely autonomous settlements—the first stage of Neolithic social development—to the second stage of simple chiefdoms, organized alliances of culturally integrated peoples. Specialized niches of craft production emerged, while the accumulation of material wealth and the development of long-distance trade led to the emergence of social stratification. "Big Men," individuals whose intelligence, energy, charisma, bravery, skill in the use of weapons, and other positive qualities gave them influence in important matters such as village defense or the organization of labor, rose to positions of wealth and power that in some cases, at least, probably became hereditary for a few generations. Similarly, individuals acknowledged to have special skills in making contact with divinities, treating illnesses, performing exorcisms, and conducting burials and other religious rituals gave rise to a class of religious or ritual specialists who claimed the right to be supported by ordinary workers (see Focus: Shamanism). Practitioners of various crafts tended more and more to specialize in producing articles that could be traded for food or other goods. Such tendencies spread and intensified as late Neolithic society gave rise to the full complex of traits that connote the concept of "civilization."

Representative Early Neolithic sites

Jiahu

The Neolithic village known as Jiahu is located on the southwestern Yellow River Plain, south of the river itself and near the headwaters of the Huai River, in present-day Wuyang County, Henan Province. It is in the same region where, it is thought, some of the earliest deliberate efforts were made by East Asian Paleolithic hunter-gatherers to tend and harvest stands of wild plants around 11,000 BCE—the first step toward actual agriculture. The Neolithic village at Jiahu, occupied from about 7000 to about 5500 BCE, is remarkable for several unusual features found to date in the excavation of the site (which is still far from complete). The Jiahu people made numerous kinds of stone and bone tools and simple but effective pottery. Jiahu flourished during the height of the Mid-Holocene Climatic Optimum, when the climate in the East Asian Heartland Region was significantly warmer and wetter than at present. Hunting and gathering apparently were still important in Jiahu culture, as indicated by the bones of numerous kinds of wild animals found at the site, in addition to fish bones and remains of wild plants. But agriculture was also firmly established. Jiahu farmers raised foxtail millet, a typical northern zone crop, but they also cultivated a domesticated form of rice—the most northerly Neolithic rice cultivation ever discovered. Residue found in a pottery jar of rice mixed with honey, hawthorn berries, and other fruit has been interpreted as some of the earliest evidence from anywhere in the world of fermentation, presumably to make a mead-like "rice ale." (In 2010 equipment of comparable antiquity for making grape wine was discovered by archaeologists in Armenia.)

Burials at Jiahu indicate a belief in some sort of afterlife, as evidenced by grave goods interred with the dead. The amount and kind of grave goods may indicate some distinctions of age, gender, and status (possibly based on political and/or religious and ritual leadership); interred goods range from a few pieces of pottery to dozens of pots and other more unusual, and presumably prestigious, items. These included, in several instances, pieces of turquoise, flutes made from the large wing-bones of cranes, and rattles made of tortoise shells (top and bottom shells fastened together, with several pebbles inside). This early evidence for music has implications for our understanding of East Asian Neolithic religious beliefs and practices. Jiahu is also the source of the East Asian Heartland's earliest known marks or "signs" engraved on tortoise shells and animal bones, widely interpreted as a very early form of Chinese writing (see Focus: Signs on Neolithic pottery). The village seems to have had a population of several hundred people on an ongoing basis, and included houses, pottery kilns, storage pits, and graves. The village was surrounded by a ditch, which has been interpreted by Chinese archaeologists as a way to keep wild animals out and domestic animals in, but which probably also served as a defense against hostile humans. The earliest stage of Jiahu culture appears to be unique, based on these features; its later stages (c. 6600–5500 BCE) are usually classified as belonging to the Peiligang Culture, known from numerous sites in the western Yellow River Plain. The ongoing excavations at Jiahu and other Peiligang sites provide strong evidence for the great antiquity and remarkable sophistication of Neolithic culture in the East Asian Heartland.

Pengtoushan

The Pengtoushan Culture arose in the marshy region around Dongting Lake in the middle reaches of the Yangzi Valley, near the confluence of the Yangzi and the Xiang Rivers. The village at Pengtoushan is one of the oldest permanent settlements known in the East Asian

Heartland Region, and the Pengtoushan Culture was one of the earliest to domesticate rice. Carbonized grains of domestic *Oriza* varieties from the site have been radiocarbon-dated to c. 8200–7800 BCE. The Pengtoushan people lived near the water, fished, ate water plants, fruit, and wild vegetables, and hunted waterfowl, deer, and small game in the surrounding wetlands and woods. They grew rice in small, wet fields, but the extent to which they controlled the flooding and draining of those fields (the defining feature of paddy-field cultivation) is not yet clear. Domesticated animals included pigs, goats, water buffalo, chickens, and ducks. Raw materials for producing pottery, stone, and bone implements could all be found locally; bamboo and other useful plants would have grown abundantly. Pengtoushan ceramics may represent a continuous tradition dating back to the very ancient Yuchanyan Paleolithic transitional pottery of the Yangzi Lakes region, but evidence for intermediate wares is lacking. Flint and hard stones for grinding may have been imported as part of trade with distant cultures. With the warm temperatures prevailing during the Early Neolithic era in the East Asian Heartland Region, rice cultivation spread northward from the Dongting Lake region along the Han River and east to the Huai River Valley. There, people of the Pengtoushan Culture and the Peiligang Culture came into close proximity to each other and interacted through competition, trade, and mutual cultural influence.

Banpo

The best-known and most representative Heartland Region Early Neolithic sites are those associated with the Banpo culture, spanning the period c. 5000–4200 BCE. The culture takes its name from Banpo Village, in the Wei River Valley near the modern city of Xi'an. Banpo Village is famous because much of the excavation site has been covered with a large hangar-like roof, turning the entire area into a site museum. Banpo culture represents an early phase of the Yangshao Culture (c. 5000–3000 BCE), often called the Red Pottery Culture because of its finely made, burnished red pottery ceramics found widely throughout the Yellow River Plain, the Wei River Valley, and adjacent parts of the Loess Highlands (Figure 3.1). Banpo village itself is especially noted for its abundant red pottery. The villagers cultivated plants, especially varieties of millet, and engaged in animal husbandry, tending pigs, dogs, cattle, chickens, ducks, and possibly sheep. They supplemented their farming produce by fishing with bone hooks and hunting with bows and arrows; the relatively warmer and wetter

Figure 3.1 Burnished red-pottery bowl with fish motif, from Banpo Neolithic village, Shaanxi, c. 5000 BCE.

climate of the time probably enhanced the abundance and variety of available wild animals, birds, fish, and plants.

The Banpo people made a wide range of specialized and finely crafted stone tools, and apparently traded with other peoples for luxury goods such as cowry shells from the far southeastern seacoast. Banpo pottery was typical of Yangshao ware generally: red in color, and hand-built from coils of wet clay. (Some later Yangshao sites have provided evidence of perhaps the earliest wheel-thrown pottery in the East Asian Heartland, but claims for the use of the potter's wheel at Banpo are disputed.) Most pottery was utilitarian and undecorated, but some pieces were beautifully polished with a burnishing tool and painted in black with designs of fish, deer, frogs, birds, human faces, nets, and other motifs, both representational and abstract. A few pieces of Banpo pottery are marked with painted "signs" that bear a general resemblance to the signs found on Jiahu Culture tortoise shells and animal bones, and which therefore might also form part of the prehistory of Chinese writing. Pottery was fired at several kilns in the village, with some evidence of craft specialization. At Banpo and some other roughly contemporary Yangshao Culture sites evidence has been found of simple metalwork in the form of small copper artifacts made from local supplies of native copper (rather than being smelted from ore), but true Bronze Age metallurgy still lay far in the future. Imprints of fabric on pottery vessels confirm that the Banpo people had already worked out the complicated technologies required to raise domesticated silkworms, unwind their cocoons to harvest silk filaments and spin them into silk thread, and weave silk cloth. Silk became and remained one of the hallmark products of Sinitic civilization from early Neolithic times onward.

Like most Neolithic villages in the East Asian Heartland, especially in the northern zone, Banpo Village was encircled by a deep, wide defensive ditch. The layout of the village centered on a public plaza, around which were houses, smaller ditches isolating sub-areas of the village, kilns, and graveyards. Small clusters of semi-subterranean round thatched dwellings were built near larger rectangular "great houses," suggesting in their overall layout that the village contained at least four extended clans or lineage groups. Dead infants were buried in pots at the foundations of these houses, while adults were buried in graveyards outside the defensive ditch. The mortuary ritual of primary and secondary burial—reburial of the bones into group tombs of relatives after the flesh was gone—suggests the existence of special ritual processes associated with care for the dead and perhaps some oral genealogical tradition to keep track of (and perhaps worship) deceased ancestors. Modern scholarly claims of early Neolithic "matriarchy" in the East Asian Heartland are clearly exaggerated and ideologically based (they rely on Marxist theories of an inevitable sequence of historical "stages" beginning with "primitive matriarchy"). But female burials that were relatively richly supplied with grave goods, at Banpo and other early Yangshao sites, offer some evidence that in relatively simple and egalitarian village cultures women may have enjoyed higher status than they did in later and more complex Neolithic chiefdoms.

Other Yangshao sites

The Yangshao Culture is seen primarily as a phenomenon of the early and middle Neolithic stages, and in much of the East Asian Heartland Region was succeeded by more advanced Neolithic cultures, such as the succession of cultural levels at Dawenkou (in the Yellow River Plain) or by later Jade Age cultures. But Yangshao cultures did persist in the Northwestern Corridor region, even as more centrally located regions made a transition to the fully developed Longshan Culture. Some of the later Yangshao sites, such as Majiayao (in present-day Gansu Province), have yielded strikingly beautiful Neolithic red pottery painted in colorful geometric designs with abstract or identifiable representations, such as people dancing in lines, holding hands.

Archaeological evidence from the Early Neolithic era hints at religious beliefs and ritual practices, but the evidence is fragmentary and difficult to interpret. Mortuary rituals are clearly implied by burials in which the dead are laid out in stereotyped fashion (face up or face down, extended or flexed, the head facing in a particular direction, etc.) and accompanied by pottery, weapons, and other funerary goods. The dead, in other words, were buried carefully and with attention to ritual details. But whether this amounts to "ancestor worship" in the sense of regular ongoing rites (such as divination or sacrifice) directed at the spirit of the deceased remains an open question. Similarly, certain kinds of imagery, such as the famous fish/mask designs found on a few pieces of Banpo pottery, seem to hint at a belief in the transformation of the soul or spirit after death, but that interpretation rests on making inferences from much later evidence.

Hemudu

The Neolithic cultures found south of the Yellow River Plain present many contrasts to the Peiligang and Yangshao Cultures of the Northern Heartland zone. A representative example is the Early Neolithic Hemudu Culture (5300–4500 BCE) and its immediate successor the Qiliangang Culture (4500–3300 BCE), found around Hangzhou Bay in the lower Yangzi River Valley. Like Banpo, part of the Hemudu excavation area has been enclosed and roofed over to create an on-site museum. The Hemudu and Qiliangang people cultivated several kinds of grain but relied particularly on rice; they had already learned to create level paddy fields and to manipulate the flooding and draining of those fields to maximize the rice harvest. Fields were worked with hoes fashioned from the shoulder blades (scapulae) of large mammals (probably cattle and water buffalo); other tools and implements were produced from stone, bone, wood, and bamboo. These were adapted to a wide variety of purposes and included knives, spearheads, arrowheads, axes, chisels, awls, needles, saw blades, loomweights, shuttles, and cooking utensils. Crops grown in addition to rice in the warm, moist environment of Hemudu included various vegetables and fruits; domesticated animals included dogs, pigs, water buffalo, ducks, and silkworms. Abundant remains of fish and bird bones show that the wetlands were fertile hunting and fishing grounds; birds and other animals were hunted with bows and arrows, and fish with harpoons, bone hooks, and (probably) fiber nets and bamboo traps. Rice and other foods were cooked in ceramic vessels. Hemudu and Qiliangang ceramics were typically decorated with impressed cord patterns, stamped designs, and incised designs, including stylized depictions of plants and animals. Many vessels were made of clay that had been deliberately mixed with rice husks and other organic materials, giving the fired pottery a dark gray or blackish color. Evidence of a certain amount of wealth, leisure, and aesthetic enjoyment comes in the form of bone and ivory carvings of birds and animals, a pottery statuette of a pig, jade and fluorite beads, and other ornaments. The Hemudu people may have been among the first to produce lacquerware, articles of thinly carved wood coated with the sap of the lacquer tree (sometimes artificially colored), which hardens to a smooth, plastic-like consistency.

A characteristic Hemudu motif, found on pottery and depicting a sun image flanked by two birds, may have had some religious significance, but any present-day interpretation of its meaning can only be speculative. The Hemudu and Qiliangang people entertained themselves and perhaps accompanied religious rituals with a variety of musical instruments, including whistles, drums, and an ocarina-like ceramic wind instrument. Villages were irregular in shape and sited to take advantage of the natural defensive topography of the land, rather than being surrounded by fortifications. The houses within those villages were adapted to a warm, damp climate subject to frequent flooding, and so were built on stilts above ground level. The houses consisted of numerous rooms and were connected to other houses by networks of raised walkways. The resemblance of these structures to the "longhouses" historically found in various parts of Southeast Asia heightens the general impression (from the shapes and decoration of ceramics, for example) that Hemudu and Qiliangang were culturally much more akin to other cultures of the southeastern coast than to cultures of the Northern Heartland Region.

The Middle Neolithic and the beginning of the Jade Age

The mid-fourth millennium saw the emergence of the first of several cultures in the East Asian Heartland Region that devoted substantial material and human resources to the production of artifacts made of jade (see Focus: Jade) (Map 3.2). This marks the beginning of what has come to be known as the "Jade Age," a uniquely East Asian variant of the Middle and Late Neolithic era. In Jade Age cultures such as Hongshan, in the northeast, and Liangzhu, in the South-Central Coastal Region, jade objects made in standardized, emblematic shapes were spread over the body of the dead in elite burials and were also employed at sites dedicated to religious rites of some kind. As the early Jade Age (Middle Neolithic) evolved into the later Jade Age (Late Neolithic), clear social ranks emerged in increasingly stratified and complex societies, with elites apparently monopolizing the use of jades, fine pottery, and other high-quality craft products, including a few small items made of copper, which were produced by artisans in workshops attached to large multi-room houses in walled towns. This was especially evident in cultures established along the middle and eastern reaches of the Yellow River Plain, such as the cultural hubs at Miaodigou and Dawenkou. Yangzi River

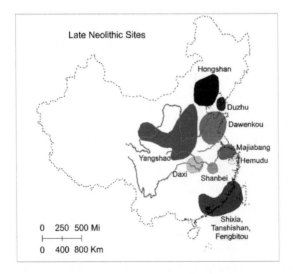

Map 3.2 Important Late Neolithic sites in the Heartland Region.

Valley cultures remained less stratified, but thrived on the production of pottery and jade, which were often traded with northern peoples.

Hongshan

The earliest Jade Age culture known thus far is the Hongshan Culture (c. 3500–2500 BCE) of the Near Northeast. Hongshan settlements, cemeteries, and ritual centers are found in the Liaoning Peninsula, the Liao River Valley, south to the northeastern fringe of the Yellow River Plain along the Gulf of Bohai, and inland to the grasslands (probably then forested) of what is now eastern Inner Mongolia. The Hongshan Culture emerged from local antecedents; during the thousand or so years of its existence it evolved from the "simple chieftainship" stage to the "complex chieftainship" stage of social organization.

The Hongshan Culture is known especially for its finely crafted jade objects, made from local supplies of high-quality nephrite. The most characteristic Hongshan jades are in the form of so-called "pig-dragons," shaped like an almost-closed capital letter "C" in which a detailed carving of an animal head is joined to a smooth, curving, unadorned body (Figure 3.2). These animal heads most commonly resemble pigs, but other types, variously interpreted as horses or dragons, are also depicted. These pieces are often about the size and shape of a bracelet, but most are pierced with a small hole in the curving body and were apparently intended to be worn as pendants, suspended by a cord around a person's neck. This is confirmed by the frequency with which they are found in tombs, resting on the chest of the deceased. Pig-dragons and other kinds of jade carving were regularly interred with the dead as mortuary offerings, and they serve as a clear marker of the culture's social stratification. Many burials contain no

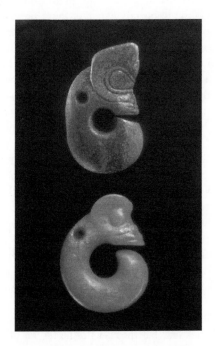

Figure 3.2 Two jade "pig-dragons," apparently worn as pendants, from the Hongshan Culture in the Near Northeast sector of the Heartland Region, c. 3500 BCE.

jades at all, others a very few pieces; in exceptional cases finely built stone-lined tombs, presumably of chieftains or lineage leaders, contain twenty or more jade objects. In addition to C-shaped pendants, Hongshan jades include images of several types of bird, cicada, fish, and turtle, as well as stylized humans.

Hongshan cultural remains include the whole range of artifacts that one would expect from a Middle Neolithic culture, including well-made pottery (red ware decorated in black, perhaps influenced by Yangshao pottery; also cord-marked red ware and gray ware with pierced and incised decorations), evidence of textile production, and a wide range of skillfully made stone tools, weapons, and implements. A few small copper items, such as rings, have been found in Hongshan sites, but evidence of significant metallurgy is lacking. The Hongshan economy was based on hunting and herding as well as on agriculture; sheep and cattle were domesticated, along with pigs, dogs, and chickens. Of particular interest is a new type of stone plow, possibly designed to be pulled by an ox, that would have been more efficient for the cultivation of fields than tillage using hoes.

A striking feature of Hongshan Culture was its penchant for large-scale earthworks. Residential and ceremonial sites were located separately, but both entailed significant investments in construction. Elite residential buildings were built on earthen platforms faced in stone. No evidence of defensive ditches or walls has yet been discovered from Hongshan Culture sites, but that might be a reflection of the limited amount of excavation of Hongshan sites done to date.

Hongshan ceremonial sites are even more impressive than the residential towns and villages. The largest and best-known is at Niuheliang, near Zhushan (Pig Mountain), in the interior of the Near Northeast, in a hilly region inland from the Gulf of Bohai. The site features elaborate, stone-lined elite graves built into step-pyramid-shaped earthen mounds faced with stone. The mounds are encircled by ceramic cylinders that have been described as drums but which perhaps are simply architectural elements. In some cases the main graves are accompanied or surrounded by smaller and less elaborate burials; whether these represent family members or sacrificial victims is a matter of speculation. Many fine jades have been recovered from these tombs. Also at Niuheliang is a large structure termed the Goddess Temple, a multi-room edifice with mural paintings on the walls of rooms and corridors. Within the structure are the remains of numerous statues depicting heavy-set (possibly pregnant) women made of clay pressed around wooden frames. Some of the statues are small, while others are as much as three times life-size. Fragments of one statue show an upper torso with a clearly depicted breast, a lower torso wearing a belt of some kind, and a mask with inlaid eyes of blue jade.

Niuheliang was clearly a key religious and mortuary center. It is impossible to know what religious rites were conducted there or what beliefs those rites enacted, but their physical manifestations are quite different from anything found elsewhere in the East Asian Heartland Region. The Hongshan people apparently traded with surrounding regions and so were not isolated from contact with other cultures, but many aspects of their own culture appear to have been unique, at least on the strength of the present evidence. It is also clear that Hongshan at its height was a wealthy and strongly stratified culture, with leaders who were able to mobilize both skilled workers for the exacting and laborious process of producing fine jade objects and large-scale teams of construction workers to build monumental residential buildings, ceremonial centers, and tombs.

The reasons for the demise of the Hongshan Culture are not well understood. One possible factor is the cooling and drying of the climate of the Near Northeast with the fading of the Mid-Holocene Climatic Optimum. The effects of that slow but inexorable climate change may have cut into agricultural production in that relatively northern region enough to undermine the economic basis of the culture's stratified, wealth-dependent society. The Hongshan people may have been displaced by, or simply absorbed into, the expanding Longshan Culture which appears to have originated in Shandong in the middle of the third millennium BCE. An interesting question that requires further investigation is the extent of the ethno-cultural links between the Hongshan people and the prehistoric cultures of the Korean Peninsula.

Liangzhu

The Liangzhu Culture (c. 3200–2300 BCE), centered in the Lake Tai area in the lower reaches of the Yangzi River, was slightly later than, but substantially overlapped in time with, the Hongshan Culture much further north. Liangzhu was a prosperous and substantial culture with numerous towns, villages, and ceremonial centers spread over an area that extended east and south to the Yangzi Delta and Hangzhou Bay, west to include much of the Lower Yangzi Valley, and north to the southeastern corner of the Yellow River Plain in southern Shandong. (As with almost all prehistoric cultures, the Liangzhu Culture takes its name from a modern place, Liangzhu near Hangzhou, near which important archaeological remains have been found. We have no idea what the Liangzhu people, or any of the other Neolithic peoples of the East Asian Heartland Region, called themselves.) Like Hongshan, Liangzhu was a Jade Age culture distinguished by exceptionally fine and beautifully crafted jade ritual objects of new and distinctive shapes and décor (Figures 3.3–3.5). Throughout the thousand years of its existence the Liangzhu Culture appears to have been characterized by significant social stratification, strong occupational specialization, and a powerful ruling

Figure 3.3 Jade *cong* (prismatic tube) from the Liangzhu Culture of the Lower Yangzi Valley, c. 3000 BCE. The corners of the *cong* are carved with a repeating pattern of a simplified and stylized version of the Liangzhu metamorphic deity figure (compare Figure 3.5).

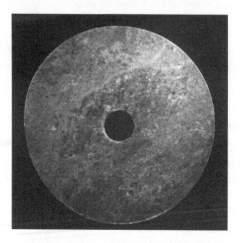

Figure 3.4 Jade *bi* (pierced disk) from the Liangzhu Culture of the Lower Yangzi Valley, c. 3000 BCE.

Figure 3.5 Metamorphic figure, presumed to be a deity of some kind, on a jade *cong* from the Liangzhu Culture of the Lower Yangzi Valley, c. 3000 BCE.

class. The area in which Liangzhu Culture predominated was, however, unlikely to have been a single polity, but rather a number of smaller complex chieftainships, holding territories of various sizes and interacting with their neighbors, whether in cooperation or in conflict. The Liangzhu rulers, who were probably hereditary chieftains supported by elite religious and military leaders, were able to mobilize the production of large quantities of expertly made jade objects as well as the labor to build elaborate public buildings, town walls, pyramid-like earthen altars, and other large structures.

Although the archaeological picture of Liangzhu society is still far from complete, it is evident from recent excavations that in addition to numerous towns and villages there was at least one city with a population of as many as 30,000 people. The city had a threefold system of massive defensive walls, comprising an inner, middle, and outer ring of pounded-earth fortifications. It has been estimated that each of the ring walls would have taken the full-time labor of several hundred workers for as much as ten years, testifying to the ability of the city's rulers to mobilize substantial labor forces and manage the logistics of employing them. The city walls were supplemented by extensive moats, demonstrating the culture's substantial expertise in water management. Excavations at various Liangzhu sites have yielded evidence of different kinds of water management systems, including moats, drainage and transport canals, and irrigation systems. True paddy-field cultivation, with flooding and draining of fields at appropriate times in the growing cycle, was the norm in Liangzhu Culture.

This intensive rice agriculture was the basis of Liangzhu wealth. A population of peasants perhaps numbering in the hundreds of thousands throughout the entire Liangzhu cultural region presumably paid some portion of their harvest to the ruling elite classes, in addition to providing labor service for elite construction projects. Agricultural products included a wide range of vegetables, fruits such as peaches and melons, and the full range of southern-zone domestic animals. Hunting and fishing in the Lower Yangzi wetlands provided abundant water-fowl, game animals both large and small, and fish, turtles, and shellfish, as well as a variety of wild plants. Silkworms were raised to produce silk cloth, and other kinds of fiber were utilized as well. Pottery was abundant and well made, and sometimes painted with signs that, like similar signs from other Heartland cultures, may be precursors of later Chinese writing. The stone tools rivaled those of the Hongshan Culture in their quality and variety, and there must also have been a wide range of bamboo implements, palm-leaf mats, and other articles made from abundant and varied (but unfortunately perishable, and thus largely invisible in the archaeological record) local plant resources. Liangzhu workers also produced high-quality lacquerware, some exceptional pieces of which were inlaid with pieces of jade. Lacquerware, the origins of which perhaps go back to the Early Neolithic era in the East Asian Heartland's southern zone, remains a highly distinctive product of Chinese culture today.

Like the Hemudu people before them, most Liangzhu people seem to have lived in multi-room stilt houses connected by walkways, but in the towns elite dwellings were raised not on stilts but on massive pounded-earth platforms and were built of log pillars with curtain walls of adobe brick. The most impressive Liangzhu structures, however, are pounded-earth plat-form altars built in the form of a three-tiered step-pyramid topped by a hall or pavilion of timber. These platform altars, which provide strong evidence of the wealth and hierarchical stratification of Liangzhu society, were built near but not within walled towns, were some-times planned so that each tier employed different colored earth (for example, gray, yellow, and red), thus showing strong attention to design qualities and marking the structures as truly special and important. Built into the platform terraces were tombs filled with extremely rich funerary gifts, especially articles of jade. Secondary burials near the elite tombs seem to give evidence of human as well as animal sacrifices as part of elite funerary rituals. Remains of burnt animal and human bones associated with the structures on top of the platform altars appear to be evidence for the practice of burning sacrificial offerings (perhaps so that their essence would ascend to the sky); this is something quite different from interring sacrifices with the dead. Such burnt offerings may imply the practice of periodic sacrifices to ancestral spirits on an ongoing basis distinct from whatever funeral rites were performed for the dead at the time of burial. If so, this would constitute some of the earliest evidence for ancestor worship in the full sense of the term, as it came to be practiced as one of the central features of Sinitic culture. The triple-walled Liangzhu city described above also included an observatory (anticipating the famous Longshan observatory at Taosi), which suggests that observations of celestial phenomena were an element of Liangzhu religion.

The most famous remains of the Liangzhu Culture are the many beautifully made jade objects found in elite burials. The high chieftains of Liangzhu were sometimes buried with dozens of jade artifacts representing thousands of hours' worth of skilled artisanal labor. Liangzhu jades were made in a number of characteristic forms, including hairpins, necklaces, pendants, and other personal ornaments, and broad-bladed axes (known by their later Chinese name, *yue*) that may have been used to decapitate sacrificial victims. An unusual jade object, known as the "Lingjiatan Jade Plaque," engraved with directional arrows in the form of a compass rose, testifies to abstract and symbolic thinking (Figure 3.6). The most abundant and striking of all Liangzhu jades are the jade tubes and disks known as *cong* and *bi*, the symbolic significance of which is a matter of lively debate (see Focus: Ritual jades and cosmic symbolism). Many of the tubes, and some other jade objects as well, are decorated with a meticulously carved image that can be read in either of two ways: as a bug-eyed monster mask or as a humanoid figure with a feather headdress standing on a platform and holding a bar-bell-like object (actually two *bi* jade disks). This metamorphic figure is highly stereotyped, showing a remarkable iconographic consistency from one example to another. How these jade objects may have been used or displayed by the living is unknown; we know them from their presence in tombs, placed around and draped on top of the body of the deceased. Whatever their religious meaning—and it seems beyond doubt that these carefully shaped and incised objects were meaningful in some way—they represent a stupendous accumulation of wealth that attests to the prosperity of Liangzhu society, the power wielded by its leaders, and the skill of its craft workers.

Recent archaeological finds in the Liangzhu region provide tenuous but intriguing evidence of written language, the form of what appear to be brief inscriptions on pottery vessels. The inscriptions consist of a small number of graphs, but whether those embody words or syllables (or, indeed, whether they encode language at all) is unknown. The graphs do not appear to be ancestral to the written Chinese characters found at Anyang and other late Shang

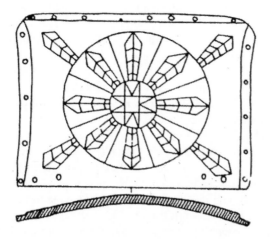

Figure 3.6 The so-called Lingjiatan Jade Plaque from the Liangzhu Culture, evidence of the importance of directional orientation in Liangzhu cultural and intellectual life.

sites, and at the present time they are completely indecipherable. The first difficulty is that no one knows what language was spoken by the Liangzhu people, and whether or not that language is related to Chinese.

The Liangzhu Culture disappears from the archaeological record around 2300 BCE, for reasons that remain unclear. Some scholars have hypothesized that a catastrophic flood, or a series of them (perhaps reflecting a short-term climate fluctuation in the waning phase of the Mid-Holocene Climatic Optimum), may have so disrupted the Lower Yangzi Region's economy that the Liangzhu Culture collapsed and never recovered. If that scenario is correct, refugees from the disaster area may have made their way north to the Yellow River Plain and were absorbed into the thriving and expanding Longshan Culture in and around Shandong. But it is clear that, during the thousand years or so of its existence, the Liangzhu Culture was one of the richest, most sophisticated, and most successful Jade Age cultures of the East Asian Heartland Region.

The Late Neolithic: Longshan

The Late Neolithic era in much of the East Asian Heartland is essentially synonymous with the Longshan Culture, which appears to have arisen in the Yellow River Plain west of Mt. Tai in what is now western Shandong Province, and spread widely to dominate and absorb other contemporary cultures. In the western Yellow River Plain, the Loess Highlands, and the Wei River Valley, for example, the archaeological record of chronological stratification consistently shows the characteristic black pottery of Longshan overlaying—that is, replacing—red pottery in what had earlier been Yangshao cultural sites. (The final phase of Yangshao Culture, identified by distinctive and beautifully painted pottery urns, retreated to the further reaches of the Loess Highlands and the Northwestern Corridor, where it continued to have a relatively autonomous existence during the Longshan Period.) In the south, the Longshan cultural sphere expanded to include the Lower and Middle Yangzi Valley, absorbing and replacing the Liangzhu Culture, and had trade relations with the Upper Yangzi, Sichuan, and other more distant regions and cultures (Map 3.3).

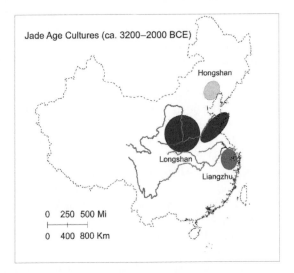

Map 3.3 Jade Age cultures in the Heartland Region.

There was undoubtedly trade, for example, between the Liangzhu Culture area and various centers of Late Neolithic Longshan Culture in Shandong and the Yellow River Plain. Contact between the Liangzhu and Longshan Cultures may have been facilitated by a shift in the course of the Yellow River in the mid-third millennium BCE. The lower course of the river swung from the south to the north of the Shandong Peninsula (emptying into the Gulf of Bohai rather than the Yellow Sea), removing the physical barrier of the wide river that had separated the two cultural areas. There is, however, no sign of an immediate Longshan surge south of the Huai River into Liangzhu territory, and the mutual impact of the two cultures seems to have been limited.

Longshan influence appears to have spread widely in the Heartland Region through several different forms of contact, both peaceful—such as trade, marriage, and gift-giving—and aggressive, through military power. By the Late Neolithic era in the East Asian Heartland it is obvious from the prevalence of weapons and walled cities that warfare was common. New weapons, such as the *ge* dagger-axe, were designed purely for military use and, unlike older dual-use weapons such as bows and arrows, were not suitable for use in hunting. The aggressive spread of Longshan Culture must have incorporated many different peoples, speaking a variety of languages and manifesting various indigenous cultures, into the Longshan sphere. Throughout the region, the Late Neolithic Period saw a rapid rise of population as a function of advances in farming techniques and more efficient territorial administration. The resulting intensification of Jade Age trends toward larger, richer, and more complex societies can be taken as the hallmark of the transition from the Middle to the Late Neolithic Period in the East Asian Heartland. By around 2300 BCE, if not earlier, the Longshan Culture area can be described as comprising a number of interacting complex chieftainships, although scholars disagree on the exact list of sites that fall into this category—an indication of how much archaeological work remains to be done on Longshan Culture. Some of the Longshan complex chiefdoms were continuing to develop toward highly stratified societies—the final phase of the Neolithic era, implying the formation of early states or proto-states ruled by dynastic lineages and supported by elite kinship networks.

Technological developments associated with Longshan Culture include advances in agricultural techniques that resulted in increased crop yields, especially given the continuing benign climate following the Mid-Holocene Climatic Optimum Period. Agriculture benefited not only from the better plows that characterized Middle Neolithic tillage but also from increasingly sophisticated water control techniques that brought more cropland into irrigation networks and paddy-field water management systems. Well-building techniques in the cities improved, and large houses even had rudimentary plumbing with clay pipes. Evidence for more widespread and skillful metalworking—producing copper tools, rings, and bells, as well as some bronze or brass objects—has been found in many sites and must have prepared the way for the full-scale metallurgy of the Early Bronze Age.

Dramatic changes in the human landscape accompanied the transition to the Late Neolithic era. Towns evolved into cities, and often had clearly defined quarters or neighborhoods for different classes of people and occupational specialists as well as increasingly large and impressive elite residences and structures for ritual purposes. Cities were linked to extensive networks of towns and villages. Together these urban–rural assemblages housed large populations and signified the ability of urban elites to control large swaths of countryside and the agrarian wealth produced there. The cities featured advanced house construction techniques. City wall construction became an art. Circular or irregular walls of pounded earth or heaped wet clay, often in conjunction with ditches or moats, had been built around villages and towns from Early Neolithic times onward, but now, in the northern zone, very large, carefully surveyed rectangular walls appeared around Longshan cities. Southern cities tended to have larger moats that functioned with the walls as protection against flooding as well as defense against attacks. Outside the city walls were burial grounds with large elite tombs. Some of the latter were characterized by wooden coffins filled with grave goods such as painted pottery, black pottery, jade implements, drums and other musical instruments, and personal ornaments of various kinds. Divination using oracle bones (dried animal bones cracked by the application of intense heat), which had been known already from some earlier Neolithic sites, became common in Longshan cultural centers, indicating the presence of specialists able to carry out the appropriate procedures.

Elaborate feasting and mortuary rituals dedicated to lineage ancestor worship (with clear evidence of ongoing, periodic rites dedicated to deceased ancestors) developed within Longshan Culture. Ceramic vessels of certain types appear to have been made especially for use in these rituals. For example, the repertoire of Longshan ceramic shapes includes tripod vessels with bulbous, hollow legs, used to heat ale made from fermented rice or millet. Also many Longshan elite tombs contain large numbers of highly refined, eggshell-thin black ceramic goblets, implying some kind of rite or ceremony of drinking toasts before the closing of the grave. Like the Liangzhu elites, the Longshan elites practiced human sacrifice as a regular feature of ritual life. A Longshan innovation in that regard was the burial of one or more human sacrificial victims in the foundations of major buildings. In some cases Longshan rites appear to have been influenced by or absorbed from the local or regional cultic practices of areas incorporated into the expanding Longshan sphere, and it is especially noteworthy that the deity-mask found on Liangzhu jade *cong* prismatic tubes continued to be an important element of Longshan iconography. Classes of artisanal, religious, civil, and military specialists became essential to the smooth practice of Longshan Culture and for its continuous spread outward to an ever-expanding periphery. Shamans, diviners, calendar managers, musicians, and ritual specialists interacted with the potters, stoneworkers, builders, copper workers, woodworkers, butchers, cooks, and many other specialists to support the elite and their increasingly elaborate ritual practices and conspicuous demonstrations of wealth, prestige, and power. As with Hongshan and Liangzhu, the Jade Age culture of Longshan produced finely worked jade artifacts in characteristic shapes, especially long blade-like objects that may have functioned as emblems of elite status. These blades, sometimes referred to as scepters, seem to have been regarded as high-value prestige items even in parts of the Heartland Region beyond the sphere of Longshan Culture, and they were traded over long distances. For example, large numbers of such blades have been excavated from the sites at Sanxingdui and Jinsha, far beyond the Yangzi River Gorges in Sichuan. Some of the blades, though manufactured in Longshan territory (probably in Shandong), were reworked locally in shape and surface decoration to suit local tastes and, perhaps, ritual requirements.

While the changes associated with the Late Neolithic are most obvious in the middle Yellow River regional cultures—the so-called Longshan or Longshanoid Complex—similar trends can be found in other regions, where economic growth seems to have been spurred by the production of particular types of luxury goods. These goods, such as jade and pottery from cultures beyond the Yangzi River Valley, were used not only by their own elites but also for trade. Trade goods almost certainly included perishable items, not directly present in the archaeological record, likely including lacquerware, silk and hemp cloth, specialty foods and seasonings, live animals and animal products such as ivory, rhinoceros horn, furs, and feathers, as well as exotic woods and raw materials such as metal, stone, and bone. As a result, distant cultures were increasingly in contact with one another, facilitating not only trade in material goods but also the exchange of ideas and cultural traits.

For example, the Shijiahe culture (2500–2000 BCE), located in the Dongting lake region of the Middle Yangzi Valley, was contemporary with the late phase of the Liangzhu Culture, and then with the succeeding widespread Longshan Culture. The large Shijiahe site at Tianmen (present-day Tianmen County, Hubei Province) is spread over an area of about twelve square kilometers, and includes a walled city about one kilometer square. It is estimated that the construction of the city wall and moat required at least 1,000 people and that the general population must have included between 20,000 and 40,000 people. Pottery was wheel-made and mass-produced. Shijiahe pottery, and probably also less durable goods including lacquerware and silk textiles, were exported north to the Yellow River Valley, east into the Huai River Valley, and south to the Nanyang Basin.

Shared cultural attributes between these regional populations gradually also came to define an emerging Sinitic culture. With the advent of the fully historical era, following on the end of the Neolithic era and the first manifestations of the Bronze Age, the emergence of Sinitic culture can be tracked by the triumph and spread of the Chinese language. It is quite possible that the people of the core Longshan Culture in western Shandong were among the early speakers of a language ancestral to Chinese, and thus in a sense were the most direct ancestral creators of what would become Chinese culture. While non-Sinitic languages have survived in pockets of what are the present political borders of China up until the present day, the earliest clearly attested writing in the East Asian Heartland Region is unquestionably an early form of Chinese. (As we have seen, the earliest coherent written language in the Heartland is now known only from late Shang dynasty oracle bone inscriptions, but earlier forms of that written language must have existed, and probably evolved from meaningful "signs" painted or incised on Neolithic pottery vessels.) All subsequent written texts in the Heartland Region derive from this core written Sinitic language, although regional variations were strong, particularly in the Yangzi Valley, Sichuan, and the Near Northeast—regions with ancient traditions that developed during the Neolithic Period.

The roots of civilization in the East Asian Heartland were widespread and diverse, and many different cultures contributed to the gradual emergence of a dominant cultural style. In this process, the importance of Longshan Culture stands out. We conclude this survey of the Neolithic era in the East Asian Heartland Region with an account of two Longshan Culture sites that point to the transition from the Neolithic to the Bronze Age.

Taosi

The Taosi cultural complex—or perhaps one should say city-state—represents a Longshan or Longshanoid culture of the eastern Loess Highlands. (The excavations are in the vicinity of present-day Xiangfen, Shanxi Province.) With an area within the walled city of about 1.1 square miles (2.8 square kilometers), it is the largest Longshan site yet discovered, although it seems probable that future excavations in the Longshan core territory of Shandong will one day turn up still larger ones. Taosi is dominated by a massively walled city dating to approximately 2360 BCE at the center of a complex of villages, cemeteries, and ritual structures. Within the city itself, some dwellings were built so as to take advantage of the special architectural properties of the loess soil; courtyards were dug down into the loess, and then caves were dug into the four walls of the courtyard to serve as rooms. Other structures were erected atop massive platforms of pounded loess.

A huge cemetery near the city, containing an estimated 10,000 graves, gives clear evidence of the social stratification characteristic of Longshan sites. A strongly hierarchical society is reflected in the size of graves and in the quality and quantity of grave goods. Less than 10 percent of the graves have been excavated. Of those, about 600 are classified as small, with few or no grave offerings. Eighty-five graves are described as medium-sized; those were supplied with wooden coffins and contained a modest amount of grave goods, including articles made of wood, stone, and pottery. The six "large" graves excavated so far, in contrast, were filled with rich grave goods, amounting to hundreds of items in each. Painted wooden coffins were entombed in large chambers the walls of which were adorned with murals and the floors strewn with powdered cinnabar. The coffins were surrounded by sacrificed animals, especially pigs, various goods made of copper, jade, lacquer, and pottery, and musical instruments such as stone chimes, pottery drums, and wooden drums with drumheads of alligator skin. Some of the ceramics were decorated with polychrome dragon motifs; others bore written signs similar to those found at a number of other Neolithic sites. Clearly these were the graves of wealthy and powerful members of the ruling elite.

The most unusual structure at Taosi is a solar observatory with a triple terrace of pounded loess forming an eastward-facing wall curving in a convex north–south arc, with twelve notches built into the top of the wall and a viewing position set back from it. The structure is designed so that an observer can precisely locate the position of the rising sun in the appropriate notch in the wall and thus verify the dates of the winter and summer solstices, the spring and autumn equinoxes, and perhaps other significant alignments as well. The structure has been dated to 2100 BCE on the basis of its astronomical alignments. It is one of the earliest pieces of evidence for the practice of calendar-making as a function of government for both practical and ritual purposes—a practice that became standard in later Chinese civilization.

Dawenkou

The most advanced society to evolve during the Neolithic Period was the final phase of the Dawenkou Culture, c. 2600–2000 BCE, located in the eastern section of the Middle Yellow River Valley. The earliest phase of culture at Dawenkou, which takes its name from the Shandong village where the culture's distinctive pottery was first found, dates back to 5000 BCE and is considered a local variant of the widespread Early Neolithic Yangshao Culture. But the final cultural phase at Dawenkou is purely Longshan. The most striking remains of this culture are tall, finely made black pottery goblets found in tombs, and tri-lobe hollow-legged cooking vessels used to heat the ale drunk from the goblets (Figures 3.7 and 3.8). Such drinking vessels, made with eggshell-thin walls and decorated with incised lines and cutout holes, have also been found in tombs of the Liangzhu Culture in the Lower Yangzi Valley, and may have been traded there in exchange for ornately carved Liangzhu jades. Hollow-legged cooking vessels came in several types and sizes, including some that were specially designed as steamers for cooking grain; they are the earliest known examples of a cooking device used for thousands of years thereafter by peoples all over the East Asian Heartland Region. Dawenkou ceramics are sometimes marked with incised signs.

The Dawenkou Culture spread throughout the lower Yellow River Basin and into the south along the coast. By 2400 BCE Dawenkou society was socially complex, with an extreme variation in burial style—ranging from simple graves with very few artifacts to log tombs filled with fine pottery, jade and ivory objects, pig skulls, and, occasionally, human sacrificial victims. Wealthy tombs belonged to powerful individuals from elite lineages. Access to or control over craft production was a symbol of power, indicated by the rich craft products displayed in the tombs of the elite. While tombs of many sizes displayed pig-wealth (sacrificed pigs), only large tombs contained the pots and implements necessary for huge clan feasts that seem to have involved a lot of drinking. This type of conspicuous consumption,

Figure 3.7 Black-ware goblet from the Longshan Culture, Shandong, c. 2500 BCE. Goblets of this kind are often found in Longshan Culture graves, sometimes on top of the corpse, perhaps giving evidence of some sort of graveside ceremony.

Figure 3.8 Pitcher for warming and serving millet ale, from a late Longshan Culture site in Shandong contemporary with the Early Bronze Age Erlitou Culture, c. 2000 BCE. The clay vessel seems to imitate a metal one, held together with rivets.

possibly used as a "send-off" feast for the deceased, has continued as a signature of East Asian Heartland mortuary culture up to the modern day.

The style and disposition of sacrificial and ritual objects placed around the body of the deceased in the Dawenkou Culture would also become typical of Sinitic culture throughout the Heartland. Generally, sacrificial victims and vessels and musical instruments such as alligator drums used in the feast were placed around the perimeter of the tomb, while items such as small axes, turtle shells, bone needles, and awls were placed around the lower portion of the body. Jewelry items, such as hair ornaments, necklaces, arm-rings, and earrings, were placed around the upper body. Some items were gender specific, suggesting different social roles. While many items of jewelry, tools, weapons, and spindlewhorls were found with both males and females, males tended to be interred with whetstones, knives, chisels, bone points, and bone spoons, while females were given head and neck ornaments. Stemmed drinking vessels for ale were placed near the upper body with the mouths facing the top of the grave. By the middle of the third millennium BCE cups were placed around the perimeter of the tomb and drinking vessels placed over the arms and legs of the corpse, suggesting, perhaps, that the corpse was the host of an afterlife feast.

Body disposition—supine, left or right side, prone, or flexed—can reflect a community's cosmology concerning the world of the dead and their relationship to the earth. Different disposition styles found in a single burial ground may reflect the social layering of different peoples and traditions or perhaps a unitary custom, such as that involving a ritual calendar, in a single culture. The Dawenkou burials included all types but most bodies were supine and facing in an easterly direction, suggesting that there was something special about those people who were buried in crouched positions or facing in other directions. If the people were buried to face the sun, north–south variations in the angle of burial can be explained as the result of burials in different seasons. Some burials may have been oriented towards high mountains.

By the end of the Neolithic Period urban civilization as exemplified by the Jade Age Longshan sites at Taosi and Dawenkou consisted of regionally dominant cities, each linked by economic ties, political and military power, and cultural traditions to networks of smaller cities, towns, and villages. These clusters in turn acted as production centers for specialized crafts that were traded with other regional urban clusters. Networks of regional interdependence clearly led to the emergence of China's earliest political states or kingdoms, although the nature of these nascent states remains a point of great debate—were the networks controlled by a single despot with charismatic and coercive powers from a central walled city or did they consist of interdependent clusters of independent settlements linked but not controlled by a single cultic center? However that question is answered, the late Longshan Period sees the Heartland poised for a transition to the Bronze Age and to a social structure dominated by dynastic states.

*

The Neolithic cultures and archaeological sites described in this chapter are only a sample of a much larger and more complicated picture. In a sense, the current state of Neolithic archaeology in China is that there is simultaneously too much and too little: Too much, because thousands of sites have been identified, and hundreds excavated; there is much more data than can readily be assimilated by the scholarly world at large. Too little, because many highly promising sites have barely been investigated at all, and many sites that have been excavated have yet to be described in formal site reports. All of China's Neolithic cultures are imperfectly understood, and there are glaring gaps in the archaeological records of even the best-known ones. Beyond that, terminological confusion is rampant; some scholars follow the now antiquated practice of dividing everything pertaining to the Neolithic in the East

Asian Heartland into either "Yangshao" or "Longshan"; others make ever finer distinctions, dividing the Longshan Culture into thirty or more sub-classifications. Many dates for cultural periods rest on very imperfect or incomplete evidence, and some are highly contested. (For example, there are several versions of the extent and periodization of the Dawenkou culture.) What can be said at this point is that every newly discovered Neolithic site in the Heartland Region adds both new data and new complexity to an already challenging picture. Our under-standing of the diversity of the Neolithic era in East Asia, the formation of Sinitic culture, and the roots of Chinese civilization continues, and will continue, to evolve.

Looking back at the Neolithic era in East Asia, we see that over a period of thousands of years the development of agriculture and animal husbandry led to a long series of techno-logical inventions—such as plows, potters' wheels, kilns, and construction methods for large buildings—and a tendency for societies to become more populous, more stratified, and more socially complex. These processes dynamically changed human history in East Asia, just as the same or similar developments led to the rise of major civilizations in Egypt, Mesopotamia, the Indus Valley, and Mesoamerica. In the East Asian Heartland the interac-tions among various regional cultures throughout time created the roots of Chinese civiliza-tion. As that civilization emerged into the Bronze Age it began more and more to take on characteristics understood throughout recorded history and up through modern times as distinctively "Chinese."

Focus: Shamanism

Shamanism is very likely the world's oldest religion. It existed at least as early as the Early Neolithic era and continues to be practiced, especially by the world's dwindling hunter-gatherer cultures, in the present day. It is found in many parts of the world but especially among the indigenous peoples of the northerly part of the northern hemisphere; the word "shaman" itself (along with its feminine form, "shamanka") is of Siberian origin. The essence of shamanism lies in the ability of a shaman or shamanka to enter a state of trance (sometimes by means of drumming and/or dancing) and, in that state, to become possessed by a spiritual being such as a deceased ancestor or an animal totem. Thus possessed, the shaman might speak with the voice of the god, giving advice or instructions from the supernatural realm about such matters as moving camp (in the case of hunter-gatherers), planting crops (in the case of farmers), treat-ing diseases, exorcising malign spirits, and responding to other exigencies. Shamans thus act as bridges between the human and the spiritual realm. They typically wear special clothing marked with symbols of various kinds and often also wear masks, symbolically transforming themselves into other beings, sometimes exhibiting a mixture of human and animal attributes. The act of entering trance is often induced or at least accompanied by the rhythmic sounds of drums, rattles, flutes, and other musical instruments.

Evidence of ancient shamanism is found widely throughout the ancient East Asian Heart-land Region and the Extended Heartland Region. Shamanism survives to the present day in parts of East Asia, especially in the north (Siberia, Mongolia, and Korea). It appears to have become nearly extinct in China itself, although it survives in some minority regions and in other scattered areas, including parts of Fujian Province and in Taiwan. Many Neolithic buri-als in the East Asian Heartland include paraphernalia associated with shamanism, such as masks, rattles, and drums, and it is a safe assumption that at least some such burials are those of actual shamans. A more difficult question is whether shamanism played a role in the evo-lution of Neolithic societies from simple villages to highly stratified societies or proto-states.

On present evidence, it appears that shamanism was an important element of the religious life of the early East Asian Heartland, but that the role of shamans gradually diminished as societies grew more complex and leadership came to be dominated by lineage-based political and military elites.

Focus: Signs on Neolithic pottery

The first clear evidence of writing in the East Asian Heartland Region appears on bones and turtle shells used in divination from the late Shang dynasty, around 1300 BCE. This "oracle bone writing" already represents a fully formed system, encoding what is recognizably an early form of the Chinese language in script that is clearly ancestral to later written Chinese characters. What are the possible precursors of this early Chinese script?

From the early Neolithic sites of Jiahu and Banpo to the Jade Age remains at Dawenkou, pottery vessels (and, more rarely, animal bones and turtle shells) containing painted or incised marks or "signs" have been found at many different locations in the East Asian Heartland Region, especially but not exclusively in the northern zone. While objects containing marks account for only a tiny fraction of excavated Neolithic pottery and bone objects, cumulatively they amount to hundreds of objects containing dozens of different signs, some of them stereotyped and found repeatedly at different places. Many scholars take the position that these signs are in some way ancestral to the archaic Chinese characters found on Shang dynasty oracle bones thousands of years later, but the precise significance of the signs, and the evolutionary path leading from isolated signs to actual written language, remain very mysterious. Some of the key questions, and their tentative answers, are outlined below.

Are the signs the same as written language?

Definitely not. Ancient signs on pottery and bones almost always appear singly, not in groups that could be taken as written phrases or sentences. (There are only a few known exceptions to this rule, including the enigmatic lines of three or four indecipherable graphs found on pottery of the Liangzhu Culture. More striking is a ceramic fragment from the Longshan Culture site at Dinggong, Shandong, belonging to the Dawenkou cultural sphere, on which eleven indecipherable graphs are incised in two parallel rows.) Even if the signs are considered "words," single words have no syntax and no grammar and so cannot be regarded as "language."

Are the signs words?

No one knows. There is no way to know whether the signs encode words, so that someone could look at a sign and pronounce it in a standard way and give it a consistent meaning. If signs were pronounced as words, why did it take people 4,000 or 5,000 years (from Jiahu to Dinggong, or even to the Shang dynasty) to think of stringing words together to make phrases and sentences?

What might the signs signify?

Some scholars interpret at least some of the signs as numbers, and others as "clan signs" denoting the identity of the maker or owner of the pot or other object on which the signs appear.

Are the signs the same as later written Chinese words?

Some of them appear to be, such as a single line meaning "one," two lines meaning "two," and so on; but the signs that seem to be the same as later written Chinese words tend to be the simplest ones, which are also the most likely to show random independent invention. This question is much debated, and the answer remains unclear.

What about the famous "sun-moon-mountain" sign from Dawenkou?

This sign has no direct counterpart among later Chinese words, but its three elements do resemble the later graphs for "sun," "moon," and "mountain." Was it pronounced as a word? We don't know. What does it mean? Maybe "sunrise" or "sunset"; maybe even "first day of the month" (because the sun and crescent moon together imply "new moon," the day on which Chinese months begin). Or maybe it is the name of a clan. We can at best make plausible guesses. This sign looks intriguingly like an early form of written Chinese, but it may not yet represent a word in a spoken language.

And what about the eleven-graph inscription from Dinggong?

This is the strongest known candidate for pre-Shang written language in the East Asian Heartland Region. It is, however, completely unreadable. One or two of the graphs bear a slight resemblance to later Shang oracle bone graphs, but most do not, and all are incomprehensible. Moreover, it is, at least at the moment, devoid of context; no comparable inscriptions have come to light. The Dinggong inscription looks very much like a kind of writing, but there is not enough evidence to say that it is for sure.

For now, the mystery of the evolution of the written Chinese language remains unsolved.

Focus: Jade

Jade has been highly esteemed in the East Asian Heartland Region since prehistoric times. There are two principal kinds of jade, nephrite and jadeite, but the Chinese word *yu*, conventionally translated as "jade," is a rather general term that can apply to both kinds of jade as well as to other hard stones such as rock crystal and agate. Both nephrite and jadeite are hard, glassy, semi-translucent minerals. The color of nephrite typically ranges through shades of green from nearly white to almost black. Jadeite, which is somewhat harder than nephrite, also exhibits a wider range of colors, including not only intense greens but also white, violet, and orange. Almost all of the thousands of jade articles known from ancient China are made of nephrite. Jadeite is not found in the Heartland Region (its principal source is Myanmar) and was rarely used in China before about 1800.

The essential characteristic of jade is its hardness. It cannot be cut with metal tools, nor can it be shaped by chipping or knapping (as early humans chipped minerals such as flint or obsidian to make tools and weapons for tens of thousands of years). Jade must be shaped by abrasion; cutting, grinding, and polishing jade requires the use of grit made of very hard minerals such as quartz or garnet. Jade can be cut into slices or blocks with a bowstring of silk or horse-tail hair used as a kind of saw to rub grit, lubricated by water, into a cutting groove. Tools made of bamboo can be used with a slurry of grit and water to grind the jade into the desired shape, and finer grit dampened and rubbed with a silk cloth gives the jade its final polish. Similar techniques had been devised in the Early Neolithic Period to work softer stone, as cutting and grinding gradually replaced knapping as the preferred method for making stone tools. Jade working then became feasible as craftsmen learned to adapt these basic methods to deal with the exceptional hardness of nephrite.

Everything about jade, from the rarity of the raw stone to the skill and laborious effort required to shape it, contributed to its appeal as the most luxurious and prestigious material available in the East Asian Heartland prior to the Bronze Age. The high value placed on jade has continued to be one of the hallmarks of Chinese culture even up to the present day.

During the late Neolithic Jade Age jade was made into a variety of personal ornaments, such as hairpins and necklaces, as well as symbolic objects of presumed religious and ritual significance. By the Warring States Period the physical properties of jade itself came to be seen as symbolic of the refined qualities of members of the elite class. Texts of the early imperial era take the smooth polished surface of jade to represent the gentleman's laboriously acquired moral education, while the fact that jade will break but not bend symbolized incorruptibility. The ability of jade to resist dirt and wear represented purity, while its hardness and durability was taken as a symbol of longevity. In pre-imperial burials bodies were often decorated with jade ornaments, with key body areas such as the face, chest, and hands covered with pieces of jade strung together. In some burials of the early imperial era, corpses were encased in suits made of jade plaques fastened together with gold wire, in the hope that doing so would render the body imperishable.

Focus: Ritual jades and cosmic symbolism

Liangzhu Culture elite burials are remarkable for the wealth of jade objects that they contain. The most distinctive of those objects are two types of ritual object that have no obvious practical purpose but which must have conveyed some kind of important symbolic meaning within the Liangzhu belief system. These objects are known by their later Chinese names, *cong* (pronounced "tsoong"), often translated as "prismatic cylinder," and *bi*, a flat disk with a hole cut out of its center. *Cong* take the form of a cylinder pushed through a square fixture, or a series of them; viewed from the end, a *cong* has the appearance of a circle within a square. *Cong* often are incised with a metamorphic image depicting a humanoid figure with an elaborate headdress, a figure that, in another view, morphs into an element of a larger monster-like mask with bulging, staring eyes.

Cong and *bi* jades may have been used by the living in various rituals; there is no evidence either for or against that possibility. We know them as grave goods, and there a pattern does emerge: *bi* were often placed near or under the head of the deceased, while *cong* are draped over the body, giving the impression that they might have been strung together on a rope or a sash and looped over the body when it was interred.

Jade objects of this kind were known to Chinese intellectuals in late pre-imperial times and throughout the imperial era, either as objects excavated from ancient tombs or as treasured heirlooms handed down over the course of many generations. They were assumed to convey some symbolic meaning, and the consensus came to be that *cong* were symbols of Earth and *bi* were symbols of Heaven, this interpretation being consistent with the standard view in Chinese cosmology, dating from the early imperial era, that Heaven is round and Earth is square. Whether that view of their symbolic meaning was shared by the Liangzhu people is impossible to know, but it seems certain that they must have meant something. Their shapes, and the manner in which they were employed as grave goods, was too standardized, or perhaps one should say ritualized, for them to have been simply meaningless, decorative luxury goods. The skill with which they are made also gives eloquent evidence of the craft workers' ability to measure dimensions, calculate angles, engrave fine lines, and perform other intricate tasks of fabrication.

The possibility that the *cong* jades were indeed symbols of Earth and the *bi* jades symbols of Heaven is bolstered to some extent by the evident cosmic symbolism on what has come to be known as the "Lingjiatan Jade Plaque" (see Figure 3.6). This unusual jade object, dating to about 2500 BCE, was found near Lingjiatan (in present-day Hanshan County, Anhui Province, west of the modern city of Nanjing), in the Middle Yangzi Region. The site is on the western periphery of the core Liangzhu area, but its archaeological context identifies the site as belonging to the Liangzhu Culture. A thin, convex rectangular jade plaque, pierced with small holes so as to be sewn onto a piece of cloth, was engraved with a design resembling a compass rose, having eight arrows within a circle and four larger arrows extending to the plaque's four corners. The motif of the circle within a square seems to recall the shape of the *cong* and *bi* jades. The design itself seems self-evidently a depiction of the eight cardinal directions, with emphasis on the four "corner" directions. In later Chinese cosmology these had special significance as the directions associated with seasonal change; northeast represented the transition from winter to spring, southeast the transition from spring to summer, and so on. The plaque was found sandwiched between the upper and lower "shells" of a jade sculpture of a turtle. This too, has possible cosmological significance; in later Chinese cosmology the combination of the flat lower shell and domed upper shell of the turtle was regarded as symbolizing the flat earth surmounted by the dome of heaven. Although, in the absence of written documents, we cannot be sure that our inferences from these jade objects are correct, it does now seem highly likely that Liangzhu religion incorporated beliefs about the importance of directional orientation and the shape of the cosmos.

4   The Early Bronze Age

Introduction

Bronze is an alloy of copper and tin (and sometimes other metals as well, such as arsenic and lead). Hard and durable, it is visually beautiful and pleasant to the touch. In molten form it can be cast to make all sorts of objects, from weapons and tools (arrowheads, axes, knives) to goblets, beakers, caldrons, and other expensive and impressive ritual vessels. Everywhere in Eurasia the invention or introduction of bronze had a revolutionary impact, as the Bronze Age superseded and subsumed the Neolithic era. In the East Asian Heartland Region bronze played an important, and sometimes dominant, role in society for almost three millennia.

A small number of ornamental copper and bronze objects have been excavated at several archaeological sites dating to the third millennium BCE in various parts of what is now China. But a radical change in the number, size, technical sophistication, and presumed function of bronze objects occurred around the turn of the second millennium, when the people of the middle Yellow River Valley region began to cast bronze vessels. This shift from producing small ornamental metal artifacts to an early state-level metallurgical enterprise represents the beginning of the Bronze Age in the East Asian Heartland Region (Table 4.1).

There are two interconnected signatures of the East Asian Bronze Age: the first is the fact that large-scale bronze manufacturing indicates a complex political infrastructure; the other is the fact that bronze items became the highest emblems of power and wealth, and symbols of the right to participate in the royal ancestral cult. These features are amply attested in the later phases of the Bronze Age in the East Asian Heartland region, and are inferred from archaeological evidence for the early phases, for which written records do not exist (or have not yet been discovered).

The Three Dynasties and the Bronze Age

Beginning with the Chinese peoples' earliest attempts in the mid- to late first millennium BCE to record their own history, and continuing throughout the imperial period, the Bronze Age was known as the era of "The Three Dynasties" (*sandai*), a term derived from tales of mythic dynastic founders with sage-like and even magical powers. These Three Dynasties are individually known by the names Xia, Shang, and Zhou. Previous to the twentieth century CE, the only dynasty with known archeological evidence was the Zhou. But after the discovery of inscribed oracle bones and a massive urban and mortuary site, known as "the Ruins of Yin" (Yinxu), near present-day Anyang, the Shang is now fully attested as an historical reality. Both the Shang and Zhou have traceable patriarchal royal lineages and hence qualify, albeit roughly, as "dynasties,"—although many questions remain, such as about the exact genealogy of the early Shang kings and how long the reigns of each of them might have been. The notion of the "Three Dynasties" is further problematized because the Zhou royal house actually lost

Table 4.1 Bronze Age polities.

	Shaanxi, North- west and Wei River	North- east	Middle Yellow River; Central Plains	Shan- dong and Northeast Coast	Middle Yangzi and Han River Valleys	Central East Coast; Huai River Valley	South- east Coastal	Sichuan
2070–1600 "Xia"	Erlitou I–III	Xinjia- dian	Erlitou I–III	Yueshi	Erlitou II			
1500–1400 Early Shang			Erligang		Erligang			
1250–1046 Late Shang			Yinxu					Sanxing- dui
1046–771 Western Zhou	Zhou		Zhou, Jin, Song, Wey, Cao	Qi, Lu	Zeng			
771–479 Spring and Autumn	Qin	Yan	Zhou, Jin, Song, Wey, Cao	Qi, Lu	Chu, Zeng	Wu, Chu	Yue	Shu, Ba
479–221 Warring States	Qin	Yan	Hann, Wei, Zhao	Qi Zhong- shan	Chu	Chu, Yue	Yue	Shu, Ba

all power during the final two-thirds of its supposed 800-year reign. The first of the "Three Dynasties," the Xia, is even more problematical, because there is no inscriptional or paleo-graphic evidence that attests to its existence. The historical status of Xia is the subject of lively and ongoing debate among scholars, with strong arguments advanced by both sides.

The Xia enigma

Many archaeologists and historians, particularly in the Chinese academic world, contend that the Xia dynasty definitely existed and that the large mortuary and urban site of Erlitou in the middle Yellow River Valley must have been its center. There are several arguments in favor of this view. The place is right; it was located in the nexus of powerful late Neolithic cultures and in between the regions in the east and west where, later, the Shang and Zhou would rise. The timing is right; Erlitou flourished from about 2070 to 1600 BCE, the period in which a predecessor dynasty to the Shang would have existed. The size and evident power of the city of Erlitou suggests a dynas-tic capital. Its rectilinear layout, defensive wall, and palaces and ritual buildings erected on tall platforms of pounded earth testify to its ability to enlist or coerce the labor of thousands of con-struction workers. That in turn suggests that the city's leaders enjoyed political and military power extending over a fairly large territory, much of it devoted to agricultural production. The consistent north–south orientation of buildings and tombs seems to testify to an ideological link between cosmology and political power. That link perhaps came into play with an unusual clustering of the five naked-eye-visible planets in 1953 BCE, a spectacular celestial event that may have been taken by people at the time as an omen legitimizing Xia rule.

Moreover, there is solid evidence that Erlitou was an early—perhaps the earliest—center of state-sponsored production of bronze vessels of shapes and types that are clearly known from later examples to have been used in the ceremonies of the royal ancestral cult. In works written later, over a thousand years after the fact, there are lists and legends of Xia kings, including lengths of their reigns. The myth explaining the founding of the dynasty became a central theme in Chinese mythology and remains famous today (see Focus: Yu the Great and China's flood myth). The case for Erlitou as the realm of the Xia dynasty has won many supporters.

But that case also has serious weaknesses. Most telling is the fact that there are no dateable written references to the Xia dynasty earlier than the fourth century BCE. That represents a span of time between the supposed founding of the dynasty and the first written mention of its name of about sixteen centuries—a very long time indeed for historical records, whether written or oral, to survive intact. It is especially striking that the name Xia does not appear on any of the tens of thousands of inscribed oracle bones of the Shang dynasty, even though the Shang supposedly defeated the Xia to establish their own dynasty in power. There are no written records of any kind from the Erlitou Period, so no artifacts self-identify as Xia by means of an inscribed or painted character. If one looks for evidence from the Erlitou Period for a state called Xia, or for a dynastic lineage of kings of Xia, it turns out that there is none. Perhaps, as was the case with the Shang dynasty, clear written evidence for its historical reality will be discovered sometime in the future. For now, many scholars remain cautiously agnostic on the historicity of the Xia, and we will refer to the period from about 2100 to 1600 BCE as the Early Bronze Age or the Erlitou Period rather than the Xia dynasty.

Erlitou

The Bronze Age in China began at Erlitou in the central valley of the Yellow River, to the southeast of modern Luoyang City in Henan Province, near where the Luo River meets the Yellow River. This is downstream from the "Three Gates Gorges," where the Yellow River makes a dramatic bend from a north–south orientation to run west–east. From there, the river and all the peoples traveling along or near it have easy access to the vast Central Plains (Zhongyuan), the heartland of Chinese civilization. The Erlitou Culture inherited, extended, and built upon the cultures of the late Longshan era, such as Taosi and Dawenkou. It seems to have evolved most directly from the Taosi Culture, and the people who elevated Erlitou from a town to a metropolis likely migrated to the area from the north. The city at Erlitou represented the center of a cultural base that influenced a broad area of the middle Yellow River Valley, with links to more distant areas (Map 4.1).

Archaeologists divide the Erlitou era into four phases. At the end of the third millennium BCE Erlitou was a town nestled into the valley of the Yi River, a tributary of the Luo River. The town evidently was located so as to take advantage of the easily defended terrain of a fertile valley. In the second and third Erlitou phases the town grew into a city that, at its height, around 1800 BCE, measured approximately 1.3 × 1.5 miles (1.9 × 2.4 kilometers) in area and supported a population of up to 30,000 residents. The city contained a number of large buildings built on pounded-earth platforms; some of these buildings were palaces inhabited by the city's rulers, while others may have been used for the performance of rituals. The city was surrounded by a defensive wall two meters thick, which is rather small compared with the massive defenses of cities of the late Longshan era. The reason for that remains unclear. It may be that the city's rulers felt secure within the natural defenses provided by the

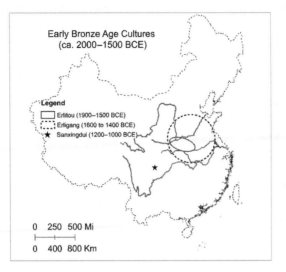

Map 4.1 Early Bronze Age sites in the Heartland Region. The geographical reach of the Erlitou
and Erligang Cultures is still undetermined and the areas shown here are approximate.
The Sanxingdui Culture was contemporary with the Shang dynasty; its origins and
geographical scope remain unknown.

city's location. Possibly the city commanded such a large hinterland that its rulers felt no
threat from neighboring peoples (see Focus: Early Bronze Age warfare).

Unlike earlier cities, Erlitou was laid out as a square, with important streets intersecting at
right angles, a pattern seen in the design of later capital cities throughout Chinese history.
Within the city walls were a number of neighborhoods devoted to the production of artisanal
goods, including jade, ceramics, and bronze; these workshops apparently operated under the
sponsorship and control of the city's rulers. The strong evidence of deliberate urban planning,
with the prominent presence of platforms for palaces and ritual structures, represents a clear
shift from the less regularized layout of pre-Bronze Age cities and seems to mark Erlitou as
the capital of a substantial state.

The final phase of the Erlitou era saw the continued construction of massive public buildings but also gave evidence of stasis leading to decline. After about 1600 Erlitou apparently
came to be overshadowed by a new city located to the east of Erlitou, near the present-day
town of Erligang, near Zhengzhou. The ancient city at Erligang is generally considered to be
the first capital of the newly rising dynasty of Shang. By 1500 BCE Erlitou was, once again,
no more than a small town.

Associated with building complexes in or near Erlitou are a number of tombs that apparently belonged to members of the city's ruling elite. These tombs were large and richly furnished with ceramic, jade, bronze, and other durable goods, and presumably originally
contained many perishable goods as well, such as food, objects made from wood or other
organic materials, and silk textiles. The size of these tombs and the richness of their contents
again testify to the ability of the Erlitou ruling elites to command the labor and skills of large
numbers of workers. The geographical proximity of clusters of large buildings with craft
centers and burial grounds suggests Erlitou's role as a religious or cult center. Archaeologists
recently uncovered a site at Erlitou consisting of groups of building foundations connected by

roads. Archaeologists speculate that one set of large buildings accompanying the largest tomb found so far at this site was linked to a founder ancestor cult (see Focus: A tomb at Erlitou).

The Erlitou economy

The basis of Erlitou's economy was agriculture. Farmers in the extensive hinterland of the city of Erlitou grew staple grains such as wheat, various types of millet, and rice (in southerly areas), as well as vegetable crops, and raised domestic animals such as chickens, pigs, and silkworms. Their farming methods were inherited from the mixed cultures of their Neolithic ancestors, but perhaps with greater reliance on irrigation and flood control works, as erosion and silting would have posed constant problems for these early farmers. A fairly extensive and well-organized bureaucratic apparatus must have existed to force these farmers to turn over a portion of their crops to support the administrative, military, ritual, artisanal, and other functions of the urban political center. We can safely infer that the urban elites, comprising one or more ruling lineages, exerted control over wealth production and craft specialization, just as such control was a key to the political and economic success of the later Shang and Zhou societies.

Trade clearly made an important contribution to the wealth of Erlitou Culture. Salt, copper, jade, cowries, turquoise, kaolin clay, precious stones, timber, animals, foods, and fine crafted goods were imported into Erlitou both from nearby towns, which may have been directly or indirectly under the control of Erlitou itself, and over long distances, from the old Taosi economic zone to the north to the Middle Yangzi River Valley to the south. Near Erlitou, the mountains provided metal, salt, and game, as well as agricultural products. The river valleys provided easy communication channels with more distant towns and their hinterlands, leading to the development of stable long-distance networks of trade. The infrastructure required to mine, transport, and process metals and other precious minerals from far distances for the bronze, jade, and other craft industries required secure relations with sources in the north and south. Imports to Erlitou would have included both raw materials and finished products; exports would have featured high-quality processed goods, especially bronzes. The discovery by archaeologists of Erlitou-style bronzes in the Wei River Valley, the Yangzi River Valley, and elsewhere in the Heartland Region suggests both long-distance trade and some measure of dominance over the natural resources essential to the Erlitou way of life and large-scale bronze production.

Bronze and bronze production

The primary trait that separates the Xia culture from its Longshan Period Taosi cultural base is the development of a system to produce cast bronze vessels and other bronze products. The large-scale production of bronze goods was fostered and supervised by an administrative structure that could control resources, transportation, working populations, and a staff of craftsmen.

In contrast to the opportunistic working of native metallic copper, bronze production requires significant technical expertise in several areas. First is mining, including the identification of ores of copper, tin, and lead and the harvesting of those ores from the earth. Pyrotechnical expertise was needed to achieve sufficiently high temperatures, probably using charcoal rather than wood, for smelting the ores to extract their metal content. Alloying the metals in different proportions (spearheads and ritual ale vessels had different requirements of hardness and malleability, calling for different alloy recipes) also required control of high-temperature procedures. Additional expertise was required to make ceramic molds, pour the molten bronze into the molds, and provide the finishing touches to the castings (see

Focus: Bronze casting by the piece-mold method). Administrative skill was needed to train, feed, and house these workers, and to supervise their work. In order to maintain a high level of production, it would be necessary to secure steady supplies of ores or refined metals, whether by territorial control or trade, and that, too, drew on the administrative and financial skills of government personnel.

Once these technical details had been worked out, the craftsmen of Erlitou were able to produce larger and more ornate bronze vessels, as well as bronze weapons, more quickly and in greater quantity than ever before. Large-scale bronze production also assumed a large elite market for these ritual objects, both in this world and in the hereafter; indeed, the majority of known Erlitou-era bronzes have been found buried in tombs over a large and varied region in the middle Yellow River Valley.

By the last third of the Erlitou Period the ruling elite routinely sponsored the production of sacrificial bronze vessels in a number of standardized shapes (and, presumably, with a number of standardized functions). These vessels were based on earlier ceramic types, but the versatility and strength of bronze allowed such vessels to evolve in both shape and surface decoration. One important vessel type was the *ding* (sometimes translated as "caldron"), a round, deep, three-legged pot that in later times (and presumably during the Erlitou Period as well) was used for cooking sacrificial meat in ritual performances affirming the legitimacy of royal power. Another standardized vessel was the *jue*, or goblet, a vessel designed to hold and pour ale; it was basically a three-legged cup that could be placed over a heat source to warm the ale and which had a long spout for pouring it (Figure 4.1). Descendent versions of Erlitou drinking and cooking vessels continued to define the Bronze Age. Inscriptions, dating from late Shang through Zhou times, explain their function in a hierarchical mortuary feast system designed to serve and placate a network of powerful ancestral spirits. The control exercised over the spirits through the correct observance of the rites by their lineage descendants was a reflection of the political power of the living kings, just as the ability to demand sacrifices and other rituals was the source of the continuing power of those kings after they died. This key religious system persisted in concert with other types of rituals involving natural spirits of the earthly and astral realms. The specialized and well-designed Erlitou vessels for cooking, brewing, eating, and drinking not only are evidence of an advanced material culture but also strongly suggest an early version of later Chinese Bronze Age religion.

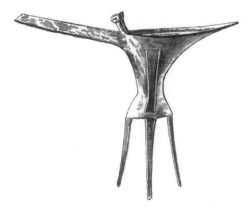

Figure 4.1 A bronze *jue* vessel for warming and serving millet ale, Erlitou Culture, c. 2000 BCE. This is one of the earliest extant bronze ritual vessels in the Heartland Region.

Religion, rituals, and cosmology at Erlitou

In the absence, to date, of inscriptions or other written evidence from Erlitou, we have no direct evidence of what the elites of Erlitou thought and believed. However, it is possible to use pre-Bronze Age and Erlitou archaeological evidence, along with inscriptional evidence from the Shang and Zhou periods—the successors to Erlitou as loci of state power in the East Asian Heartland Region—to make reasonable inferences about a range of Erlitou beliefs and practices.

It seems clear, for example, that religious rituals were performed beyond the simple burial of the dead. Already in the third millennium BCE Yangzi Valley Liangzhu Culture, altar-like structures placed in close proximity to elite graves seem to imply some sort of ongoing devotions involving the entombed person. The existence of structures identified as temples at Erlitou likewise testifies to ongoing religious observances. Whether this amounted to ancestor worship of the kind known later from the Shang and Zhou periods is a matter of speculation, but the evidence is suggestive. The continuity in shape and function of ritual vessels—such as the *ding* and the *jue* for presenting meat and alcohol offerings—from ceramic types in the pre-Bronze Age period up through Erlitou and later may imply some continuity of belief and practice. In other words, the Erlitou elites, like those of later Bronze Age dynasties, may have practiced a religion in which sacrifices of animals (raw, cooked, and in soups) and grain (raw, cooked, and brewed as alcoholic drinks) were made to deceased ancestors. As in later times, these offerings were likely made according to a regular schedule associated with a repeating sixty-day cycle or according to the seasons. In exchange for the offerings—which represented hunting and harvest bounty—the ruler, on behalf of the people, prayed for abundant harvests, long life, children, and other blessings.

The Erlitou peoples continued the Longshan tradition of using oracle bones—that is, specially prepared animal bones that were cracked by the application of heat to give affirmative or negative answers to questions addressed to supernatural powers of some kind (such as nature gods or deified ancestors). Unlike the Shang and Zhou peoples, who used tortoise shells and ox bones for divination, the Erlitou peoples divined using pig and sheep bones. Also unlike their successors, the Erlitou diviners did not inscribe the divinatory questions on the oracle bones. Nevertheless, it seems likely that the later use of oracle bones as a means of consulting deified royal ancestors reflects practices associated with Erlitou and other early proto-states. The oracle bones, together with finely wrought drinking and feasting vessels and other ritual items, attest to a highly developed symbolic system for communication with a pantheon of supernatural entities.

Furthermore, some scholars who accept the historicity of the Xia dynasty point to textual evidence—admittedly dating from over a millennium later—suggesting that key elements of the Chinese calendar system were already in place by the Erlitou Period. Distinctive features of this calendar system include the ten-day "week" (which, during the Shang, was used to keep track of sacrificial rites directed at specific ancestors on specific days of the week); the repeating cycle of sixty days that remained in place throughout later Chinese history as a way of keeping track of days; and perhaps even the twenty-five-month period of ritual mourning between the death of one king and the accession of the next (see Focus: The sixty-day cycle and the ten-day week). While this evidence is open to dispute, it is beyond question that physical evidence from the Jade Age, such as the Liangzhu-Period Lingjiatan "compass rose" jade plaque and the solar observatory at Taosi, denotes a strong cultural commitment to spatial orientation and celestial observation that continued into the Erlitou Period and beyond. The astronomers of Erlitou must have been well aware, for example, of the disparity between the lunar "year" (twelve lunar months, equal approximately to 354 days) and the 365-and-a-fraction days of the solar year. They might, in addition, have had to reckon with the agricultural calendar (twenty-four fifteen-day "fortnights" tuned to the rhythms of plants and seasons; this comprised 360 days, equal to six sixty-day cycles), well known in later times. However, the extent to which this knowledge existed in the Early Bronze Age is unclear. Material evidence suggests that some people, perhaps those in charge of rituals, were already experimenting with calendar keeping (see Focus: The Erlitou sky).

One visually striking symbolic device found in a number of Erlitou Culture tombs consists of a tadpole- or dragon-like figure composed of turquoise mosaic (Figure 4.2). Sometimes this figure appears as a long serpentine form with brightly outlined nose and eyes, possibly once fastened onto a hemp cloth backing, accompanied by a small bell and placed like a shroud over the deceased. In another variation the mosaic was attached to a bronze shield-like plaque; the dragon figure is squat, crouched as if looking up at the viewer. Once again, the eyes are the most prominent feature. Variations of the animal mask and the reptilian dragon form dominate the imagery of late Shang bronze décor and continue in one form or another through the Zhou period. The meaning of this imagery has been and continues to be the subject of scholarly debate; very likely its meaning was not constant, but evolved over the course of millennia. On the one hand, the dragon image may owe some elements of its depiction to real-world animals such as snakes and alligators, both of which, like dragons, were associated with watery environments. On the other hand, when dragons appear on early artifacts they tend to be depicted as distinctively mythical beasts quite unlike any actual snake or alligator. In later Chinese thought dragons were also situated among the heavenly constellations and were able to fly (albeit they were never depicted with wings).

Figure 4.2 Ornament representing a dragon, made of turquoise inlay. Erlitou Culture, c. 1800 BCE. Several examples of this kind of plaque are known from Erlitou tombs, where they were placed on the chest of the deceased.

The placement of turquoise mosaic dragon plaques on the chests of the deceased in elite Erlitou tombs, somewhat like shields, suggests a protective function. No early text explicitly explains the meaning of dragon-like iconography, which appears in various cultural contexts in the East Asian Heartland Region since the Neolithic. Some scholars suggest a relationship of dragons with shamanistic communication with celestial or ancestral spirits; in other words, the spirits of the deceased could ride the dragons up into the sky. Others theorize that the dragons represented the ancestral spirits themselves, endowing those who wore the images with symbolic transcendence. The prolific appearance of dragon-like imagery on sacrificial vessels beginning in the late Shang era suggests a spirit-like role in the consumption of food offerings, an interpretation hinted at in texts a millennium later. Whatever the exact meaning of this imagery (and its exact meaning might never be known), it does seem to involve a relationship to the divine.

Erlitou in context

The elites in Erlitou and in cities in and even beyond its political and economic orbit had access to specialists—today we would call them engineers—who were able to manipulate earth and water on a large scale. To the north of the Yellow River ores were mined in the mountains and salt processed from the lakes. Rivers were tamed with dikes and diverted into irrigation ditches. Fields were cleared and plowed. Fire was controlled to cook food and to transform earth and stone into ceramics and metals for use as vessels, weapons, tools, musical instruments, and ornaments. We know from later inscriptions and texts that citizens (those accepted as "people" (*min*), as distinct from those with different belief systems as well as, perhaps, different languages and customs) viewed their state—either the Shang or the Zhou—as inhabiting the cosmic center, occupying "All Under Heaven" (*tianxia*). We have no idea what the people at Erlitou believed; we can, however, see them as ancestors to the later cultures defined as Shang and Zhou.

Focus: A tomb at Erlitou

In one Erlitou tomb the deceased was clearly powerful enough in life to merit burial with a large repository of jades, bronzes, turquoise, and other luxury goods. While these funerary goods reflect his wealth and power during his life, they also must have had a purpose in providing for his afterlife. Analysis of his burial goods thus provides us with a picture of the inner beliefs and values of the people at Erlitou. This thirty- to thirty-five-year-old man was placed on his side facing east, with his head pointed northward. North was a direction linked with death by the Late Bronze Age. Like the Xia people, the Zhou also oriented burials of their dead to the north. East, on the other hand, the direction later associated with rebirth or deathlessness, was the direction toward which the Shang buried their dead, a custom shared much later with the powerful Yangzi Valley Chu culture from the sixth through third centuries BCE. A rich literature concerning transcendence over death rose with the Chu. Recently excavated documents suggest the antiquity of those ideas and the accompanying spirit worship practices.

The ground of the tomb had been prepared with cinnabar, considered a preservative of the corporal aspect of the self up through the Tang Period (618–907 CE). On top of the cinnabar, the deceased had been laid out carrying a bronze bell and inlaid turquoise dragon (with a white jade nose pointing to the northwest, the direction by Han times linked to transcendence). He had a necklace of ninety cowries around his neck, a symbol of wealth and used for trade in the late Shang and early Zhou period. His earrings were turquoise beads. Around his skull were placed three fine white pottery objects with more turquoise beads—possibly part of a headdress. He was facing a panoply of lacquer and pottery vessels set out as a feast. Some vessels were placed above and behind his head. These ritual preparations are common to later tombs (although the bodies of the Shang and Zhou were placed in supine positions) and suggest a shared conception of the afterlife.

Focus: Yu the Great and China's flood myth

Like many other cultures of early Eurasia, the early Sinitic people of the East Asian Heartland Region had a myth about a great flood that threatened to destroy the world. In the Sinitic version, trouble began when the (legendary) sage-ruler Shun expelled a rebellious group, the Three Miao tribes, from the Heartland for contravening the norms of civilized behavior. This shift of peoples somehow upset the cosmic balance, so that a great, world-engulfing flood ensued. Shun then appointed a being named Gun, who perhaps was a composite human–animal (fish/dragon) figure, to control the raging waters. Gun tried to do so by building dams and dikes, but those efforts failed, and Gun was punished by being exposed on a mountain peak. After some time, his son Yu (also perhaps a composite dragon-like figure; in some versions of the myth he is able to transform himself into a bear) burst fully grown from Gun's body. Shun entrusted Yu with the task of flood control, and Yu successfully drained away the waters by dredging and deepening the existing channels of rivers and marshes.

When the floodwaters had flowed away to the sea, Yu surveyed the land and laid out the boundaries of nine provinces into which the Heartland was divided. Then Shun retired from the throne and, rejecting his own son as unworthy, acquiesced to the demand of the people for a righteous king and that Yu should ascend the throne. When Yu died, after a long reign, the people demanded that his son should succeed him, thus establishing the principle of hereditary rulership in the Heartland Region. Yu is regarded as the founding ruler of the Xia dynasty, and thus the progenitor of 3,000 years of dynastic rule.

It is impossible to know how ancient parts of this myth may be. Yu's name appears in one bronze inscription from the middle Western Zhou Period (around the ninth century BCE), but there is no reference to the flood myth per se, simply to his re-engineering of mountains and rivers. There are no earlier written references to a flood myth, yet oral tradition may have preserved some memory of early water management, irrigation, and flood control.

The prevalence of flood myths in ancient Eurasia suggests a possibility that those myths preserve a cultural memory of some actual flood disaster. Some scholars have suggested that the event commemorated by the myth is an ancient one indeed: the melting of the glaciers of the last Ice Age, around 18,000 to 12,000 years ago, which raised the level of the oceans by about one meter per century for several thousand years and permanently inundated vast amounts of land. Some other interpreters suggest that the flood myths should be understood metaphorically as explanations of celestial phenomena (see Focus: The Erlitou sky). Others point out that the myth of Yu as dynastic founder can be seen as a way of mediating between the ideal of rule by a supremely virtuous sage and the reality of hereditary rule in a dynastic system—an active controversy during the last centuries of the Zhou. The myth formed part of the ideology of the Mandate of Heaven that rulers invoked to legitimize their sovereignty. And some philosophers of the early imperial era pointed to Yu's labors as proof of the wisdom of literally "going with the flow" of natural phenomena rather than seeking to dominate and manipulate the natural world to human ends.

In other traditions, Yu had a magical function. He was associated with a particular gait (like a cripple or a bear). Texts dating as early as the late Zhou note that performing the Steps of Yu three times was a common ritual for exorcising demonic presences, such as was necessary to safely pass through a city gate. Thus Yu, like some of the early dragon imagery, perhaps had a protective role.

It is in the nature of myth to convey important cultural information and to admit of various interpretations. The myth of Yu the Great in some rudimentary form may go back to the Early Bronze Age. Like many later myths it sheds light on the cultural roots of the East Asian Heartland Region.

Focus: Bronze casting by the piece-mold method

The Bronze Age began in Sumer, an ancient Middle Eastern civilization based in Mesopotamia, modern-day Iraq, around 3300 BCE. The technology of blending, smelting, and casting bronze alloys spread to Anatolia and other parts of the Middle East, and to Egypt, within two or three centuries. Thereafter, bronze-working continued to spread eastward through Iran and Central Asia, reaching the northwestern fringe of the Extended East Asian Heartland Region by about 2200 BCE. Along with the "recipe" for the bronze alloy came a method for casting simple objects, such as knives and spearheads, using two-part ceramic molds. But Middle Eastern Bronze Age methods for casting more complex shapes never made it to, or at least were never adopted by, the metallurgists of the East Asian Heartland Region. Instead, those craftsmen developed a unique process of bronze casting known as the piece-mold technique. This seems to have evolved from the Heartland Region's long and highly sophisticated ceramic-making tradition.

The first step in the piece-mold process was to make an exact model in clay of the eventual bronze object—say, for example, a three-legged *ding* ceremonial cooking vessel—including all surface decoration. The clay model was then fired in a kiln to create a sturdy ceramic form. Then soft clay was packed around the model, picking up its every shape and detail. This packed clay was then allowed to harden, but not to complete dryness; then it was sliced into segments and carefully removed from the model. The segments then could be reassembled and tied together, forming a precise mold of the clay model. A clay core was inserted to form the interior of the final bronze vessel; small clay spacers were used to determine the thickness of the bronze body. (These spacers left gaps in the bronze body that were later filled in using a soldering process.) When the mold was fully assembled molten bronze was poured into the narrow space between the mold and the core, and allowed to cool and harden. The mold could then be broken off the cast bronze vessel, and any necessary finishing could be done by hand.

In the hands of skilled craftsmen the piece-mold method was capable of producing bronze works of complex shapes and highly sophisticated décor. At the height of the East Asian Bronze Age vessels that today rank among of the world's greatest bronze masterpieces were made using this method.

Focus: The Erlitou sky

The five planets visible to the naked eye—Mercury, Venus, Mars, Jupiter, and Saturn—conspicuously move against the background of the stars. But the so-called "fixed stars," as viewed from Earth, also appear to move in a much longer time scale. This is a consequence of a "wobble" in Earth's axis of rotation; the axis, projected onto the dome of the heavens, inscribes a circle in the northern sky, taking about 26,000 years to complete one circuit. The spot toward which this projected axis points at any given time is known as the Celestial North Pole. At any given time during the 26,000-year cycle there might or might not be a star at or near that spot. Our own polestar, Polaris (α *Ursa minoris*, the first star in the "handle" of the Little Dipper) began to be used for navigation during Roman times and moved into position close to the true pole around 1100 CE; it is now moving away from the pole. The star Thuban (α *Draconis*) served as the polestar from about 3800 to about 1900 BCE, and would have marked the north pole for the late Neolithic cultures of the East Asian Heartland Region. It was succeeded by Kochab (β *Ursa minoris*). The palace foundations and elite tombs of Erlitou are oriented a few degrees west of true north, probably indicating that the Erlitou rulers continued to use the nearly obsolete Thuban as their polestar. Tombs of the succeeding Shang dynasty, in contrast, are oriented a few degrees east of north; the likely explanation for this is a shift to Kochab as the polestar, even though it had not yet achieved its closest approach to the pole. This shift tells us that the ancient people of the East Asian Heartland were meticulously observing the night sky and using those observations to conform their earthly realm to the patterns of heaven. Probably already in the Erlitou Period celestial phenomena were linked to earthly counterparts. In later Chinese astrology the Milky Way was called the Sky River, and certain constellations were paired with terrestrial states or provinces.

Another consequence of the wobble of Earth's axis of rotation is that the stars which accompany the sun at sunrise on any given day of the year, such as the spring equinox, slowly shift over time. This phenomenon, technically known as the "precession of the equinoxes," is familiar in Western astrology with the shift from one "age" to another, such as the transition from Taurus to Aries around 1800 BCE, and from Aries to Pisces around 1 CE; the Age of Aquarius will dawn around 2700 CE. Western astronomy and astrology were consistently oriented toward the ecliptic (the apparent path of the sun against the fixed stars), while East Asian astronomy and astrology were polar and equatorial in orientation. Rather than the Signs of the Zodiac, East Asians divided the celestial equator (the Earth's equator projected onto the fixed stars) into twenty-eight unequal segments called Lodges; the number twenty-eight is probably derived from the (approximately) twenty-eight-year orbital period of Saturn. This system probably dates to the beginning of the Bronze Age; the movement of the sun, moon, and planets through the Lodges was held to have astrological significance. The planet Jupiter, which takes about twelve years (actually 11.86 years) to complete one orbit through the Lodges, played an important role in Chinese astrology at least from the Warring States Period onward; this feature of Chinese astrology also may have very ancient roots.

In February 1953 BCE the five planets visible to the naked eye gathered in a tight cluster in the constellation Pegasus; all five were packed together in a space about the size of the full moon. This was a rare and spectacular sight that would certainly have been interpreted as an omen of some sort. In later times, the gathering of the planets in a single Lodge was understood to mark the beginning of a new celestial cycle and, by implication, a new dynastic cycle as well. If the planetary cluster of 1953 BCE legitimized the establishment of the Xia dynasty, the dynasty's end may have been signaled by a less-dense but still impressive gathering of the planets in December 1576 BCE that perhaps coincided with and ratified the replacement of the Xia by the Shang.

The doctrine of the "Mandate of Heaven," claiming that dynastic legitimacy is conferred by celestial powers, was first articulated by the Zhou kings to justify their overthrow of the Shang in the eleventh century BCE. The inference from the planetary clusters that a similar idea already existed a millennium earlier is necessarily somewhat speculative. But in any case it is clear that the Bronze Age peoples of the East Asian Heartland were acutely aware of the complex phenomena of the night sky, and tried to make sense of how those phenomena affected their lives.

Focus: Early Bronze Age warfare

There is little direct evidence for early Bronze Age warfare in the East Asian Heartland Region—no archaeologically investigated ancient battlefields, no mass graves of bodies with battle injuries, and of course no contemporary accounts of warfare in that still preliterate phase of Sinitic society. But the indirect evidence is very strong, and it allows us to draw confident conclusions about ancient warfare.

Most obviously, the massive fortifications characteristic of Late Neolithic (Longshan) and Early Bronze Age cities and towns testify to the prevalence of warfare or the threat of war. The enormous effort required to build and maintain these defensive earthworks is inexplicable otherwise. The apparent expansion of the area under the control of the Erlitou polity was probably accomplished at least in part by military force, indicating that attacking armies could sometimes overcome those defensive works. By analogy with massively fortified cities in other historical cultures, we may surmise that the fortified cities of the East Asian Heartland Region served as places of refuge for people fleeing the countryside in the face of an attack, and as citadels in which to mount a defense against an attacking army. Fortified cities and towns also might well have served from time to time as redoubts for urban elites trying to survive uprisings in their own countryside.

Testimony for Late Neolithic and Early Bronze Age warfare is also found in the large number of weapons placed as grave goods in tombs of the time. These weapons included bows and arrows and spears, essentially unchanged from their alternate, and probably prior, function as hunting weapons. The ability of the bronze workshops of the Erlitou Culture to replace stone arrowheads and spear points with sharper and more durable bronze versions would have given the Erlitou armies a significant advantage. The most prevalent Bronze Age weapon, however, was not a repurposed hunting implement, but a pure military weapon. This was the *ge* dagger-axe, a uniquely Sinitic weapon that remained the mainstay of infantry warfare for centuries (Figure 4.3). Sometimes (misleadingly) called a halberd, the *ge* consisted of a broad triangular dagger, generally six to eight inches (fourteen to nineteen centimeters) long and sharpened on both edges, mounted transversely near the end of a wooden pole approximately three feet (around one meter) long. Adapted for

Figure 4.3 Bronze blade for a *ge* dagger-axe, Shang dynasty, c. 1200–1100 BCE. The dagger-axe was the standard infantry weapon in the Heartland Region from the Neolithic era to the Warring States Period.

both slashing and stabbing, the dagger-axe could be wielded either one-handed, like a tennis racket, or two-handed, like a baseball bat; it was effective both for forehand and backhand strokes. Some training and practice must have been necessary to ply the dagger-axe skillfully, and in particular to avoid leaving one's own body exposed after a missed or ineffective stroke. Dagger-axe heads also made the transition from stone to bronze versions, and this remarkable weapon remained in use for some 2,000 years, with both the shape of the blade and the length of the pole evolving over time. Broad-bladed stone or bronze axe heads are also sometimes found in Erlitou- and Shang-era tombs; these were probably not battlefield weapons, but rather were used to decapitate prisoners of war to serve as sacrificial victims.

With the exception of a relatively small number of professional palace guards who provided personal security for members of the elite, Early Bronze Age armies probably consisted mainly of peasants conscripted for relatively short campaigns and provided with only rudimentary training. The prevalence of massively fortified towns and cities testifies to the relative ineffectiveness of such armies, which would have had only limited abilities to mount prolonged sieges or to scale city walls.

Conspicuous by their absence from Early Bronze Age battlefields were three weapons that became characteristic of warfare in the ancient Heartland Region. The war chariot was a West Asian invention that reached the Heartland Region no earlier than the mid- to late Shang era. Swords were rare or absent in the Early Bronze Age, and the use of swords in the Sinitic culture area seems to have originated in the East-Central Coastal Region and spread to the Yellow River Plain during the Spring and Autumn Period. And the crossbow, adapted from hunting weapons employed by cultures situated in the mountains and forests southwest of the Heartland Region, did not enter the arsenal of the Sinitic states until the late Warring States Period. Written texts from Warring States and Han times preserve a cultural memory of Early Bronze Age warfare as small-scale and relatively primitive, and archaeological evidence bears out that view.

Focus: The sixty-day cycle and the ten-day week

Prior to the introduction of the Western (Common Era) calendar in the early twentieth century, the Chinese did not employ a calendar that maintained a continuous, cumulative count of years, beginning with a Year 1 and continuing indefinitely into the future. (The so-called Yellow Emperor Calendar, which, for example, designates 2015 CE as Year 4652, is a modern invention with no historical relevance.) The early peoples of the East Asian Heartland Region devised several different ways of keeping track of the passage of days and years.

Probably the most ancient method, because it is based on such a conspicuous natural phenomenon, is the lunar month (of approximately twenty-nine and a half days, from new moon to new moon) and, by extension, the lunar year—twelve lunar months or approximately 354 days. The lunar year would have been complemented by the solar year of 365.25 days, marked by the return of the rising sun to a designated point on the eastern horizon. These two cycles are incommensurable; at some point, lost in antiquity, people learned to insert intercalary months (leap months) from time to time to keep the solar and lunar years in reasonable proximity. By the Late Bronze Age, astronomers of the East Asian Heartland Region discovered that adding seven lunar months per nineteen solar years served to coordinate the two cycles over fairly long periods of time. (This is known as the Metonic Cycle, after its Greek inventor, Meton of Athens.)

By long-standing convention, probably extending back to prehistoric times, East Asian months were held to begin with the new moon. Accordingly, each new year began on the new moon of a designated first month. In ancient times the first month varied, and one of the tasks of a new dynasty was to designate the official first month. Throughout imperial times, and down to the present day, the Chinese new year begins on the second new moon after the winter solstice. Another solar calendar, also of great antiquity, divided the year into twenty-four named fifteen-day periods, starting with "Spring Begins," forty-six days after the winter solstice and continuing on through the seasonal round. This calendar, with its periods named for natural and agricultural phenomena, approximated the year as 360 days, so five (or sometimes six) days had to be inserted at intervals to maintain synchronicity with the true solar year. Neither of these calendars included a cumulative year count from a putative Year 1.

Another ancient, and unique, system for keeping track of cycles of time was the sexagenary cycle (i.e. a cycle of sixty). This was used from prehistoric times to define a repeating cycle of days; only much later was it applied to a cycle of years as well. The sexagenary cycle was particularly important for scheduling the endless round of sacrifices to the royal ancestors at least as early as the Shang dynasty (as we know from oracle bone inscriptions). The technique for keeping track of the days combined two sets of ordinal numbers, known in imperial times as the ten Heavenly Stems and the twelve Earthly Branches, in such a way as to select a repeating cycle of sixty of the possible 120 combinations. One might visualize a small gear with ten teeth rotating inside a larger gear with twelve teeth, engaging one pair of teeth every day. The gears then reach the initial pair of teeth again on the sixty-first day. The set of sixty having been completed, the cycle begins anew. (For the Heavenly Stems, the Earthly Branches, and the complete cycle of sixty pairs see Tables 4.2 and 4.3.) The origin and meaning of the so-called Stems and Branches are lost in the mists of time; one plausible hypothesis is that the Stems referred to the readily perceptible changing phases of the moon over ten three-day intervals in the course of a lunar month. The Branches may refer to the twelve lunar months of the lunar year, or to the twelve earth-years in one Jupiter year (an important cycle in Chinese astrology). Remarkably, the sixty-day count appears to have been maintained in an unbroken sequence from the Early Bronze Age to the present day.

Table 4.2 The ten Heavenly Stems and twelve Earthly Branches.

Stems	Branches
Jia	Zi
Yi	Chou
Bing	Yin
Ding	Mao
Wu	Chen
Ji	Si
Geng	Wu
Xin	Wei
Ren	Shen
Gui	You
	Xu
	Hai

Table 4.3 The Sexagenary Cycle for days and years.

A1	A11	A9	A7	A5	A3
jiazi	*jiaxu*	*jiashen*	*jiawu*	*jiachen*	*jiayin*
1	11	21	31	41	51
B2	B12	B10	B8	B6	B4
yichou	*yihai*	*yiyou*	*yiwei*	*yisi*	*yimao*
2	12	22	32	42	52
C3	C1	C11	C9	C7	C5
bingyin	*bingzi*	*bingxu*	*bingshen*	*bingwu*	*bingchen*
3	13	23	33	43	53
D4	D2	D12	D10	D8	D6
dingmao	*dingchou*	*dinghai*	*dingyou*	*dingwei*	*dingsi*
4	14	24	34	44	54
E5	E3	E1	E11	E9	E7
wuchen	*wuyin*	*wuzi*	*wuxu*	*wushen*	*wuwu*
5	15	25	35	45	55
F6	F4	F2	F12	F10	F8
jisi	*jimao*	*jichou*	*jihai*	*jiyou*	*jiwei*
6	16	26	36	46	56
G7	G5	G3	G1	G11	G9
gengwu	*gengchen*	*gengyin*	*gengzi*	*gengxu*	*gengshen*
7	17	27	37	47	57
H8	H6	H4	H2	H12	H10
xinwei	*xinsi*	*xinmao*	*xinchou*	*xinhai*	*xinyou*
8	18	28	38	48	58
I9	I7	I5	I3	I1	I11
renshen	*renwu*	*renchen*	*renyin*	*renzi*	*renxu*
9	19	29	39	49	59
J10	J8	J6	J4	J2	J12
guiyou	*guiwei*	*guisi*	*guimao*	*guichou*	*guihai*
10	20	30	40	50	60

Capital letters = Heavenly Stems, numbers = Earthly Branches. The chart is read vertically from left to right, from *jiazi* (A1) at the top of column one to *guihai* (J12) at the bottom of column six. This pairing of the Stems and Branches selects exactly sixty of the possible 120 combinations. After the cycle reaches the pair *guihai*, it begins again with *jiazi*.

5 The Shang dynasty

Introduction

With the Shang dynasty (c. 1600–1046 BCE), the East Asian Heartland Region makes the transition from proto-history to history, from interpretations based on inferences from non-verbal archaeological evidence to direct accounts based on contemporary written documents. The Shang continued the Neolithic and Early Bronze Age practice of using animal bones in divinations designed to diagnose present problems or to predict effective solutions for the future, but added the innovation of carving the divination questions into the bones themselves (Figures 5.1 and 5.2). In this way, the Shang rulers and their divination specialists created a body of written work that speaks to us across a time gap of more than 3,000 years (see Focus: Oracle bones). While these "oracle bones" limit our view to certain ritual activities, the subjects and concerns expressed reveal previously unknown aspects of early Chinese government and religion. Of great significance is the fact that they corroborate some of the later written accounts of the Shang, allowing that evidence to be used, with due caution, in understanding Shang history.

Archaeological evidence continues to play an important role in understanding the Shang era, which was one of dynamic change in the East Asian Heartland. Innovations included the increasing cultivation of wheat and the large-scale raising of domestic sheep, goats, and bovines. Also key was the introduction, via the steppelands of Central Asia, of the war chariot (with associated technologies covering everything from horse breeding and training to the crafting of wheels and harness). The casting of bronze ritual vessels reached a level of technical mastery and aesthetic brilliance that has seldom been equaled throughout world history. Shang officials engineered large structures above and beneath the ground, managed an extensive economic and manufacturing network, and formed a complex government aligning multiple lineages and a hierarchy of officials.

New archaeological work is extending our knowledge of the Shang kingdom's early period, including the locations of its shifting capitals, and of the territorial reach and far-flung trade networks of the Shang at its height (Map 5.1). The ongoing study of oracle bone inscriptions continues to enrich our understanding of Shang religious beliefs and practices. For the first time in the history of the East Asian Heartland a few individual people, such as King Wu Ding (c. 1250–1192 BCE), emerge from the sands of time, known to us by name and deed; here we see biography just beginning to replace mythology. With the Shang it can be stated, perhaps for the first time, that we are looking at a society that is unquestionably directly ancestral to later Chinese culture. Yet Chinese culture evolved dramatically in later centuries; as we look closely at the Shang, we see much that is familiar, but also much that seems archaic and strange (see Focus: The discovery of the Shang dynasty).

Figure 5.1 Bovine scapula used as an oracle bone, Shang dynasty, Anyang period, reign of King Wu Ding (twelfth century BCE).

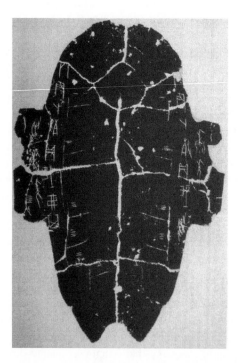

Figure 5.2 Rubbing of a turtle plastron used as an oracle bone, Shang dynasty, Anyang period, reign of King Wu Ding (twelfth century BCE).

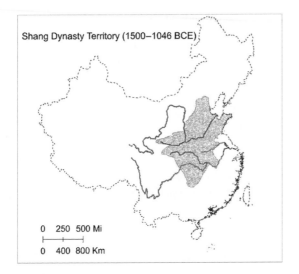

Map 5.1 Territory under the direct or indirect control of the Shang kings during the late (Anyang) phase of the Shang dynasty.

An overview of Shang history

By 1600 BCE Erlitou was in serious decline. The city, within its reconfigured defensive walls, had grown physically smaller, and its population had shrunk. Whether this was wholly or in part due to the misrule, as legend would have it, of the stereotypically depraved King Jie, or whether the decline was due to more mundane factors, Erlitou—the putative Xia dynasty—was nearing the end of its time as the ruling power in the Yellow River Plains. At the same time, a new power was rising at Erligang, about seventy miles downstream on the Yellow River, near the present-day city of Zhengzhou. Most scholars today understand Erligang to be the home of the nascent Shang culture, if not the beginnings of a kingdom.

A major source for Shang history is the "Basic Annals of Yin" of Sima Qian's monumental *Shiji* ("Records of the Grand Historian"; "Yin" is an alternative name for Shang, perhaps with pejorative connotations, used by the succeeding Zhou dynasty). Sima Qian's genealogy of the Shang kings begins with the clearly mythical founding ancestor, Xie, whose mother gave birth to him after swallowing the egg of a black bird. The genealogy lists fourteen pre-dynastic ancestors; whether these were to be understood as chieftains of an ethnic group or rulers of a state subordinate to the (possibly Xia dynasty) realm of Erlitou is unclear. The genealogy enters the realm of probable history with Cheng Tang (Tang the Accomplished), who is portrayed as overthrowing the Xia and executing its last ruler, the supposedly depraved, debauched, and impious King Jie. Tang's role as dynastic founder may have been advanced by a clustering of the five planets that are visible to the naked eye (Mercury, Venus, Mars, Jupiter, and Saturn) in December 1576. This gathering of planets was similar to, though not as tightly bunched together as, the event of February 1953 BCE that may have accompanied the Xia dynasty's rise to power (allowing, for the moment, the historicity of the Xia). The 1576 event may have been taken as an omen that the Xia's era had come to an end and a new dynasty had arisen. We know from archaeological evidence that the Late Neolithic and Bronze Age peoples were keenly interested in celestial events (witness, for example, the observatory at Taosi), and such rare, spectacular sights as these planetary clusterings would surely have been observed and interpreted as important omens.

From Cheng Tang, the first dynastic king, to Pan Geng, the eighteenth of the royal line, the Shang are said to have moved their capital multiple times. Pan Geng's move, in around 1300 BCE, was the final one; thereafter the capital remained in "Shang" (later known as Yinxu). In recent years Chinese archaeologists have excavated a number of Early Shang cities in the Yellow River Plain, and various proposals have been made to match these excavated cities with the early Shang capital cities named in later historical records. As these late written sources suggest, some of these early Shang walled cities date to a time long before the reign of Pan Geng.

The pre-Yinxu sites are culturally consistent with the city at Erligang, which, in turn, as we know from artifacts unearthed there, was influenced by the Erlitou ("Xia") culture. The early Shang cities seem to have dominated the Yellow River Plain from c. 1500 to 1300 BCE. To fit with the traditional Xia–Shang–Zhou "Three Dynasties" (*sandai*) paradigm, many scholars insist that the Erligang phase must represent the early Shang Period, ruled by the kings who preceded Pan Geng in the received Shang genealogy. One site, located at Yanshi, in present-day Henan Province north of the Luo River and south of Mang Mountain, is about four miles (six kilometers) east of the Erlitou site. In an attempt to match later historical records, many Chinese scholars claim that this site must have been an ancient capital, perhaps even Xibo, the legendary capital of the Shang founder Cheng Tang. There are no inscribed oracle bones in this or other Erligang-phase sites, so the actual identity of such sites can only be surmised. The bronze and jade types at Erligang-era sites belong neither to purely Erlitou nor to purely Yinxu styles, but show a shared evolutionary history with both.

The enclosed city at Yanshi was small, covering only three-quarters of a square mile (1.9 square kilometers). The irregularly shaped wall—suggesting perhaps periodic additions or repairs—had seven gates and several crisscrossing wide avenues. A smaller walled-in section inside the southern side of the wall had been filled with purposefully designed, and perhaps ritually organized, architecture: a central palatial structure, flanked on the east and west with buildings in rows. Another enclosure reveals a building with a rudimentary plumbing system, including drainage ditches along the east and west sides, suggesting bathing or food preparation operations. City life was complex and typical of urban centers of the time, no doubt engaging peoples of different socio-economic levels and skills as well as being sites for trade and ceremony. The fact that there were other cities suggests a dynamic exchange between regions perhaps governing a variety of resources. How the early Shang kings did or did not rule these centers is unclear.

As the Shang influence waxed and waned and waxed again, urban cities and towns built high walls of pounded earth. The existence of these walls implies a fear of attack or invasion, likely from confederations of coastal, northern, and northwestern peoples whose relationship with the Shang was unstable. Ancient peoples from the northern and western edges of the old "Xia" world may have been relatively well organized and not fully convinced of Shang legitimacy, even assuming that there was a clear Shang identity at that time. Some scholars suggest that the walled towns were actually garrison towns erected by the Shang army as outposts. The relationship between an isolated army brigade and the local people may have been both economically symbiotic and emotionally hostile. Anthropologist and archaeologist K. C. Chang argued that Shang Period settlements exhibit an "ecosocial interdependence among specialized communities," which included centers for administration, redistribution, and ceremony as well as villages organized under a central power.

While the earliest phases of the Shang dynasty, and its several successive capital cities, still pose many unanswered questions, the final phase is attested by abundant archaeological and oracle-bone inscriptional evidence, and is comparatively well understood. The establishment of the new capital at Yinxu by King Pan Geng is generally accepted as an historical fact, and credible evidence exists for the eleven Shang monarchs who followed him on the throne (though the legendary accounts of Zhòu, the twelfth and last Yinxu monarch, leave much room for doubt). (Note that, while they are spelled alike in romanization, Zhòu [the last Shang king] and Zhōu [the new dynasty] are written with different characters and pronounced differently in the modern tonal Chinese language.)

The royal center at Yinxu lies near the modern city of Anyang, along the Huan river, a tributary of the Yellow River in northeastern Henan. The new Shang capital was established immediately to the south of a Middle Shang Period city at Huanbei, which appears to have subsequently been abandoned as the new city at Yinxu grew. There, elite and commoner residences, workshops, chariot burials, storage pits, and cemeteries were clustered around a large rammed earth structure believed to be a palace or temple. Here, the Shang kings performed sacrificial rites directed at the royal ancestors and a host of major and minor deities embodying natural phenomena, rites that asserted and reinforced their power at the apex of a pyramid that defined the roles of everyone from royal kinsmen to slaves. The kings controlled a complex economic network that provided everything from staples such as grain and cloth to the bronze and jade implements that were the universally acknowledged emblems of power (see Focus: Shang bronzes).

The greatest of the Shang kings was Wu Ding, the twenty-first Shang monarch and the fourth to rule at Yinxu. His dates, known only approximately, are often given as c. 1250–1192 BCE, but might be later than that by a few decades. Regardless of the precise dates, he apparently had a very long reign—traditionally said to have been fifty-nine years—and he brought the Shang state to its pinnacle of power in the world of the East Asian Heartland Region. For centuries before the discovery of the Shang site at Yinxu he was already a famous historical figure because a chapter in the classic called the *Documents* (*Shangshu* or *Shujing*) extols his concern with proper ritual. Other historical legends relate his battle prowess. Modern scholarly knowledge about the reign of Wu Ding is greatly enhanced by his heavy, almost obsessive, reliance on oracle bone divination to guide his every action. The inscriptions on oracle bones from his reign tell his story (see Focus: What is Chinese writing?). Wu Ding seems to have been particularly concerned with confirming the goodwill or disapproval of his ancestral spirits concerning everything from running his government and executing wars to the success of harvest, the fecundity of his wives, and even his own physical aches and pains (apparently he suffered from poor dental hygiene). Although most divination records were positive, rare records from Wu Ding's reign showed that prognosticated events that did not turn out exactly as the king predicted were sometimes recorded, perhaps in the hope of refining procedures so as to reduce the incidence of such false outcomes.

Another important source of information on the Wu Ding era is the tomb of one of his consorts, Lady Fu Hao (see Focus: The tomb of Fu Hao). The only known Shang royal tomb that escaped plundering by robbers, her tomb is a huge structure that has yielded thousands of artifacts relating to her life. Other information about her life has been found on inscribed oracle bones that reveal details of her activities. Wu Ding had many wives; he made a practice of marrying women from various tribes and polities on the periphery of the area under Shang control, so initially Fu Hao was simply one of many living symbols of Shang diplomacy. But she seems to have been an extraordinary person. She was one of the few women in Chinese history to become a significant military leader. Her tomb contained battle-axes and other weapons, and oracle bone inscriptions depict her as leading armed forces against various neighboring peoples. Perhaps because of her military prowess, her son was named heir apparent to Wu Ding, giving her a position of considerable power and prestige at the Shang court. Unluckily, her son predeceased his father, and so never served as king, and Fu Hao died before Wu Ding also.

In the century or so after the reign of Wu Ding the Shang state seems to have entered a period of prolonged decline, probably including the diminution or loss of control over some peoples on the periphery of the Shang domain. In the Shang capital things proceeded much as before, with the same cycle of sacrifices to royal ancestors and the use of oracle bones to guide royal policy. Ritual reforms during the reign of Zu Jia (c. 1170–1151 BCE), referred to by some scholars as the "New School" of Shang administration, involved a more rigid schedule of ancestral cult practices linked to the ritual calendar. Previously, the oracle bones were interpreted as being able to give both positive and negative responses to proposed human actions set forth in the paired questions inscribed on the bones. Under Zu Jia and his successors negative answers were suppressed and not presented to the ancestral spirits for confirmation, and the range of topics presented to the oracle bones was narrowed.

By the time of the decline and fall of the Shang court in the eleventh century BCE, the political power of the royal lineage had gone through repeated waves of expansion and retraction. Some eras, such as those of Pan Geng and Wu Ding, expanded the territory under Shang control; at other times, the domain shrank inward toward the Shang core area. Archaeology attests to two or three different periods of Shang artifacts found far afield, including westward into the Wei River Valley and southward to the Middle Yangzi River Valley, before long-term decline set in during the last century or so of the dynasty's existence. Under Wu Ding's successors the decline seems to have become pervasive and unstoppable. Putting aside for now an account of the exact circumstances and sequence of events, we can at least say with some confidence that in or about 1046 BCE the Shang dynasty was overthrown by a people called the Zhou, whose homeland was in the Wei River Valley. This was not simply a case of one royal family replacing another; the Zhou conquest, as we shall see, had momentous consequences for the development of Chinese civilization.

Characteristics of Shang government and society

Histories written during the Han dynasty (206 BCE–220 CE)—more than a millennium after the fall of the Shang—provide a gloriously detailed account of the Shang era, but that account is not necessarily to be trusted. Many of its details are likely to be purely legendary. Discrepancies between the Han historical accounts and the archaeological reality continue to fuel a debate among historians and archaeologists over the organization and geographical reach of the Shang state. How was political control maintained and what were its actual limits? Were far-flung territories ruled, directly or indirectly, by the Shang kings, or was there simply a spread of Shang high culture to various non-subject or non-allied peoples? Some scholars understand Shang as an empire with an elaborate bureaucracy of ranked officers and others simply as a shifting alliance of city-states based on kinship ties. The truth probably existed somewhere in between and varied over time.

The majority view of the Shang state, at least in its final (Yinxu) Period, has been that it directly controlled a relatively small area of the northern Yellow River Plain, and that it was surrounded by a region it referred to as the Four Quarters (Sifang)—a term that scholar Sarah Allan has shown also applied to the Shang supernatural cosmic model. The surrounding regions, partly or not at all under Shang control, were inhabited by actually or potentially hostile peoples. In recent years the discovery and archaeological excavation of a number of walled cities—of Shang date, and marked by characteristic Shang cultural remains—in the territory of the Four Quarters has led to a reconsideration of the size and territorial control of the Shang state. It now seems possible that such walled cities represent regional capitals of Shang dependent territories, perhaps ruled by members of the Shang royal family or members of the high Shang aristocracy, perhaps even with some titles of nobility similar to those seen in later times. For the moment the evidence for a Shang polity in which dependent states were ruled by Shang royal kinsmen or allied members of the nobility is incomplete and ambiguous. If the evidence holds up, however, it will mark a major shift in our historical understanding of both the Shang kingdom and its successor, the Zhou dynasty, overturning the conventional view that territorial control via dependent aristocratic states was a Zhou invention. The existence (or not) of Shang-era dependent aristocratic states may be resolved as further archaeological evidence comes to light.

The late Shang capital at Yinxu was a metropolitan region consisting of different lineage neighborhoods, workshop areas, palatial structures, and residences located among extensive areas dedicated to elite burial. The ritual center may have been someplace near the royal burial grounds, an expanse of massive tombs guarded by the spirits of sacrificed warriors and other human victims (see Focus: Human sacrifice). Extensive archaeological excavations in the area have revealed caches of oracle bones nearby as well as numerous finely worked bronze and jade objects in the tombs (Figures 5.3 and 5.4).

Evidence from the oracle bone inscriptions provides information about the structure of the Shang government and the nature of Shang society. There is clear evidence of a royal family, headed by a king whose power and actions were upheld but also constrained by a network of

Figure 5.3 Small jade sculpture of a woman with a fish-like or reptilian tail, possibly representing the soul of the deceased person; tomb of Lady Fu Hao, Shang dynasty, Anyang period (twelfth century BCE).

Figure 5.4 Bronze axe of the type used to behead human sacrificial victims; tomb of Lady Fu
Hao, Shang dynasty, Anyang period (twelfth century BCE).

relationships with powerful aristocratic lineages. Members of the royal and aristocratic lineages sought cohesion and stability through marriage alliances. The Shang polity was an example of what is sometimes called a "palace state" or a "ceremonial state," meaning that royal power was expressed largely through the performance of symbolic ritual functions, with the king occupying the symbolic center. Certainly the king acted as a state-builder, protecting and, when possible, expanding the territory under royal control through the use of military power; but, in addition, and perhaps more importantly, he was the chief celebrant of the royal ancestor cult and the interpreter of the will of the ancestors and other deities expressed through divination by means of oracle bones. He also appears to have presided over, and probably participated in, court ceremonials involving music and the performance of masked dances. In these ways the Shang state was strikingly different from the highly bureaucratized, and to some extent meritocratic, governments familiar from later periods of Chinese history.

A particularly high-profile performative role of the Shang kings was their leadership of royal hunts. These were large-scale quasi-military operations that involved the participation of members of the nobility (and an invitation to participate was undoubtedly a sign of royal favor) as well as hundreds of beaters and other workers. The actual hunting took place in areas of many square miles and resulted in the killing or capture of hundreds, or even thousands, of wild animals. Royal hunts were by definition a privilege restricted to the king, and they affirmed his royal power and prestige. Hunts were often staged as part of royal processions to inspect the borderlands, where they were presumably intended to inspire awe and admiration in the rulers of peripheral states. Numerous oracle-bone inscriptions testify to the hunt as a key feature of the king's symbolic role.

Subordinate to the elite classes were skilled workers of all kinds, who belonged to heredi- tary lineages. They were patronized, supported, and regulated by the king and his noble sup- porters, for whom they produced various goods. The king used the services of many kinds of religious specialists. Some prepared oracle bones for use, cracked the bones to perform the divination, and inscribed the divination record on the bones themselves. Others supervised the raising of special animals for use in sacrificial rituals and oversaw workers who slaugh- tered, butchered, and cooked the beasts and offered them on the ancestral altars, along with grain and ale. Other religious specialists were in charge of the calendar, astronomical obser- vations, and astrological interpretations. Still others organized and helped to carry out royal hunts; these workers would have included dog handlers, horse wranglers, chariot drivers and maintenance workers, butchers, handlers of wild animals caught alive, and many others. Within the capital city and other urban areas, hereditary specialist workers (again under elite supervision and patronage) included metal workers (ore smelters, mold-makers, and bronze founders); bone, stone, jade, shell, wood, and ceramic artisans; brewers; wheelwrights; weav- ers and other textile workers; and designers and builders of structures, roads, and walls. Elites acting on behalf of the king also mobilized and oversaw the work of laborers, captives, conscripts, and other low-status workers. One may summarize by saying that the Shang elites commanded all of the resources necessary to the running of a major city and the supplying of the needs of the ruling class.

The oracle bones tell us that some of the inhabitants of the Shang domain were enrolled in groups or classes of people designated as the "Many Fathers," "Many Sons," "Many Archers," "Many Artisans," "Guard of the Many Horse-chariots," "Many Dog Officers," and "men," again no doubt under elite supervision. The military was organized into armies composed of "men," divided into "left, central, or right" units. An elite guard made up of royal relatives, attested for the early Zhou Period and surmised for the Shang, was tasked with protecting the king. Senior members of elite lineages probably had their own guard units, but large-scale military force was the prerogative of the king.

The rural population was highly regulated as well, with officials, acting in response to calendrical calculations and oracle bone divinations, commanding the commencement of major agricultural operations such as plowing, planting, and harvesting. Other officials supervised and controlled animal husbandry. Still others enforced the obligation of peasants to supply grain and other produce to the government, or to perform corvée labor or military service. Some of these government offices engaged junior officers, called *chen*—a word that a millennium later also would refer to a government minister—whose jobs may have ranged from highly esteemed occupations requiring literacy or music skills to lowly positions as simple factotums. How widely writing, for religious or other purposes, was known among the elite or the officer class is a mystery. Scholars suggest that certainly accounting in trade, agriculture, and craft production was required. Scribes may have used bamboo strip scrolls or silk fabric for records other than the ancestor-cult-related bone and eventually bronze inscriptions. But these texts, if they existed at all, did not survive the vicissitudes of time.

Shang society shared many characteristics with other early civilizations in Egypt or Mes- opotamia. It was hierarchical, with a defined elite class that controlled groups of specialists linked to the political, military, religious, and handicraft production spheres. Political organi- zation appears to have consisted of multiple inter-related lineages, all patriarchal, that revolved around a central royal lineage, that of the Shang king and his ancestors. The original meaning of the word for "king" (*wang*) may have been "the man with the axe" (used for chopping off heads), or, alternatively, something like "big man," a kind of chief patriarch in a federated alliance of other patriarchs. The Shang king was probably not the only high chief claiming authority over parts of the East Asian Heartland Region at the time, as there is evidence of other sophisticated civilizations beyond the reach of the Shang court, such as those in the Chengdu basin in the far west, and southern coastal cultures. Artifacts found in these places reveal independent economic and religious systems, but also obvious signs of contact with the Shang civilization.

Shang religion

Religion during the Shang era was exclusively an elite pursuit—if commoners had any religious beliefs and practices, we have no idea what they might have been—and the principal Shang cult, worship of the royal ancestors, was the prerogative of the king himself, assisted by many ritual specialists and functionaries. The other most important elite cult was the worship of Shang Di, the "High God," who presided over such matters as agriculture, weather, and health. There is some debate as to whether the term Shang Di represented a single high god or a group of astral deities, and whether it or they represented the highest, more remote ancestral spirits or nature spirits, or perhaps both. Many oracle bones were cracked to learn the wishes and intentions of the High God, and many sacrificial rites were performed to beseech and propitiate him. In addition, from the oracle bones we know that the Shang worshipped a wide range of nature deities and performed rituals that involved fire (burning victims at key sites, such as on a riverbank), water (sinking sacrificial items into the river), and earth (burying human and animal victims under building foundations and along tomb ramps).

Shang life was controlled by the hierarchy of Shang Di, royal and other powerful ancestral spirits, and deified supernatural environmental forces. While these spirits seem to have controlled separate realms, their powers could overlap. Prayers for rain might be addressed to Shang Di or certain sacred mountains or rivers, but ancestral spirits were queried about rain as well. The dead ancestral kings were also referred to as Di. The succession of kingship under the Shang is a source of much scholarly speculation and dispute. There was clearly no rule of primogeniture, whereby the eldest son inherited his father's throne. Succession was sometimes from father to son (not necessarily the eldest), sometimes from brother to brother, sometimes from uncle to nephew. Some scholars, notably K. C. Chang, have argued that succession alternated between two royal sub-lineages, but others have found flaws in that theory. Whatever the case, all deceased kings were recognized as royal ancestors and were worshipped as such.

Upon dying, kings and their wives were given posthumous names (and we generally refer to Shang kings by those names), consisting of a given name and one of the ten denominators of the Heavenly Stems (see Focus: The sixty-day cycle and the ten-day week, in Chapter 4). That second element of the posthumous name indicated the day of the ten-day "week" on which that particular royal ancestor was worshipped. So, for example, we can interpret the name Wu Ding as "the martial king (*wu*) who receives worship on day 4 (*ding*)." For unknown reasons, probably having to do with lucky and unlucky days, some day-indicators, such as *bing* and *ding* (days three and four of the ten-day cycle), were favored in posthumous names, while others, such as *wu* and *ren* (days 5 and 9) tended to be avoided. In any case, an entire royal department was charged with carrying out the ancestral sacrifices on an ongoing basis, each royal ancestor being worshipped on his proper day.

Besides maintaining a regular calendar of services to the ancestral spirits, diviners had to manage extraordinary events that might require special sacrifices or exorcism rituals. The appearance of a rainbow, or a certain cloud pattern, or a vivid dream were omens that diviners had to interpret. Curses upon the royal family, most likely from the most recently deceased ancestors, but also possibly from distant kings or environmental spirits, had to be dealt with. First the spirit responsible had to be found, then the proper sacrifices determined. Finally, if the sacrifices did not have the desired effect, one of several types of exorcistic rituals had to be determined and performed. A dismembering sacrifice, often of a dog, killed and buried, was performed when beginning the construction of a building or a tomb, or as part of an exorcism to clear an area of malign influences. Time itself, particularly the days associated with ancestral spirits, was filled with spiritual agency. For example, if bandits raided Shang territory it was considered a curse as well as a military emergency, and the king, with the help of his diviners, asked the spirits how many days the curse would last.

Issues of daily life such as agriculture and health required exorcisms and sacrifices to the ancestral spirits and a range of environmental deities, such as winds, directions, mountains, and rivers, or to various lesser gods. They, perhaps under the aegis of the High God, controlled the weather, the harvest, illness, crime, and numerous other aspects of life. Many oracle bone texts show an anxious concern to ascertain the correct deity to whom to offer sacrifice, and the details of the offering, which were often quite substantial: texts speak of "a cutting sacrifice of three penned cattle," "a burnt sacrifice of ten sheep," "a sacrifice of three [human] captives," and so on. Over 2,000 pits with animal and human remains were distributed among the royal tombs (Figure 5.5).

Bronze vessels were an integral part of Shang worship, and their possession was a sign of power and prestige. The number of finely crafted and artistically rendered bronzes put in a tomb reflected the social and political power of the individual. Elaborate rules governed the sacrificial offerings owed to various ancestors, but in general they included both material goods that signaled wealth and magical access to the supernatural, such as jades and bronzes, and food offerings. The sacrifice of animals—especially cattle, pigs, and sheep, but occasionally wild-caught creatures such as deer—represented wealth and power. So, too, the offerings of grain and ale represented control over aspects of the Shang economy. Bronze vessels were needed to cook the meat and the grain and to warm and pour the millet ale. Vessels were made in specific shapes to carry out these various functions.

Figure 5.5 Sacrificial burial of a chariot with its team of horses; tomb of Lady Fu Hao, Shang dynasty, Anyang period (twelfth century BCE).

Shang bronzes, especially those from the Yinxu Period, are typically decorated with mask-like composite images combining features of various animals: the image on a vessel might combine the horns of a water buffalo or a deer, the staring eyes of a predatory beast, the snout and fangs of a tiger, and, often, stubby grasping arms tipped with claw-like hands. For decades scholars have argued about what (if anything) these mask-like images mean. No Shang or early Zhou inscription gives any hint of an answer to the question. Some scholars, now a distinct minority, have argued that the images have no symbolic meaning, but are simply decorative. Others have used the traditional (but much later) Chinese term for the images, *taotie* ("glutton"), to link the composite animal mask to hybrid or chimerical images from Chinese mythology. One recent and attractive hypothesis holds that the image represents a metamorphic transformation of the deceased ancestor into a fierce but protective beast with an insatiable appetite for sacrificial offerings. In this view, to perform the physical act of placing meat, grain, and ale in their proper vessels was literally to feed the ancestor. There is much later evidence of powerful human spirits going through a process of being part animal, but essentially no one really knows how the Shang "read" these images. Attempts have been made, without success, to read the various composite parts of the image—horns, ears, jaws, and so on—as a "vocabulary" that can convey specific information about the ancestor portrayed.

Bird imagery is also common as part of the décor of both Shang bronzes and jades. The legs and handles of bronze serving vessels were often composed of bird images. An important example of a jade representation is a Xin'gan amulet-like object featuring a half-bird/half-man figure in a fetal position. It attached originally to a belt or an article of clothing and almost certainly conveyed some symbolic meaning, perhaps relating to a magical power to transform like a fetus into a person or a person into a bird. Similar jade figures appeared later in Zhou tombs. Birds were also associated with birth. A Shang origin myth preserved by the Zhou claims that the first Shang queen had been impregnated by a bird. A related image that appeared on bronze vessels dating to the late Shang through early Zhou is the half-human, half-animal (for example, tiger or bird) composite. Some scholars associate that figure with shamanistic powers employed during ancestor cult rituals. No specific text explains this, but later tales of shamans and magical birds, as well as shamanic imagery on bronzes, lacquerware, and silk paintings, suggest some belief in transcendence and travel to and from the sky or the realm of the ancestors in half-animal forms (see Focus: Were Shang kings shamans?).

We may never be able to understand all of the specifics of Shang ancestor worship, but it is clear that it was both one of the Shang king's most important obligations and one of his most potent sources of authority. All Shang royal tombs contained rich arrays of funerary goods, including items of silk, jade, and other luxury materials, sacrificial victims (including decapitated humans and entire chariots with their horses in harness), and sets of bronze ritual vessels. A plausible explanation for the bronzes in particular, which were often placed close to the body of the deceased, is that they enabled the spirit of the dead king to continue to sacrifice to his own deceased ancestors. Even death, it seems, was not enough to release the kings from the duty of serving their ancestors.

Shang and its neighbors

The royal domain—the area directly ruled by the Shang kings—in the last (Yinxu) phase of the Shang Period was not large. It seems to have extended westward as far as the confluence of the Luo and Yellow Rivers, northward into the old Taosi cultural region, southward into modern Henan, and southeasterly into the Huai River basin. The royal domain inhabited the symbolic center of the cosmic model that the Shang called the Four Quarters. Some people in the surrounding regions may have been governed by members of the Shang royal family or at least by wealthy lineages allied with the royal family. Beyond those subordinate states (if that is what they were) stretched a vast area of the East Asian Heartland Region inhabited by peoples who were culturally, and most likely linguistically, different from the Shang people. The Shang kings tried to maintain their economic control over the larger area under their indirect control and, where possible, expand their sphere of influence. Access to raw resources for activities such as metal and jade working required long-distance trade and control over the supply chain. The Shang kings accomplished this through military coercion and the setting up of allied control over key posts, as at the site of Panlongcheng, north of the Yangzi River. They also established a network of allies that were incorporated into the Shang belief system, including the worship of the Shang ancestral god-kings through feasting and gift-giving. Hence, archaeologists have discovered Shang craft products, including ritual vessels and jades, distributed over a region much larger than that controlled directly from Yinxu (Figure 5.6).

The diffusion of Shang ritual bronzes and other metal products west into the Wei River Valley (homeland of the later Zhou state), south of the Yangzi River, and to the southwest all the way to Sichuan supports the image of ancient Yinxu as a center of complex networks of relationships with peoples beyond the sphere of Shang control, who in turn were in contact through either trade or warfare, or both, with even more distant peoples. The Shang search for metals to supply the needs of the Yinxu bronze industry may have reached into what is now Yunnan Province, the site of later non-Sinitic bronze cultures; there is archaeological evidence for an ongoing trade in ingots of tin and lead from mines in the far southwest to the Shang capital region. Shang bronze weapons were traded in all directions. Among other places, they have been found at Xin'gan (in present-day Jiangxi), in the

Figure 5.6 Bronze *fang zun* vessel with decoration of four rams, from a Shang-era tomb near Changsha, Hunan Province, a good example of Shang bronze-working technology used to produce a vessel in a distinctive provincial style.

southeastern section of the Yangzi River Valley; at Chenggu (in present-day Shaanxi), in the mountain passes leading to the Zhou homeland in the northwest; and at Sanxingdui (near Chengdu in present-day Sichuan), in the far west of the Heartland Region near the eastern ranges of the Himalayas.

Of these three sites, Xin'gan in the southeast reveals the strongest Shang influence. There, Shang-style bronze vessels, often locally produced, were interred in sets in tombs, along with goods such as pottery, jades, tools, and weapons. Subtle differences from Yinxu norms in the style and contents of tombs suggest adherence to local cultural values. Some scholars contend that a unique style of axe buried with tomb occupants reflects a southern practice that can be traced back to the Neolithic. Unlike the bronze sets favored for interment with the occupants of Yinxu tombs (and, oddly, more in line with later Zhou customs, albeit with a greater focus on grain), the funerary goods interred at Xin'gan valued caldrons over vessels for heating, pouring, and drinking ale. The Xin'gan people also appear to have clung to a retro style of bronze décor that harked back to pre-Yinxu times. Their artisans modified Shang bronzes by adding sculptural details, such as small tigers standing on top of the caldron handles, that presumably reflected local aesthetic taste or religious symbolism. Cooking methods employing the vessels may also have departed from Shang norms. Some Xin'gan caldrons had double bottoms, presumably to create a chamber that could be filled with burning embers to keep foods hot. A similar cooking tradition continued much later farther north, where vessels with fire chambers and braziers have been discovered. Another example of a deviation from standard Shang style found in locally produced bronzes is in the design of the flat high legs on the caldrons. Instead of birds, the Xin'gan caldrons featured fish or tigers.

In what is now southwestern Shaanxi province, in the western site of Chenggu in the area near the Three Gates Gorges (where the Yellow River make a sharp turn from south-flowing to east-flowing), numerous late Shang bronzes manufactured at Yinxu were found, along with vessels from as far away as Sichuan and Xin'gan, suggesting that Chenggu served as a transit area for long-distance trade. This site was no doubt connected to the long-term Wei River Valley network of relationships that had ebbed and flowed ever since the Erlitou Period.

Indigenous bronze cultures in Sichuan may have developed in response to early contact with Erlitou Culture. By the late second millennium BCE the people of Sanxingdui had developed a highly advanced Bronze Age culture quite different from anything else known from the East Asian Heartland Region. The presence of a number of actual Shang bronzes in the Sanxingdui ritual caches testifies to some (probably indirect) trade contact with the distant Shang-era polity, but that contact strikes a relatively minor note in comparison with the utterly unique products of the local bronze industry. It is unknown why so many bronzes were buried together, but it is clear from the large standing figures with massive mask-like heads that the ritual functions of the bronzes did not belong to the Shang world. Some scholars have proposed that they might have been carried in ritual processions. The masks have heavy-featured faces with fearsome bulging eyes and thin-lipped smiling mouths (Figure 5.7). Known examples were found buried in sacrificial pits together with items made of gold, jade, ivory, and other materials. Ancient script samples from Sichuan (usually dated later) cannot be deciphered. What religious beliefs the Sanxingdui people had, what language they spoke, and how far their political sway extended are all unknown. The distinctiveness of Sichuan culture continued well into the Zhou Period, although it is also evident that the peoples of Sichuan were in continuous contact with cultural centers in the Middle and Lower Yangzi River basin and the Yellow River Plain. Some scholars have identified the indigenous bronze cultures with the states of Shu and Ba mentioned in Zhou-era documents.

The people of the Heartland Region also had long-standing contact with cultures beyond their northern frontier, spread in an arc from northern Hebei through Shanxi, Shaanxi, and

Figure 5.7 Gilt bronze head from Sanxingdui, near Chengdu, Sichuan province, the work of a
culture contemporary with the late Shang dynasty (eleventh century BCE) but culturally quite unlike the Shang.

the Ordos Plateau. Some of these peoples were nomadic herdsmen rather than farmers, and
they engaged in both trade and opportunistic raiding along the Shang frontier. These northern
cultures were almost certainly the intermediaries that introduced into the Sinitic cultural
sphere such innovations as the basic technology of bronze-working, sheep-herding, and char-
ioteering. Although how influential non-Sinitic bronze technology really was is a subject of
great debate, it is clear that the war-chariot and its associated technologies came to the late
Shang via Inner Asia (see Focus: The chariot). The northern cultures maintained their own
indigenous bronze industries, producing mainly weapons and small decorative items. Northern tombs often contained weapons sets consisting of knives with animal-head pommels and
tubular-socket axes, plus a sword. Some of these northern-style weapons have been found in
the Heartland Region, including at Yinxu, but usually as isolated single items rather than in
sets. This seems to indicate that the weapons were acquired piecemeal through trade or military plunder rather than being produced locally by Shang bronze workers. In general, contact
between the Shang state and its northern neighbors seems to have involved a mixture of trade
and hostility, and was of comparatively low importance to the Shang elites.

The decline and fall of Shang

Under King Wu Ding's successors Shang power began to unravel. A weakening Shang center
found itself surrounded by increasingly organized and sophisticated peoples who eventually
shook off the yoke of loyalty to the Shang kings. These peripheral peoples had for decades or
centuries demonstrated their loyalty at the cost of unknown amounts of tribute in the form of
local agricultural crops, wild and domestic animals, slaves, and various other local products.

Their rulers began to wonder if loyalty to the Shang was worth the price. By around 1100 BCE the Zhou people, who lived in the Wei River Valley to the west of the Shang heartland, had organized a federation of former Shang allies, successfully taken control, and worked slowly to shift the flow of tribute to themselves. These steps were the first moves in what would become a plan to overthrow the Shang.

Later Zhou accounts of these events contain a great deal of moralistic spin. They portray the Shang kings as weak and depraved, rescued from their own ineptitude by noble and wise subjects such as the dynastic founder King Wen of the Zhou. The Zhou preserved (or created) many mythical narratives about the Shang, many of which appear in texts dating to the fourth century BCE. For example, a popular narrative concerned a virtuous minister named Yi Yin who had to take charge when Tai Jia, one of the earliest Shang kings, misbehaved. Many magical qualities were attributed to Yi Yin. Most famously he was the mighty archer who shot down nine of the ten suns (which normally appeared one at a time in the course of a ten-day "week") that appeared ominously on a single day. Some scholars suggest that this was symbolic of the Shang effort to systematize an earlier calendar. In other myths, Yi Yin acts as a shaman-doctor with all-seeing powers, capable of healing illness.

The last Shang king, Zhou (written with a different character than the "Zhou" of the Zhou dynasty; he is also known as Di Xin), is a notorious figure in Chinese history: the paradigm of a drunken, violent, cruel, lascivious, and impious last ruler of a dynasty whose evil actions precipitate his own and his dynasty's demise. Among other atrocities, he allegedly cut open the abdomen of a pregnant woman to see what a fetus looked like, and hacked open the chest of one of his virtuous ministers to see if the heart of a sage looked any different from that of a normal man. At licentious outdoor picnics he had groups of naked women bathe in pools of ale and hung cuts of meat from trees. But the last straw came when his lewd behavior caused him to forget to present the required annual sacrifices to the High God. Outraged, and favored by Heaven with an omen of a celestial red bird associated with another massing of the five planets in 1059 BCE, the kings of Zhou rose up in righteous rebellion. Demoralized, some units of the Shang army refused to fight to defend their king.

But Di Xin may never have existed. It is entirely possible that he is a figment of Zhou dynasty propaganda, a stick figure set up and knocked down to justify the Zhou conquest of Shang and their establishment of a new dynasty. If he existed, he was unique among the Yinxu Shang kings in leaving behind no oracle bones or bronze vessels inscribed with his name. Further, surveys of Muye (near present-day Luoyang, Henan Province), the site of the supposed decisive engagement in which the Zhou destroyed the Shang, have not yielded any physical remains of a great battle, though, being in the flood plain of the Yellow River, any post-conflict artifacts would probably long since have been washed away or buried beneath layers of silt. Even if Di Xin was a real person, it is almost certain that the catalogue of his wickedness was greatly exaggerated by Zhou propagandists. One way or another, however, the Shang dynasty was reaching the end of its line, and it had surely ceased to exist by the mid-eleventh century BCE.

In the next chapter we will consider how much of the Zhou narrative of the demise of Shang reflected reality, how much was polished propaganda, and how much was purely mythical.

Focus: Oracle bones

The term "oracle bone" refers to the practice in the East Asian Heartland Region of using heat-cracked bones to answer questions about the future. Most of the bones employed were the bottom shells (plastrons) of turtles or the scapulae of large mammals such as domestic cattle or water buffalo, but occasionally the scapulae or other bones of other animals, including deer, goats, sheep, tigers, and even human beings, were used. Oracle bones are found in sites dating back to the Neolithic Period, and most scholars assume a substantial continuity of practice: a question is posed, and a bone is cracked by the application of heat to provide an answer.

The use of tortoise plastrons, an imported and presumably more exotic or expensive product than the bones of large mammals, flourished with the Shang. That and the addition of writing distinguished Shang practice from earlier and other regional practices. The higher-level organization of Shang society is reflected to some degree in the increased regularity and patterning of the practice. In the fully mature system of oracle bone use that characterized the late Shang Period the bones were carefully prepared. The shoulder joints of scapulae were removed to make a flatter, smoother surface. Small pits were carved into one surface of the scapula or plastron, with an equal number and symmetrical distribution of pits on the left and right sides of the bone, leaving thin areas of bone on the other surface. A pair of questions was posed, allowing alternative outcomes, for example, "Crack-making on such-and-such a day, should the king make a burnt offering of one penned ox?" and "Crack-making on such-and-such a day, should the king perhaps not make a burnt offering of one penned ox?" The language of the bones was formulaic and organized into multiple propositions. Heat was then applied, probably with a hot bronze poker, to a number of the pits on the lower surface of the bone, causing them to crack with a popping sound, and this yielded answers (whether through the shape of the cracks, or the sound of the bone cracking, or some other way that we no longer understand). Diviners read the pattern of these cracks on the right and left sides of the front side of the bone as omens of divine will. There is some evidence that other forms of divination, perhaps involving the manipulation of stalks of plants to produce series of numbers, were used to verify some of the results obtained from the bones. Dated inscriptions recorded the who, what, and when of the divination, specifying the question or questions asked as well as the results and verifications. Judging from later practices, it is likely that the entire divination process involved prayer, chanting, the employment of sacred spaces, and other aspects of the ritual process that remain undocumented.

In the late Shang Period oracle bones were consulted frequently about all sorts of issues affecting the king, his household, and his administration. Bones and shells were often used over and over again until their surfaces were completely covered with cracks and writing. Some bones were revered; the writing was filled with cinnabar and they were highly polished. Used bones were treated with respect and archived in pits that sometimes contained hundreds of pieces. There, fortunately, the oracle bones and their inscriptions awaited discovery by archaeologists some 3,000 years later, transforming scholarly understanding of ancient Chinese history. The oracle bone inscriptions have given us a tremendous amount of information about Shang government, religion, cosmology, trade, warfare, and many other topics. Of course, there are subjects about which the bones are silent, and about which we would like to know much more: the daily lives of the common people, for example. But, with respect to the subjects that the Shang diviners were interested in, we hear for the first time the people of the ancient Heartland Region speaking to us in their own words.

Focus: The discovery of the Shang dynasty

In the early decades of the twentieth century Gu Jiegang, Liang Qichao, and other iconoclastic young historians launched what came to be known as the "Doubting Antiquity Movement." They noticed that the traditional written accounts on which China's understanding of its own ancient history was based were found in documents written centuries after the events that they purported to describe. Moreover, they showed that the traditional founding heroes of Chinese civilization—figures such as the Yellow Emperor and the flood-tamer Yu the Great—tended to appear in inverse order in the written record: the earlier the supposed "sage-ruler," the later his name appeared in written accounts. The antiquity-doubters proclaimed that all of China's ancient history was false, that the cultural heroes were figures of myth rather than flesh and blood, that the supposedly ancient documents were later forgeries, and that the earliest dynasties, including the Shang, never existed.

The antiquity-doubters were right about a great many things, but, in one of history's ironies, their proclamation that the Shang dynasty never existed coincided with the emergence from the soil of the Yellow River Plain of physical proof of the dynasty's reality. Around the turn of the twentieth century a number of scholars noticed that traditional Chinese pharmacies were selling what were described as "dragon bones," some of which contained inscriptions in an archaic script. These supposed dragon bones were being ground up for use as medicine. Recognizing the script as an early form of Chinese writing, scholars traced their source to the village of Xiaotun, near Anyang in Henan Province, where local peasants were supplementing their income by digging up the bones and selling them to dealers in medical materials. An officially sponsored archaeological expedition to Anyang in 1928 turned up hundreds of inscribed bones, as well as richly furnished royal tombs. As scholars began to be able to read the archaic oracle-bone script, they found that the kings mentioned in the inscriptions matched much of the Shang royal genealogy in Sima Qian's *Records of the Grand Historian* (*Shiji*, c. 100 BCE). Without a doubt, the Shang dynasty was a real part of China's antiquity.

Focus: Shang bronzes

The most durable artifacts of Shang civilization were bronze vessels, weapons, and tools. A large metallurgy workshop operated west of Yinxu city and produced bronze ritual vessels as well as the weapons and tools required in warfare, craft occupations (such as wheel-making), building, and food production. Bronze vessels and bells used in the ancestor cult or other official ceremonies were more ornate, and more individualized in design for different lineage rituals, than most weapons and tools. The religious metal goods required a highly skilled and experienced staff capable of precise smelting, incising, measuring, casting, and finishing skills. Of course, weapons and tools required skilled artisans also, but those in control of the production of religious goods also had to pay attention to the special features of full ritual sets. These sets could include caldrons for meat stews, storage vessels for grain and liquids, and drinking and ablution vessels. Special care was also required for the design and production of upward facing bells (*nao*), which may have set the mode and rhythm of ritual music, while tuned sets of stone chimes and other instruments played intricate pentatonic melodies.

The artisans crafted finely wrought animal heads in bands around the neck or covering the belly of a vessel, as well as abstract décor of spirals and dots. Vessels were often raised on high legs shaped like birds. Animal faces also decorated the weapons (designed more for display than for use in combat) of the elite. Although the décor and exact styles would vary over the following millennia, the Zhou continued the production of bronze vessels, weapons, and tools. The social roles of these goods also reflected cultural constancy over time. The use of bells and stone chimes in ceremonies continued to be critical to royal performances throughout the Zhou Period. Likewise, state expansion required effective metal weapons, helmets, and tools: axes, knives, arrowheads, and chariot fittings; adzes, chisels, awls, shovels, cooking vessels, and spinning whorls. Shang metallurgical technique represented an artistic pinnacle of early civilization that all surrounding cultures and subsequent artisans would imitate but never quite attain.

Some Shang bronzes bear inscriptions, most commonly a single character cast into the bronze as part of the manufacturing process. Many of these single characters seem to reflect an older stage of Chinese writing than that used on oracle bones, and are sometimes difficult to decipher. The graphic signs are assumed to be names or titles of the person commissioning the vessel, or of the ancestor in whose service it would be employed. Toward the end of the Shang era some bronzes were produced with longer inscriptions of several words, also usually dedicatory in nature, often to specific ancestral spirits. The practice of inscribing texts onto bronze vessels continued and was amplified during the Western Zhou Period into a precious medium for preserving documents. Such inscriptions are a major source of evidence for Zhou history.

Focus: What is Chinese writing?

Chinese writing was invented during the Shang dynasty. Before the Shang, some artifacts bore inscribed sets of symbols that may have represented verbal communication, but there is no clear evidence of graphic representation of the Chinese language until the late Shang Period oracle bones. The graphic symbols on the oracle bones clearly represent an ancestor of the modern Chinese language. Many aspects of the language represented by the oracle bones have been carried down into modern Chinese. Some symbols representing words are exactly the same, although the exact meaning of the word may have changed over time. The basic sentence structure is subject–verb–object; grammar is expressed primarily through word order. One symbol represents one syllable. Nouns are not gendered; verbs are not conjugated to indicate case, nor inflected to indicate past, present, or future. These features of the language have remained unchanged since the earliest writing, 3,500 years ago.

The development of this written language had a revolutionary impact on the societies of the East Asian Heartland Region. Among other effects, inscriptions on oracle bones probably enhanced the perceived spiritual power of divination. Writing made possible more sophisticated accounting and other record-keeping functions of government, and enabled accurate communications over long distances via couriers carrying written messages. Eventually it would propagate through a vast range of human activities.

Since the Shang Period writing continued to be developed over time. New words and written characters sometimes replaced older words and graphs that had become obsolete. The art of writing became important, as did the composition of written texts. Not only were some texts, especially ritual texts, inscribed into metal vessels, bells, or weapons, written in a highly ornate calligraphy, but the arts of prose, poetry, and parallel rhyming prose were increasingly refined over the centuries. During the Western Han dynasty (206 BCE–7 CE) scholars complied dictionaries for interpreting the archaic and ornate language preserved in songs and documents. Not long afterwards, the scholar Xu Shen (c. 55–149 CE), in his pioneering work *Explaining Words and Analyzing Characters* (*Shuowen jiezi*), categorized Chinese graphic signs or characters into six types: those that indicate an action or idea; those that convey an image of a thing; those that contain an element indicating the sound associated with the character; those that convey both phonetic and semantic information simultaneously; those that evolved out of an earlier character to represent a new word or meaning; and phonetic loans, where the character for one word is borrowed to write another. Linguists today generally agree that the great majority of Chinese characters are logographs containing both phonetic and semantic information (as in Xu Shen's "form and sound" category).

The writing system that we know from the late Shang Period is already a mature system. Its orthography was reasonably standardized, so that what one literate person wrote, another could read. It demonstrates a clear and consistent grammar. And a mechanism was in place for adding new written words based on the spoken language. Written Chinese characters are sometimes referred to, mistakenly, as pictograms, or, equally inaccurately, as ideograms. It is true that a minority of Chinese characters are stylized pictures of actual things: the ancient character for "horse" is a sketchy picture of a horse (modern form 馬), and the character for "fish" is a picture of a fish 魚 (modern form 魚). Likewise, some characters are pictures of ideas; for example, "up" depicts a dot above a straight line (modern form 上) and "down," conversely, shows a dot below a line 丅 (modern form 下). But the key fact about Chinese characters is that they represent *words*, not pictures of things or ideas. Every character represents a word, derived from the spoken language. And Chinese script is in principle mostly phonetic—that is, the written character contains information about its pronunciation.

At an early stage of development scribes apparently began to "borrow" pictographic or ideographic characters to write similar-sounding words that were not easy to write as "drawings" of things or ideas. For example, a word pronounced *li* 豐, meaning a particular type of bronze vessel, was written as a drawing of that distinctive vessel with some unidentified substance, probably an offering, on top of it. 豐 That character could then be borrowed to write another word, also pronounced *li*, that meant "ritual" (Note that archaic Chinese words were pronounced very differently from the modern pronunciation given here). But such borrowing could lead to great confusion: in a given instance, did the character represent a *li* vessel, or did it mean "ritual"? The anonymous scribes who were engaged in inventing the written Chinese language came up with an ingenious solution: borrowed characters were given an added element, called a "radical" or "classifier," that indicated the general realm of meaning of the written word. A fairly small number of such radicals gradually became standardized. Thus, to continue this example, adding the radical "to divine" 示 丅 to the character *li* "bronze vessel" immediately told any literate person that "this is the word *li* 禮 that means 'ritual.'" (The "to divine" radical serves to disambiguate a whole family of written characters having to do with religion, such as *si* 祀, "sacrifice" 祀 (phonetic *si* 巳); *shen* 神, "spirit" (phonetic *shen* 申); and *xiang* 祥, "good omen" (phonetic *yang* 羊).) The vast majority of Chinese characters are formed in this way, by adding a radical to a phonetic element. The system was in use by the late Shang Period, and over the course of time made possible the creation of a vocabulary of thousands of written words. During that time the form of Chinese characters has evolved considerably, but the principles behind the written language have remained unchanged. This can be seen in the form of the character "spirit" used in bronze inscriptions (神), the "small seal" form used to write bamboo documents in the Warring States Period (神), and the modern kaishu form (神).

Focus: The tomb of Fu Hao

Fu Hao was one of King Wu Ding's many wives and concubines. Her status rose abruptly when she gave birth to a son, who seems to have been appointed heir apparent to the throne. (Both the son and his mother died while Wu Ding was still alive, however, so that line of succession was broken.) But she seems to have been an extraordinary person in her own right. We know something of her life and career because her name appears in quite a few oracle bone inscriptions. Often these concern worries about her pregnancies and illnesses, but some deal with her very unusual role as a military commander: a true "woman warrior," she appears in the oracle bone inscriptions as the leader of several military expeditions. The oracle bone inscriptions also depict her as participating in various rituals that were normally the prerogative of men. Her richly endowed tomb reflects her high status during her lifetime.

The tomb, designated M5 in the Shang cemetery at Xiaotun, near Anyang, is the only known Shang royal tomb that escaped the depredations of tomb robbers. Its intact contents thus represent a precious window into life at the top of the Shang hierarchy. Fu Hao's tomb might be considered modest in size when compared with the eleven tombs (all extensively robbed) at Xibeigang (also near Anyang) that held the remains of the Shang kings of the Yinxu Period. But, by most other standards, it was both large and lavish. The tomb pit at ground level measured five meters (about sixteen feet) by 3.5 meters (about eleven feet), tapering down to a slightly smaller wooden chamber that once held Fu Hao's lacquered wooden coffin (now completely decayed). The remains of six dogs were found below the wooden chamber, and the skeletons of sixteen human sacrificial victims were arranged around it.

The tomb contained a great wealth of funerary goods. These included about 130 bronze weapons of various kinds and twenty bone arrowheads, testimony to her unusual role as a female military leader. There were more than 200 bronze ritual vessels; some of these were probably used by Fu Hao during her lifetime, but some, inscribed with her posthumous name Mu Xin, must have been made after her death and were intended exclusively as mortuary offerings. The grave also contained more than 700 jade items, including some dating from around Fu Hao's lifetime and others from the late Neolithic Hongshan and Liangzhu Cultures; these were already ancient by the time of the late Shang Period and may have been treasured family heirlooms. There were also more than 500 bone hairpins, almost 7,000 cowrie shells (used as money during the Shang Period), and miscellaneous items of ceramic, stone, and ivory. The latter included a beautifully worked ivory cup with elaborate turquoise inlay.

The oracle bone inscriptions that provide some details about Fu Hao's life and career, along with the contents of her tomb, give a vivid picture of the wealth and sophistication of the Shang court at its height under King Wu Ding.

Focus: Human sacrifice

Many religions, around the world and throughout history, have involved the presentation of offerings as an aspect of worship. In a subset of those religions, offerings included the sacrificial slaughter of living creatures, and, in a further subset, the sacrificial victims included human beings. Human sacrifice was a regular and routine part of the religious rites of ancient China. The practice gradually diminished over time, and had largely faded into disuse by the beginning of the imperial era, but it took a surprisingly long time to be abandoned altogether and was practiced under extraordinary circumstances until comparatively recent times.

Human sacrifice as a regular practice in the East Asian Heartland Region seems to have begun in the Neolithic Period, when the burials of members of the elite (identified by rich grave goods) sometimes contained one or more extra bodies, presumably killed in order to serve the master of the tomb in his afterlife. The prevalence of human sacrifice can be inferred from the pervasive presence in elite Shang tombs of a particular kind of broad-bladed bronze axe, the design of which seems intended specifically for cutting off heads. These grisly instruments are sometimes decorated with a grinning monster mask that suggests the ritual consumption of these offerings by spirits. By the time of the late Shang dynasty human sacrifice was practiced on a large scale under two different sets of circumstances (Figure 5.8). One was a continuation of the Neolithic practice of providing servants to be entombed with a member

Figure 5.8 Pit with human sacrificial victims, Shang dynasty, Anyang period.

of the ruling class; the other was the use of (often headless) human victims to help sanctify a built space, such as the walls and entry ramps of large tombs. The two types of victim likely differed in origin: the former may have been intimates of the Shang elite, whereas the latter were captives from other peoples who did not practice Shang religion and were thus not members of the Shang in-group, and were perhaps not even considered as "human."

Human sacrificial victims were often prisoners of war, captured in the incessant border wars that the Shang kings pursued with their unruly neighbors. When the supply of war prisoners was insufficient the Shang kings would sometimes mount raids across their frontiers with the express purpose of capturing victims. The Qiang, a pastoral people living beyond the Shang state's northwestern frontier, were often the target of such raids. Naturally, before undertaking such a raid, the kings used oracle bones to divine the suitability of the planned raid and its prospects of success.

There seems to have been essentially no difference in the treatment of animals and people in propitiatory sacrifices. Some animals were specially raised for sacrifice and others not. In the case of the latter group the diviners simply asked about the number and kind of victims— three male cattle, eight pigs, two humans, or whatever—and the way in which they were to be sacrificed. The use of humans in such ad hoc sacrifices was characteristic of the Shang, but declined rapidly under Zhou rule and eventually disappeared, even though sacrifices of animals continued much as before. Late Zhou handbooks of ritual contain elaborate instructions for raising animals intended for sacrifice and for ensuring their ritual purity. In the early imperial period it came to be widely believed that members of the ruling elite should be paragons of virtue and benevolence, and the manifest cruelty of human sacrifice violated that self-image. In addition, the definition of who qualified as "human" had broadened as the early empires encompassed many earlier states and diverse cultures. Gradually tomb figurines of clay, wood, or (eventually) paper replaced both human and animal victims in the graves of the elite; tens of thousands of such figurines have been excavated from tombs dating from the Han dynasty onward. Still, the practice of human sacrifice took many centuries to disappear altogether. Even the emperors of the Ming dynasty (1368–1644 CE) took with them in death some of their favorite concubines and musicians. Accompanying a superior in death was a symbol of loyalty.

Focus: Were Shang kings shamans?

As we saw in Chapter 3, shamanism appears to have been widespread in the East Asian Heartland Region during the Neolithic and the Early Bronze Age. One influential body of scholarly opinion holds that shaman priests played key political roles as Neolithic societies went through the process of developing ever-greater complexity and social stratification. Some scholars regard the kings of the early historical Shang dynasty as shamans, pointing to their heavy involvement in the use of oracle bones to make contact with and seek the advice of gods and royal ancestors. Arguments in favor of viewing the Shang kings as shamans include the existence of some oracle-bone characters that appear to show figures in ritual postures wearing masks, sometimes masks augmented with antlers. Masks of that type have been firmly associated with shamanism in other cultures. Remains of drums found in archaeologically excavated Shang tombs might hint at drumming as a technique for achieving trance, but this evidence is ambiguous and subject to alternative explanations.

Moreover, there are strong arguments against the view that the Shang kings were shamans. In contemporary societies where shamanism is still practiced shamans are socially marginal figures whose seeming magical powers create fear and respect but result in little actual political power. Shamans in the ancient East Asian Heartland may have been limited to healing rituals, working with diviners to isolate sources of curses or spells and especially to define the proper ritual techniques for curing illnesses. The most elaborate elite burials do not yield evidence that their occupants practiced shamanism. Nor is there anything to suggest that the Shang kings entered into trance or out-of-body travel when performing oracle-bone divination; and, while there is evidence for masks and music in some Shang rituals, trance and spirit travel are defining characteristics of classical shamanism that cannot be proven archaeologically for the East Asian Heartland. The oracle-bone records reveal that the Shang kings did function as intermediaries with the spirit world, but how they did so apart from the use of oracle bones is unclear.

Focus: The chariot

The chariot, widely distributed in the ancient world, was a lightweight vehicle drawn by two or more horses and consisting of a box-like platform mounted between two large spoked wheels. The box was large enough to accommodate a driver and two fighters, typically an archer for offense and a spearman to defend the chariot and its personnel. The chariot appears to have been invented around 1800 BCE in the steppelands of Western Asia, north of the Caspian Sea and east of the Ural Mountains. It presumably evolved from the heavy, solid-wheeled oxcarts used by the nomadic peoples of that region on their migrations. The chariot was specifically a military vehicle, and one that conferred such advantages on those who possessed it that it rapidly spread throughout the ancient world, from North Africa to the East Asian Heartland. It seems to have reached the East Asian Heartland around 1300 BCE—that is, a generation or so before the Shang moved their capital to Yinxu. The chariot would remain an important component of Chinese military force for over 1,000 years thereafter.

The adoption of the chariot involved a major transfer of technology. If a Shang army had happened to capture a chariot in a battle with their steppe-dwelling neighbors to the north it would not have done them much good without access to a number of associated technologies. The most important, and probably the most unfamiliar, of these were, first, the various skills involved in breeding, raising, and training horses; and second, the techniques of the wheel-wright involved in making spoked wheels and fitting them onto axle hubs. Other material technologies, adaptable from those already known to the Shang, including carpentry (for making the chariot box and other wooden components), bronze casting (to make metal fittings), and leather-working (for making the harness). And, of course, the techniques of driving a chariot, and fighting from its moving platform, had to be learned and perfected. The implication is that the Shang rulers, or their agents, were in close enough contact with chariot-using peoples to be able to learn and transfer these technologies to the Shang domain, perhaps through peaceful trade or, more likely, through territorial expansion or coercion of chariot-savvy prisoners of war.

The chariot had three separate but overlapping military applications. It served as a command-and-control vehicle for officers in charge of a battle, giving them an elevated view of the battlefield and enabling them to move quickly from place to place if necessary. Chariots, even when standing still, also provided an elevated platform from which archers could fire more accurately and effectively. Finally, chariots could serve as heavy assault vehicles, charging the enemy infantry and spreading destruction and panic. The chariot assault could not work effectively in hilly or broken terrain, but on level ground it could be quite devastating. It was possible for infantry to stand up to a chariot charge, with spearmen aiming to kill or disable the enemy's horses, but to do so took uncommon bravery and discipline. Overall, the possession of chariots conferred a significant advantage over armed forces that lacked them. The inclusion of chariots and their horses among the grave goods in many Shang royal tombs testifies to the value and prestige of these formidable weapons.

In Shang times chariots were deployed in relatively modest numbers. At the climactic battle of Muye, in which the Shang suffered their final defeat (if much later sources can be believed), the insurgent Zhou forces are said to have fielded 3,000 chariots. In later times the number of chariots possessed by a state became a sort of shorthand for the state's military power; the largest states were said to possess 10,000. By the time China was unified by the First Emperor of Qin in 221 BCE, the creation of massive infantry armies, the adoption of mounted cavalry, and the widespread use of the crossbow sharply reduced the military effectiveness of chariots, but they retained their role as battlefield taxis for the general staff and as prestigious vehicles for both civil and military officials.

6 The Western Zhou Period

Introduction

With the collapse of the Shang dynasty in 1046 BCE its successors, the Zhou, began a reign that would last nearly eight centuries. That statement requires immediate modification, however, because for most of that period the Zhou kings had symbolic status but little power. Increasingly, as time went on, they were treated by the rulers of the quasi-independent states that made up the Zhou realm as being politically irrelevant. By the time the last Zhou king died without an heir in 256 BCE the royal dynasty was a faint vestige of its former self. Hardly anyone noticed that it was gone.

Historians divide the Zhou era into two periods, the Western Zhou and the Eastern Zhou, so called because the dynasty's ritual capital was initially in the west, in the Wei River Valley. In 771 BCE the Zhou court moved, under duress, eastward to a site near the present-day city of Luoyang, in the Yellow River Plain. The Western Zhou was on the whole a time of cohesiveness and dynastic strength; the Eastern Zhou marked a sudden diminution of the power and prestige of the Zhou kings. The Eastern Zhou itself is divided into two periods. The first is the Spring and Autumn Period, named for a chronicle called the *Springs and Autumns* [i.e. the passage of time] kept by the rulers of the state of Lu, spanning the years from 722 to 481 BCE; for convenience the Spring and Autumn Period is usually defined as extending from 771 BCE to the death of Confucius in 479. The second half of the Eastern Zhou is called the Warring States Period, extending from the death of Confucius through the formal end of the Zhou monarchy in 256 to the unification of China by the ruler of the state of Qin in 221 BCE. (These designations are, of course, all retrospective, coined long after the periods that they describe.) In this chapter we will be concerned with the Western Zhou Period.

In thinking about the Western Zhou, or indeed any period of ancient Chinese history, it is important to remember that, as archaeological evidence reveals, Chinese civilization evolved out of competing regional cultures. Many of these were as culturally rich as the historically attested northern cultures, but they left no history and were forgotten. Only the Xia, Shang, and Zhou—the so-called Three Dynasties—were known from literary sources before the advent of modern archaeology. These northern cultures of the Yellow River Plain over time produced a hybrid and relatively unified culture both typified and aided by the use of writing and a shared belief system. The Zhou kings, or more probably their court ritual specialists, chronicle-keepers, and scribes, bequeathed to posterity an elaborate narrative concerning political legitimacy, setting out the justification for extinguishing Shang rule and replacing it with a dynastic line founded by one of its former subjects. The narrative of the founding of the Zhou dynasty includes China's first formulation of a political theory. While hints of it survive in the bronze inscriptions cast during the 300 years of Western Zhou hegemony, the political argument is transmitted most expansively in texts known to have been written down during or even after the late Warring States Period, many centuries after the events they purport to describe. The extent to which this narrative is based on historical facts, and the extent to which it represents political propaganda spun by the Zhou royal house, is one of the most persistent and vexing problems in early Chinese history. We will take a close look at that founding narrative in this chapter.

Beyond the controversial narrative, the Zhou Period, from the early days of the Western Zhou onwards, is attested by hundreds of inscriptions on bronze vessels. Unlike the brief and uninformative inscriptions sometimes found on Shang bronzes, the Zhou inscriptions are often full of information, especially on matters at the intersection of politics and ritual. While also subject to the political goals of their patrons, the bronze inscription texts, many excavated from tombs or ancient caches, reflect views of the events unvarnished by the officials of later ages (see Focus: A Western Zhou tomb).

One key aspect of the political narrative for legitimacy was tied to Zhou religion. Whereas Shang kings became deities or Di after death in a supernatural hierarchy headed by the Shang Di (High God or High Gods), the Zhou worshipped Tian (Heaven), the Sky itself, with Shang Di being one aspect of this larger power. The power of sky gods, including at first many of the established Di from Shang Times, influenced Zhou politics. According to Zhou mythology it was the "Mandate of Heaven" (Tianming—that is, the *ming*—"command" or "mandate"—of Tian), that led the ordinarily peaceful first kings of the Zhou to rise up against the unworthy last king of Shang. According to later narratives a key feature of the shift of Heaven's mandate from the Shang to the Zhou people involved a concept of spiritual power called *de* (see Focus: What is *De* 德?). Heaven was the ultimate source of *de*, and it was earned by the founder-kings Wen and Wu by their accomplishments. Later royal heirs earned *de* by imitating Wen and Wu, and bequeathed it to the dynasty's subsequent kings as a precious heirloom. Thus the dynasty remained in power.

The first few reigns of the Western Zhou dynasty were preoccupied with the ritual, administrative, and military needs of the post-conquest period, but gradually a new Zhou identity arose, forged through an evolving mythology of its own kings and showing less concern for the lingering but fading authority of the old Shang gods. This is reflected to some extent in the changing role of bronze vessels in sacrifices. Not only was there a shift in the types of vessels—each type designed to present on the altar a different food or alcoholic beverage, prepared and offered in ways that differed from the old Shang rituals—but bronzes were also produced in new shapes and with new décor. While, on the one hand, finely wrought examples continued to be produced, there was, on the other hand, a general tendency for greater and greater plainness. Instead of the intricate art of finely crafted single vessels, beginning with the reign of King Mu (c. 957–917 BCE) there was a tendency to cast matched sets of single types, sometimes in graduated sizes. Also after this time, tuned sets of musical bells started to be used in rituals, along with the older chime-stones, suggesting the performance of sacrificial feasts that included new types of dance, song, and instrumental orchestration.

The Zhou court continued to make use of oracle bones for divination, but they played a much smaller role in Zhou ritual than they had done during the Shang Period. Although there is not much physical or inscriptional evidence for the practice in the early Zhou, scholars believe that the Zhou kings favored a different method of divination that used the stems of the yarrow plant to derive oracular figures. The results of the manipulation of the yarrow stalks could then be interpreted by specialists to suggest the advisability, or inadvisability, of undertaking some course of action. It appears that the Zhou kings made extensive use of this system of divination, which came to be associated with a text called the *Yijing* or *Zhouyi* (*Book of Changes*) (see Focus: The *Book of Changes*, in Chapter 7).

As part of their consolidation of power, the early Zhou kings set up a new administrative capital near the intersection of the Yellow River and the Luo River, called Luo Yi (near modern Luoyang), also called Cheng Zhou, the "Created Zhou." This contrasted with Zong Zhou, "Ancestral Zhou," the city of their ancestors in the Wei River Valley. There are many legendary accounts of the establishment of this new center by the third Zhou King, King Cheng, with the help of his uncle and protector, Zhou Gong. Zhou Gong was a younger brother of King Wu, who had died shortly after the conquest, while his heir, King Cheng, was still a minor. Bronze inscriptions attest to the forced immigration of Shang officials and artisans to the new city and to the king ritually occupying the "center" (*zhong*)—a move that required divination. The notion of the king occupying the "center" in the middle of the Four Quarters (Sifang) or the Four Territories (Siyu) would eventually lead to the term Zhongguo, the "Central Kingdom," for China. The archaic words for "kingdom" and "territory" were related and distinguished in writing only by the addition of semantic signs representing "earth" or "boundary" to the core graph for "territory."

Zhou considered its capital the center of the cosmos, and itself the ruler of "All Under Heaven" (*tianxia*), a term that appears commonly in later texts and in bronze inscriptions towards the end of the Zhou. The term *tianxia* can also be read as "Those who were descended from Heaven," although this is not a common modern understanding of the word. But that nuance reminds us that only elite participants in the Zhou belief system qualified as *min*, a word that later came to mean "the people" but which in early Zhou time meant something more like "fully human beings." All other lesser beings, such as workers, servants, slaves, and non-Sinitic tribal peoples, could be used as members of the Zhou elite saw fit. However, as with so much of the intellectual history of the ancient East Asian Heartland Region, textual evidence for the notion that elite humans were descended from god-kings who had themselves descended from Heaven is found only in relatively late sources. That such a belief existed in earlier times is a matter of inference.

In addition to harnessing Shang talent, the early Zhou kings had to bring order to the lands they now controlled. This involved military coercion (constant suppression of rebellious individuals and groups), ritual inclusion (awards to allies), and land distribution. According to later texts that support the ideology of the early Zhou as a Golden Age of good and moral government, land redistribution was done in an almost mandala-like unfolding of planned investitures, involving estates with control over hunting preserves and farmland. This gave rise to the now outdated idea of Zhou feudalism (see Focus: Zhou "feudalism"?). In fact, the greatest priority of Zhou kings was military protection and control over the economy.

Military protection involved not only the larger Zhou army but a core of loyal male relatives that protected the king, known as "tooth-and-claw" soldiers or the Tiger Guard. Outer protection included layers of territorial states that were built up over generations and governed by aristocrats who had proven, mostly through their military prowess, to be both loyal to the Zhou way and powerful. These included men who were either members of the Zhou royal family, relatives by marriage, or local rulers of polities that existed before the rise of the Zhou but maintained an allegiance to the new government. The lords of the protectorates were called Hou, and later became known as "territorial lords" (*zhuhou*, "the many Hou"), a term that earlier generations of scholars often interpreted as "feudal lords." The protectorates were mostly located along the eastern and southern borders of the Zhou core: this might suggest that peoples to the West and North of the core were either no threat during the first half of the Western Zhou or were allies; on the other hand, it could signify that leaders of polities in those regions were unwilling to accept Zhou hegemony.

Membership of the Zhou religio-political order required service, either military, ritual, or administrative, as well as the regular payment of tribute in the form of goods. In exchange the Zhou king rewarded them with greater responsibilities and items of status and prestige within the Zhou ritual system, such as fine bronzes, special ales, jades, and red robes, knee covers, and slippers (Figure 6.1). Other rewards included items of adornment for chariots and horses. In addition, some were also rewarded with land and its occupants, as well as slaves. These gifts are documented in bronze inscriptions as part of ceremonies that reinforced participation in the Zhou belief system and in the Zhou mission of perpetuating the original Mandate of Kings Wen and Wu.

At some point in the early first millennium BCE the term "Hua-Xia" began to be used to denote the Zhou realm and the various territorial states that made up the Zhou political and social world. It is not clear exactly what the term originally meant—*hua* by itself means "flowery" or "ornate"; *xia* means "summer"—but is also the character used to write the name of the Xia dynasty, and it may have been an ancient place-name. Whatever its origins, Hua-Xia is the first word that can reasonably be translated as "China" or "Chinese." It denoted the Sinitic peoples and their expanding territory, increasingly called "All Under Heaven," and considered to be ruled by the Son of Heaven. It had connotations of adhering to the Zhou Mandate of Heaven, to worship of the Zhou ancestors, to participation in the spoken and written Chinese language community, and even to certain standards of conduct, ritual, manners, and dress.

By establishing the central Yellow River Plain and the Wei River Valley as the royal domain, and parceling out the territory on its periphery to members of the nobility, the early Zhou kings greatly expanded the area under their control—although the exact extent of their

Figure 6.1 Bronze covered container for sacrificial food. Bronzes of the early Western Zhou Period retain, in shape and decoration, many features of late Shang bronzes.

control at any given time is still a subject of debate. Certainly it fluctuated, so much so that by the ninth century BCE former protectorates and allies had become formidable regional powers, some with competing agendas to the Zhou. Some of these regional powers evolved out of territories of Sinicized peoples who originally contested the early Zhou state.

Numerous non-Sinitic peoples lived in territories surrounding, and widely scattered within, the world of Hua-Xia. They were viewed as uncivilized by the Hua-Xia elites, and called by a variety of names, all of which had connotations of "barbarism." The people of Hua-Xia tended to refer to these non-Sinitic peoples by generic names, assigned according to their geographical location. No one knows what they called themselves, or whether the names used by speakers of Sinitic languages were based to any extent on those appellations. During the first half of the Western Zhou the Yi peoples in the east and southeast were most troublesome; later, difficulties arose with the Manyi in the south and, finally, the Qianyun in the west. The Di and Rong peoples in the north eventually swept down and destroyed the Zhou in the eighth century. It is unclear how culturally or ethno-linguistically different these various peoples were from the amalgamated descendants of the Xia, Shang, and Zhou who occupied the Central Plains and formed the core of what would become Chinese culture. It is likely that at least several dozen languages, many of them linguistically unrelated to Chinese, were spoken within the East Asian Heartland Region in Zhou times, and dozens more in the transitional lands of the Extended Heartland Region. (Even today, the Chinese government officially recognizes more than fifty minority languages in use within the country.) But the long-term trend was for non-Hua-Xia peoples to become Sinicized over the course of time, and to become integrated into the expanding Chinese realm (Map 6.1).

Archaeological evidence confirms later literary sources in suggesting that in the course of the Western Zhou Period the dependent polities numbered 100 or more, with smaller states ringing the Zhou domain and larger ones farther away. One long-term theme in Zhou history is the process of consolidation of these states, sometimes peacefully through traditions of

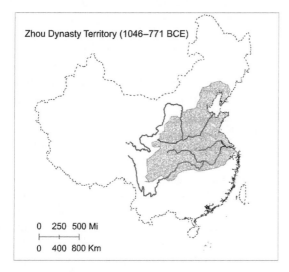

Map 6.1 Territory under the direct or indirect control of the Western Zhou dynasty. The Zhou greatly increased its territorial reach by governing indirectly through as many as 100 dependent polities. The Zhou royal domain embraced territory in both the Yellow River Plain and the Wei River Valley.

intermarriage, and sometimes violently, as larger states vanquished, extinguished, and incorporated the territory of their smaller and weaker neighbors. The rulers of these larger states, often belonging to the class of *zhuhou*, territorial lords, would play a major role in early Chinese history, down to and even into the early decades of the imperial era. Although no Western Zhou bronze inscriptions attest to Zhou efforts to preserve the sacrifices of surviving members of destroyed royal houses, later texts often claim that the early Zhou kings had consciously set aside lands to support the continued worship of the dead lords of once-powerful states. For example, a surviving branch of the Shang royal family was granted the small eastern state of Song and the descendants of Zhou Gong were set up nearby in Lu.

The Zhou economy relied on the subservience of near and far allies to provide raw materials such as metals, jade, furs, leather, grain, meat, salt, and shell, as well as crafted goods such as silks, ceramics, lacquerware, body ornaments, clothing, weapons, and prepared foods (such as dried meats and fruits). Animals, slaves, and numerous other goods came to the Zhou along trade routes or as the result of military plunder. Taking over and expanding the trade and tribute networks of the earlier Shang state would have been key to early success. By the last century of the Western Zhou, however, Zhou central authority weakened as the aristocratic polities established beyond the Zhou state grew stronger. Bronze inscriptions and songs about this later period also suggest some sort of environmental disaster, perhaps in the form of a severe drought, which might have been interpreted by local rulers as signifying that the Zhou kings were losing the favor of Heaven. The invasion and loss of sovereign lands—an increasing problem—had since Shang times been understood as a sign of a lack of spiritual favor or even a "curse." Bronze inscriptions reveal a wavering kingship surrounded by officials establishing their own lineage narratives.

The Zhou founding myth

The story of the pre-dynastic Zhou, and of their defeat of Shang and establishment of their own dynasty, is told in the great Han-era history the *Records of the Grand Historian* (*Shiji*), and in other transmitted texts compiled centuries after the fall of the Zhou. The First Ancestor of the Zhou royal house was said to be an agricultural deity named Hou Ji, often translated as "Lord Millet" (*ji* means "grain"). As the story is told in the song "Birth of the People" in the *Shijing* (*Book of Odes*, Ode 245), his mother Jiang Yuan stepped in the footprint of a god and became pregnant with Hou Ji. Although the birth was smooth and troublefree, thanks to the aid of that god (perhaps understood to be Shang Di), the fact that the baby was conceived as the result of a fertility ritual in the wilds, rather than from a named husband, led to his abandonment. But the magical protection of the baby by animals revealed his special role and he was rescued. Eventually, he would teach the Zhou people to raise millet and to brew millet ale, allowing the Zhou farmers to establish a strong state (see Focus: A Zhou ancestral hymn from the *Book of Odes*). The historical Zhou kings regarded themselves as descendants of Hou Ji. Indeed, while we must understand Hou Ji as an earth god, the ancient idea that Zhou had its beginnings as an agricultural power might be preserved in the earliest graph representing the name Zhou, a square divided into four (a classic sign for "cultivated field,") but with an added dot in each square perhaps representing grain kernels.

The earliest Zhou kings were praised in later histories for their morality. One of the pre-dynastic Zhou kings was "Great King Danfu," who ruled Zhou people in a more northern homeland. When the Zhou state was attacked by northern "barbarians" he considered it a sign of his own failure as a leader and so went into exile. But, as he walked away from the Zhou capital, carrying all of his possessions on his back, the people all followed him to set up a new homeland, wanting no other ruler. The Great King Danfu was the grandfather of the legendary King Wen, also known for his civil virtue.

According to myth, a number of supernatural events signaled the coming shift of Heaven's Mandate from the Shang to the Zhou. First a red bird alighted on the roof of the ancestral shrine, and then the five naked-eye-visible planets (possibly understood as gods or ancestral spirits) massed together (the old texts say "conferred") in the sky just before dawn on the first day of the sixty-day calendrical cycle in 1059 BCE. Such omens signified divine, cosmic sanction of the Zhou goal to re-establish proper ritual and civil behavior by a Son of Heaven. King Wen publicly claimed that the Mandate had passed to Zhou, and began preparing for his own dynasty to assume the throne. In planning the succession, King Wen was "assisted" by a sage advisor, Lü, who, through his extraordinary personal virtue, rose from the lower ranks of commoners to become King Wen's most important minister. He was later awarded the title Tai Gong, "Grand Patriarch," and given the state of Qi as his personal territory. There are no bronze inscriptions or other earlier evidence for any of these figures or events, other than reverence expressed for King Wen and a possible oblique reference to the astronomical event (still a subject of debate). The conjunction of the planets in May 1059 BCE really did take place, as proven by modern archaeo-astronomers, but whether or not it was observed by Zhou people on that day in the Wei River Valley is unknown.

King Wen died before the conquest of Shang was complete. The task of overthrowing the Shang state fell to King Wen's son, King Wu, who carried out a series of military engagements culminating in the Battle of Muye in the spring of 1046. On that famous battlefield the outnumbered Zhou force of 3,000 chariots prevailed because the Shang had lost the Mandate, and the Shang troops had lost the will to fight for their corrupt king. Kings Wen and Wu thus became the heroes of the founding of Zhou: Wen for peacefully claiming the mandate (King Wen = the Civil King), Wu for consolidating it militarily (King Wu = the Martial King).

King Wu died around 1039 BCE, just a few years after the conquest. This led to the rise of the third hero of the founding of Zhou: Dan, entitled Zhou Gong, a younger brother of King Wu (often known in English translation as the "Duke of Zhou"). In King Wu's legendary redistribution of territory after the conquest Dan was appointed ruler of the large eastern state of Lu. Immediately after the conquest he addressed the surviving remnants of the defeated Shang aristocracy, explaining to them the theory of the Mandate of Heaven and assuring them that their defeat was the inevitable consequence of the last Shang king's depravity and impiety (see Focus: The Duke of Zhou lectures the nobles of Shang). In articulating the theory of the Mandate of Heaven, the Zhou leaders not only stressed its applicability to their own takeover from the Shang but projected it back in time to the founding of the Shang state itself. The Shang dynastic founder, Cheng Tang (Tang the Accomplished), they said, took over from the Xia because he had inherited the Xia's Mandate. In the process of describing the establishment of Shang, the Zhou propagandists may have invented an entirely fictitious Xia king, Jie, for whose existence there is no concrete evidence at all. If he did not exist he had to be invented, because the theory of the Mandate of Heaven required that there be a "bad last king" of Xia who lost the Mandate. In the much later texts that purport to give an historical account of these mythical or at least mythicized events, King Jie is described in similar terms (drunkenness, depravity, lasciviousness, cruelty, listening to the political advice of women, abandoning the ancestral sacrifices) as those used to portray the misdeeds of the last Shang king.

Equally mythical is the tendency of these later tales to emphasize the role of loyal ministers, the so-called Tai Gong and then Zhou Gong. This emphasis was a product of a Warring States Period controversy over who was better equipped to rule: a king who received power simply through inheritance or a highly educated and more virtuous official (such as Confucius). These are examples of later historians using ancient historical "events" in arguments over political debates of their own time period. For this reason, historians treat transmitted texts and their transmission of historical events with caution. It seems that Western Zhou bronze inscriptions record a number of "Zhou Gong" over different generations, as it was an important position in the Zhou government that possibly included the idea of an uncle as both protector and tutor of the royal heir.

On King Wu's death, Zhou Gong's most important legendary role was as regent for the young son of King Wu. Two other brothers, who had been given lands in the East, objected to this and rebelled, allying themselves with remnants of the defeated Shang nobility. Zhou Gong's second most important legendary role was thus to suppress the eastern rebellions (although bronze inscriptions continue to record rewards granted to officers for their battles with Yi peoples in the east). As a symbol of loyalty to inherited kingship and rule, Zhou Gong nobly stepped aside when King Cheng came of age. Later he was much praised for this by Confucius and his followers—he could have seized the throne himself but righteously relinquished it, thereby setting the Zhou royal succession on a firm footing.

Another famous story of Zhou Gong's loyalty is expressed in a tale preserved in two versions: a chapter in the *Book of Documents* and a recently discovered bamboo text. Although the details differ, essentially the tale is moralistic. When the health of his brother, King Wu, was failing, Zhou Gong secretly swore a request to the spirits to spare King Wu and take him instead. He put this prayer inside a metal casket and hid it away. Unfortunately, King Wu died anyway and, in the fight over the throne, Zhou Gong was at one point exiled by an ignorant King Cheng. Later on his true loyalty to rightful kingship was discovered and he was restored, but only after Heaven caused a vicious hail storm that knocked over trees and destroyed fields of grain. After Zhou Gong was reprieved (and the other two brothers exiled) nature righted itself again.

The mythology of righteous Kings Wen and Wu likely evolved out of Western Zhou ancestor worship rituals. The creation of the Zhou state and its military mission to expand and "spread" its Mandate in the Four Quarters is repeated like a mantra on bronze inscriptions up until the eighth century BCE. How many of the more elaborate tales could be traced back to oral histories, perhaps performed in contexts other than the ceremonies of award documented in the inscriptions, many never be known. Or perhaps many songs and narratives, representing the beginning of poetry, fiction and history itself, were early on recorded on perishable materials, such as bamboo strips, that have not survived the ravages of time. Scholars have many different opinions but no proof. The ceremonial details recorded on bronze inscriptions suggest a system of record keeping for the meting out of rewards and punishments. It is possible that there were lineage records and perhaps annals of the king's movements, as years were often denoted with reference to some royal event in the course of the year (e.g. *Springs and Autumns*, Lord Xi [of Lu], fifth year [655 BCE], "Winter; the Heavenly King left and resided in Zheng"). There may have been divination manuals and ritual liturgies. Any bamboo texts have long since rotted away, and repeated flooding and silting of the site in the Yellow River Plain would have covered up or scattered physical evidence of the conquest and other important battles.

The idealized formation of the Zhou state as described in the Han histories is not fully borne out by archaeological evidence. Scholars have struggled to find traces of the ancient heroes and the early Zhou states, coming up with a bronze inscription here and a settlement outline there. Evidence of palaces and shrines in Ancestral Zhou, along with massive lineage caches of precious bronzes, many inscribed, has been discovered, but not a single royal tomb.

Even though most of the Shang royal tombs at Yinxu had been plundered over the ages, the monumental layout of the sacred mortuary site dominated the city; the tombs were very conspicuous. While from time to time a Western Zhou Period elite burial ground is discovered, usually showing clear influence of earlier Shang burial styles, it is a mystery why the royal Zhou mortuary ground has never been found.

An historical overview

Accepting, perhaps with some reservations, the historicity of Kings Wen and Wu, we can begin to put together an historical overview of Zhou. The founders, Kings Wen and Wu, came to power in part by promulgating the theory of the Mandate of Heaven, according to which they were cosmically empowered to take over from the Shang. King Wen, the master of civil engagement, and his son, King Wu, the master of righteous chastisement, set up the foundation for a sophisticated earthly government designed to re-establish the broken connection with the High God and Heaven. This renewed patriarchal order revealed itself in geographical terms as land (with the peasant population attached to it) parceled out to worthy kin and close allies. Every chief of the Zhou federation was no doubt awarded land and Shang booty. Part of any Zhou king's duties to his ancestors consisted in expanding the territory under Zhou rule. Military expeditions to the Four Quarters (a spatial concept inherited from the Shang) forced local rulers into tribute relationships or "opened" new lands that could be given to royal kinsmen or loyal supporters to govern and in which to set up their own lineage shrines. The Shang economic and government system was incorporated into Zhou rule.

The Western Zhou Period spanned the reigns of thirteen kings, from King Wen (the dynastic founder, who died before the takeover from Shang was complete, but is still regarded as the first dynastic Zhou king) to King You, who presided over the turmoil that brought the Western Zhou Period to an end. The earliest kings consolidated the takeover from the Shang dynasty. These early reigns began with King Wu (r. c. 1049–1043 BCE), who is credited with completing the conquest of Shang. He was succeeded by his son King Cheng (r. c. 1043–1005 BCE), who was still a minor at the time of his father's death. Zhou Gong, a younger brother of King Wu, served as regent for King Cheng and continued to work on consolidating control over the East. King Wu's grandson, King Kang (r. c. 1005–978 BCE), then inherited the throne, and generally followed the policies of his predecessors; internally the kingdom was largely at peace, and border wars, sometimes defensive and sometimes in pursuit of territorial expansion, were small-scale and generally successful.

King Zhao (r. c. 977–957 BCE) personally led a campaign down the Han River Valley in an attempt to subdue the lower Han Basin and part of the central Yangzi River Valley, occupied by peoples who were culturally and ethno-linguistically distinct from the Sinitic population of the Central Plains. The goal was not simply to expand the state but also to control access to metals such as tin and lead, which since the beginning of the Bronze Age often were imported from the South. Eventually, this region would develop under Zhou influence into the state of Chu, a cultural center combining high Zhou culture with many local customs—a typical evolution for peoples on the fluctuating Zhou borders. The early Zhou kings considered that large region to be part of their realm of "All Under Heaven," but in fact they exercised little or no control there; it was not until the Eastern Zhou Period that Chu was incorporated into the multi-state system of the Heartland Region. King Zhao's attempt to impose royal authority in this southern region was a fiasco. In a pitched battle, the Zhou army was annihilated by the southern defenders, and the king himself drowned in a river.

His successor, King Mu (r. c. 957–917 BCE), is famous for something that probably never happened. He is the hero of a narrative called the *Tale of the Son of Heaven Mu* (*Mu tianzi zhuan*), written several centuries after his death but probably based on old legends, that describes a journey he made to the West, far beyond the Heartland Region. He was searching for a magical fairyland presided over by Xi Wang Mu (the Dowager Queen of the West; the term *wangmu* actually meant "granny" but the goddess is thought of as a powerful fairy queen), who possessed the elixir of immortality. While that pilgrimage was clearly a later fantasy, perhaps just as his father went off in battle into the southern lands King Mu may have journeyed to the west, inspiring the later legends. For centuries, down to the present day, some scholars have taken the *Mu tianzi zhuan* as an actual record of the king's travels and have tried to trace his itinerary—some believed he made it as far as the eastern Mediterranean—but all such attempts have proven unconvincing.

In general, the reign of King Mu seems to have been a time of transition, from an earlier era of consolidation to one of growth and self-confidence. Worship of the Zhou founders, Kings Wen and Wu, was established, with a clear spread of the worship among local lords. After King Mu the bureaucratic organization of the government also grew more complex. Particular lineages provided governmental functionaries over generations, so that certain families specialized in particular jobs. Ritual ceremonies for promotion and award were standardized and criminal law began to be codified. Some officials were promoted on merit and not just as a result of their family connections.

As ties of kinship and obligation loosened over time and space the Zhou court found itself relying increasingly on professional functionaries to carry out the business of government. Although the Zhou seem to have been less sophisticated than the Shang at first, merely imitative rather than innovative, over the 300 years of Zhou hegemony two major advances occurred. One was the spread of writing and literacy from the central court into the local courts. The other was the development of a professionalized, though often still hereditary, governing bureaucracy.

Like the Shang, the Zhou court maintained and developed its own army, branches of which were often led by career officials trained in the Tiger Guard. These young men, most likely drawn from blood relatives and allied families, were the key line of defense for the king when he was at court or out on a hunting or military expedition. Some of these men rose to become army captains or royal officials who acted as liaisons between the central and local courts. There were also central and local supervisors of land, punishments, labor, and horses that reported to their respective courts. They managed corvée labor, military conscripts, horses, agricultural land, punishments, trade and negotiations, hunting preserves, and the handicraft industries, working with local lineage elders to settle disputes and punish offenders.

Essential to court life were the scribes, diviners, astrologists, musicians, and other ritual officers who officiated at the award and gift-giving ceremonies and the annual sacrifices, and generally oversaw the harmony between the human and spirit worlds. It is unclear whether literacy was limited to members of these groups or if a certain portion of the young elite males, particularly the royal heirs, might also have been educated in certain songs and performance texts. Bronze inscriptions suggest that ritual officers, like officers in many other functions, inherited their jobs at court. The calculation of the calendars, the keeping of court records, and the performance of Zhou songs and dances during sacrifices to the ancestors were essential activities for maintaining and enriching the historical memory that composed Zhou identity (see Focus: A Zhou bronze inscription).

Long after the reign of King Mu, towards the middle of the ninth century BCE, the star of Zhou glory began to fall. The monarchs did not often last very long and appeared as the head of ceremonies recorded in bronze inscriptions less and less often. States that would later evolve into major contenders for power after the fall of the Western Zhou began to emerge out of obscurity. These included Qin, Jin, Qi, and Chu. While many of the Zhou kings during this period were nondescript, one king became notorious in later legend as a symbol of what could go wrong with power that is simply inherited rather than earned through virtuous learned civil behavior. He represents the beginning of the end for the Zhou state.

Bad King Li

The decline of Zhou royal power during the ninth century BCE was accompanied by increasing political chaos. In later histories this period is portrayed as a time when the Zhou hold on the Mandate of Heaven began to weaken. This decline was exemplified by the actions and policies of King Li (r. 877–841 BCE), who is depicted as a stereotypical bad king—not so bad as to lose the Mandate altogether, but bad enough to call its possession into doubt. He is said to have acted cruelly and inhumanely towards his people, to have ignored the advice of loyal and worthy ministers while listening to sycophants and women, and to have been personally licentious and careless of his royal duties. In many ways, stories about King Li match those of the last kings of the Xia and the Shang.

Using categories of "humaneness" and "inhumaneness" characteristic of Confucian thinkers in the Warring States Period, traditionalist philosophers and historians who wrote about the Western Zhou era described King Li as lacking the true Way of Kingship (*wang dao*). A late third-century BCE bamboo text describes King Li as causing "great suffering while at Zhou [i.e. the western capital, Zong Zhou]" to the point where "the ministers and lords tried to correct him and the myriad peoples couldn't bear it so they sent him to Zhi." The *Shiji* account of King Li notes that he reigned for thirty years but tended to follow the bad advice of one minister. The *Shiji* quotes a speech of another minister, Rui Liangfu, who predicted the Zhou downfall because of its lack of respect for nature and bad economic policies, which led to horrendous famines. Instead the king focused on what benefited himself the most, and employed wizards and corrupt officials to control the people instead of pursuing a sound agricultural policy. He believed all the slander whispered to him by unscrupulous evil officials to discredit upright ministers; he refused to listen to righteous criticism and tried to repress all dissent. Finally, a popular revolt chased him to a place called Zhi, where he died in exile, leaving behind a seriously weakened royal government.

The evidence that survives from King Li's own time paints a different picture, though not necessarily a more reliable one. Western Zhou bronze inscriptions during and after the time of King Li sometimes mention suffering; however, it is not attributed to the king but rather is portrayed as the consequence of natural disasters "sent down" from Heaven. However, perhaps as a testament to King Li's self-serving nature, the only inscriptions on bronze vessels that were cast by and for a Zhou king that are known to exist today are those from his reign. In them he congratulates himself on taking charge of the Mandate of Heaven. Whether this type of inscription is typical or atypical we may never know, unless we find the burial ground of the Zhou kings, which will yield more examples. The fact that King Li's inscribed bronzes have been handed down by collectors for generations suggests that his tomb or personal treasury was plundered long ago.

Overall, later accounts of the reign of King Li probably exaggerate his failings by depicting him as having all of the characteristics of a bad king, but it is safe to say that his reign was not a successful one.

The disaster of 771 BCE

Zhou royal power recovered to some extent under King Li's son, King Xuan, who reigned from c. 827 to 782 BCE. (An elder named Gong He acted as regent during the first fourteen years of this reign, until King Xuan was old enough to take over.) But apparently King Xuan, like his father, had no respect for the rites and did not "register the fields," a practice involving ritual plowing that was said to have been established at the royal ritual center of Qianmu by King Wu. This plowing ritual was an appeal to the High God Shang Di and other environmental spirits to provide protection and continued good harvests. Despite his neglect of this rite, however, King Xuan managed to reign for forty-six years.

King You succeeded King Xuan on the latter's death in 782 BCE but was extremely weak in both domestic and external policy. A number of bad omens are associated with both his reign and the fall of the Western Zhou. A major earthquake in 780 BCE likely caused considerable damage and enough chaos to allow the Rong people from the north and west to successfully invade. In addition, like many "bad kings," King You allegedly tried to please a woman at the expense of good government. He is depicted as being besotted by his concubine (later made official consort) Bao Si, whose fickle self-centered demands caused the invasion of the capital. Apparently, she enjoyed watching the rush of troops preparing for battle after a signal fire was lit as a warning. After three false alarms the troops stopped responding and, naturally, it was the fourth warning that was real. In 771 BCE a non-Sinitic group called the Quan Rong attacked and sacked the western capital. King You was killed and Bao Si was taken as war booty. The surviving remnants of the Zhou court evacuated the western capital with the help of the neighboring states of Qin and Jin. (The Qin would eventually chase out the Rong and occupy the old Zhou homeland themselves.) The Zhou monarchy was re-established in the eastern capital at Cheng Zhou by King Ping (r. 771–720 BCE). But the loss of their homeland, and presumably access to their ancestral shrines, caused the Zhou to suffer a permanent loss of power and prestige; the dynasty continued for another 500 years in name only, bolstered by legend and myth but with no real power.

Inscriptions and literacy

The signature artifact of the Western Zhou Period is the inscribed bronze vessel. By the time of the Zhou conquest bronze technology was thoroughly embedded in Sinitic culture, and the Zhou initially continued the production techniques and the forms and manner of use of the ritual vessels established by the Shang. For the Zhou, as for the Shang, bronze vessels were quintessentially used to communicate with deceased ancestors and other spirits, and the majority of all vessels cast bore no inscription. However, after the Zhou consolidated their hold over the Central Plains they began to change the ritual sets of vessel types and to inscribe long narrative texts on bronze vessels.

The characteristic written document of the Shang dynasty is the oracle bone inscription, and Shang bronzes are often inscribed only with a word or two—such as a clan name or personal name—or are not inscribed at all. The Zhou kings, in contrast, promoted the use of bronze inscriptions to record important events (Figure 6.2). The inscriptions seem to have been intended to deliver messages to the ancestors and other spirits in the course of sacrificial rituals—for example, informing the ancestors of a military victory by inscribing an account of it onto a bronze vessel that was then employed in ancestral sacrifices. But the inscriptions also served to record history for future generations; by choosing to create records on an extremely durable material, the Zhou kings ensured that the events recorded would continue

Figure 6.2 Inscription on the interior of the Duoyou *ding*, a bronze vessel discovered in 1980 in Chang'an County, Shaanxi Province. The inscription, of 288 characters arranged in twenty-two lines, commemorates the defeat of a people called the Yan Yun by the Western Zhou general Duoyou, in a series of battles in which the Zhou forces killed 350 enemy troops and captured 127 chariots. The vessel was awarded to General Duoyou by Zhou King Li (r. 877– 841 BCE).

to be read into the indefinite future. They also added prayers to the ends of these records, swearing to their ancestors that, in exchange for long life, 10,000 years of descendants, and good fortune, they would eternally provide sacrifices. The creation of narrative history, in other words, came about in the context of religious rituals and was itself a sacred act that spanned the arc of time: commemorating the past within the context of a present award with promises into the future. This was done with great enthusiasm and a conspicuous expenditure of resources; during the Western Zhou Period thousands of bronze vessels were cast and hundreds of them were inscribed. The intersection of writing and ritual suggests, too, that the recitation of historical narratives and prayers during the sacrificial ceremonies may also have contributed to the creation, preservation, and transmission of legend and history. Over the centuries, writing on bronze vessels became more diverse, encompassing everything from simple dedications to ancestral spirits through records of meritorious service to the king to long legal pronouncements. The longest-known bronze inscription, on the ninth-century BCE Mao Gong *ding* (a round or square caldron, elevated on three or four legs, used for cooking meat in sacrificial rituals), is just less than 500 characters in length. The possession of bronze vessels signified wealth and honor. During most of the Western Zhou the right to cast a bronze reflected merit awarded by the king. By the time of the Lord (*gong*) of Mao, many inscriptions no longer directly quoted the king or referenced his involvement. The longest inscriptions belonged to rich clans with powerful positions and the ability to garner their own resources and perhaps cast vessels without the consent of the king.

Most scholars agree, however, that on the whole the quality of Zhou bronzes deteriorated over time. After a period in the middle third of the Western Zhou Period marked by curly-plumed birds and extravagant animal imagery, the skills of bronze artists seem to have declined. High social rank was represented by the display of multiples of a single form as a set, foregoing the earlier emphasis on fineness of workmanship or the intrinsic beauty of the individual caldrons, tureens, flasks, bells, and so on. Clearly, while feasts and sacrificial rituals employing bronze vessels remained key activities defining Zhou and Zhou-influenced culture, the more secular competitive concern with display among local lords intensified.

The spread of inscribed bronze vessels from the central court to local courts during the Western Zhou Period reflected the expansion of literacy. Under the Shang dynasty literacy was probably a near-monopoly among lineages of ritual specialists who inscribed divination records on oracle bones and scribes who may have kept records of other events by writing on bamboo strips. (As with presumed Western Zhou bamboo texts, none survive.) It is unknown if even the king could read, much less write, although he did have a role in interpreting the divinations. The situation changed during the Western Zhou Period. Although actual writing may have remained in the hands of bronze-engravers and scribes, it is reasonable to suppose that Zhou elites were able to read the inscriptions on their treasured bronzes, or at least parts of the texts, particularly those that rhymed and could be sung and were perhaps memorized or even performed as part of ceremonies of award and sacrifice. Most scholars believe that portions of transmitted literary texts, such as are preserved in the *Book of Odes* (*Shijing*) and the *Book of Documents* (*Shangshu* or *Shujing*), can be traced back to the Western Zhou. The complexities of administering a far-flung kingdom partly divided into regional territorial states demanded a corps of literate functionaries.

Although no bamboo texts earlier than the fifth century BCE have survived, bronze inscriptions recording award and gift-giving ceremonies sometimes refer to records preserving an account of the merits of the recipient's lineage. It is likely that legal statutes such as have been found in abundance from the third century BCE onward already existed in written form in early Zhou times, along with accounting records of agricultural produce and other material goods owed as tribute from the regional lords to the royal court. The chronicle of the various affairs of the rulers of Lu that gives the Spring and Autumn Period its name probably had counterparts in the form of chronicles of royal visits and other significant events in the territorial states. There may also have been divination manuals and liturgical texts for sacrificial and ritual performances.

The written Chinese language, which emerged fully developed by the late Shang Period, has continued to exist and evolve up to the present. During each era old words were dropped and new were added, and over time the script was standardized and sometimes simplified. Yet, because a Chinese character had to adapt to many different pronunciations, dialects, and even languages over time, it developed an universality that allowed it to bind all the different peoples assimilated into the Sinitic world together. The roots of that literary heritage are firmly planted in the Western Zhou.

The ritual state

The Zhou royal court and, by imitative extension, the local courts, employed dozens of functionaries to attend to the business of government, comprising ranks ranging from senior advisors to keepers of the royal kennels. But these offices were a far cry from the highly structured, professionalized bureaucracy that characterized Chinese government in later times. Instead, the Zhou system is an example of what is sometimes called a "ritual state." High offices were held by members of the nobility and were often hereditary. Relations between rulers and functionaries were personalized and cemented by the conferring of gifts from the sovereign to his officials and by manifestations of loyalty and deference on the part of the officials. The king's legitimacy flowed from his charisma as possessor of the Mandate of Heaven and his power to authorize its extension through a process of "command" (*ming*). The possession of vessels used in the service of the ancestors represented the receipt of the king's *ming* and an award for merit in the service of the holy Zhou mission of expansion. Bronze vessels also signified the possession of a cosmic power that came with *ming* called *de*. Later understood as a "moral force" or "integrity derived from proper ritual behavior," *de* was the force that came from Heaven first to the Zhou founder and then by means of the *ming* process from king to king and from king to official and finally from official to official. Young men trained in military and ritual skills could earn *de* for their lineage; only with enough *de* did a royal heir, a local heir, or even an officer's son take up his inherited ancestral position. This process is documented in the bronze inscriptions. This power, like an ancestral blessing, signified the ability to act in a manner described as "awesome decorum"—a kind of dignity reflecting the awe-inspiring nature of spirits, and hence the ability to govern. During the Western Zhou, *de* implied also physical health and political and economic control over resources. Much later, in the Warring States Period, the followers of Confucius would recreate this ritual concept as an individual program of self-cultivation that prepared a person to govern. They used as models the legendary King Wen and Zhou Gong; *de* would be generated as a moral force acquired by imitating those paragons.

One aspect of the Zhou kings' claim to legitimacy and paramount power was their ability to grant access to the spirit world through gifts of bronze vessels (Figure 6.3). For a nobleman fortunate enough to be granted a bronze vessel by the king the receipt of that favor was a momentous event, and the vessel itself became an important heirloom, handed down through the generations. The largess of the Zhou kings extended to sites far distant from the Zhou homeland, because conferring bronze vessels on rulers of distant places effectively brought them into the Zhou political orbit. Eventually, as the central court weakened over the course of the Western Zhou era, local lords assumed the power of patronage, dispensing bronze vessels to their own adherents and allies. After the fall of the Western Zhou, the rulers of territorial states increasingly instituted worship of their own ancestral deities in imitation of the rites once monopolized by the Zhou kings and asserted their own claims to legitimacy by promulgating ancestral narratives that competed with the Zhou founding narrative.

Sovereignty, whether of the Zhou kings or the territorial lords, involved the frequent performance of rituals and the giving of grand feasts accompanied by music, dances, entertainment, and the bestowal of gifts. Sumptuary laws preserved in later texts specified in detail who could wear what kinds of clothing, how many rows of dancers could perform at courts of one rank or another, and various other details. Court sessions presided over by the king or the territorial lords began in the dim light of dawn. The assembled nobles and functionaries wore formal robes and headgear appropriate to their rank. They knelt in the presence of the ruler, wearing special knee-pads to ease the strain. The ruler entered, seating himself on a mat on a raised platform (chairs would not come into use in the Sinitic world until many centuries later), facing south. He, too, wore formal robes and an elaborate hat with strings of beads hanging down in front of his face; this shielded his visage from the eyes of lesser persons and also served to remind him that his view of the world was necessarily partial. He did not speak; royal decorum demanded that he sit silent, remote, and motionless. A select high official ushered in the awardee, who stood in the center of the court facing the king. At a signal, a scribe spoke on the king's behalf, perhaps to confer a bronze vessel on the nobleman. The music of bells, drums, and chime-stones accompanied the movement of officials and the king into, around, and out of the ritual space. Musical performances included plucked string instruments, mouth organs, panpipes, flutes, bells, drums, and chime-stones, as well as singing and dancing.

Rituals were directed toward a wide pantheon of deities and spirits. The most powerful belonged to Heaven ("those up above"), lesser deities to Earth ("those below"). The

Figure 6.3 Drawing of a square *ding* vessel from a tomb at Baoji. Early Western Zhou vessels
such as this one diverge in shape and decoration from their Shang antecedents.

ancestors' spirits ascended to the sky to dwell with the High God after their bodies were
buried in the ground and years of rituals performed. The dead were mourned for "three years"
(in practice, for twenty-five months: that is, "into the third year"), during which time the
principal heirs wore special mourning garments, abstained from sex and eating meat, and
performed other austerities. All natural phenomena, such as mountains, rivers, planets, stars,
and perhaps time itself (the seasons, the days of the calendar) had spiritual agency.

A good harvest symbolized spiritual approval, and harvest rituals offering up fine grain
ales were annual events. The Zhou word for "year" depicted a grain plant bowed over, heavy
with seed. The annual harvest festival, celebrated with purified millet ale and ritual bird hunting in a sacred pool, was a multi-day event hosted by the king. The bounty from agriculture
and hunting was offered to the ancestors by placing it in bronze vessels, in direct contact with
the written testimonials of earthly merit in service of the Zhou king that were inscribed on
the vessels. As the spirits consumed the offerings they also absorbed the documentation and
prayers of their descendants. During the second half of the Western Zhou prayers and blessing decorated the striking surfaces of sets of tuned hanging bells called *yong*. The importance

of music, and especially of bells (sets of bells being expensive prestige items), in ancestral sacrifices and to the preservation and performance of cultural memory indicates that, in the Western Zhou, the conduct of government was inseparable from ritual behavior.

Women, commoners, and slaves

Much less visible than male nobles in the ancient inscriptions and texts are women, commoners, and slaves. Elite women were traded as brides among the ranking lineages and sent off with (often inscribed) bronze dowry vessels and entourages of maids and sisters. The early queens, all from a clan named Jiang, married into the Zhou royal clan, named Ji. Only women carried the clan names as part of their own titles, which often included words designating their birth rank. Although children inherited their father's clan names, the women did not change their clan names on marriage. However, they might be known to history only as the X-clan woman of such-and-such a lord (her husband) of such-and-such a place; their personal names are often unknown. Early queens may have been quite powerful, presiding over their own gift-giving and award ceremonies, particularly when the king was away on hunting trips, military expeditions, or royal progresses through the territorial states. Although we have few records of elite women venturing out on expeditions or being put in charge of projects outside of the palace, such as the Shang records provide for some of their elite women, we cannot assume that Zhou elite women were always hidden behind palace walls, as they were in later imperial society. Female chastity was undoubtedly valued and protected, however, as it provided a guarantee to the husband that any offspring were most likely his own.

Later records suggest that elite women often traveled between courts and engaged in other quasi-public activities. Although elite women in early Zhou times may have had some opportunities for independent action that were denied later elite women, early Sinitic culture was resolutely patriarchal and hierarchical and there is no doubt that the primary social function of elite women was the production of male heirs. Yet, at least in some cases, their social role also seems to have included some ritual and administrative duties. They may have been in charge of some sacrifices at ancestral shrines. Female-made goods, such as silk and ramie cloth, were important emblems of wealth and (like furs and pelts obtained by male hunting) functioned as a kind of currency for intra- and inter-regional trade. Their production (though not necessarily their trade) was presided over by elite women. Wealthy women were buried alongside their husbands in adjacent tombs. This was somewhat different from the Shang Period, in which queens seem to have had tombs and shrines independent and smaller than those of their husbands.

The least visible people in ancient society were the male and female slaves, captives, conscripts, ordinary laborers, and other minions who worked behind the scenes erecting shrines and palaces, building walls and dikes, clearing land, farming, and serving in the armies and courts. There was no such thing as an independent landowning peasantry (some scholars argue that in fact all land was legally the king's); agricultural workers were attached to the land that they farmed. Except for when they were awarded, along with land and houses, to Zhou officials and mentioned in the inscriptions celebrating those awards, there are no records of their lives. Slaves, often criminals or prisoners of war, are even less visible in the historical record. Only their bones are occasionally dug up from the access ramps and foundations of large tombs, where they were sacrificed as offerings to the spirit of the tomb occupant (a practice that was widespread during the Shang and diminished over time during the Zhou, disappearing by the Han era).

The Western Zhou legacy

Even if the archeological remains of Zhou cities are meager in comparison to the late Shang capital, the impact of the Zhou stamp on the Shang cultural legacy was lasting and strong. Not only were Kings Wen and Wu (and eventually Wu's son, King Cheng, and his uncle, Zhou Gong) firmly established as icons by imperial times, but archaeological sites all over modern-day China attest to the reach of the Zhou kingdom's bronze ware and trade networks. Early Zhou bronzes, some inscribed, have been discovered far north and northeast of the Zhou royal domain, in old Shang strongholds such as Shandong and in the vicinity of modern Beijing. To the south, down the Han River into the central Yangzi River Valley, in modern Henan and Hubei, burial grounds of local aristocrats, such as the Zeng people, employed elaborate Zhou-style bronze ritual sets in their own rites, although some pieces had local decorative touches, such as exaggerated retro-Shang animal mask iconography. The southern fondness for in-the-round sculptural details and exuberantly elaborate surface décor evolved into a lively and distinctively southern bronze style during the Spring and Autumn and early Warring States Periods.

The Western Zhou Period in many ways contributed to the long-term distinctiveness of Chinese civilization. Building on Shang foundations, the Zhou developed a model of aristocratic government that lasted for several centuries, even if it eventually proved to be unstable and untenable. They devised a theory of government, the Mandate of Heaven, that informed public policy in China down to the end of the imperial era in 1911 CE. Indeed, the modern word for "revolution," *ge ming*, literally means "changing the Mandate." While they continued oracle-bone divination, a practice that goes back to Neolithic times, they also invented and popularized divination by means of yarrow stalks, the basis of the *Book of Changes* and a practice that retains worldwide currency today. For the first time in the Sinitic world they pioneered the creation of written texts comprising histories, ritual liturgies, poetry, and other genres that went beyond bare-bones oracle records. With the Western Zhou Period one can truly say that the familiar outlines of Chinese civilization were beginning to take form.

Focus: A Western Zhou tomb

An ancient burial ground of Yu people crisscrossed east–west and north–south in the hills east of the Qingjiang River in Shaanxi. This is located west of the Zhou homeland region, in the Loess Highlands to the north of the Wei River Valley. These people may have first benefited from relationships with late Shang colonists, but clearly blossomed as allies of the Zhou. The site of the old city may have been to the northwest of the burial grounds. During the first half of the Western Zhou Period the elite members of this area were buried in tombs reflecting hierarchical relationships of wealth and power. Some of the tombs even had accompanying human and horse sacrificial burials. Among the largest is Tomb Number 13, located high in the northeastern section of the hillside. It consisted of a main burial and an attached burial (Figure 6.4).

The body of the main tomb occupant, probably that of a man, was placed flat on its back, oriented as if overlooking the river. The body had been covered with cinnabar dust, a red colored mineral (mercuric sulfide) that acts as a preservative. The probably female body in the shallow burial attached on the southwest side of the main burial was placed on its side, as if facing the person in the main burial. Bodies and shrouds have disintegrated, leaving only the accompanying bronze and jade ornaments. The main tomb occupant had a wooden, probably painted lacquer, coffin placed inside a wooden coffin chamber constructed in the main

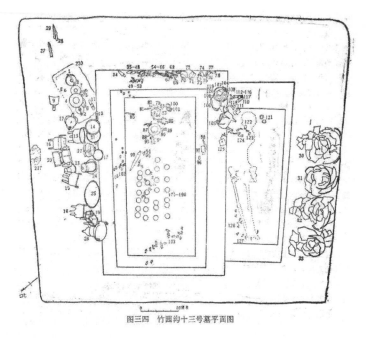

图三四 竹園沟十三号墓平面图

Figure 6.4 Diagram of Baoji Tomb 13.

rectangular pit. A jade knife and other small jade ornaments, some shaped like fish, were at the waist. What had been a shroud over the waist had been held down with bronze roundels shaped like coiled snakes. Jade ornaments such as fish, silkworm cocoons, beads, circles, drills, and other small objects had been placed over the torso, face, and hands. The body may have held a metal goose-head staff in its left hand and a wooden staff fitted with a large, highly ornamented bronze hatchet head in the right hand. The staff of the hatchet included a face with a design akin to a Mohawk hairstyle sticking up over the haft and the blade itself was decorated with intertwined animals and eyes. The cover over the body's feet had small bronze pendants. A number of bronze horse and chariot ornaments and little bells were near its feet.

The probable woman was placed only in a wooden chamber with a jade necklace of beads and a semi-circlet. On a ledge above the head had been placed an object that once sported many jade hairpins and a jade circlet. The foot cover was similar to that in the main burial, and both bodies had two round circlets of jade placed to the upper right of their heads. A small of array of sacrificial vessels placed on the ledge of the main tomb, but near the face of the secondary burial, may have been intended for its use. Clearly the body was buried after the person in the main chamber.

The main tomb chamber also had a sacrificial ledge surrounding the chamber. The narrow ledge above the head of the body in the main burial held an array of small bronze items, including cap ornaments, small bells, axe-heads, arrowheads, hairpins, and cups. Surrounding the entire double tomb complex, the main tomb chamber and its attached chamber was a large sacrificial ledge containing arrays of objects to the left and right of the dead. The biggest, placed along the entire left side, consisted of a huge sacrificial banquet display of bronze and lacquer vessels along with bells and a tortoise shell. In that array, the vessels for serving and drinking ale had been placed on a tray closest to the main burial's head. To the right of the burials were placed four large ceramic storage jars.

Like many groups that made up the old Zhou network of peoples, the occupants of this cemetery maintained their local traditions. This burial ground, like all Western Zhou burial grounds, reveals a combination of classic late Shang/early Zhou bronze styles with some unique arrangements, such as the attached burial.

Focus: What is *De* 德?

The word *de* represents a critical concept in ancient China but it is difficult to translate into English because it takes on new meanings at different time periods. The two critical time periods of its varied use can be roughly divided into Western Zhou and Warring States contexts. The difference between the two contexts is political and religious. During the Western Zhou Period all participants in the Zhou system had to worship Heaven as defined by the Zhou royal house, as well as the Zhou founder kings and only those of their own ancestors who had served the Zhou kings. By the Warring States Period this system had lost all legitimacy and the spiritual hierarchy had collapsed; *de* took on a range of new meanings. In its most basic sense *de* was an inner spiritual attribute required of anyone who expected to work in government, including the king. In either context, Tian (Heaven, or, by the Warring States Period, Heaven/Nature) was the ultimate source of *de*. It is ironic and not a little curious that the ancient pronunciation of *de* was a near homophone for Di, god, but we cannot prove that the words were in fact understood by ancient people as related concepts. In any case, although the source of *de* was the same in either context the method of transmission from Tian to the individual was different.

In the Zhou system the first kings received the designation of *de* concurrent with Heaven's Mandate. From that time on future kings had to prove through good civil and military government (in imitation of Kings Wen and Wu) that they also had enough *de* to rule. *De* could be received through service to the ancestors. Earning *de* over time required the repeated imitation of ancestral patterns in both warfare and ritual. Zhou bronze inscriptions describe performances in which a man "grasps" *de* in his "opened heart." Earned *de* was also represented by awards, such as ritual bronze vessels. Officers and other elite men earned *de* for their lineage each time the king awarded them or commanded (*ming*) them to continue or enhance their role in service of the Zhou mission to expand. During the Western Zhou *de* was primarily tied to military achievements.

During the Spring and Autumn Period the same understanding of *de* remained in place, but with the difference that political power and the charisma of *de* by then had devolved from the Zhou kings to the territorial lords.

During the Warring States Period no state held Heaven's Mandate. Civil behavior was more valued by the literary elite—many of whom had no connection to a particular king—than warfare. Competing religious systems and cultural conflicts resulted in the evolution of a new cosmology, one based on *qi*, a cosmic vapor or "breath" that imbued all aspects of reality. *De* in this system represented the internal accumulation of positive, properly channeled *qi*—through musical and ritually prescribed behaviors—inside one's heart.

In both contexts, *de*, while an inner force, was displayed externally, sometimes physically in a musical performance and other times simply as a dignity of proper movement and behavior. In both contexts this displayed behavior was called *weiyi*, "Awesome Decorum." Initially, it was meant to represent a Zhou fierceness that, in imitation of the fearsome aspect of the ancestors, would frighten Zhou enemies. Later, because *de* was closely associated with King Wen, it acquired moralistic connotations. Thus *de* can mean "virtue" in some Warring States and later texts. As political and cosmological thought continued to develop in the Western Han Period *de* remained a key, but disputed, term that covers a range of meanings including "virtue," "power," "potency," "benefit," "accretion," and "reward"; the exact sense of the word can only be understood with careful attention to context.

Focus: Zhou "feudalism"?

The Zhou dynasty is often described as an era of "feudalism" and, indeed, some aspects of Zhou rule seem to justify that term. The form of Zhou government described in later texts (though not fully corroborated by contemporary bronze inscriptions), such as the parcel-ing-out of territory to members of the Zhou royal family and its close allies and the imposi-tion of stated obligations on the part of the territorial lords—such as attending the Zhou court when summoned, presumably providing corvée laborers on a regular basis, and supplying chariots and troops on command—suggest a feudal model of government. Nevertheless, we avoid the term "feudal" in this book and the use of feudal titles and terms such as "fief" to describe the territories under aristocratic governance.

In part our decision not to use these terms is a reflection of the confusion that they are likely to cause. There is no generally agreed upon definition of feudalism and it is thus impossible to use the term with any degree of clarity. On one end of the spectrum of defini-tions is the focus on political matters emphasized by the late Joseph Strayer. In Strayer's view, based on practices in medieval Europe, feudalism was characterized by a fragmentation of power and authority, political power as a private possession, a militarized society, and the provision of military force by the vassals to the ruler by private agreement. At the other end of the spectrum is the Marxist definition of feudalism, which emphasizes the concentration of land ownership in the hands of a minority and the existence of a large population of exploited landless peasants. In the Marxist periodization of history the Chinese Bronze Age was a pre-feudal "slave society," while the feudal era lasted throughout the imperial period, from 221 BCE to 1911 CE.

One feature of classic European feudalism of the medieval period that has only an approx-imate counterpart in Bronze Age China is the practice of *subinfeudation*, whereby a vassal holding a fief granted by the sovereign had the right to enfeoff vassals of his own. So, for example, a king could enfeoff (grant a fief to) a baron, and a baron could enfeoff a knight. As government evolved in early China there was a consolidation of territorial states by military conquest and a tendency for administration to flow into the hands of bureaucratic functionaries. But there is no clear evidence of a ritual of subinfeudation in the Western Zhou period.

One issue that arises in the context of supposed Zhou "feudalism" is the translation of titles held by the Zhou aristocracy. Five such terms occur regularly (*gong*, "patriarch"; *hou*, "archer"; *bo*, "eldest brother"; *zi*, "son"; and *nan*, "male"): in addition to their conventional meanings, these came to be used as titles for rulers of territorial states, beginning perhaps as early as the late Shang Period and certainly current by the mid-Western Zhou. There is no evidence that these five originally formed a hierarchy; for example, the difference between a *bo* and a *nan* might have been a reflection of regional or dialect usage rather than a difference in status. But by the Spring and Autumn Period they were definitely hierarchical; when the *Springs and Autumns* refers to a number of territorial lords in the same entry (as, for example, listing the participants in a conference), it is always in the order *gong*, *hou*, *bo*, *zi*, and *nan*. And later books of ritual, such as the late Warring States or early Han *Li ji* ("Record of

Rites"), set out elaborate sumptuary rules for the five grades of territorial lords. On the other hand, some titles, such as *zi* and *nan*, do not appear in the Western Zhou bronze inscriptions. Also, the titles *gong* and *bo* seem to have indicated lineage roles first and political roles second. Only *hou* was clearly political, but it also had inherent military implications.

The issue of translation arises because, by long-standing convention, these titles are usually translated as duke, marquis, earl, viscount, and baron—terms inextricably bound up with European feudalism that inevitably carry connotations inappropriate to the Chinese situation. The problem is that, if one decides not to use these admittedly misleading terms, there are no good alternate choices. Our decision is sometimes to leave the terms untranslated, and in other cases to translate the titles uniformly and without distinction as "lord," putting the actual title in parentheses when doing so seems appropriate.

Focus: A Zhou ancestral hymn from the *Book of Odes*

"King Wen" (*Odes* no. 235)

King Wen up above shines in the Sky
Zhou is an old country but its Mandate is just new
Oh Zhou so illustrious and Di's Mandate so timely
King Wen ascends and descends from the sides of Di

Busy busy King Wen whose renown is endless
Displayed awards, ah, to Zhou and to King Wen's descendants
King Wen's descendants branching out for 100 generations
All the officers of Zhou, so illustrious for generations

Generations of such illustrious men, their strategies so strong yet reverent
So bright the many officers born here in the royal kingdom
The royal kingdom so produces such pillars of Zhou
Marching in line the many officers, making all tranquil for King Wen

Somber and grave is King Wen glittering and respectful
The blessing, ah, Heaven's Mandate once belonged to the descendants of Shang
The descendants of Shang, their glory numbering in the thousands
But the High Gods commanded them to become subjects of the Zhou

To become Subjects of the Zhou, Heaven's Mandated is inconstant
The Yin officers fine and diligent present libations in the capital
When they initiate the libations, they always brocade skirts and special caps
Loyal subjects of the king, endlessly think of your ancestors

Endlessly thinking of your ancestors, display and cultivate their *de*
Forever enact the matching of their commands and from them seek much good fortune
Before the Yin lost their armies, they were the ones who matched the High Gods
Reflect you upon the Yin and keep the Mandate from changing to another

Not changing the Mandate endlessly exhaust yourself to the cause
Bright and shiny righteous and well-known ponder what Yin's received from Heaven
The works of High Heaven have no sound or fragrance
Those whose decorum is modeled on King Wen enables the trust of the ten thousand countries trust you.

Focus: The Duke of Zhou lectures the nobles of Shang

The *Shangshu* or *Shujing* (*Book of Documents*) contains a speech called "Duo shi" ("The Many Nobles") that was supposedly delivered by Zhou Gong (a title traditionally translated as the Duke of Zhou), speaking on behalf of King Wu, to those members of the Shang aristocracy who survived the Zhou conquest. (Shang here is called by its alternative name, Yin.) The speech is famous for explaining the theory of the "Mandate of Heaven" (*Tian ming*), the authority to rule. The theory contends that rulers are empowered by Heaven (*Tian*, the Sky, referring both to the location and the supernatural power of Shang Di, the High God). If Heaven is disgusted by immoral behavior or offended by inadequate or improper sacrifices it will transfer the authority to rule to another man. The notion of "command" (*ming*) could also connote one's allotted time on earth (also determined by Heaven); the term can also refer to a mantic statement in a divination text. The following translation has been abbreviated by cutting out a long middle section.

Duo shi ("[Speech to the] Many Nobles")

In the third month, Zhou Gong inaugurated the new city of Luo, and on that occasion made an announcement to the royal nobles of Shang: "The king has spoken thus: 'You, the surviving many nobles of Yin! Merciless and severe Heaven has greatly sent down destruction on the Yin. We Zhou have assisted the decree, and taking on ourselves Heaven's bright majesty we effected the royal punishment and rightly disposed of the mandate of Yin. It was terminated by (the High) God. Now then, you many nobles, it was not that our small state dared aspire to Yin's mandate. Heaven's not giving favor (to Yin) was definite. It was not that we took advantage of the disorder (of Yin), but that Heaven helped us. It was in this way that we have dared seek the throne. (The High) God did not give favor (to Yin); what we inferior people held on to and did was (the expression of) Heaven's discernment and severity.

I have heard it said that the High God would guide the wayward, but the lord of Xia did not moderate his ways. Then (the High) God descended and ascended (i.e. visited the shrine to enjoy the sacrifices) and approached that Xia (king), but (the king) did not care about (the High) God. He was greatly licentious and dissolute and so there was talk about him. Then Heaven did not care about or listen to him. And when he neglected (Heaven's) great Mandate, it sent down and applied punishment. And so Heaven charged your ancestor Cheng Tang to depose the Xia, and use talented men from among the people to regulate the (lands of) the Four Quarters. From Cheng Tang to Di Yi there were none who did not make bright their virtue and carefully attend to the sacrifices. Heaven also grandly established them, and protected and governed the lords of Yin. Of the Yin kings also none dared neglect (the High) God. There were none who did not match (their actions) to Heaven's (pattern) to benefit (the people). (But) their successor in our time greatly lacked a clear understanding of Heaven. Still less was he willing to think of how the earlier kings toiled for their royal house. He was greatly licentious in his dissoluteness. He had no consideration for Heaven's clear laws, nor for the respect due to the people. So the High God did not protect him, and sent down destruction as great as this. Heaven did not give him favor (because) he did not make bright his *de*. . .."

"The king has spoken thus: 'You, many nobles of Yin, now our Zhou king grandly and excellently has assumed responsibility for (the High) God's affairs. There was the Heavenly charge, saying: destroy Yin. And (now) he has reported to (the High) God his work of regulating Yin . . . . I will tell you: It is you who have been greatly lawless. It was not me that caused your move (to this new city); this originated in your (own) city. I am aware that Heaven has (already) inflicted upon Yin a great punishment, therefore I shall not punish you (further).'"

"The king has said: 'I shall explain to you, many nobles, that I have in a timely way followed (Heaven's command) and transferred and settled you in the West. It is not that my own character is unruly; this was the command of Heaven, so do not disobey it. I dared not be dilatory. Do not bear resentment against me . . . .'"

"The king has said: 'Now I tell you, many nobles of Yin, I have refrained from killing you. I repeat my orders. Now that I have made this big city of Luo, there are none in the Four Quarters whom I reject. And what you, many nobles, should do is to serve us, with haste and obedience. Then you may have land and peace in your occupations and your dwellings. If you behave reverently and carefully, then Heaven will favor and pity you. If you cannot, then not only will you not have any land, but I shall also apply Heaven's punishment to your persons.'"

Modified [JSM] from Bernard Karlgren, *The Book of Documents*
(*Bulletin of the Museum of Far Eastern Antiquities* 22 (Stockholm, 1950), pp. 55–6.

Scholarly opinion about the authenticity of this and other supposedly ancient texts in the *Book of Documents* has long been, and remains, sharply divided over the past century. Some dismiss such texts as outright forgeries of the late Warring States or early imperial era, while others accept these texts as authentic, either passed down orally over a period of centuries (a prodigy of memorization and transmission) or handed down in written form on perishable materials such as silk fabric or bamboo strips. The language of the text is archaic, so it is possible that parts of it are ancient, but how ancient is debatable, as there is no evidence for such long narratives in the bronze inscriptions until late Western Zhou, over 200 years after the original event. The highlighted role of Zhou Gong might also be the result of Warring States mythology, born out of the worship of Zhou Gong in the state of Lu by Confucius and his followers. In any case, for most of Chinese history many chapters in the Zhou section of the *Book of Documents* have been accepted as "authentic," and they thus constitute an important element of how the Chinese have understood their own history.

Focus: A Zhou bronze inscription

The Da Yu *ding* was discovered in a mud bank in the Zhou homeland around 1821, where many large caches of inscribed bronze vessels with long inscriptions have been discovered. These caches, possibly made as secret storage pits when the Zhou aristocracy fled eastward from the Rong invasion of 771 BCE, contained precious vessels collected by lineage heads for many generations. It is possible that this early Zhou vessel (with its unusually long inscription for that time) had been stored by a later descendant of Yu, the man who was given the right by King Kang to cast this vessel. This vessel was a large caldron cast in the twenty-third year of King Kang (1003 BCE), and it awards Yu for his protection of the king when young and for his military success.

The award ceremony begins with a typical testimony of the Zhou king to uphold the Heavenly Mandate inherited from the Zhou founders, Kings Wen and Wu, a lineage narrative that was also recorded in transmitted texts such as the *Book of Documents*. Other key aspects of

Zhou lineage narrative alluded to in this inscription include the "creation of the state" by King Wen after the last Shang king lost Heaven's approval through excessive drinking. Heaven protected "the boy" (a reference to the young King Wu of Zhou) and King Wen when he conquered the Shang, thereby "spreading (the mandate or law of) Unifying *de* to the Four Quarters." The present king may also have been alluding to his own protection and duties as king to maintain the Zhou state. Both the tales of the Yin loss due to excessive drinking and the protection of a future Zhou leader by Heaven are found in later texts, such as the *Documents* and the *Odes*.

The inscription proceeds to document the king's award to Yu, who was an elder and possibly the king's teacher (much in the way that Zhou Gong was for King Cheng), for his loyalty and his military and ritual aid in the role of Grand Subduer. The specific occasion for the award was the date on which Yu ascended to the position of his ancestor, Patriarch Nan (Nan Gong). This position came with a particular flag, ritual costume, special alcoholic brews, special vessels, and a chariot with one or more horses. Numerous peoples and their lands also came under his jurisdiction. Many historians take this as evidence for an early Zhou Period state made up of land grants awarded to relatives and situated around Zongzhou ("Ancestral Zhou") as a protective "fence," as described in the *Zuozhuan* (*Zuo Commentary*) and the *Shiji* (*Records of the Grand Historian*). This assumption has led many scholars to read the ancestor's name Nan as a mistake for Dan, a name mentioned in the later accounts as a son of King Wen, known as Zhou Gong.

The lines include a fair amount of rhyming, suggesting that perhaps music was a part of the ceremony and that parts of this inscription may have been sung.

Translation

It was the ninth month, when the King was in Zongzhou (Ancestral Zhou), that he commanded Yu.

The King, agreeing [to Yu's promotion], spoke [possibly through an intermediary]: "Yu, the Greatly Manifest King Wen received Heaven's Aid and the Great Mandate. When King Wu succeeded King Wen and created the state, he cleared the land of noxious presences and spread [the Mandate] throughout the Four Quarters, correcting their peoples. No one among his military vanguard, when presenting alcoholic brews [to the spirits], dared get drunk; and, when presenting burnt and grain offerings in sacrifice [to Kings Wen and Wu], no one dared to offer toasts. For this reason, Heaven sheltered and watched over the boy (King Wu) and provided a model of behavior and protection for the Former King so that he could spread the Mandate throughout the Four Quarters. I have heard that when Yin let the Mandate fall, it was a case of having lost the army due to the fact that Yin's border lords and Yin's correctors, amounting to one hundred leaders, followed each other in lining up for alcohol!

"Ah! You are active in the position of Grand Subduer all day.

"As for me, when it was the case of my being a young acolyte, you would not cut me—your only ruler—down. Now I have already reached the stage when I have modeled myself upon and stored up the corrective *de* of King Wen. And, just like King Wen, I am commanding second and third military attacks.

"Now I command you, Yu, to join Zhao and Rong in respectfully enacting [the Zhou law of] unifying *de*: energetically enter the court to advise me at any point in the day. When presenting the memorial feasts, hasten about to express fear of Heaven's awesomeness."

The King said: "So I charge you, Yu, to model yourself upon your ancestor Patriarch Nan whom you have succeeded."

The King said: "Yu! When it comes to guiding and aiding me, take over the supervision of warfare and energetically recommend punishments and submit pleas [for justice]; from dawn to dusk, help me, the One Man, present grain sacrifices to the Four Quarters so that I can make an inspection trip of the peoples and lands bequeathed by the Former Kings.

"I award you with a vessel of sacrificial millet ale, a head-cloth and a cloak, knee-covers and slippers, and a chariot with horses.

"I award you the flag of your Ancestor Patriarch Nan to use in hunting.

"I award you the elders of four states as supervisors and six hundred and fifty-nine slaves ranging from charioteers to common men.

"I award you the management of thirteen royal servants, a thousand and fifty slaves moved from their land."

The King said: "Yu! You should act respectfully in your corrective military campaigns and not disregard my charge!"

Yu took this opportunity to respond to the King's gifts and used [the opportunity] to make a treasured caldron for Ancestor Nan Gong.

It was the time of the twenty-third annual sacrifice performed by the King.

7   The Spring and Autumn Period

Introduction

The Spring and Autumn Period takes its name from the *Springs and Autumns* (a poetic reference to the passage of time), a chronicle kept for the lords of the state of Lu. Its first entry dates to the equivalent of 722 BCE and the final entry corresponds to 481 BCE. The chronicle records, in brief and formulaic language, significant events in Lu and events in other states that affected Lu in some way. In practice, the Spring and Autumn Period is usually taken to include a slightly larger span of time, from the end of the Western Zhou Period in 771 BCE to the death of Confucius in 479. The choice of an ending date for the Spring and Autumn Period is somewhat arbitrary; the Spring and Autumn Period elides into the succeeding Warring States Period through a series of significant events in the mid-fifth century BCE. Often given short shrift in histories of China, perhaps in part because of the brief and seemingly uninformative nature of the *Springs and Autumns* records themselves, the Spring and Autumn Period, on closer examination, proves to be an era of great interest and historical importance (see Focus: A year in the *Springs and Autumns*).

The defining characteristic of the Spring and Autumn Period was the decline of the Zhou royal house to a status of relative insignificance. Prior to 771 BCE the Zhou, though clearly in the throes of a long-term decline, retained significant territorial holdings, military power, and the charisma that flowed from the possession of the Mandate of Heaven. With the loss of the western capital and the move of the royal court to the east the Zhou royal domain was reduced to a small fraction of its previous size and the kings' ability to raise and maintain military forces dwindled. While the territorial lords continued to acknowledge the Zhou kings as holders of the Mandate of Heaven, it was apparent to everyone that the dynasty's grip on the Mandate was tenuous and slipping. The Mandate stayed with the Zhou only so long as power among the territorial states was more or less in balance, so that no single state was powerful enough to claim the Mandate and try to seize it by force. With a near-vacuum at the heart of the Zhou royal system of government, the territorial states had to work out other arrangements to carry on the business of government and try to maintain some measure of peace and harmony among the rulers of the territorial states. The failure to find a durable solution to this challenge led eventually to the each-against-all politics and warfare of the Warring States Period.

Important changes took place within the territorial states as well. The process of larger states encroaching upon, and swallowing up, smaller ones—seen already in the Western Zhou Period—continued at an accelerated pace. The *Springs and Autumns* records the extinction of fifty-two territorial states (or clan-dominated polities) over a period of 241 years. The Eastern Zhou royal domain and a number of small "interior" states occupied the lands around the middle reaches of the Yellow River Plain; several large states on the periphery of this core region—Qin in the northwest, Jin in the north, Yan in the northeast, Qi in the east, Wu and Yue in the southeast, Chu in the south—increased in power and importance. A number of states, both large and small, experienced a change in aristocratic leadership as ruling families failed to produce viable heirs or were overthrown in coups d'état by ministerial families. Being the ruler of a territorial state was a dangerous business; the *Springs and Autumns* records the assassinations of thirty-six rulers.

The social changes within the ranks of the aristocratic elite brought about by this political turmoil were accompanied by changes in religious practices, which, in turn, were reflected in new types of bronze vessel. The worship of the Zhou founder kings Wen and Wu had become a fundamental part of aristocratic religious belief and practice by the end of the Spring and Autumn Period, and the mythologized heroic version of the Zhou conquest of Shang became firmly embedded in Chinese culture.

Confucius (Kongzi), whose lifetime coincided with the last few decades of the Spring and Autumn Period, exemplifies a number of other important changes in Chinese society in the mid-first millennium BCE. One of the most significant of these changes was a shift in the status and social function of the lowest ranks of the aristocracy, the *shi*, a class to which Confucius belonged. The *shi* (a word often translated as "knights") were minor nobles, the lowest-ranking class of people authorized to perform sacrifices to their ancestors and trained to perform ritual and military roles within local government. During the Western Zhou Period they were primarily a military class, trained in chariot warfare, archery, and other martial skills; at the same time some *shi* had begun to perform bureaucratic functions both at the royal court and in the territorial states. By the Spring and Autumn Period the transition of the *shi* from "knights" to "men of service" or "men of affairs" was well advanced. Some *shi* failed to adapt to the new circumstances and dropped down into the ranks of the commoners; others acquired new skills, including literacy, and had successful careers in government service. Accompanying this metamorphosis of the *shi* class were the first signs of a literati class; the first evidence of systematic thought about government and society; and the first trickle of what would become a flood of new written documents of all kinds, from social thought through poetry and prayers to government records and codes of law, and much else besides. Confucius also exemplifies a new tendency in early Chinese history: the emergence into the light of history of a few individuals who appear as actual personalities, with hopes, fears, ambitions, and disappointments. With the Spring and Autumn Period, history begins to seem more "real," because it is played out by actual human actors rather than mythical heroes.

Regional cultures and the rise of the peripheral states

Beginning with the decline of the Zhou hegemony during the eighth century BCE, regional cultures embodied in states that had been dominated politically and economically by the Zhou began to loosen those ties and compete with the "inner" polities clustered in the middle Yellow River Plain around the old eastern administrative capital of Zhou. The archaeological record reveals strong cultural resurgences in the Chengdu Basin, the Middle Yangzi and Han River Valley region, the Dongting Lake region, the Lower Yangzi and Huai River Valley region, and the Shandong Peninsula and adjacent parts of the Yellow River Plain. Although some polities identified with these regions had varying fates after the fall of the Western Zhou and before the military conquest and unification of all of China by Qin in 221 BCE, a handful of early states maintained their cultural prominence in each region. Most of the ruling lineages of these territorial states had long-term contact, including intermarriage, with the Zhou lineage and thus continued their respect for the once powerful Zhou connection to Heaven. But while the Zhou kings retained titular spiritual power they lost almost all of their secular potency. For most of the Spring and Autumn Period rulers of the largest of the territorial states competed to be acknowledged as the "protector" of the Zhou kings, instituting a new political phenomenon in the developing Sinitic world: the office of *ba*, "hegemon," first among equals of the territorial lords and putative defender of the Zhou kings' interests. The hegemons, nominally protectors of the Zhou royal family, actually enriched themselves at the expense of the Zhou court and the small "inner" states clustered around the reduced Zhou royal domain over the course of the Spring and Autumn Period (Map 7.1).

The inner states

Foremost among the "inner states" clustered around the middle reaches of the Yellow River was, of course, Zhou itself, much reduced in territorial extent and political and military power, but still at least nominally acknowledged as the holder of the Mandate of Heaven. Only the Zhou sovereign was allowed to use the title "king," to have nine rows of dancers at court ceremonials (lesser lords presumably, as described in later ritual texts, had fewer rows of dancers: seven for *gong*, five for *hou*, and so on), and to enjoy other ceremonial privileges and monopolies. All of these privileges were violated during the Spring and Autumn Period by one or another of the powerful territorial lords, but in theory they still applied to the Zhou sovereigns and their hierarchy of aristocrats.

Lying mainly to the east of the Zhou domain, a number of small states with ancient lineages survived precariously, hemmed in by large and powerful neighbors. Among these were Cao, Wey, and Song. With relatively small territories and no room to expand, these states nevertheless were active participants in the multi-state system of the Spring and Autumn era, attending covenant meetings and included in all high-level negotiations. Their rulers are recorded as having attended conferences of the territorial lords, where they were treated with

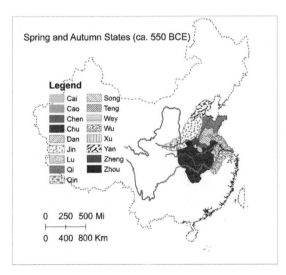

Map 7.1 During the Spring and Autumn Period the consolidation of Zhou dependent polities was well under way. *Ba* hegemons attempted to maintain order on behalf of the Zhou kings.

respect. Wey, being an historic lineage of long standing, appears often in the *Springs and Autumns* and seems to have enjoyed considerable prestige.

Song was one of the largest of the inner states, sharing a border with the state of Lu, to its east. It had special status because of its ruling house's reputed exalted lineage; according to later histories a surviving branch of the Shang royal family was given the rulership of Song in order that the ancestral sacrifices to the Shang ancestors would continue to be maintained. Song was also a regular participant in the conferences of state rulers and was capable of marshaling significant military force. Although its long-term trajectory was one of decline, Song was a state to be reckoned with for much of the Spring and Autumn Period. Lord Xiang of Song (r. 650–637 BCE) is generally considered to have been the third *ba* (hegemon), a testament to Song's continued importance in the early Spring and Autumn Period.

Oddly, in literary works of the Warring States Period about the Spring and Autumn era Song also became the butt of many jokes, and a "man of Song" was the comic equivalent of a foolish country bumpkin. To give one of several possible examples, a well-known ancient Chinese joke tells of a man of Song who, while tending his fields of grain, happened to see a rabbit carelessly run into a stump and knock itself silly. The farmer took the rabbit home and made a good meal of it; thereafter he gave up farming and kept a close eye on the stump, hoping for more rabbits. This story gave rise to a Chinese saying that is still current today: "Guarding the stump, waiting for rabbits." It describes someone who neglects practicalities while hoping for an unlikely stroke of good fortune. Whether or not its people were unusually feckless, Song lost both territory and status during the later decades of the Spring and Autumn Period and declined to insignificance during the Warring States Period.

Zheng was one of the most important of the inner states. Relatively young, it was established in 806 BCE, in the waning years of the Western Zhou Period, when King Xuan of Zhou gave a grant of royal land near the western capital to his younger brother, who then became known as Lord (*gong*) Huan of Zheng. Lord Huan initially established his capital in the Wei River Valley, just east of the Zhou ceremonial capital, but he soon began to concentrate on developing the largely vacant portion of his territory that extended eastwards beyond the passes at the great eastward bend of the Yellow River. He established a new capital east of the passes, near the city that still, in the present day, bears the name Zhengzhou. The rulers of Zheng were thus in a position to help smooth the transition of the Zhou court after the calamitous defeat of 771 and the shift of the Zhou capital from west to east. Successive lords of Zheng became high advisors to the Zhou court, but in an effort to consolidate their power they crossed the line between protecting the royal court and encroaching on it. When King Ping appointed high advisors from other inner states to balance the power of Zheng, Lord Zhuang of Zheng responded by demanding, successfully, that the Zhou king send one of his sons to the Zheng court as a hostage to ensure royal compliance with Zheng's demands. Such requests were common among states as collateral for upholding military covenants, but it was unusual for a territorial state to make such a demand of a Zhou king. Under King Ping's successor, King Huan, relations with Zheng became overtly hostile. King Huan assembled a coalition of allies and launched a punitive expedition against Zheng in 707 BCE, but was humiliatingly defeated. The reign of Lord Zhuang marked the high point of Zheng power, however. Upon his death in 701 a civil war broke out between two of his sons, both claiming to be their father's chosen successor and both forming alliances with other inner states. After twenty years of civil war Zheng was exhausted. As the Spring and Autumn Period went on, Zheng, squeezed between powerful neighbors to the north and south, devolved to the status of a minor state. It was extinguished and its territory absorbed by the state of Hann in 375 BCE, during the Warring States Period.

The state of Lu was located east of Song and southwest of Qi in the lower Yellow River drainage area. It encompassed the foot of the Shandong Peninsula, west of the sacred Mt. Tai. Its territory was land-locked and offered no scope for expansion. Lu was a relatively large inner state that enjoyed prestige beyond what one might expect from its military and economic power. Claiming direct descent from Zhou Gong Dan, the "Duke of Zhou" himself, its rulers regarded themselves as being especially high-born and privileged; for example, they claimed some prerogatives in ceremonial rituals, such as the right to use certain types of sacrificial animals, that otherwise belonged only to the Zhou Sons of Heaven. Lu looms large, and perhaps undeservedly large, in accounts of early Chinese history because of two factors: its *Springs and Autumns* is the only state chronicle to have been transmitted from antiquity substantially intact, revealing a clear bias regarding the lords of Lu and their affairs; and Lu was the native state of Confucius, lending it a gloss of prestige that has endured through the ages.

Although Lu gloried in the exalted lineage of its rulers, its genealogical proximity to the Zhou royal house could also cause problems. A case in point is King Xuan's intervention, near the end of the Western Zhou Period, in a succession dispute in Lu. King Xuan, for reasons that are unclear, commanded Lord Wu of Lu (r. 825–816 BCE) to name his younger son as heir apparent, skipping over the heir's elder brother. When Lord Wu died the younger son indeed succeeded to the throne, taking the title Lord Yi, but was deposed by a rebellion a decade later. The elder brother's son, Bo Yu (also known as Boya), was then placed on the throne by the rebels, but was not recognized by King Xuan, who regarded him as a usurper. After dithering for more than a decade, in 796 BCE the king dispatched an army to invade Lu, bring its succession into line with the preferences of the Zhou royal house, and punish the Lu rebels. Bo Yu was killed and was succeeded by a different younger brother of Lord Yi, known as Lord Xiao. These struggles, played out over a period of some twenty years, left Lu weakened and vulnerable.

Lu suffered permanent damage from another succession dispute a century later. Three sons of Lord Huan (r. 711–694E) contended with one another for the throne. One of them finally became Lord Zhuang, but the two brothers would not desist. They set up competing lineages that in effect carved out two independent polities in what had been Lu territory, leaving the nominal Lu lords to preside over a shrunken and weakened state. In this reduced condition Lu held on almost to the end of the Warring States Period, when in 249 BCE it was conquered and absorbed by Qin.

The outer states

The political life of the Spring and Autumn Period was dominated by a handful of large outer states that aggressively expanded their territory through both the conquest and absorption of smaller states and the colonization and absorption of territory on their porous outer borders, often incorporating into their populations large numbers of non-Sinitic peoples. Commerce, marriage relations, and war created a vacillating scenario of new political players, some with ancient and deep connections with the old Zhou court and others with lively local cultures bursting through a veneer of Zhou cultural overlay. Our tour of the outer states will proceed clockwise, beginning with Qin in the northwest.

The state of Qin arose in the Loess Highlands of the northwestern East Asian Heartland Region and extended to ill-defined boundaries to the north and west. It had a mixed population that included Sinitic people but also non-Sinitic peoples, such as Rong and Qiang, whose exact identity remains unknown. (The Qiang are regarded by some scholars as "proto-Tibetans.") The Qin rulers claimed a lineage going back to the Western Zhou Period, but Qin became a player in Zhou politics only with the Zhou defeat of 771 BCE, at which time the lords of Qin and its neighbor Jin facilitated the escape of the Zhou court from the western capital to the eastern one. This was a strategic move on the part of the Qin state, because it left vacant the extensive Zhou domain centered on the Wei River Valley. Qin soon defeated and expelled the Rong tribes that had killed King You and drove the Zhou court from its ancestral homeland, and incorporated that territory into the Qin domain. Successive lords of Qin also expanded the state's territory by forcibly incorporating some of the tribal lands to its north and west. Qin became a formidable military power, and it may be that this frequent border warfare served to keep its armies in perpetual fighting trim. Like the large territorial domain of Jin, and for the same reason—proximity to horse-riding nomadic northern peoples—Qin was one of the earliest Sinitic states to integrate cavalry into its armed forces.

The Qin rulers moved their capital several times during the first century of the Spring and Autumn Period before settling down in 677 BCE at Yong, in the ancestral lands of the Zhou, which remained the Qin capital until 383 BCE. Qin grew rich from the excellent farmland of the Wei River Valley and, with irrigation, the Loess Highlands. Archaeological excavations at Yong have revealed palaces and other buildings constructed with ornate bronze fittings and fine roof tiles. Qin cemeteries reveal some cultural differences from the inner states; in particular, bronze vessels interred with the dead were often thin and shoddily made, or were replaced by ceramic replicas. This practice of using objects specially made as grave goods, rather than sending the dead to the afterlife accompanied by sacrificial bronzes and other precious objects, appears to have begun in Western Zhou times, but it did not become common until the Warring States Period.

Qin seems to have been regarded by the older Zhou territorial states as a semi-barbarous upstart state, but its growing power made it impossible to ignore. Having played an important role in saving the Zhou monarchy from extinction in 771, Qin seems to have held an exaggerated sense of its own importance. This is reflected in their rhetoric of receiving the Mandate of Heaven and following in the footsteps of Sage King Yu (no mention of the Zhou) cast into a set of finely wrought bronze display vessels early in the Spring and Autumn Period. Indeed, this early sense of self-importance continued as it became a bigger and bigger player in the Eastern Zhou Period.

Just east of Qin, across the southward-plunging section of the Yellow River before its dramatic eastward bend, and north of the Eastern Zhou royal domain, was the state of Jin. The lords of Jin claimed that their state had been created by one of the sons of the Zhou founder, King Wu, but that is very likely a retrospective fabrication. Jin did have a long prehistory; archaeology tells us that its territory, including the imposing late Neolithic city of Taosi and other settlements in the region along the Fen River in present-day Shanxi, had been settled since before the Erlitou Period. Local peoples produced and exported minerals and salt craved by the emerging states of the Central Plains. On the other hand, a wealthy burial ground of Jin lords with inscribed bronzes dating from the Western Zhou Period attests to a clear Zhou relationship beginning as early as the tenth century BCE. This cultural connection, along with its economic advantages, led to the rise of a powerful state that lasted until the very end of the fifth century BCE.

Early Spring and Autumn Period Jin royal bronze inscriptions reveal a militarized state with clear cultural connections to Qin to the west, by then ensconced in the old Zhou homeland. Contemporary inscriptions written by the leaders of both Qin and Jin talk of expansion and punishing enemies. Like Qin, Jin incorporated populations of Rong and other tribal peoples, and had an ill-defined northern border reaching into the Extended Heartland Region, lands more suited to pastoralism than to agriculture. The resulting cultural interplay in Jin's northern territories seems to have made Jin the first Sinitic state to include warriors on horseback (in contrast to using horses just to pull chariots) as a significant element of its armed forces.

Throughout most of the Spring and Autumn Period Jin was one of the most powerful states in the East Asian Heartland Region. Jin's power was consolidated and extended by Lord (*hou*) Wen (r. 636–628 BCE), who was recognized by the territorial lords as the second *ba* ("hegemon,"), succeeding Lord Huan of Qi in that position (see below). Before ascending the Jin throne Lord Wen, then known as Prince Chong'er, spent nineteen years in exile as the result of a succession dispute (see Focus: Chong'er). During his wanderings he visited most of the other great powers of the day, gaining valuable intelligence that he put to good use in his brief reign. His immediate successors maintained Jin's eminence, but toward the end of the Spring and Autumn Period Jin entered a long phase of decline brought about by competition among its high aristocratic lineages for influence over or succession to the throne. For most of the fifth century BCE Jin was wracked by near-continuous civil war, and the state itself dissolved into three successor states—Hann, Wei, and Zhao—in 403 BCE, early in the Warring States Period.

The state of Yan, located in the far northeast of the Heartland Region and stretching from the coast of the Gulf of Bohai inland to the Xinggan Mountains and northeastward to the Liaodong Peninsula, was apparently established early in the Western Zhou Period as a garrison state to protect the Central Plains from attack. The early state of Yan is known from an elite cemetery at Fangshan, near present-day Beijing, where a number of inscribed bronze vessels were found; included in the inscriptions were references to Tai Bao, a half-brother of Zhou King Wu, and to Yan Hou, the "Lord of Yan." Shang-style artifacts in the tombs attest to a historic connection of the local people to the earlier dynasty. The northeast, with a largely non-Sinitic population, thus seems to have been brought at least nominally into the Sinitic orbit at an early date. It is interesting to note that the population of the coastal region west of the Liaodong Peninsula probably included speakers of Old Koguryoic, regarded by some linguists as ancestral to Korean and Japanese.

Despite its ancient heritage, the state of Yan played relatively little part in the affairs of the Spring and Autumn Period, though it gained in importance during the succeeding Warring States Period.

The state of Qi occupied most of Shandong, from the eastern slopes of Mt. Tai to the peninsular seacoast, with the exception of some coastal enclaves of a non-Hua-Xia people known as the Eastern Yi. Over the course of the Spring and Autumn Period Qi expanded its territory at the expense of some of its smaller neighbors in the lower Yellow River Plain. Qi rose up out of the remnants of the old late Shang economic and political network. There is a good deal of rhetorical and historical evidence of deep cultural ties to the Zhou court dating back to at least the ninth century BCE and probably earlier. The hybrid nature of Qi cultural history is reflected in a lengthy late Spring and Autumn Period bell inscription. The preservation in that inscription of speech patterns and archaic graphs characteristic of the Zhou homeland at least four centuries earlier suggests a reverence for Zhou ritual language. Yet, oddly, this same inscription traces the Qi lineage back to Cheng Tang, the legendary founder of the Shang, with no direct reference to the Zhou (which by that time had been reduced to the vestigial Eastern Zhou domain) at all. This strategy of employing high cultural rituals and rhetoric (associated with the glory days of the Western Zhou) and local heroes (associated with the Shang, persisting into or revived in later times) is typical of many local cultures of the Eastern Zhou Period.

In later accounts we find a different version of Qi origins. According to the Han *Records of the Grand Historian* (*Shiji*), the first Qi ancestor aided Yu the Great, tamer of the great flood, in founding the Xia dynasty. Later, men of the Jiang clan aided King Wen and his father as they prepared the Zhou conquest of the Shang, and were rewarded with the rulership of Qi. Bronze inscriptions confirm that the early Western Zhou kings used to marry Jiang women, but no doubt from a western branch of that large clan. The Jiang family was famous for its strong-minded women whose tales of love affairs and general disobedience to their husbands were collected in *Mr. Zuo's Commentary* to the *Springs and Autumns* (*Zuozhuan*).

Whatever its origins—and the state of Qi probably does date back to the early Western Zhou Period—by the early decades of the Warring States Period the Jiang royal family of Qi weakened and was challenged by a rival family, surnamed Tian. In 410 BCE the Tian clan took over, ruling the state of Qi until it was conquered by Qin in 221 BCE.

The state of Qi rose to prominence during the seventh century BCE following the decline of the state of Zheng. Qi's rise to power came under the auspices of its long-reigning and accomplished ruler Lord (*gong*) Huan (r. 685–643 BCE), aided by his chief minister and advisor Guan Zhong (c. 730–645 BCE), one of the most famous and influential figures of the entire Spring and Autumn era. (Such was Guan Zhong's fame that his name was attached to the *Guanzi*, an eclectic work on statesmanship compiled, in part from earlier sources, in the second century BCE. In fact the book has little or nothing to do with the historical Guan Zhong, but borrowing his name as the putative author added to its aura of authority.) Guan Zhong, with the approval of Lord Huan, was one of the pioneers in creating a bureaucratic and merit-based system of government, taking the first steps toward replacing the old aristocratic and ritual-based Zhou system. Lord Huan was one of the first Sinitic rulers to promulgate a code of laws, written by Guan Zhong. At the same time Qi armies fought to bring recalcitrant Eastern Yi enclaves under Qi rule, strengthening the state's ability to respond to external challenges. Qi also instituted policies to improve the management of craft, marine, salt, and grain production and distribution, thus increasing the wealth of the state. These policies were so successful that Lord Huan was recognized by his peers, the rulers of other powerful states, as the first *ba* ("hegemon"), empowered to protect and act in the name of the Zhou king (for example, in convening multi-state conferences or authorizing military punitive expeditions). The Qi program of reform faltered somewhat after the deaths of Guan Zhong (645 BCE) and Lord Huan (643 BCE), but Qi remained a major power throughout the rest of the Eastern Zhou Period.

The southeastern states of Wu and Yue were outside the orbit of the Western Zhou, but were organized as states at least partly on the Zhou model during the Spring and Autumn Period. Wu occupied the lower Huai River Valley, extending southward to the northern banks of the Yangzi River and its delta. Yue lay to the south of Wu, and apparently included in its population many non-Sinitic peoples, although its rulers aspired to membership in the Spring and Autumn multi-state system. They promoted a claim, no doubt bogus, that they were descended from the royal house of the Xia dynasty. In part reflecting their outsider status, the rulers of Wu and Yue referred to themselves as "kings" (*wang*), although the Zhou kings granted them only minor titles of nobility.

Wu became integrated into the Spring and Autumn multi-state system through the patronage of Jin. With the great southern state of Chu starting to recover from its humiliating defeat by Jin in the Battle of Chengpu (632 BCE), Jin looked to the growing military power of Wu to act as a brake on Chu's expansionist ambitions. Beginning around 580 BCE, Jin launched a series of attacks on Chu, annexing some minor states that formerly had been conquered by Chu. Thereafter, throughout the sixth century BCE, Chu had to defend not only its northern border against Jin but its eastern border against Wu. During those decades Wu began attending inter-state conferences with the backing of Jin, as Wu became increasingly inte-grated into the Sinitic world. In 506 BCE King Helü of Wu launched a full-scale invasion of Chu, inflicting another resounding defeat on the great southern power. At the same time Wu engaged in a series of battles against Yue in a struggle for control of the Yangzi delta. In 496 BCE King Helü was mortally wounded during an invasion of Yue.

King Helü's son, King Fuchai, followed in his father's ambitious footsteps. In one of the most famous episodes of Spring and Autumn history (no doubt considerably embroidered in the retelling), King Fuchai inflicted a devastating defeat on Yue in 493 BCE. Yue's king, Goujian, was captured; his wife was made one of King Fuchai's concubines and King Gou-jian himself was forced to be one of King Fuchai's personal servants. In the wake of this victory Fuchai demanded to be recognized as hegemon and, in that role, he presided over an inter-state meeting in 482 BCE. But his triumph was short-lived. King Goujian, pretending to accept his humiliation, had actually been plotting revenge with loyal supporters in Yue. The Yue armies mounted a series of invasions of Wu, culminating in a three-year siege of the Wu capital beginning in 473 BCE. Defeated, King Fuchai hanged himself. Yue then claimed the office of *ba*, but by then the whole system of hegemony had little meaning, and the title itself lapsed from that time onward. In Wu, meanwhile, a series of usurpations and assassi-nations marked succession to the throne, so that the state's once-formidable power declined during the remainder of the fifth century BCE.

One long-term effect of the partial incorporation of Yue into the Eastern Zhou political world was the adoption of swords by the armed forces of the Central States. The *ge* dag-ger-axe, known from the Late Neolithic Period and the Early Bronze Age, had remained the infantry weapon of choice in the East Asian Heartland, but during the early sixth century BCE swords made by the expert smiths of Yue were recognized both as prestige items and as highly effective weapons. They were cast from an unusual mix of metal alloys in geometrical patterns that made them not only striking to look at but also famously strong and sharp (Figure 7.1). They must have been highly regarded, as Yue swords are found in archaeological sites through-out the Yangzi River Valley.

The large and powerful state of Chu dominated the southern Heartland Region. Archaeo-logical evidence suggests that the earliest Chu elites lived in the upper Han River Valley and were in contact with the Zhou farther north. The first Chu capital, Danyang, was probably located in the Han River Valley, though its exact location is a matter of dispute. Chu steadily expanded southwards along the Han River and then eastwards into the middle reaches of the

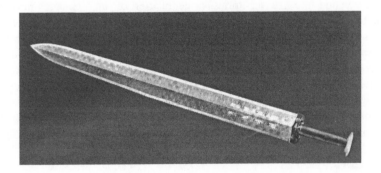

Figure 7.1 Bronze sword which, according to its inscription, was made for the personal use of King Goujian of Yue, ca. 510 BCE. Careful control of different alloys accounts for the beautiful patterning on the surface of the blade, and its extreme sharpness.

Yangzi River. The Chu people, usually characterized as "barbarian" by northern writers, built up a major metropolis in the Jiangling Region on the north side of the Yangzi River, upriver from modern Wuhan and the Dongting Lake region. Over the centuries the Chu rulers pushed eastward, culturally dominating the entire north side of the Middle and Lower Yangzi River Valley. Its expansion eastward was checked for a time, as we have seen, by the coalition of Jin and Wu, but that obstacle eventually gave way. As was the case in other powerful outer states, in Chu a Sinitic elite presided over a large population of non-Sinitic peoples.

The rulers of Chu sought to enhance their prestige by claiming an illustrious remote ancestry. During the Eastern Zhou Period origin tales of the territorial states clearly varied according to the times and the teller. We see this again for the state of Chu. While the *Records of the Grand Historian* traces the genealogy of the Chu ruling house back to the mythical Yellow Emperor (*Huangdi*), a recently discovered bamboo text describing the origins of the Chu people, like the earlier Qi bronze bell inscription, emphasizes a family connection with the royal house of Shang. The Chu bamboo text claims that a god descended from the sky to a mountain, then traveled up a river to meet with the Shang king, Pan Geng, founder of the Shang capital at Yinxu. Pan Geng gave him a daughter in marriage; their offspring fathered the Chu people.

Chu was an economic and military powerhouse, thriving on its control of a major trade route between the Central Plains and regions to the south. It had control over and access to natural resources, especially tin and lead used in bronze production, but also cowry shells, ivory, rhinoceros horn and rhinoceros hide (the preferred material for making armor), and other exotic southern products. Chu traded with the supposed states of Ba and Shu in the southwestern part of the East Asian Heartland Region. Ba was located in the Three Gorges region of the upper Yangzi River, and seemed not to participate in the Zhou cultural overlay, as their people were buried in boats placed in caves high up a cliff face—a style completely unknown in the Heartland. Shu occupied lands in the Sichuan Plateau, where the very distinctive Sanxingdui culture, contemporary with the late Shang Period, had held sway. During the Spring and Autumn Period both Ba and Shu lay outside the Zhou multi-state system and were known to the Central States only through long-distance trade.

Although Chu territory included vast marshes that would not be drained for conversion to agricultural production for several centuries to come, Chu was already a major producer of rice, as well as of silk, goldware, and lacquerware. As early as the Western Zhou Period Chu had developed a regional style in ritual bronze vessels, with distinctive shapes and surface décor, and that continued to be true during the Spring and Autumn Period.

Along with Qi, Chu was a pioneer in administrative reform. Beginning in the seventh century BCE Chu expansion into new territories, or acquisition of satellite states through conquest, gave rise to a new kind of administrative district called a *xian* (in later contexts, usually translated as "county"). These districts were governed by officials—who were not necessarily members of the upper ranks of nobility—appointed directly by the ruler. This gave the central government much more control over taxes, registration of the population (for taxation, corvée labor, and military service), trade, and other functions of local rule than was the case with territory under traditional aristocratic administration. *Xian* districts were organized in Jin and Qin in the sixth century, and in other states soon afterwards: a further step in the bureaucratization of government in pre-imperial China.

The *ba* "hegemons"

As we have seen, the office of *ba*, conventionally translated as "hegemon," was an innovation of the Spring and Autumn Period designed to bring some sort of order to the chaotic competition of the territorial states. The idea of the office of *ba* is said to have originated with the great statesman of Qi, Guan Zhong, and the first of the hegemons was Guan Zhong's employer, Lord Huan of Qi. Among the duties of the hegemon were to "protect lineages that were failing and revive those that had been extinguished"—in other words, to prevent and even reverse the relentless process of smaller polities being extinguished and absorbed by larger ones. The mechanism for doing this was to wield the power supposedly granted to the hegemon by the reigning Zhou king to convene inter-state conferences and to mount military actions—characterized as "punitive expeditions"—against states that transgressed others' borders or disturbed the structure of the old order. In broader terms, the role of the hegemon was to protect the Zhou monarchy and act on its behalf in matters of inter-state relations. In practice, the designation of hegemon recognized the paramount power, at least temporarily, of one or another of the major states.

The *ba* system is taken as a matter of historical fact in a wide range of texts from the War-ring States and Han Periods. Nevertheless, some scholars have argued that the whole notion of hegemons was an invention of later writers, and that the office of hegemon never existed. And in fact there are reasons to doubt at least the details of the hegemon system. For one thing, later texts do not agree on the list of hegemons. One common reckoning begins with Lord Huan of Qi and continues with Lord Wen of Jin, Lord Xiang of Song, Lord Zhuang of Chu, and Lord Mu of Qin. Other lists take Lord Xiang of Jin to have been the third hegemon; still other lists omit Lord Mu of Qin and add King Helü of Wu, King Fuchai of Wu, and King Goujian of Yue. This variation is not necessarily fatal to the historicity of the *ba* system, however. The rank of hegemon was conferred by the general consent of the most powerful territorial lords, and variation in the lists of hegemons might reflect claims to that office that were not fully ratified by the territorial lords of the time. A second difficulty is that the word *ba* does not appear at all in the *Springs and Autumns* text, only in Zuo's later commentary on it. This, again, is not necessarily a problem, however, because it might simply reflect disap-proval of the hegemon system on the part of the lords of Lu. For example, the *Springs and Autumns* seems to question the validity of any inter-state conference convened by anyone but the Zhou king himself. In general, the *Springs and Autumns* is silent, or evasive, on subjects that offended the sensibilities of the rather conservative lords of Lu. The most serious chal-lenge to the reality of the hegemon system is the absence of the word *ba* as a title from all known bronze inscriptions of the Spring and Autumn Period. Those inscriptions are a rich source of history and one might suppose that, if the hegemons were really an important factor in inter-state relations of the time, some author of a bronze inscription would have mentioned them. But the inscribed vessels are silent on this subject. It is hard to reconcile that silence with the universal belief in later times that there had been hegemons and that their deeds and accomplishments were well known. As with many aspects of early Chinese history, more evidence is needed before coming to a firm conclusion.

Agriculture, technology, and commerce

In the Western Zhou era and, presumably, even earlier in the Shang all land in principle belonged to the king, and the peasants who worked the land had no rights to either the land or its products. The entire harvest belonged to the king, and his functionaries collected the crops and then doled out grain and other food, clothing, tools, and other necessities to the peasants. The same system prevailed under the governments of the territorial lords at the beginning of the Spring and Autumn Period. But things changed around the beginning of the sixth century BCE when Lu, followed by other states, instituted a tax on crops, generally in the range of 10 to 20 percent, replacing the old system of state ownership of the entire harvest. This immediately improved the efficiency of farming, as farmers could keep the greater part of their harvest and so had an incentive to grow more.

This system of taxation probably formed the basis for the idealized system described by the fourth-century BCE Confucian philosopher Mencius (Mengzi). Land was supposedly marked out in units of nine fields configured as 3 × 3 grids (similar to a tick-tack-toe game layout); peasants worked the central field collectively, and its harvest was paid as tax. Each family was assigned one of the outer eight fields and kept its harvest for themselves. This system, called the "well field" system because the configuration of the fields resembled the Chinese character for "well" (井), did not yet amount to private ownership of land with the right to inherit or sell it, but it was a step in that direction. The extent to which this system was actually implemented is unclear. But, together with other improvements in agriculture, including new varieties of millet and rice, more widespread cultivation of soy beans, improved irrigation, the introduction of iron tools, and more widespread use of oxen or water buffalo for plowing, it is very likely that new systems of taxation contributed to steadily increasing crop yields throughout the Spring and Autumn Period.

The most significant technological development in the Spring and Autumn Period was the widespread use of iron, both from meteoric raw iron and mined ores. The use and control of very high temperatures was already familiar in the East Asian Heartland Region from the bronze and ceramics industries, and was easily adapted to the smelting of iron. The Sinitic emphasis on bronze casting as the principal form of metallurgical work no doubt contributed to the early adoption of cast iron (rather than wrought iron, as in western Eurasia) as the most common way of making iron implements. Well into the imperial era, however, bronze remained the metal of choice for weapons, chariot fittings, ritual vessels, and other high-status goods. (In addition, bronze swords and dagger-axes could be sharpened to a keener edge, and were less brittle, than cast-iron versions.) Iron was used for more ordinary purposes, and greatly improved the efficiency of plows, spades, sickles, knives, and other tools.

Commerce flourished during the Spring and Autumn Period. During the Western Zhou commerce had been largely controlled by the royal establishment and the courts of the territorial lords; it was closer to a ritual exchange of gifts or tribute than mercantile activity. Trade in goods, sometimes over long distances, was increasingly privatized in the Spring and Autumn Period. New roads and canals facilitated travel for territorial lords going to interstate conferences (or committing aggression against their neighbors) and merchants engaged in the transport of goods. Check-points and tariffs controlled and impeded, but did not stop, such trade. A wide variety of goods became increasingly available throughout the Heartland Region. Merchants officially recognized by one local court carried tallies like passports that allowed them to cross borders and trade with other regions.

Money made its first appearance in the Heartland Region toward the end of the Spring and Autumn Period. Previously, cowrie shells, imported from the South China Sea, were used as a medium of exchange from Shang times. But cowrie "money" seems to have been used more for the display of wealth than for the purchase of goods, and was often incorporated into clothing or horse gear decorations. Also, since the Shang Period, metal and stone blades may have served as a medium of exchange and, by the late sixth century BCE, bronze coins shaped like double-bladed spades began to circulate in Jin and nearby territories of the inner states. This first step at monetarization, involving the use of objects representative of precious goods rather than the goods themselves, encouraged trade and made it more efficient.

Literature, music, and intellectual life

The expansion of literacy that began during the Western Zhou continued during the Spring and Autumn Period. As the administrations of the territorial lords became more bureaucratized there was an increasing demand for literate officials who could keep records, draft documents, maintain archives, and perform other, similar functions. These duties came to be united in the persons of scribes (*shi*, a different word from the *shi* meaning "knight"), who were also responsible for interpreting omens and making astrological readings. Below the scribes were copyists, who made copies of documents but did not necessarily understand the texts they were copying. Rather, they had the technical skills needed to prepare the rolls of bamboo strips that were the common medium of writing at that time, and to make ink, prepare brushes, and write with a legible hand.

In addition to the *Springs and Autumns* of Lu, which has been transmitted through the ages, at least a few other states also kept chronicles that are known through quotations in such works as *Mr. Zuo's Commentary* to the *Springs and Autumns*. Whether all, or even most, states maintained such chronicles is unknown. Beyond that, not much that we would describe as literature has come down from the Spring and Autumn Period. It is safe to assume that people of that era told stories to one another; some of those may have been transmitted in writing to become part of the great fund of historical anecdotes that we know from Warring States, Qin, and Han times, but, if so, the originals have been lost. Similarly, there is every reason to suppose that people composed songs and recited poetry; some of the content of the *Book of Odes* (*Shijing*) appears to date from the Spring and Autumn Period, although that anthology was still several centuries away from achieving the form in which we know it today. But, with those tantalizing exceptions, the literary life of the Spring and Autumn Period remains to be discovered.

We know more about music in the Spring and Autumn Period because physical evidence for it remains in the forms of archaeologically recovered bells, chime-stones, drums, and other instruments, and pictorial representations of musical performances on bronze vessels. The most significant of the various musical instruments were bells. Several kinds of bells were known in Shang times, including *bo*, which were hung from stands, and *nao*, which balanced, mouth upwards, on thick stems. Bronze founders had already discovered that, cast in the proper shape, a bell could play two notes, depending on where it was struck. But these bells were made singly and do not seem to have been tuned to any particular note. Musically they may have functioned more like gongs, to beat out a rhythm or to punctuate a musical phrase.

Arrays of tuned bells (*yongzhong*) began to be produced in the mid-Western Zhou Period. Originally a product of the south, they quickly spread throughout the Heartland Region. At first comprising just a few bells, by the late Spring and Autumn Period arrays of finely tuned bells might span three octaves or more and be capable of carrying a complex melody. These arrays were prestigious luxury items and featured elements of the instrumental music played at the courts of territorial lords (Figure 7.2). The bell arrays were often complemented by arrays of chime-stones made of resonant, fine-grained stone, shaped and sized to the proper tuning, suspended like bells from wooden racks, and played with wooden mallets. Other musical instruments in Spring and Autumn orchestras were ocarinas, various kinds of flutes, drums of several shapes and sizes, and zither-like stringed instruments (*se*) or laplutes (*qin*).

In the absence of relevant written materials it is difficult to talk about the intellectual life of the Spring and Autumn Period. Certainly there must have been debates over policy matters, such as the appropriateness and content of law codes such as the one promulgated by

Figure 7.2 A set of twenty-six tuned bronze bells from Tomb 2, Xiasi, Xichuan, Henan.

Lord Huan of Qi on the advice of Guan Zhong. The last seventy-five years of the period, however, coincide with the lifetime of Confucius, and accounts of his career as a social critic and teacher give us an idea of the issues that occupied concerned minds at the time and some of the ways of addressing them (see Focus: Confucius and the *Analects*). He gives us a picture of someone who was widely educated through access to works on history, ritual, music, and poetry; of a milieu in which rulers were at least willing to listen to, if not to adopt, radical proposals for improving society; and of the possibility that a learned and thoughtful person could live a rich life of the mind and attract students to share it with him. In the culture of the Spring and Autumn Period Confucius appears as an isolated case, but he ushered in, with the advent of the Warring States Period, a vigorous and widely shared intellectual life that profoundly shaped the future of Chinese thought and society.

Focus: A year in the *Springs and Autumns*

The *Springs and Autumns* records, in brief, laconic statements, events in the state of Lu, as well as events in other states that potentially might affect Lu. Here is the entire text for the twenty-eighth year of Lord Xi of Lu (Lu Xi Gong):

- In the twenty-eighth year, in spring, the lord of Jin made an incursion into Cao. He also invaded Wey.
- Mai, the son (of the late Lord Zhuang of Lu) was guarding (the frontier of) Wey. Because he did not do so successfully, the lord (i.e. Lord Xi) executed him.
- A person from Chu (attempted to) relieve Wey (from the attack by Jin).
- In the third month, on the day *bingwu*, the lord of Jin entered (the capital of) Cao, captured the lord of Cao, and handed him over to a person from Song.
- In summer, in the fourth month, on the day *jisi*, the lord of Jin, with armed forces from Qi, Song, and Qin, fought with a person from Chu at Chengpu. The Chu army was disgracefully defeated.

- Chu executed its great officer, De Chen.
- The lord of Wey left his state and fled to Chu.
- In the fifth month, on the day *guichou*, the lord (of Lu) met with the lord of Jin, the lord of Qi, the lord of Song, the lord of Cai, the lord of Zheng, the lord of Wey, and the lord of Ju, and made a covenant at Qingtu.
- The lord of Chen attended the meeting.
- The lord (of Lu) paid a court visit to the (Zhou) king where he was (i.e. at a temporary palace at Qingtu).
- In the sixth month, Lord Zheng of Wey returned from Chu to Wey. Yuan Xuan of Wey left the country and fled to Jin.
- Lord Kuan of Chen died.
- In autumn, the lord's (i.e. the late Lord Zhuang's) eldest daughter (widow of the late lord of) Qi came to Lu.
- The lord's (i.e. the late Lord (Zhuang's) son Sui went to Qi.
- In winter, the lord (i.e. Lord Xi) met with the lord of Jin, the lord of Qi, the lord of Song, the lord of Cai, the lord of Zheng, the heir-designate of Chen, the lord of Ju, the lord of Zhu, and a person from Qin, at Wen.
- The king (Son of) Heaven held an audience at Heyang.
- On the day *renshen*, Lord (Xi) paid a court visit to the king where he was.
- A person from Jin captured the lord of Wey and returned with him to the capital.
- Yuan Xuan of Wey returned from Jin to Wey.
- The territorial lords then besieged (the capital of) Xu.
- Lord Xiang of Cao was restored to his state, and joined the territorial lords in besieging Xu.

Modified from James Legge, *Shoo King* (*The Chinese Classics*, Vol. 5), p. 207.

This year—equivalent to 632 BCE—was a momentous one. As the *Springs and Autumns* records, in the summer of that year Chu was disastrously defeated by a coalition of states, led by Jin, in the Battle of Chengpu. This put an end to Chu's ambitions to extend its territory into the Central States in the middle Yellow River Valley. Chu remained a great power, but its days of expansion northward were finished. It is notable that the *Springs and Autumns* uses the loaded word "disgracefully" in connection with Chu's defeat, and records also (without specifying the connection) that Chu executed the general whose incompetence precipitated that defeat.

This quoted passage conveys some of the abbreviated, matter-of-fact style of the annals. Without further information it would be difficult, or sometimes impossible, to identify the people and events recorded here. Fortunately, the classic commentaries on the *Springs and Autumns*—the *Zuo*, *Gongyang*, and *Guliang Commentaries*—draw on both orally transmitted stories and now-lost written documents to provide such identifications, and often flesh out the brief records of the annals with fuller (though unverifiable) anecdotal accounts. For example, *Mr. Zuo's Commentary* expands on the first sentence of the *Springs and Autumns* text as follows:

In the spring of the (Lord of Lu's) twenty-eighth year, the Lord of Jin planned to invade Cao, and asked permission to travel through (the territory of) Wey. A person (i.e. the ruler) of Wey denied permission. (The Jin army) retraced its steps and crossed the Yellow River at its most southerly point. It then attacked Cao and invaded Wei. In the first month, on the day *maoshen*, they captured Wulu. In the second month, Xi Hu of Jin died, and Yuan Zhen took command of the second army (division), while the lord (of Jin) rewarded Xu Chen by making him deputy commander of the third army (division). The lord of Jin and the lord of Qi met at Hanyu to conclude a covenant. The lord of Wey requested to be included in the covenant, but a person (i.e. the ruler) of Jin denied (the request). The lord of Wey then wanted to align his state with Chu, but the people (of Wey) did not want that, and deposed their ruler in order to curry favor with Jin. The lord of Wey then departed and made his home at Huainiu.

Not readily visible in the translated text are some of the special conventions followed by the annalists over the course of centuries. For example, when the text refers to the death or burial of the ruler of a state, it uses special terms for "to die" and "to bury" that apply only to rulers; other deaths and burials use more common terms. The text uses the term "a person" (as in "a person from Qin") as a sign of disapproval, suppressing the person's name when the individual in question has acted in a ritually incorrect way (such as invading a neighboring state without royal authorization or trying to attend a conference of territorial lords without having suitably high status). And when several states are mentioned together they always are listed in rank order (not visible in our generic translations as "lord"); *gong, hou, bo, zi*, and *nan*. (Here the text makes an exception; normally the *gong* of Song would be listed ahead of any *hou*, but here we have, among the signers of the covenant of Qingtu, "Our lord" (the *gong* of Lu, always listed first—the *Springs and Autumns* is a Lu document); the *hou* of Jin, the *hou* of Qi, the *gong* of Song, the *hou* of Cai, the *bo* of Zheng, the *zi* of Wey, and the *zi* of Ju. (Normally the *gong* of Song would out-rank any *hou*; the special status granted to Jin and Qi seems to have been a recognition that rulers of both those states had served as hegemons,) Thus, despite the terse and seemingly uninformative entries in the *Springs and Autumns*, a close reading of the text can reveal a great deal about the ritual/political life of the period.

Focus: The *Book of Changes*

Just as oracle bones are indelibly associated with the Shang dynasty, the *Book of Changes* (*Yijing* or *Zhouyi*) system of divination is firmly associated with the Zhou. The system involved a manipulation of stalks to derive a series of numbers that were transcribed into one of eight trigrams (three lines), which are then combined into sixty-four hexagrams (six lines). By Han times the numbers had evolved into a system of broken and unbroken lines representing cosmic forces. Once the hexagram (called a *gua*) was obtained it was necessary to find the figure in the divination manual, the *Yijing*. There one would find a mantic "statement" associated uniquely with that hexagram, which provided an overall reading of the six-line figure and a supplementary reading of each of its six lines. The texts are frequently enigmatic or obscure, and require further expert interpretation. They may have been drawn from now-lost fragments of song, liturgy, or mythological tales.

Mythology firmly associates the *Changes* with the Zhou people. The precursors of the hexagrams, three-line figures of solid or divided lines (trigrams, also called *gua*), were said to have been invented by Fu Xi ("Tamer of Beasts"), one of the mythical "sage-emperors" who were supposed to have ruled the Sinitic world in high antiquity. Mathematically, there are eight (2^3) possible arrangements of three lines that can be either solid or divided, ranging from three solid lines to three divided lines, with six possibilities in between. As the myths have it, the trigrams were found to be insufficiently specific to yield accurate divination, so King Wen, the founder of the Zhou dynasty, invented the hexagrams, each of which may be thought of as two trigrams piled on top of one another. There are sixty-four (2^6 or 8×8

trigrams) possible arrangements of six lines that can be either solid or divided. The sixty-four hexagrams of the *Yijing* can thus be thought of as exhausting all possible interpretations of all possible phenomena in the world: they are complete and comprehensive.

Archaeological evidence suggests that the original *gua* were not sets of solid or divided lines, however, but series of numbers. Such series, often of six numbers and usually different combinations of 1, 5, 6, 7, 8, and 9, have appeared on oracle bones, ceramics, bronzes, and other objects since the Shang Period, possibly indicating the use of "stalk divination" to verify bone divination results. At some point, probably around the beginning of the Han dynasty, the numbers began to be replaced by solid lines (for odd numbers) and divided lines (for even ones); these figures were taken as representations of the cosmic forces of yin and yang. Fourth-century BCE numerical *gua* (referring to trigrams or hexagrams) seem to represent a stage in between the old Shang and Western Zhou stalk divination rules and the Han simplification into yin and yang (Figure 7.3).

The *Yijing* divination system is definitely associated with the Zhou dynasty (as the alternate name of the system, *Zhouyi*, indicates), but it is highly unlikely that it was invented by King Wen personally. Indeed, the link between divided or undivided lines and the cosmic powers of yin and yang was not clearly in place until the early imperial era. The importance of yin and yang as concepts in the known text of the *Yijing* is evident in the fact that, among the sixty-four possible combinations of trigrams, many hexagrams are presented in pairs, with one representing the opposite configuration of the other. Though the *Yijing* system

Figure 7.3 Section 24 of a fourth-century BCE trigram divination manual written on bamboo strips. Originally from Chu, the text has been given the title *Shifa* ("Stalk Divination") by the team of researchers at Tsinghua University, where it is preserved. The manual rolls out like a map and has thirty sections with different charts and divination subject sample types that a diviner could consult at one time. In Section 24 the Eight Trigrams are arrayed according to the directions and provided with yin yang/ Five Phase correlates. Redrawn by Lala Zuo after Li Xueqin, ed., *Qinghua daxue cang Zhanguo zhujian* (Warring States bamboo-slip documents preserved at Qinghua University), Vol. 4 (Shanghai: Zhongxi, 2013), p. 76.

undoubtedly evolved to a significant extent during the long centuries of the Zhou era, the texts assigned to each line do seem to preserve old mantic statements from an earlier age.

Whatever its origins, the system came to be widely used and has lasted down to the present day, and not only within China. One begins by asking a question. A Zhou king might have asked, "Is the next cyclical day *xinhai* an auspicious day to attack the Rong (northern 'barbarians')?" According to later texts the divination expert would then divide a group of fifty stalks into various numbers of groups, holding remainders in certain ways between different fingers to indicate the various factors in complicated equations used to derive the odd and even numbers or solid or divided lines. The process had to be repeated and calculated numerous times to evolve a single line, much less a hexagram. In fact, there is much controversy as to how exactly the lines were derived now that recent archaeological manuscripts show that all lines in pre-Han times were originally numbers and these numbers do not match up with later theories of line calculation.

The two examples below are the first and second hexagrams in the *Yijing*. They represent pure yang power and pure yin power because one is all 9s, a yang number, and the other is all 6s, a yin number. *Qian* in some interpretative traditions represents Heaven and the Father, while *Kun* represents its reflective opposite, Earth and the Mother. Generally, hexagrams in the *Yijing* tradition are read from the bottom line upwards.

☰ *Qian*: Supreme, Felicitous, Advantageous for prognostication.
Nine in the first position:
  A dragon lying low. Do not employ it.
Nine in the second position:
  See a dragon in the field. It is advantageous to see a big person [a person of higher rank].
Nine in the third position:
  A gentleman is active and forceful all day but at the end of the day must be apprehensive and compliant. Danger. No harm.
Nine in the fourth position:
  It will be as if leaping up inside an abyss. No harm.
Nine in the fifth position:
  A flying dragon in the Sky. It is advantageous to see a big person.
Nine in the uppermost position:
  A blocked dragon will have regrettable consequences.

☷ *Kun*: Supreme, felicitous. It is advantageous to prognosticate on a mare. When the gentleman goes out, if he goes first, he'll get lost, but if he follows, he'll make it to the host. It will be advantageous to go southwest, where he'll make friends. If he goes to the northeast, he'll lose friends. It is safe to prognosticate. Auspicious.
Six in the first position:
  Tread on frost. Firm ice is coming.
Six in the second position:
  Straight, square, and big. With no repetitions, everything will be advantageous.
Six in the third position:
  It is possible to prognosticate on the display held inside. If engaged in the king's service, then without accomplishing (the project), it will be finished.
Six in the fourth position:
  A tied up sack. No harm. No praise.
Six in the fifth position:
  A yellow skirt. Supreme auspiciousness.

Six in the upper position:
   Dragons battle in the field. Their blood is black and yellow.

Two features of the *Yijing* are especially notable: First, it is not designed to yield a simple yes or no answer to a question; rather, the texts evoked by the hexagrams are generally ambiguous and obscure, and serve as vehicles for introspection, contemplation, and interpretation. They can be seen as a source of advice rather than of easy answers. Second, it came to be firmly text-based, in keeping with the general Zhou tendency to evoke and rely upon the written word. Undoubtedly the line interpretations and overall hexagram interpretations were closely guarded oral traditions passed down through generations of hereditary diviners; but sometime in the Warring States Period, if not before, these interpretations began to be written down. The bare text then, over time, attracted a large number of written commentaries that sought to clarify the enigmatic divinatory texts. In later times the *Yijing* became one of the thirteen orthodox classics of the Confucian tradition, and was seen by many Chinese scholars and philosophers as the ultimate repository of wisdom.

Focus: Chong'er

One famous Jin ruler, whose stormy career is recounted in numerous tales, was Chong'er, posthumously known as Lord (*hou*) Wen of Jin (r. 636–628 BCE). During his lifetime Wen Gong was called Chong'er ("Double Ear"), presumably reflecting some unusual physical attribute. He is often described in tales as being physically handicapped, with a malformed ribcage and/or spine. The last years of the reign of his father, Lord Xian, were turbulent because of a succession crisis. His original heir apparent, Shensheng, was deprived of his status as heir through the influence of the ruler's favorite concubine, Li Ji, who wanted her own son to succeed to the throne. Under duress, Shensheng committed suicide in 656 BCE. Lord Xian then initiated a series of military campaigns against his sons by other wives who were potential candidates to inherit the throne of Jin, driving several of them, including Chong'er, into exile. Chong'er fled the state in 655; when Lord Xian died in 651 Chong'er declined to return to Jin to compete for the throne. His half-brother Yiwu became Lord Hui of Jin.

Chong'er became a wanderer. He and his entourage, no doubt consisting of a military escort, advisors, and servants, first spent several years at the court of Qi, the powerful eastern state that was his mother's native place. Later he passed through the small states of Cao, Song, and Zheng, where the burden of hosting the unwanted guests undoubtedly put a strain on their resources. Chong'er kept track of the willingness or otherwise of other rulers to help him; on one occasion, the ruler of Cao forced Chong'er to partly disrobe so that people could see his deformity, and years later he repaid the insult by extinguishing the state of Cao. After leaving Zheng he next went to the powerful southern state of Chu for a prolonged visit. The last stage of Chong'er's wandering took him to the northwest to visit the state of Qin, now firmly under the control of the old Zhou homeland in the Wei River Valley. When Lord Hui of Jin died in 636, Qin provided a sizeable army to escort Chong'er back to Jin, where he finally ascended the throne.

After Chong'er took the Jin throne in 636 BCE he confronted what he saw as a growing threat from Chu in the south, using the knowledge he gained in his travels to reform Jin military and civil administration. Although in the end Chu would last much longer than Jin as a state, Chong'er led the Jin army against the Chu army in the famous Battle of Chengpu, defeating them in 632 BCE and effectively blocking Chu's northern expansion for a decade or more.

In a set of tales drawn from Spring and Autumn Period historical lore and recorded in *Mr. Zuo's Commentary* to the *Springs and Autumns*, we learn something about Chong'er's personality. Despite his bravado during feasts at the various courts during his travels, he was very frightened of the supernatural, a trait that was typical of many lords of that time. For example, he believed that the music and dance costumes at one particular feast performance might invoke ancient spirits that clashed with his own ancestors, causing him illness. Therefore he employed diviners and exorcists to diagnose and treat any problems of that sort. In other tales these same experts on the spirit world were consulted to interpret his nightmares, explain the prophetic meaning of his being chased by a demon, or interpret the conversation between ancient demonic spirits lodged deep within his body in order to diagnose his medical problems.

Focus: Confucius and the *Analects*

His name was Kong Qiu, or, more formally, Kong Zhongni; in texts he is usually called Kongzi, "Master Kong." "Confucius" is a Latinized form, devised by seventeenth-century Jesuit missionaries, of an unusual version of his name, Kong Fuzi. He was born around 551 BCE in Qufu, the capital of the state of Lu. His grandfather is said to have come from Song, and had ties, many centuries in the past, to the royal house of Shang. Some of his other ancestors may have belonged to the Eastern Yi, the indigenous people of the Shandong Peninsula. He was from a family of minor aristocrats, members of the *shi* class—a class that, throughout the Heartland Region, was being redefined from "knights" to bureaucrats and administrators—"men of service." According to legend, his mother raised him in poverty but took pains to assure that he received a comprehensive education, studying all of the texts he could find, with an emphasis on music, ritual, and historical documents. He was particularly interested in accounts of King Wen and King Wu of Zhou, and of Zhou Gong Dan, the "Duke of Zhou," revered in Lu as the founder of that state. But he was no ivory tower intellectual; true to his *shi* heritage he studied the martial arts and was an expert archer and charioteer.

He had visions of becoming a high minister/advisor to the lords of Lu (perhaps with the example of Guan Zhong of Qi in mind), but as he approached middle age he found himself stuck in a routine bureaucratic position. In his fifties he began to travel from one court of the Zhou inner states to another, hoping to find a ruler who would put his ideas into practice. Along the way, he began to attract disciples—tradition says that there were seventy-two of them—who traveled with him as an entourage, and who lived in the Kong family compound when they were back in Lu. Confucius became a full-time teacher; he reasoned that if he could not succeed in high office himself, he could at least train a cadre of potential civil servants, some of whom might be able to put his ideas about good government into practice. And in fact some of his disciples, and their later followers, did have successful administrative careers.

Our principal source of information about Confucius is the *Lunyu*, which means "Discussions and Sayings"; the title is conventionally translated as the *Analects*, an unusual word that means "literary gleanings." The long-held conventional view is that the *Lunyu* was written down by Confucius's disciples shortly after his death in order to have a record of his teachings, but recent scholarship has shown that the book comprises many layers. Some of the earliest can be attributed to the first generation of Confucius' disciples, but others were written over the course of a couple of centuries, so the book as we know it was finalized as much as 200 years after the Master's death. The text itself is a jumble of short passages which has preserved layers of ancient language, including some "dialogue." Caution is therefore required in reading the *Lunyu*; some of its teachings reflect the views of later followers rather than of Confucius himself. Stories about Confucius that appear in other works of the Warring States or Han Periods must be taken with even more grains of salt, because such stories often advance an agenda quite at variance from the teachings of Confucius himself.

Confucius rejected the idea that he was a reformer or an innovator; he described his mission as one of recovering and reinstituting the era of good government and lasting peace that he thought was exemplified by Kings Wen and Wu and by Zhou Gong Dan. He attributed the excellence of the early Zhou rulers to their conformity to *ren*, "benevolence," a term that describes the kind of generous, polite, understanding, spontaneous conduct that prevails in relationships between people of goodwill. Confucius saw this quality as something that was quite rare in his own time, but which was a very powerful social force. The personification of *ren* was the *junzi*, a term that Confucius redefined for his own use. *Junzi* literally means "son of a ruler," but Confucius explicitly said that it really didn't have anything to do with ancestry or noble birth. An actual son of a prince who behaved badly was no *junzi*, while a person of humble birth who conducted himself in a princely fashion truly was one. Other virtues praised in the *Lunyu* include *yi*, "righteousness," intentionally acting in a moral and upright fashion; *li*, "ritual," a word covering everything from ordinary etiquette and an orderly personal life to a knowledge of the liturgies and gestures of royal sacrificial rites; *zhi*, knowledge, described by the famous Confucian formula "to know something, and to know that you know it, and to not know something, and know that you do not know it"; *xin*, "trustworthiness," to be a person of one's word, and never deceitful or devious; and *zhong*, "loyalty." All of these came together in the practice of *xiao*, "filial piety," the obedience, love, and care one owes one's parents. Filial piety in turn forms the foundation for what later followers of Confucius called the "five relationships": father to son, ruler to minister, husband to wife, elder brother to younger brother, and friend to friend (because each friend defers to the other as an elder brother).

Confucius's ideal world, then, was one of hierarchy and obligation, a world in which every person knew his or her place and knew to whom he or she owed deference. It was harmonious, moderate, and stable. It stood in glaring contrast to the treachery, turmoil, warfare, and social fluidity of the late Spring and Autumn Period in which he lived. Confucius might have regarded himself as a failure because he neither attained high office nor found a ruler who was willing to put his sociopolitical ideas into practice, but his teachings—interpreted, extended, and sometimes altered by later followers—became the dominant ideology of China throughout the imperial period. And for more than 2,000 years he has been hailed as "China's First Teacher," and an embodiment of all that is best in Chinese culture.

8   The Warring States Period

Introduction

The Warring States Period was a time of continuous violence that began and ended with series of dramatic events. Throughout the fifth century BCE, the state of Jin was racked by civil warfare among a roster of powerful aristocratic clans (Map 8.1). In a series of shifting alliances involving deadly battles, one by one most of those clans were exterminated. The outcome, in 403 BCE, was the fall of the legitimate ruling family of Jin and the partition of the state into the successor states of Hann, Wei, and Zhao (named for, and ruled by, the three clans that managed to survive the century of civil war). At the end of the Warring States Period the state of Qin, having adopted a policy of the comprehensive militarization of society, used its new-found strength to challenge and defeat each of the separate states of the Heartland Region, uniting all under Qin rule in 221 BCE.

In response to the political chaos and uncertainty that was a hallmark of the time, however, the Warring States Period was also an era of unprecedented cultural brilliance and creative innovation in the arts, literature, and intellectual life. Texts written with brush and ink on wooden or bamboo strips proliferated explosively and promoted the circulation of new ideas in a wide range of fields. The decorative arts, from inlaid bronzes to painted lacquerware to embroidered textiles, reached new heights of design and execution. Freelance intellectuals, known as "traveling persuaders," found ready audiences as they expounded their theories at the palaces of the elite.

Nevertheless, people who lived during the Warring States Period experienced it as an era of chaos, violence, and constant anxiety. At the pinnacle of society territorial lords feared being assassinated, or overthrown by their ministers, or having their state invaded, conquered, and perhaps annihilated. By the end of the Spring and Autumn Period most of the polities that had been established during the Western Zhou had already been extinguished, their territory absorbed into a handful of powerful states once on the periphery of the early Zhou state system. During the Warring States Period most of the surviving small states were turned into powerless dependencies of these great states, or abolished altogether. In many states, great and small, usurpers had overthrown the original aristocratic ruling clans. These usurpers were often from the ranks of the state's own high officials.

At the other end of the social spectrum ordinary peasants might suddenly find themselves conscripted for military service, perhaps to perish on a battlefield far from home. Farmers in hamlets or villages faced starvation when a passing army trampled their crops and stole their stores of grain. Displaced peoples added to the economic difficulties of smaller states, which relied on annual tributes from farmers. Governance involved not only agricultural management but also a means of protecting their resources from other coercive powers.

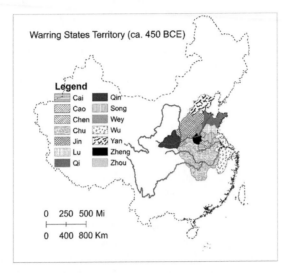

Warring States Territory (ca. 450 BCE)

Legend

Cai	Qin
Cao	Song
Chen	Wey
Chu	Wu
Jin	Yan
Lu	Zheng
Qi	Zhou

0   250   500 Mi

0   400   800 Km

Map 8.1 The early Warring States Period was dominated politically and militarily by the large peripheral states. In the late fifth century BCE the powerful state of Jin broke apart into three states, Hann, Wei, and Zhao, further complicating the political turmoil of the time.

As the larger states grew in wealth and power their armies also became larger. Rulers and their generals abandoned old-fashioned aristocratic codes of warfare that had limited the scale of fighting; new weapons and tactics made battles fiercer and bloodier than ever before. The question on every ruler's lips was, "How can I preserve my state?" Rulers supported roving military strategists and legal advisers in attempts to stave off collapse.

The states at war

Jin

Even by the turbulent standards of the Spring and Autumn and Warring States Periods, political life in the state of Jin was chaotic and dangerous. Aristocratic lineages empowered by their earlier relationships with the Zhou court competed for influence at the Jin court. Throughout the Spring and Autumn Period Jin was racked by a series of succession crises as clans vied to put their favorite candidates on the Jin throne. By the beginning of the fifth century BCE the dozen or so battling clans had been reduced to six: Zhonghang, Fan, Zhi, Hann, Wei, and Zhao. In further civil warfare the Fan clan was exterminated and Lord Wen of Zhonghang was driven into exile, whereupon his territory was divided among the surviving clans. Lord Yao of Zhi then engineered a complicated series of alliances and betrayals by which he hoped to induce the Hann, Wei, and Zhao clans to wipe one another out. But Lord Yao's naked ambition induced those clans to unite, under the leadership of Lord Xiao of Zhao, to defeat the Zhi clan instead. Lord Yao of Zhi, who was killed in 453 BCE, has been remembered throughout Chinese history as a colorful symbol of unchecked ambition coming to a bad end.

Finally, the large and powerful state of Jin was divided into three successor states of Hann, Wei, and Zhao in 403 BCE. Zhao was located farthest north, with Wei in the middle. Small and weak, Hann was located near the old Zhou "inner states" and, like them, played only a marginal role in Warring States inter-state affairs. Zhao borrowed warfare styles from its northern, more nomadic neighbors and proved the most aggressive. The Wei rulers traced their ancestry back to a son of founder king Wen of the Western Zhou, an aristocrat of the Bi lineage. Both Zhao and Wei fought Qin expansion, with Wei succumbing in 225 BCE and Zhao in 222 BCE.

Lu

In the waning years of the Spring and Autumn Period power in Lu had been usurped by three separate lineages descending from the Huan clan. The Ji (or Jisun) lineage dominated. These three sometimes fought one another and sometimes cooperated, but always at the expense of the lords of Lu. By the early Warring States Period the legitimate rulers of Lu, who traced their ancestry to the legendary Zhou Gong Dan, controlled less than half of their nominal territory. An attempt on the part of the old ruling lineage to regain power through an alliance with the state of Wu failed, and Lu played essentially no role in inter-state affairs thereafter. Instead Lu was dominated by its neighbors, particularly Qi to the north and east. Lu did not formally succumb to Qin until 249 BCE.

Qi

Unlike other states, Qi underwent the replacement of its ruling clan, named Jiang, with little effect on its power and influence. In a series of coups and civil wars in the years 485–481 BCE the Tian family first murdered the heir apparent of Qi and installed their own puppet instead. When that child-ruler was overthrown the head of the Tian clan arranged for the murder of his replacement and then proceeded to wipe out most of the legitimate ruling family, along with its allies. The old ruling family was allowed to remain in nominal control of the capital city, Linzi, for several more decades, but was extinguished in 386 BCE. Qi remained a powerful player in inter-state affairs and the Tian rulers became famous for their patronage of guest-intellectuals, who gathered at the Jixia Gate of Linzi, a site of intellectual exchange and learning that became known as the Jixia Academy (see Focus: The Jixia Academy). Qi was the last state to succumb to Qin in the wars of unification in the third century BCE.

Yan

Qi's northern neighbor, Yan, like many other states of that era, was racked in the late fourth century BCE by civil war between upstart usurpers from the ministerial class and upholders of the old aristocratic ruling lineage. Both Qi and Zhao took advantage of that turmoil to invade Yan, though neither succeeded in conquering it beyond short-term victories. The situation stabilized under King Zhao of Yan (r. 311–279 BCE), who instituted administrative and military reforms. The state of Yan survived through the rest of the Warring States Period and was among the last states to capitulate to Qin.

Wu and Yue

In the southern Heartland Region the late Spring and Autumn Period saw a complex struggle for domination among three large and powerful states, Wu, Yue, and Chu. Wu and Yue were both coastal states; Wu was based in the fertile Huai River Valley, extending southwards to the Yangzi River; Yue lay to the south of Wu. Chu dominated an extensive territory north of the Middle Yangzi River Valley. To recapitulate some key events of the Spring and Autumn Period: Wu, under King Helü, temporarily gained great-power status after inflicting a series of defeats on Chu in the late sixth century BCE and absorbing some of its eastern territory. Helü's heir, King Fuchai, crushed the Yue armed forces in 494 BCE and reduced Yue to the status of a tributary of Wu. But Yue, under King Goujian, avenged that defeat in 482 BCE, annihilating the Wu army, occupying Wu's capital city, and seizing the heir apparent. Wu's attempt at resurgence in 473 BCE ended in disaster, when Yue abolished the state of Wu and absorbed its territory. Yue remained a player in the struggles for survival and expansion until the middle of the Warring States Period. After its defeat of Wu, Yue expanded northwards by absorbing some minor states in the lower Yellow River Plain. But Yue was extinguished as a state in the mid-fourth century BCE; most of its territory was absorbed by Chu in 334 BCE, with some northerly areas taken over by Qi.

Chu

Chu itself, blocked in the east by Yue, absorbed or reduced to tributary status a number of small states in the Middle Yangzi and Upper Huai River basin, such as the minor states of Zeng and Cai. It even threatened old states such as Song and Lu. But Chu was plagued by rivalries among the ruling clan's various lineages and by continuing turmoil in the upper ranks of its bureaucracy. Despite its size and wealth, Chu, unlike Qin, was incapable of dominating the Heartland Area, despite conquering many small states south of the Yellow River and splitting up Yue (with Qi). Although Chu had made significant strides in reforming the structure of its government and military forces, it, like Yue, continued to be looked down upon by statesmen of the northern Heartland Region. Their performance of Zhou-style rituals was disparaged. Mencius described their speech as "shrike-tongued" and "barbaric." By the late fourth century Chu was forced to abandon its capital, Ying, as its territory shrank eastwards. Chu was finally defeated by Qin in 223.

Ba and Shu

In the southwest and west the polity or people of Ba, in the Three Gorges area of the Upper Yangzi Valley, continued to play little or no political role among the states of the Heartland Region. Its neighbor Shu, however, in the high, fertile, mountain-ringed Chengdu Plain of Sichuan, was forcibly drawn into the multi-state system of the Warring States Period by the necessity of resisting the expansion of Qin into Sichuan. A series of Qin campaigns, beginning in the mid-fifth century BCE, encroached on the northern edges of Shu territory; the process of conquest culminated in 316 BCE when the entire Sichuan Basin, including some territory identified as belonging to Ba, was taken over by Qin. This long and successful campaign added enormous agricultural resources to Qin's treasury and helped to fuel Qin's relentless campaign to bring all of the Heartland Region under its control. Qin invested in considerable infrastructure projects in the former Shu territory, such as water-management projects to enhance its productivity and new roads to create easier routes of travel between Sichuan and the Wei River Valley. The most famous of these projects, the Dujiangyan, a water-management project that diverts part of the flow of the Min River for irrigation purposes, remains in use today.

Qin

The state of Qin, in its northwestern stronghold, continued to be regarded by the Central States as a semi-barbarian polity, perhaps because of its large population of non-Sinicized Rong people, but it played an increasingly important role in the Warring States Period and ultimately emerged successful as the conqueror and unifier of China. Qin's power temporarily declined at the end of the Spring and Autumn Period and, for the first century of the Warring States Period, its administration was chaotic, weakened by a succession of young rulers dominated by dueling factions of ministers. Qin's rise to power began in 385 BCE, when a pretender to the throne mobilized supporters among the Rong and returned from exile in Wei. He arranged for the murder of the current child-ruler and his mother, and mounted the Qin throne as Lord Xian (r. 384–362 BCE). Applying reforms that he perhaps had become familiar with during his exile in Wei, Lord Xian began the systematic registration of the population, amplified the law code, and established commandery and county (*jun* and *xian*) governments ruled by bureaucrats directly responsible to the state, a key bureaucratic reform that had begun in Chu and spread to other states during the fifth century BCE. (Commanderies were so called because they were originally frontier districts under military command.)

The reforms instituted by Lord Xian of Qin were greatly extended under his successor, Lord Xiao (r. 362–338 BCE), on the advice of his remarkable prime minister, Shang Yang (also known as Lord Shang, d. 338 BCE). Lord Shang's overall aim was to mobilize the state for warfare. He saw the great mass of commoners as a resource of the state to further its military objectives; common people were to devote themselves to agriculture to support the army and were also subject to military conscription and corvée labor. They were to be kept ignorant, docile, and obedient, and were kept in line by a code of laws that provided ferocious punishments for all infractions (such as mutilation or being torn apart limb by limb). Household registration was also a form of control. Households were registered in groups of five; each was responsible for the others. If a crime occurred and was not reported by the miscreant's neighbors in their household group, all five would be subject to punishment along with the actual criminal. Explicit regulations also governed the conduct of government officials, who could be punished both for failing to carry out their stated responsibilities and for encroaching on the duties of others. In general the civilian government was subordinated to the armed forces and the chief means of advancement in rank was prowess on the battlefield, measured by the number of enemy heads taken. In the end Shang Yang overreached himself and, by amassing too much power, incurred the jealousy of others. After the death of Lord Xiao, Shang Yang was accused of treason and executed by being tied to two chariots and torn apart. But his reforms endured, launching Qin on a century-long drive for power and continuing to form the basis of Chinese law during the imperial age.

Warfare

The trajectory of military affairs in the Warring States Period favored the mobilization and deployment of ever-larger forces, the substitution of infantry and cavalry for war chariots, the development of more efficient weapons, longer campaigns, and few or none of the old ritualistic restraints on military engagements.

Cavalry was introduced into the Sinitic Heartland by Jin around the beginning of the Warring States Period, initially as a way of equalizing battlefield forces in conflicts with mounted northern nomads. Mounted warfare soon spread to other states and gradually replaced chariots accompanied by foot soldiers as a way of projecting overwhelming strength in combat, cavalry being faster, more maneuverable, and less limited by terrain than chariots. (Chariots continued to be used as transport vehicles for senior staff and as battlefield command-and-control vehicles.) Mounted soldiers were equipped with lances, swords, and the same type of recurved compound bows as had been used in chariot warfare. These changes provoked an arms race, and a new weapon was soon developed to counter the use of cavalry. This was the crossbow, thought to have been adapted from a hunting weapon of non-Sinitic peoples in the far southwest and redesigned for military purposes. In its military form a crossbow could fire a short, heavy arrow with an armor-piercing point, capable of bringing down a horse. (The crossbow could not be used as a cavalry weapon because it was too difficult to reload on horseback.) It also required less strength and training than the compound bow, a useful feature with conscript armies; on the other hand, its rate of fire was slower than the compound bow. Crossbows were soon manufactured in large quantities to a standard design; the bronze crossbow trigger exemplified the use of standard, interchangeable parts (long before the nineteenth-century inventions attributed to the American Samuel Colt; Figure 8.1).

City walls had been a feature of polities in the Heartland Region since Neolithic times. In the Warring States Period they were enlarged and strengthened in response to the increased size of armies in that period and the willingness of commanders to lay siege to cities for years at a time. Massive city walls could seldom be breached, but a prolonged siege could starve defenders into submission. An innovation of the Warring States Period was the building of frontier walls, both in the north (by Qin, Zhao, and Yan) to guard against invasion by nomadic peoples and along interior boundaries (by Yan, Zhao, and Chu), often following the line of a major river. In an era of massed infantry, such walls offered some protection against, and at least some advance warning of, invasions by other states before they could get close to besieging the capital city.

References to armies numbering in the hundreds of thousands become commonplace in historical accounts of Warring States warfare, along with accounts of the slaughter of tens of

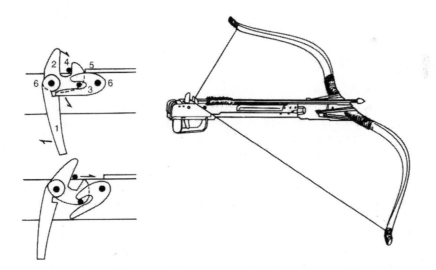

Figure 8.1 Schematic drawing of a crossbow trigger and a crossbow, one of the key weapons in Chinese warfare in the Warring States Period. Triggers were mass-produced with standardized, interchangeable parts. 1) trigger; 2) combined rear sight and bowstring holder; 3) lock; 4) bowstring; 5) arrow; 6) assembly pins.

thousands of soldiers of defeated armies. These numbers probably reflect some exaggeration, but it is clear that massive armies were typical of the period. The part-time efforts of generalist bureaucrats were no longer adequate to direct the movements, deployment, and battlefield tactics of such huge forces, and by the mid-fourth century BCE military specialists began to devote their careers to their management. Some of those specialists were not only battlefield commanders but also military theorists. The legendary sixth-century BCE general Sun Wu is a figure about whom little reliable information is known; his name was borrowed some two centuries later as the nominal author of the *Art of War* (*Sunzi bingfa*). But such fourth- and third-century military specialists as Sun Bin (who led a successful Qi battle against Wei), Wei Liao (an acolyte of Lord Shang in Qin), and Bo Qi (a Qin general) were genuine historical figures associated with the writing of military treatises. The late Warring States Period saw the development of a rich literature on the use of military power.

In the face of constant threats of invasion and annihilation states often sought to protect themselves by forming alliances. Prompted by the increasing power of Qin after the mid-fourth century BCE, rivalry among the leading states tended to be played out through so-called "horizontal and vertical alliances." The horizontal alliances were east–west groupings of states under the leadership of Qin, usually including Yan as well as some of the smaller states of the middle Yellow River Plain, aimed at checking the power of Wei, Zhao, Qi, and Chu. The vertical alliances, conversely, were anti-Qin coalitions bringing together northern and southern states, particularly Chu and Qi. These alliances were unstable, and sometimes the partners were coerced into participation. In the Battles of Guiling (353 BCE) and Maling (341 BCE) Qi troops led by Sun Bin decisively defeated the army of Wei, which thereafter became an unwilling and subordinate ally of Qi. This exposed Wei to the hostility of Qin, which inflicted several crushing defeats on Wei in the second half of the fourth century BCE. A vertical alliance between Qi and Chu did not prevent the catastrophic defeat of Chu by Qin in the Battle of Danyang in 310, as a result of which Qin wrested away control of the Han River Valley from Chu. This left Chu seriously weakened while allowing Qin to solidify its control over all of the Sichuan Plateau. A complicated series of shifting alliances and bitter military engagements left Qin and Qi as temporarily dominant powers at the beginning of the third century BCE.

Administrative reform

By the end of the fourth century BCE, amid incessant warfare and threats of war, almost all of the states of the Heartland Region had enacted reforms similar to those initiated in Qin by Shang Yang, though no other state became so single-mindedly oriented toward agriculture and war. The systematic registration of state inhabitants became commonplace, with officials registering individuals by name, birthplace, residence, occupation, and official status (if any). The practice of forming households into mutual responsibility groups became widespread. Land surveys noted the size and productivity of fields. All of these reforms facilitated the collection of taxes, payable in grain and in silk. Trade was also taxed and subjected to government control.

Trade prospered in the Warring States Period, buoyed by increasing wealth and facilitated by the development of new and better roads (primarily for military purposes). Merchants required appropriate documentation when crossing state boundaries, and were often assessed for customs duties at frontier posts. Large markets developed in cities, displaying goods from far and near; market officials recorded the names of merchants, assessed taxes, and sometimes imposed price controls. The methods employed to keep track of and control farmers, merchants, artisans, and other commoners were probably not uniform across the various states of the Warring States Period, but most if not all of the states enacted rules of that general kind. Such administrative procedures also facilitated the application of legal codes and the prevention, detection, and punishment of crimes.

Law

The promulgation of codes of law supposedly began with Guan Zhong of Qi in the Spring and Autumn Period, but by the Warring States legal codes proliferated—despite the vigorous opposition by Confucian scholars, who felt that rulers instead should embody moral models that people would naturally emulate. In the absence of transmitted legal codes or archaeologically recovered legal documents for most states it is not possible to say with certainty that every state in the Warring States Period promulgated a legal code, but historical anecdotes preserved in transmitted texts of the period give the impression that most did so. Laws typically divided crimes into the categories of "malicious harm," encompassing crimes of violence including assault, homicide, rape, brawling, rebellion, and treason; and "misappropriation," covering robbery, bribery, fraud, embezzlement, and other property crimes as well as social crimes such as adultery. Malicious harm was typically punished severely, including by branding, amputation of limbs, and execution with various degrees of severity. The most drastic punishment involved the extermination of the criminal's entire family, sometimes including even first and second cousins.

Misappropriation was more often punished with fines, shaving the beard (a form of public humiliation), floggings, and hard labor during a term of government slavery. Failure to report a crime was itself a criminal offence, as were various kinds of official misconduct. Making false accusations was severely punished, as was giving false testimony. The laws were formulated in such a way as to reinforce the social hierarchies implied by a cultural commitment to filial piety. Thus a child who murdered, or even accidentally caused the death of, a parent was executed with maximum severity, whereas a father who beat his son or his servant to death was subject only to light punishment, or sometimes not punished at all. Rebellion was considered not just a crime of violence but a crime against the social order, and was punished accordingly. Regardless of other evidence, conviction required that the accused culprit confess to the crime; in extreme cases a confession could be extracted through torture, within the boundaries of administrative regulations.

As the Warring States Period drew to a close, and into the Qin and Han periods, the administration of the law gave rise to a large legal-affairs bureaucracy. County magistrates were assisted by judicial secretaries, who knew the details of the laws and the regulations governing trials, and who knew how to carry out criminal investigations. The judicial secretaries were also in charge of hiring and supervising assistants who functioned as a kind of police force. An appeals procedure was developed whereby doubtful or difficult cases could be referred from the county magistrates' courts to prefectural and higher courts. The ruler was the ultimate judge, and might agree to hear appeals; no further appeal was possible. The general principles of these early legal codes and procedures continued to inform the administration of justice throughout the imperial period.

The expansion of literacy

The great expansion of government functions entailed by these administrative reforms and innovations created a huge demand for literate bureaucrats. These were often drawn from the old *shi* class of minor aristocracy, whose original military functions had become obsolete.

One striking feature of this new class of literate bureaucrats was professional mobility. It became commonplace for trained individuals, known as "traveling persuaders," to seek employment anywhere within the Heartland Region and to serve any ruler that would support them. This was quite contrary to the norms of the old aristocratic society, where the nobles of any one state were expected to serve the ruler of that state. It was also a reflection of the general breakdown of aristocratic lineages and power networks.

The careers of Confucius's own disciples strikingly illustrate this phenomenon. To take just a few examples: Ran Qiu, known as Ziyou, stayed within the state of Lu, the home of Confucius; he served as an administrator and advisor to the upstart Jisun clan. Zhong You, known as Zilu, first served the Jisun clan in Lu, then the Kong clan (not related to Confucius's Kong family) in Wey. Zilu's fate shows the dangers of this kind of bureaucratic employment: he found himself on the losing side of a succession dispute in Wey and was executed; his body was minced and pickled, and supposedly served at a banquet. Zai Yu, known as Ziwo, allied himself with the Tian clan of Qi and served as magistrate of the Qi capital city, Linzi. And Duanmu Ci, known as Zigong, held high office in several states, including Lu and Wey.

Although the Warring States was an era of political disunity and chaos it was a rich period for philosophical, religious, and political speculation, with many extremely diverse views competing for local court sponsorships. Traditionalists favoring a "Confucian" practice of archaic "Zhou" ritual (as they understood it) competed with pragmatic economic and warfare specialists. Some persuaders advocated the worship of ancient kings, others offered ways to placate fearsome local spirits, while still others advocated a life of nihilistic selfishness in a cosmos in which individual human lives were meaningless. Humorists, too, wandered around, cracking jokes and satirical puns. The roads from state capital to state capital were full—not only of would-be political advisors but also of military theorists, alchemists, soothsayers, astrologers, swords-for-hire, craftsmen, and other migrants.

In an era of danger, treachery, and uncertainty, but also of boldness and opportunity, such traveling persuaders often found a warm welcome at the courts of rulers of the territorial states. Rulers provided housing, stipends, and other guest privileges to freelance advisors, who might stay in one state for a brief visit or a long tenure before leaving to seek audiences at other courts. The state of Qi appears to have been unusual in its welcome to roving intellectuals, housing—the historical sources allege—hundreds or even thousands of thinkers and theorists near the Jixia Gate of the capital city, Linzi. These included revolutionary naturalist thinkers who rejected the traditional focus of a cosmos run by high gods and ancestral spirits. Most rulers, however, were willing to give a hearing to wandering advisors who might provide a political or military edge in the struggle for state survival. As King Hui of Liang famously said to the prominent Confucian Mencius (Mengzi), "Sir, you have not minded traveling a thousand *li* to visit me; I assume you have something that will profit my kingdom." (Mencius stiffly replied that he dealt in humaneness and righteousness, not "profit.") Some persuaders were more akin to skilled debaters than political theorists; for example, the semi-legendary Su Qin was said to be able to argue with equal conviction in favor of both vertical and horizontal alliances. Many traveling persuaders offered well-thought-out and consistent teachings during the Warring States Period, and so a tradition of Chinese philosophical discourse began.

Intellectual life

The demand for literate bureaucrats had the effect of widening the market for lower-level literate elites. The upsurge in literacy, in turn, was reflected in new forms of intellectual life and a blossoming of written texts of all kinds during the Warring States Period. The spread of literacy is largely connected to the Confucian tradition, which emphasized education, and to Confucius, who in the closing decades of the Spring and Autumn Period was portrayed as devoting himself to the collection of texts associated with Western Zhou history and the idealization of that era as a golden age. These texts included songs and documents linked to historical events and prescriptions for conducting rituals. Confucius' own legacy was preserved by successive generations of disciples in a text called the *Analects* (*Lunyu*). The creation, duplication, and transmission of texts advocating a plethora of different political and religious views became one of the most distinctive features of the Warring States Period.

Until fairly recently, historians studying the Warring States Period grouped the various ideas and theories of these ancient advocates into distinct "schools," such as Confucianism, Legalism, and Daoism. But this has changed with the discovery of many new texts from the Warring States era that had been preserved underground in tombs until modern times. Essentially, now scholars understand that there was a tremendous overlap and sharing of ancient ideas and beliefs. We can distinguish trends, but not distinct schools, a concept which would imply a purposeful education in and transmission of a select body of knowledge. So, for example, in the collection of texts once supposed to belong to a "Legalist School," including the *Book of Lord Shang* (*Shang jun shu*), *Shen Buhai*, *Hanfeizi*, and *Shen Dao*, among others, we find many ideas linked to Daoism and Confucianism regarding, on the one hand, the passivity, and, on the other hand, the exemplary moral behavior of the ruler. Although these texts emphasize laws regarding agriculture, taxation, and the recruitment and deployment of bureaucrats, many of their ideas regarding human nature are shared with other thinkers.

There is some evidence that successive generations of descendants of Confucius maintained the Kong family mansion as a center of Confucian education (students and disciples of which were self-styled as *Ru*; see Focus: Who is a *Ru*?). The perpetuation of a Confucian academy at Qufu seems to have been at least in part due to the efforts of Kong Ji (known as Zisi), the grandson of Confucius and a significant thinker in his own right. Manuscripts linked to his teachings, as quoted in other works, have been found in tombs in the southern Heartland Region. This suggests that there was a frequent and large-scale circulation of ancient texts and ideas originating from different regions and groups of thinkers and their disciples.

The followers of Confucius' great rival, Mozi, seem to have been organized in quasi-military fashion, with formal membership requirements, initiation rituals, and obligatory obedience to superiors. Their focus was on the peasant rather than the elite. But the Mohist model was very much the exception, not the rule. In addition, the evidence for the Mozi organization was not well preserved, mostly consisting of negative comments in transmitted texts. The text of Mozi itself had to be reconstructed from fragments preserved in the Daoist Canon (the *Daozang*). (The Daoist Canon itself was the result of four separate attempts, over a period of centuries, to collect all extant texts in the "Daoist" tradition; the final version dates to the Ming Dynasty, around 1444 CE.)

Most intellectual life in the Warring States Period seems to have been organized around individual masters and their disciples. In some cases, the transmission of ideology or knowledge was centered on the creation or transmission of written texts. In other cases, this is unclear. The leader of a sect, the "master," instructed and trained disciples (who might be drawn from a variety of backgrounds) in the ideas and rituals that he felt would help solve the political chaos of the time. Many texts from the Warring States Period are linked to one particular "master" or another and were probably collected (or created) by his disciples, even many generations after the death of the original master. Often texts were ascribed to some semi-legendary figure from the remote past, who was held up as the model of behavior and the basis for instruction. Some masters stayed at home, acting primarily as teachers; others were in the ranks of traveling persuaders, taking to the road accompanied by an entourage of disciples. Disciples, like the political leaders that the masters occasionally served, often shifted their allegiance from one master to another, and had many diverse fates. Some became masters themselves either of the original ideology or of a splinter group. Many took positions as officials in one territorial state or another, finding practical situations in which to employ their lessons.

Little is known about the processes whereby texts were copied and circulated, but it seems clear that there were various ways in which this was done. Some texts were handed down from master to disciple, either orally or in writing. Copies of various qualities would proliferate over the course of generations, being carried by the literate and semi-literate all over the ancient lands. The artisanal trade of a scribe no doubt evolved from workers employed in the ancient states to inscribe ritual texts on bone and bronze. Scribes wrote out texts with brushes and ink onto slips of wood or bamboo cut into strips of uniform size and with a smoothed writing surface. Small bronze knives were used for correcting mistakes (by shaving off "typos" from the surface of the strip). Whether these scribes were limited to working for courts, as in the Shang and early Zhou, or could privately freelance in copying texts is not clear. Obviously the ability to write was involved in the creation and transmission of a master's text. The precise mechanism for "publishing" the text, and whether a professional scribe played a role in this, is unknown, but, whatever the exact process, it clearly resulted in many more texts in circulation, and in private hands, than ever before.

Texts and trends

The Warring States Period produced many different types of texts covering topics from tomb inventories and divination to historical tales and philosophy. Some continued to influence Chinese intellectual history, while others disappeared completely. In this section we will briefly introduce some of the most significant thinkers of the Warring States Period.

Intellectuals of the Warring States Period of all philosophical persuasions were faced with the problem of finding language that conveyed their ideas clearly and accurately. Words used by one thinker were often used in a different sense by another. Philosophers of the Warring States Period struggled to define the relationship between words and things or actions. Word play was a way of investigating the problem of truth (considered to be immutable) and the language used to convey the truth (words being arbitrary and contingent). The principle of "the rectification of names" attempted to ensure that the meaning of a word as it was generally understood actually matched the phenomenon to which it referred. Thus when Confucius says in the *Analects* "let the 'father' act like a father, and the 'son' a son" he is affirming the key Confucian value of proper behavior within a traditional hierarchy. When "father" and "son" truly live up to the words that name them, their loyalty to each other will trump any externally imposed legal framework. The *Analects* and the *Mencius* use the word *Dao*, "Way,"—originally used by the naturalists to describe a non-anthropomorphic or non-human-centered cosmos—to describe an orderly, harmonious, hierarchical vision of society, which Confucius and his followers associated with ancient sages. *Dao* is a particularly vivid example of a word that was adopted by every group of thinkers and understood with a wide range of different meanings. That term and several others will come up repeatedly in this survey of Warring States thought.

The Confucian lineage of thinkers includes Mencius and Xunzi. Mencius is the most famous of Warring States Period followers of Confucius, although their lifetimes did not overlap. ("Mencius" is a latinized form of Mengzi, "Master Meng"; his personal name was Meng Ke. His dates are approximately 391–303 BCE.) He was said to have studied with Confucius' grandson, Zisi, and to have been a member of the intellectual community of Jixia for several years. The book that bears his name records his conversations with rulers that he met in the course of his travels throughout the Heartland Region. The graceful prose style and extended arguments of these presumably "recorded" conversations contrast sharply with the fragmentary snippets of teaching and dialogue found in the *Analects*. Mencius based his teaching on humaneness and righteousness (*ren* and *yi*), qualities that could be brought to sage-like perfection through self-cultivation. This involved "nourishing one's *qi*"—that is, the breath or vital essence that animates living things.

The concept of *qi* came into use in philosophical discourse in the fourth century BCE and was a key concept in the naturalist vision of the cosmos, in which *qi* was understood as a primordial undifferentiated substance that divides spontaneously, in accordance with the intrinsic principles of the *Dao*, to become everything in the world (known as "the myriad things" (*wanwu*). Like *Dao*, *qi* acquired a broad range of meanings as it was adopted by disparate thinkers. For philosophers such as Mencius, one's inner nature (*xing*) was composed of *qi*, and proper cultivation of it led to specific desired social behaviors.

Mencius believed that human nature is inherently good, using the example of a child who falls down a well—any bystander would immediately attempt to rescue the child, without stopping to make calculations about kinship or material rewards. Because of this fundamental goodness, everyone has the potential to cultivate the "sprouts of virtue" in their own natures. He also formulated a version of the concept of government by consent of the governed, arguing that people would flee a badly governed state but would flock to live under the rule of a humane and righteous ruler. Mencius' rather idealistic views were not adopted by rulers in his own time as the basis of political policy, but they were very influential in the later development of Confucian philosophy.

Xunzi (c. 310–215 BCE), the third great thinker in the early Confucian tradition, directly contradicted Mencius' belief in the goodness of human nature. He believed that people are inherently bad, but that they can be transformed by education and the good example of a righteous ruler (backed by the threat of punishment to deal with the recalcitrant). He taught that social order is a reflection of cosmic order, urged rulers to cultivate ritual and righteousness as keys of a proper (hierarchical) social order, and reaffirmed Confucius' doctrine of the rectification of names. Scholars believe that much of his beautifully written text actually came from his own brush. His thought is among the most sophisticated of the late Warring States Period, distinguishing and engaging the multiple strands of competing ideologies. Although he was not politically successful during his lifetime, his writings were clearly influential in the application of ritual to government bureaucracy and to the canonization of certain key texts of divination, poetry, historical narratives, music, and ritual into "classics" of Confucian learning. Xunzi's historical reputation has always been slightly tarnished because he doubted that human nature could be good without strict educational discipline and because his two most famous pupils, Han Fei and Li Si, are strongly linked to the policy of controlling society through severely punitive codes of law rather than trusting model kings to exhibit ideal "humane" behavior.

The most influential of anti-Confucian thinkers was Mo Di (c. 480–390 BCE; see Focus: Mozi and Mohism). The book of *Mozi* is a highly disparate and unevenly preserved text, but it is clear from the vituperative criticism by Confucians of Mozi's thought and the actions of his generations of disciples that Mohism once was widely popular and influential. Unlike the Confucians, who equated filial loyalty with the performance of expensive mortuary rituals, the Mohists emphasized frugality. While the Confucians preferred to focus on the social role of ritual, the Mohists warned against ignoring the supernatural world of ghosts and spirits. Finally, most repulsive to the Confucians, the Mohists did not respect the traditional social hierarchy of rulers and servants, fathers and sons, superiors and inferiors. Instead, they advocated "impartial caring." Status, kinship, and social relations, in Mozi's view, should not affect how one cares for other people. Also associated with the Mohist text are chapters dealing with logic, defensive warfare, and other technical subjects.

The canon of texts linked to an emphasis on law as the basis of social control included the *Book of Lord Shang* (*Shang jun shu*, ascribed to Shang Yang, ?–338 BCE). This book describes the reforms instituted in Qin by its supposed author; most of its content is now regarded as the work of later followers. The mid-fourth-century BCE reforms, including registration of the population, the formation of five-household mutual responsibility units, the mobilization of the state for agriculture and warfare, and the use of rewards (especially for battlefield achievements) and punishments (for any infraction of the laws), played a crucial role in the rise of Qin to a position of overwhelming political and military power. Lord Shang's chilly totalitarian vision marks him as one of the most original thinkers of the Warring States Period.

Shen Buhai (c. 400–c. 337 BCE) is often described, along with Shang Yang, Han Feizi, and some others, as belonging to a "Legalist School," but that label obscures important differences among these political theorists that vitiate the concept of "Legalism" altogether. The book ascribed to Shen Buhai has not survived in its entirety, but is known from quotations in other works that have been collected by Qing dynasty scholars. The surviving fragments show Shen Buhai, who supposedly held high office in Hann, to have been primarily concerned with administrative matters, such as the appointment, evaluation, and promotion of officials.

Shenzi (attributed to Shen Dao, c. 350–c. 275 BCE) is another of the many Warring States texts that survives only in quoted fragments. Shen Dao, like Shen Buhai, is often, but unconvincingly, described as a Legalist. Rather than emphasizing punitive law, he begins with the premise that people have different talents and capacities but all act to benefit their private interests. Social order, therefore, requires a clear and consistent set of rules that everyone can understand and that can be followed without hardship or resentment.

The author of *Han Feizi* (Han Fei, c. 280–233 BCE) was related to the ruling family of Hann. He studied with Xunzi, along with his fellow-student Li Si, who became prime minister of Qin during that state's great campaign of conquest and unification. Invited to Qin, Han Fei was soon accused of being a Hann agent and was coerced into committing suicide. The book that bears his name, written in clear, polished prose, is highly diverse in subject matter, including political essays, historical anecdotes, and even a commentary on the *Laozi*. Han Fei advised the ruler to be remote and aloof, trusting no one, using expediency and strategic advantage as necessary, and taking rewards and punishments to be the "two handles of government." His work is characteristic of late Warring States political thought in that it draws heavily and eclectically from a wide range of thinkers and texts.

The *Laozi* or *Daodejing* was traditionally attributed to Lao Dan, a possibly imaginary figure contemporary with Confucius, about whom—if he existed—nothing is known. Its mix of political strategy and naturalist thought is now regarded as a work of the fourth century BCE; it is known to have circulated widely, in a number of variant or incomplete versions, at that time. The received text is probably the work of a Han dynasty editor. (In the Warring

States versions of this text, the *De* section precedes that on *Dao*. This order of the text was reversed during the Han, possibly as a response to the primacy placed on *de* by Confucian scholars.) The *Daodejing* introduced the concepts of *Dao* as the unitary force pervading the universe, and of yin and yang—female/male, dark/bright, moist/dry, cool/warm, and so on—as complementary opposites through which change occurs. The text shows a strong preference for yin, using the analogy of water that over time wears down the hardest stones. In a curious echo of the vision of Lord Shang, the ruler in the *Daodejing* is a remote and awesome figure ruling a population of ignorant peasants; but here he rules not with law and administration but through a benevolent and mysterious "power" or "virtue" (*de*). This suggests another term that came to be widely used in Chinese philosophy, "non-action" (*wuwei*). Because the sage-ruler is perfectly attuned to the cosmic *Dao*, he need not take any purposeful actions; "he does nothing and yet nothing is left undone."

The *Zhuangzi* is often grouped with the *Laozi* as a "Daoist" work, though it is not clear what exactly that term means in the Warring States context as every thinker subscribed to one definition or another of the *Dao* (often polarized into two competing conceptions of *Dao*: "the Human Way," *Ren Dao*, and the "Cosmic Way" or "Way of Heaven," *Tian Dao*). As reflected in the *Daodejing* and the *Zhuangzi*, the "Daoists" believed that the world is a manifestation of the all-encompassing cosmic *Dao*; what we understand as reality is the effect of a constant process of transformation of *qi* (see Focus: Zhuangzi on death and transformation). Traditionally attributed to Zhuang Zhou (c. 370–300 BCE), the text is divided into seven "inner" chapters, fifteen "outer" chapters, and eleven "miscellaneous" chapters, each possibly reflecting different temporal layers of composition. The inner chapters are possibly by Zhuang Zhou, perhaps recorded by his followers; the outer and miscellaneous chapters are often ascribed to a "primitivist" (or naturalist) author (chapters 8–11), a "syncretist" author (chapters 12–16 and 33), and "later followers." The *Zhuangzi* shares the *Laozi*'s concept of the Way and the necessity for a self-cultivated sage ruler, but it also emphasizes the importance of remaining free of worldly entanglements; its vision of an ideal society is a cheerful but unrealistic anarchism. The text is marked by a strong commitment to relativism; binding judgments are impossible. The work's most famous passage depicts Zhuang Zhou taking a nap beneath a tree and dreaming of a butterfly; when he awoke, he could not tell if he was Zhuang Zhou dreaming he was a butterfly, or a butterfly dreaming he was Zhuang Zhou. The *Zhuangzi*'s lively and idiosyncratic prose style has made it a favorite of later poets and painters, who embraced the idea of freedom from social obligations and wandering in nature as a path to transcendence (see Focus: Zhuangzi on death and transformation).

The *Yangzi*, which exists only in fragmentary quotations (including some in the *Zhuangzi*), is attributed to a shadowy figure named Yang Zhu (fourth century BCE). Sometimes termed a "hedonist," he took an extreme view of the necessity of preserving and extending one's own life and of avoiding worldly entanglements. He is famously reported to have said he would not give a single hair from his head to save the world. Ignoring the mortal world and its problems as illusory, and striving for personal immortality (with an implied belief in a more real supernatural sphere) would continue to be a popular path chosen by Daoists, Buddhists, and others throughout Chinese history as an alternate life path to the more engaged Confucian social ideal.

The books of Hui Shi (late fourth century BCE) and Gongsun Long (c. 320–250 BCE) are sometimes grouped together as "Logicians" or "Dialecticians." Their works are known only from quoted fragments. Hui Shi is known for a set of paradoxes, such as "the sun at noon is already descending, a living person is already dying." (This invokes the Daoist idea that any aspect of a concept naturally embodies its opposite: maximum ascent implies descent; life implies death. As the *Daodejing* puts it, "Reversal is the movement of the *Dao*.") Gongsun Long explored verbal puzzles, most famously "a white horse is not a horse." (The concept "horse" does not specify color, so "a white horse" does not coincide perfectly with "a horse.") Through such seemingly trivial utterances, they were exploring the possibilities and limitations of language. They may have been responding to the confusion resulting from intellectuals using the same words to convey different meanings. Another factor may have been increased exposure to regional dialects of Chinese as long-distance travel in the Heartland became more common.

The work of naturalist master Zou Yan (c. 305–240 BCE) is also known only by quoted fragments. A guest at the Jixia Gate in Qi, he was an early theorist of the correlative cosmology that would be brought to a high state of sophistication in the Western Han dynasty. He is said to have introduced the concept that dynasties ruled by virtue of one or another of the Five Phases (*wuxing*, i.e. five paradigmatic forces of nature: wood, fire, earth, metal, and water), and that dynasties succeed one another in the conquest cycle of the Five Phases: metal conquers wood (cutting), wood conquers earth (growth), earth conquers water (damming), water conquers fire (extinguishing), and fire conquers metal (melting). He also visualized the earth as being formed of nine great continents, with China occupying the southeastern one. This was a schematization of the nine provinces supposedly laid out by Yu the Great after he conquered the great flood, as described in the "Tribute of Yu" ("Yu gong") chapter of the *Book of Documents*.

The *Shizi* is purportedly the work of Shi Jiao (c. 390–330 BCE), a traveling persuader about whom little is known. The text of the *Shizi* is damaged, with many missing pieces and brief fragments, but it is of great interest as the earliest self-consciously syncretic work in the Warring States Period; it deliberately picks and chooses elements from a wide range of other texts and traditions to formulate a hybrid doctrine intended to be superior to its sources. It deals, among other things, with administration, self-cultivation, yin and yang, and cosmology.

The *Lüshi chunqiu* is attributed to Lü Buwei (?–235 BCE), prime minister of Qin in the mid-third century BCE. Probably he was the sponsor and editor of this almanac-like book, which was written to his specifications by a team of anonymous scholars and completed in 239 BCE. Despite its title (*Mr. Lü's Springs and Autumns*), it is not a chronicle, but a syncretic work dealing with cosmology, administration, agriculture, and other subjects drawn from a variety of Warring States sources. It is notable for including a version of the "Yue ling" ("Monthly Ordinances") calendar, which specifies different activities and policies for each month and season using Five Phases criteria, and for following Zou Yan's theory of the conquest sequence of dynasties. It also provides the earliest source of correlative cosmology that matches some of the material in the almanacs or "day books" (*rishu*) that have been discovered in excavations of several tombs. The *Lüshi chunqiu* was a model for, and influence on, Former Han dynasty syncretic works such as the *Guanzi* and the *Huainanzi*.

There are many thinkers whose names have come down to us but whose works are lost, known only from brief fragments. The texts that do remain exemplify the diversity, argumentativeness, and sheer energy of Warring States intellectual life, in spite of (or perhaps in part because of) the political turmoil and military danger of that era.

Literature

Most of the texts that have come down to us as part of the received tradition were apparently written as teaching tools, intended to be expounded upon by a master of that text. They are therefore generally regarded as essays in social or political philosophy, and for the most part have been studied for their content rather than for their literary form. The exceptions would be divination and song texts, which inspired many later imitations.

Two important literary genres are found in texts of the Warring States Period: historical anecdotes and poetry. Historical anecdotes, found in such works as *Mr. Zuo's Commentary* to the *Springs and Autumns*, *Discourses of the States* (*Guo yu*) and the *Intrigues of the Warring States* (*Zhanguo ce*), have traditionally been studied as sources of historical information, and have only recently attracted the attention of scholars for their literary value. Short narratives amounting to a few tens or a few hundreds of words, they draw on commonly known historical events to present lively, well-crafted stories that engage the attention of the reader or listener and often feature a noble minister or political strategist. Masters probably used these tales to teach lessons about values and conduct. They could also be used to teach students models for future use while in official positions. Literati working the regional courts had to show off their knowledge of songs, ritual, historical precedent, and divination. Sprinkled throughout the historical narratives are quotations from the *Book of Odes* (*Shijing*) and the *Book of Changes* (*Yijing* or *Zhouyi*), both already "classics" in the Warring States Period.

The texts respected as sources of knowledge valuable for government service were those associated with the Zhou and the "Northern" or Yellow River culture, such as the *Book of Documents* and the *Book of Odes*. Yet "Southern" culture, focused around the Yangzi River, was thriving and lively. It would eventually eclipse the stale worship practices of antiquity and initiate, among other things, a birth of poetry (beyond song). The haunting poetry preserved in the *Elegies of Chu* (*Chu ci*) tapped into ancient practices ignored or disparaged by conservative northern philosophers. The romance of invoking spirits by shaman-like flower-garbed singers at natural sites such as swamps, lakes, and mountains vividly portrayed a relationship between the poet-minister and the supernatural. The most famous of these Chu poems is "Encountering Sorrow" ("Li sao"), said to have been written by a semi-legendary Chu official, Qu Yuan, who, in a state of despair at being slandered by corrupt officials, wrote this poem and then drowned himself in the Miluo River. Written in a difficult but beautiful literary style, it is an elaborate allegory describing the out-of-body experience of a shaman who takes flight across the heavens. Another early poem in the *Elegies of Chu* is "The Summons of the Soul" ("Zhao hun"), a literary treatment of a common ritual designed to tempt the soul of a recently deceased person to return to his or her body and live again. The lush, elaborate language of the *Chu ci* poems, and their air of exoticism, proved very attractive to a northern audience and influenced the development of new poetic genres in the Han dynasty.

Besides texts of songs and poetry, divination manuals for interpreting stalk divination may also reveal cultural differences between the south and north. The oldest manual known is the *Book of Changes*; versions of it have been found in southern tombs. By the end of the Warring States Period this book evolved from a manual instructing the average elite male in how to deal with day-to-day issues to a philosophical tract for understanding the Way of Heaven. Each hexagram integrated mythical and religious lore into their reading of the six yin and yang lines. Other hexagram texts found in southern tombs, however, use an entirely different style of lore, such as ancient figures and images of shamanistic flight, both unknown in the *Book of Changes*. Other stalk divination manuals have also come to light that contain no lore at all. They combine eight yin and yang trigrams and other symbols of correlative cosmology, such as the season, numerology, directions, etc. to provide practical answers to the elite householder on whether certain actions would be auspicious or not. In this sense, they function similarly to the archaeologically recovered "day books" (*rishu*) which use astrological day signs, rather than trigrams and stalk divination, to determine auspicious or inauspicious implications of actions taken on any particular day.

The fact that day books have been found in the Chu area as well as in the territory of Qin serves as a useful reminder that some apparent regional cultural differences may simply be artifacts of textual preservation rather than actual differences in regional cultural heritage. Tombs containing texts have been disproportionately found in Chu (where the anaerobic waterlogged soil acts as a preservative of organic matter) and Qin (located in the dry northwest, where organic materials also tend to survive in good condition). Tombs in the Yellow River Valley did not preserve their contents as well. Whether they reflect widespread cultural similarities or regionally specific traits, the contents of these tombs have opened our eyes to layers of ancient Chinese culture previously invisible.

Texts from tombs

Many previously unknown texts, as well as the earliest known versions of some transmitted texts, have been archaeologically recovered from tombs of the Warring States, Qin, and Han Periods, dramatically improving our understanding of intellectual life in early China. The texts include everything from technical books covering subjects such as medicine, divination, mathematics, agriculture, and law, to philosophical texts and historical narratives. Many newly discovered texts dating to the Qin and Han Periods may have had roots deep in writings of the Warring States era. Texts dating to the end of the Han and later tend to be recognizable fragments of transmitted texts associated with legendary masters, but earlier tombs reveal many new discoveries with no clear attribution of authorship.

Although few scholars question the early existence of texts written on bamboo strips, silk, or wooden planks, the earliest example that survives today was found in the 433 BCE tomb of Lord Yi of Zeng. This text, archaeologists would learn, represented an example of the most common type of text to be found in Chu regional tombs, an inventory. These "tomb inventories" listed the objects collected for the funeral and presumably buried in the tomb with the deceased (the lists sometimes do not perfectly match the actual tomb contents). These objects included everything from ritual vessel sets to boxes and jars packed with food, clothing, cosmetics, and articles of jade. The Zeng records noted which items were donated to the recently deceased by those of his family, friends, or political connections (see Focus: Lord Yi of Zeng's tomb).

Another extremely common type of text found in Chu tombs comprised records of divination and sacrifices performed during the last few years of the deceased's lifetime (see Focus: The death of Shao Tuo). Teams of diviners kept these records of their efforts to cure patients of illness. They reveal the various methods of stalk and shell divination, as well as different types of exorcistic ritual, employed, as well as the panoply of different spirits—both natural and human—appealed to for a cure. It was believed that unhappy spirits could cause illness and death. Placing the record in the tomb (for they obviously failed in their efforts to save the deceased) may have been because it was considered contaminated with the names of ghosts and spirits, or because it would show the spirits in the otherworld that, even though they failed, they had sincerely tried. Thus reassured, unhappy ghosts should have no excuse to afflict them. These texts augment our understanding of ancient notions about health, the body, and the afterlife. The proliferation of texts in tombs reinforces the impression that there was an upsurge of literacy at all levels in the Warring States Period, and—to the extent that grave goods were intended for the enjoyment of the deceased—the texts give evidence of the importance of possessing and reading written materials of various sorts.

The beginning of a trend to bury administrative records and law texts is also first evident in Chu tombs. Later, this became common in Qin and Han elite tombs, many found in the old Chu region. Other manuals and texts on technical subjects, such as divination manuals, religious treatises, almanacs, and mathematical calculators—possibly those used by the deceased—were also buried in tombs. By Qin and Han times certain elite tombs contained books on medicine, agriculture, and legal statutes, accompanying texts on divination, ritual law, military strategy, historical records, and historical anecdotes. Many of these types of text have their roots in Warring States times. A trove of texts in the possession of Tsinghua University includes many such texts, including different versions of songs and tales that appear in later collections, such as the transmitted *Book of Odes*, *Book of Documents* and *Lost Zhou Fragments* (*Yi Zhou Shu*). Some of the texts in the Tsinghua collection are merely variants of transmitted versions, but most are new discoveries of texts that left only traces in previously known materials, or more likely none at all.

Among such texts found in Chu tombs are philosophical texts that were not preserved into the Qin and Han. Some of these explore concepts that were also debated by masters such as Laozi, Mencius, Xunzi, Han Feizi, Zhuangzi, and followers of Mozi. They were concerned with inner human nature (*xing*) and how the cultivation of one's "intention" (*zhi*) through the practice of music might affect one's allotted lifespan (*ming*). Others concerned the effects of ghosts and spirits, the nature of the cosmos and birth of the "ten thousand things," proper social relations, proper dress, debates on circumstances that would make it necessary for a ruler to abdicate, and many tales involving mythical sages, linked to mythologies about Xia, Shang, or Zhou, acting in exemplary ways.

The plethora of texts reveal a rich literary and diverse philosophical culture in which traveling persuaders competed for influence in Warring States Period courts. The texts found in tombs reinforce our mental image of political and philosophical thinkers roaming the ancient world with cartloads of texts and an entourage of disciples, stopping at courts willing to support them, where they acted as advisors, teachers, and perhaps sources of amusement.

The two transmitted works that existed during the Warring States Period in versions most completely resembling the known texts were the *Laozi* (traditionally known as the *Daodejing*) and the *Book of Changes* (*Yijing*). Sections of what would become known as the *Ritual Records* (*Liji*) were also found. Several copies of the *Liji* chapter "Black Robes" ("Ziyi") were found. It specifies rules dictated by a "master" (in this case, generally thought to be Confucius) on the proper behavior between a ruler, his ministers, and the people. During the Han Period the *Ritual Records* was one of three collections of ritual laws, records, and discussions, including the *Zhou Ritual* (*Zhouli*), an idealized description of a ritual bureaucracy (with sections similar to the *Xunzi*), and the *Etiquette Ritual* (*Yili*), the latest and most detailed compendium of sumptuary law. These three ritual texts, edited during the Han Period, preserved old fragments of earlier texts. Texts found in tombs help us identify and assess these older sections and the ideas found in them.

Some historical texts have increased our understanding of the chronological sequence of events in early China (although they give few or no dates, only the names of famous and infamous people). One, called *The Succession of Years* (*Xinian*), describes on 138 bamboo strips events from the time of the Zhou conquest up to about the middle of the fourth century BCE. It provides many new details not preserved in transmitted accounts, but also skips others. It summarizes the rise and fall of the Western Zhou and then moves on to how the states of Jin, Chu, Qin, Qi (and other less long-lived states, such as Zheng and Wey) replaced it. Then it moves through the Spring and Autumn and early Warring States Periods in a more detailed manner, sometimes comparing it to the "present" state of events, seemingly from a Chu perspective. Another clearly Chu text is the *Chu Residences* (*Chu ju*), which lists the capitals of all Chu rulers up to about the same time as when the *Xinian* ends. The text begins with an origin myth of the Chu people who, it says, descended from a god who married a Shang princess.

Texts in Warring States tombs that clearly exhibit a naturalist bent include early versions of the Daoist classic the *Daodejing*, as well as one previously unknown text called *Taiyi Gives Birth to Water* (*Taiyi sheng shui*). *Taiyi* was a late Warring States term, widely attested in texts from Chu, that seems to have replaced the term Shang Di for the High God. (*Taiyi* is surprisingly difficult to translate. *Tai* means "great" or "grand," and *yi* is the number "one," but "Great One" or "Grand One" have misleading connotations in English. A paraphrase, "The Great Undifferentiated One" perhaps comes closest to the real meaning of the term.) Uncoupled from theocratic links to ancestral lineages, *Taiyi* was a completely natural cosmic force, located perhaps up in Heaven (*tian*), that operated organically and not with the arbitrary whimsicality of an anthropomorphic deity. Another Warring States text, *Ur-Eternity* (*Hengxian*), describes the birth of the world, but, unlike the older sections of the *Laozi* (as seen in the recently discovered reversed *Daodejing* versions), it removes any reference to human birth from a metaphorical "mother." In the highly abstract cosmology of *Ur-Eternity* the idea of becoming an "enlightened king" (*mingwang*) is mocked. Prior to the time of the Great Void (another term also found in the *Laozi*) was an even more profound nothingness. *Qi* had not yet begun to congeal and split into *yin* and *yang* and thereby produce "something." There is no mention of a cosmogonic force such as *Taiyi*. The philosophical impulse behind these texts was clearly part of a movement to transform the old Zhou deities into abstract forces, leading to the correlative and organic Han dynasty cosmology of yin–yang and the Five Phases (*wuxing*).

While the newly discovered texts are revolutionizing the scholarly view of ancient China and the nature of its classical texts, one aspect of these texts is disturbing. Many of them have come to light through illicit means. Grave robbing for precious materials is a serious problem in modern China, possibly involving high-level corruption. Chinese museums and universities have been forced to rely on private donors to purchase these materials from dealers, usually in Hong Kong, in order to preserve them and make them available to scholars. While scholars are amazed at the contents of these manuscripts, they mourn the fact that all the information available from the original excavation has been stripped away. This has also created the opportunity for forgers to enter the market. Nevertheless, a comparison of the content and writing style of legitimately excavated texts with those obtained from the antiquities trade shows that most of the latter are authentic. Forgeries tend to stick to imitating famous classics.

The arts

Because of the special geology of the Yangzi River Valley, tombs from the state of Chu have yielded more artifacts to modern archaeologists than those of any other early Chinese polity. Remains from tombs in the Yellow River Plain are relatively scarce. The lack of materials from the north to compare with the abundant remains from the south means that it is often difficult to know to what degree the Chu materials are examples of styles and techniques that were in use throughout the Heartland Region, and to what extent they represent a local or regional Chu culture. One thing that is clear, however, is that, contrary to the prejudicial northern view of the Chu people as crude, shiftless barbarians, Chu civilization was sophisticated, with a fine aesthetic sense.

A distinctive southern style of ritual bronze vessels, featuring natural or chimerical animal figures cast in relief or in the round, was evident as early as the Shang dynasty. Chu continued to produce innovative décor on bronzes throughout the Eastern Zhou Period. Some of the

Heartland Region's earliest examples of lost-wax casting are found on sixth-century BCE Chu bronzes, which depict kinetic surfaces of intertwined wriggling snake-dragons and other animals (Figure 8.2). These vibrant vessels built upon and extended the more traditional piece-mold casting techniques and clearly contrasted with bronzes produced in the northern style, which had become stodgy and technically inferior to the earlier Shang and Western Zhou ritual vessels. Another southern innovation, known as the Huai Style (from the Huai River Basin between the Yellow and Yangzi Rivers), emerged during the Spring and Autumn Period and continued into the Warring States Period (Figures 8.3a and 8.3b). It featured lidded vases, basins, bowls, and other bronze vessels decorated with narrative reliefs showing hunting, fighting, feasting, and other activities. Another innovation in bronze, not necessarily limited to the south, was the proliferation of a wide variety of bronze objects, including vessels, oil lamps, chariot fittings, and sash-hooks and other personal ornaments, decorated with inlay of gold, silver, or turquoise. "Money trees," apparently produced uniquely in the Upper Yangzi Valley in Sichuan, feature delicately cast bronze "branches" festooned with coins and images of gods and immortals. Yet another manifestation of bronze objects as decorative luxury products was the development of bronze mirrors, polished on one side to a high degree of reflectivity and decorated on the other side with elaborate patterns, such as stylized leaves or variations on the character for "mountain" (*shan* 山)—perhaps suggestive of the magic mountains represented in later incense burners (Figure 8.4). China's Late Bronze Age had moved very far from the Shang and Western Zhou model of using bronze primarily for ritual vessels and weapons, employing bronze instead as a symbol of wealth and luxurious good taste expressed in a very wide range of objects.

Another Chu specialty was finely painted lacquerware vessels. The soil, water, and climate of the Yangzi River Valley were conducive to the growing of lacquer trees (*Toxicodendron vernicifluum*). Chu artisans grew adept at working with the trees' toxic sap, which hardens into a plastic-like substance, adding pigments in colors such as red, black, and green and painting it, layer by layer, on wooden substrates. Although lacquerware had been used at least

Figure 8.2 A *Zun* (jar) and *pan* (basin) bronze drinking set from tomb of Lord Yi of Zeng, 433 BCE. The intricate surface decoration of these vessels testifies to the technical skill in bronze-casting in the Chu cultural region.

Figure 8.3a A Huai-style bronze *hu* covered vessel with narrative decoration, from the late Spring and Autumn Period.

Figure 8.3b Rubbing of décor from the vessel in Figure 8.3a. The activities portrayed include hunting, fighting, and feasting.

Figure 8.4 A bronze mirror with décor of four characters for "mountain" (*shan* 山) that delineate a "square earth" within the "round Heaven" of the mirror itself.

since the Shang Period and was in widespread use by the end of the Bronze Age, works by
Chu artisans were known to be especially beautiful and well made. Lacquerware recovered
from Chu tombs has included everything from massive coffins to large animal statues (used
to hold drums) to finely painted round and square boxes for holding personal items such as
food or cosmetics. The increasing lack of bronze vessels in tombs reflects not only the lack
of social and political organization required to control the access to metals and the artisans
required to cast it but also the priority given to the production of metal weapons. Finely
crafted lacquerware thus replaced bronze as a signifier of wealth and social esteem in burials.
While access by the rich to the best lacquer workshops required political connections, access
to lacquer manufacturing did not conflict with the need for weapons and did not require
long-distance supply chains. Lacquerware was also exported from Chu (perhaps sometimes
in the form of diplomatic gifts), and has been found as far afield as modern northern Korea.

Jade, the most distinctively characteristic luxury material of the Heartland Region since
late Neolithic times, continued to occupy an important place in the arts of the Warring States
Period. Elaborate jade ornaments such as necklaces of multiple jade elements held together
with silk cord or gold wire have been found in elite tombs of both men and women, along
with jade hairpins, earrings, and other personal items. Small jade objects, such as carvings of
dragons, tigers, and domestic animals of various kinds, were decorative and may also have
functioned as protective talismans.

Domesticated silkworms (*Bombyx mori*) were raised throughout the Heartland Region.
Judging from later records, we can understand that farms usually included a stand of mul-
berry trees (the leaves of which form the exclusive diet of silkworms), and farm buildings
typically included a shed in which silkworms were raised and silk processed. The techniques
of boiling the cocoons, unwinding the silk fibers, spinning them into thread, and weaving silk
cloth were required skills for women throughout the Sinitic culture area. Silk cloth was produced as early as the Neolithic Period in the Heartland Region, but the Warring States Period
saw the development of a wide range of weaving techniques used to produce luxury fabrics.
Warring States silks found in tombs include dyed plain weaves, brocades, figured gauze, and

various types of embroidery. Fashionably dressed members of the elite, wearing splendid robes of dyed and woven silk accessorized with inlaid bronze sash-hooks and ornaments of jade, must have made a magnificent spectacle.

Paintings are under-represented in the early Chinese archaeological record; most paintings were presumably done on perishable materials such as wood, plaster, and possibly silk, and have been lost in the course of time. No above-ground wooden buildings survive in China from the pre-Tang (seventh century CE) period, but fragmentary evidence indicates that, as early as the Shang and Western Zhou, buildings associated with the elite were brightly and elaborately painted, with pillars, walls, beams, and ceilings covered with colorful figurative and abstract designs. A few examples of murals from tombs of the Warring States, Qin, and Han periods, often deteriorated and sometimes fragmentary, give some idea of what palace walls of the time may have looked like. But the most abundant and best-preserved early paintings are on lacquer objects, such as coffins, baskets and boxes, vases, and small decorative pieces, which sometimes are decorated with scenes of daily life or what may be depictions of a celestial realm (Figure 8.5). The visual effect of elite buildings in early China was overwhelmingly one of color and pattern to an extent that is now hard to imagine.

Architecture of the Warring States Period continued long-standing Heartland Region traditions in the construction of palaces and other significant structures. Such buildings were

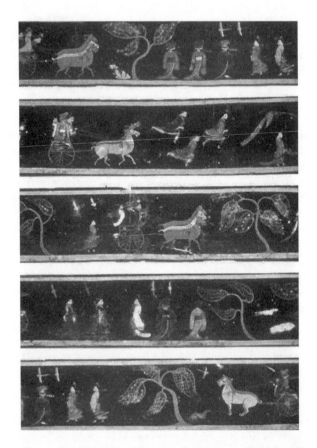

Figure 8.5 Panel from the side of a lacquer-painted box from a Chu tomb at Baoshan, Hubei
    Province, c. 300 BCE, depicting elite figures traveling in chariots.

built on platforms of pounded earth reached by staircases. The construction technique was post-and-beam, with massive columns made from the trunks of single trees holding up a heavy bracketed roof. Early Bronze Age roofs were thatched, but by the Warring States Period heavy tile roofs had become standard. The space between columns was filled by non-load-bearing walls. In the Warring States Period most state capital cities were double-walled, with an outer wall encircling the city itself and an inner wall demarcating and defending the palace compound. Two innovations became conspicuous at that time: the first was the "plat-form" or "terrace" (*tai*), a very tall pounded-earth platform surmounted by highly ornamental buildings, a kind of showpiece architecture; the second was the watchtower (*guan*), a tower of perhaps four or five stories, often built on or adjacent to the terrace. In general, palace buildings grew larger and more ostentatious during the period. One exception was the leg-endary "Hall of Light" (*mingtang*), a ceremonial building usually located outside the city wall. This was a very austere structure, made of unpainted wood and with a thatched roof. Various floor plans are suggested in early texts, usually with either nine or twelve rooms. The ruler was supposed to carry out monthly rituals in the Hall of Light to ensure that his policies and activities were in harmony with the months and seasons.

One aspect of early Chinese art is conspicuous by its absence: there are few depictions of gods or other supernatural beings, and nothing at all like the heroically large and idealized images of deities found in other early cultures: the winged bulls of Assyria, the larger-than-life pharaoh statues of Egypt, or the idealized marble sculptures of the Olympian gods of ancient Greece, for example. A few images of deified kings and astrological gods, such as *Taiyi*, appear in silk paintings and the carved stone panels of Han tombs. It is possible that we simply have not found or identified earlier imagery of high gods. So far as we know, there are no sculptures of the Shang celestial god Shang Di, nor of its Zhou equivalent, *Tian*, nor of any of the divinized supposed sage-kings of antiquity, such as the Yellow Emperor. This may reflect the fact that the early Chinese envisioned divinity as a complex network of integrated supernatural influences rather than power represented in the figure of a single anthropomor-phic deity.

Burials and funerary practices

Tomb architecture and associated funerary practices underwent significant change in the Warring States Period. From the Erlitou Period onwards, or perhaps even earlier, down through the Spring and Autumn Period, elite tombs in the Heartland Region were gathered in cemeteries. Tombs consisted of vertical pits, sometimes fifty feet (fifteen meters) or more in depth, with access ramps and sometimes terraced steps; a wooden structure at the base of the pit held the coffin of the deceased as well as grave goods of various kinds. When the pit was filled in with earth its surface was level with the surrounding land, and it was sometimes topped with a very modest structure that was presumably used to conduct rites for the dead. (Such surface structures tended to become larger and more elaborate over time.) The focus of ancestral rites during the Zhou Period was the ancestral temple, which was a separate build-ing or complex of buildings within the city wall and not connected to the cemetery.

In the Warring States Period elite tombs were sometimes still sited in cemeteries, but, especially late in the period, were often individually sited (perhaps indicating an increased influence of geomancy as a set of techniques for identifying auspicious locations). The tombs themselves continued to be of the vertical pit type, but now were typically crowned with a high mound rather than being filled to ground level. (Scholars debate the source of this new trend for tomb mounds; one likely hypothesis traces them to the *kurgan* mounds of elite burials in the steppelands beyond the Heartland Region.) The mound was often flanked with separate pits holding additional funerary offerings and fronted with a substantial temple in which ongoing ancestral rites would be performed (Figure 8.6).

The wooden burial chamber also changed. In earlier times the majority of the burial goods were placed on an earthen ledge or platform that surrounded the wooden chamber holding the coffin. During the Warring States Period the platform disappeared and the burial goods were placed in different wooden chambers inside the pit, one of which contained the coffin and others that contained goods associated with the various aspects of an elite person's life: war, government, travel, feasting, home life, and so forth (Figure 8.7).

The type and quantity of grave goods changed along with these changes in tomb architecture. A trend that grew in importance during the Warring States Period was the use of guardian figures (*zhenmushou*) in the eastern chamber of the tomb (Figure 8.8). These were especially prevalent in Chu tombs and may also have been associated with fecundity and renewed life. Often of lacquered wood, they typically featured bug eyes, a long, protruding tongue, and antlers—all features that suggest influence from the shamanistic heritage of Yangzi River Valley cultures. A belief, perhaps originally southern, took hold that the human body was animated by two souls: an ethereal soul (*hun*), and a material soul (*po*). The ethereal soul left the body at the moment of death, perhaps to fly up to the sky, but the material soul remained with the body and accompanied it in the tomb. Thus there was a continuing need to nurture and cherish the indwelling soul of the deceased. Offerings within the tombs tended to replicate, or improve upon, the kinds of things that the deceased would have enjoyed in his or her lifetime. These often included texts, as we have seen, but also bronze and jade luxury items, lacquer boxes holding food and cosmetics, clothing and textiles, musical instruments, domestic animals, and a large number of servants—increasingly, no longer actual animal and human sacrifices, but wooden or clay figures representing animals and people. This was part of a more general trend toward the use of "luminous objects"

Figure 8.6 Local residents looking at the excavation of a tomb at Baoshan, Hubei Province, c. 300 BCE. The figures standing around the edge of the excavation give an idea of its scale.

Figure 8.7 A side chamber of the underground wooden structure of a tomb at Baoshan, showing some of the offerings interred with the deceased.

Figure 8.8 A *zhenmushou* tomb guardian figure. Tombs in the Chu cultural area often include such figures, apparently intended to deter malign spirits from entering the tomb.

(*mingqi*)—items made specifically for use as funerary offerings, rather than actual objects of daily use. Notable examples of *mingqi* were ceramic vessels coated with dark green glaze as substitutes for bronze vessels, and simulated, often miniaturized, musical instruments that resembled the real thing but were not actually playable. This is not to say that tombs contained no actual, usable offering goods, but the trend was toward simulacra, especially the use of wooden or ceramic figurines. Toward the end of the Warring States Period, large tomb retinues of soldiers and servants pointed the way toward the famous terra-cotta warriors from the tomb complex of Qin Shihuangdi.

Focus: The Jixia Academy

In 386 BCE the Tian Clan, which had by then dominated Qi politics for more than a century, formally overthrew the last ruler of the legitimate Jiang lineage that had ruled the state since Western Zhou times. Under the leadership of the Tian patriarch Lord Huan of Qi (r. 374–355 BCE) Qi began to offer hospitality and stipends to large numbers of intellectuals and thinkers of various persuasions. Because they gathered in the neighborhood of a particular gate of the walled capital city of Linzi, these intellectuals came to be known as "gentlemen of Jixia" ("below the Ji Gate," the gate itself presumably being named for Hou Ji, "Lord Millet," an ancient Zhou agricultural deity). In modern times many scholars have referred to this gathering of thinkers as the Jixia Academy. That term is highly contentious, however. Some scholars point to the lack of any organization or infrastructure that justifies the term "academy," while others insist that the intellectuals of Qi were no different from the motley collections of astrologers, alchemists, herbalists, magicians, good talkers, military strategists, swords-for-hire, and general hangers-on that could be found at the court of any Warring States polity.

The scholarly consensus now is that while there was no formally structured academy at Jixia, something special was indeed going on there. Under a succession of Tian Clan rulers of Qi lasting for the duration of the fourth century BCE, the ranks of subsidized guests in Qi seem to have been dominated by wandering intellectuals and philosophers, who not only were supported financially but were encouraged to propose and debate their various theories in an atmosphere of unprecedented openness and what we would now call freedom of expression.

It is surely not accidental that Qi was the home state of the esteemed minister–advisor Guan Zhong, whose wise counsel helped in the rise to prominence of the earlier Lord Huan of Qi, the first Spring and Autumn era hegemon. The establishment of the patronage community at Jixia would have been an effective way of honoring Guan Zhong and perpetuating his legacy. Nor was it accidental that in the neighboring state of Lu there had arisen an institution that really could be called an academy: the headquarters, at the Kong family mansion at Qufu, of the followers of Confucius, who were engaged in defining, and refining, the meaning of the *Ru* intellectual lineage and curating its sacred texts. The openness of the Jixia establishment stands in probably deliberate contrast to the doctrinal orthodoxy of both the *Ru* and their intellectual adversaries, the Mohists.

The two outstanding features of the Jixia patronage community were its size and its diversity. If the standard historical sources are to be believed (and they undoubtedly exaggerated to some extent), the "gentlemen of Jixia," not to mention their families, disciples, and servants, numbered in the hundreds. Supporting all of them implies a huge expenditure of funds on the part of the Tian rulers of Qi; the payoff, in prestige and the occasional useful idea, was immeasurable but presumably substantial. As for diversity, the names and ideas of most of the Jixia scholars have been lost to history, but we do know that among the many thinkers who visited or resided at Jixia were the Confucians Mencius and Xunzi, the cosmological theorist Zou Yan, the eclectic intellectual Shenzi, the political theorist Yan Ying, and the debater Tian Ba. Their interactions were undoubtedly lively, and may have been a valued source of intellectual entertainment for the Tian rulers.

That the intellectual diversity of Jixia mirrored the explosive growth of text-based knowledge in the Warring States Period is strikingly confirmed by the large number of texts that have been discovered in archaeologically excavated tombs of that period. Most tomb texts are archival (lists of grave goods, lists of attendees at the funeral) or practical (almanacs, medical recipes). Only a minority can be considered philosophical or theoretical. Contrary to the expectations of many scholars, the latter seldom form coherent collections of works of one "school" or another; rather, they tend to be quite diverse. On the whole, these excavated texts indicate that the tomb occupants had wide-ranging interests, valued different points of view, and participated in a richly varied intellectual life.

Focus: Who is a *Ru*?

The term *Ru*, denoting a person in early China who adheres to a conservative set of doctrines, has become an important point of contention in modern scholarship on Chinese thought. The origin of the word is obscure. In its earliest usages it seems to refer to a group of post-Western Zhou ritual specialists who, by the Warring States Period, referred to themselves as "Weaklings" or "Flexible Ones"—a term that some scholars suggest describes one aspect of their ritual performance of music, dance, and song, involving a great deal of bowing and bending.

Another quite different theory notes that the first sustained use of the term comes in the *Mozi* chapters 38 (lost) and 39 ("Against the *Ru*, Parts A and B"), where the followers of Confucius are systematically criticized and their doctrines refuted. *Ru* in the *Mozi* is a pejorative term, something like "Weaklings" or "Spineless Ones." It is quite possible that the followers of Confucius then appropriated the term for themselves, giving it a new sense of "Adaptable Ones" or "Flexible Ones," contrasting themselves to the ideological rigidity of the Mohists. An analogous case is a familiar one: some Americans at the time of the Revolutionary War gleefully referred to themselves as "Yankees," appropriating the term from the lyrics of the British marching song "Yankee Doodle," which mocked the soldiers of the Continental Army as a bunch of ill-dressed country bumpkins.

Whatever its origins, by the time of the Western Han dynasty the term *Ru* generally applied to thinkers who accepted Confucius as a great sage and an authority on the correct conduct of rituals. It included, but was not necessarily limited to, the successive generations of followers of Confucius who refined and extended the teachings of the Master at the Kong family mansion in Qufu. Another defining characteristic of the *Ru* was their acceptance of certain texts—the *Springs and Autumns*, the *Book of Documents*, the *Odes*, the *Book of Changes*, and the *Ritual Records*—as authoritative sources of doctrine and conduct. Many *Ru* believed that Confucius had personally written or edited these texts. The association of *Ru* with the followers of Confucius was strong enough that, by the early Han dynasty, the term *Ru Mo* was a standard shorthand for "Confucians and Mohists," denoting the two leading schools of thought at that time.

How, then, should one translate the word *Ru*? Many scholars feel uncomfortable with the translation "Confucian," at least when referring to the Warring States and early imperial eras, because it seems to carry too much baggage from Confucianism's later development as a philosophy and quasi-religion. The great Victorian translator James Legge consistently translated *Ru* as "scholar." Some modern authorities prefer to translate *Ru* as "classicist." The problem is that both of these translations are too broad: in Warring States, Qin, and Han China, there were clearly scholars who were not *Ru*, just as there were people who regarded non-*Ru* texts (for example, the *Daodejing*) as "classics." Some other modern scholars "translate" *Ru* as "Ruist," which is accurate but uninformative. Despite misgivings about translating *Ru* as "Confucian," no one has yet come up with a better solution.

Focus: Mozi and Mohism

Mohism is the philosophical tradition named after Mozi (Master Mo, personal name Mo Di, c. 479–381 BCE). Mo Di's origins and early life are obscure. He does not seem to have belonged to the lower level of the aristocracy (*shi*, "knights" or educated "men of service") that produced so many thinkers in the Warring States era; many scholars have speculated that his family belonged to the artisan class. His followers formed a tightly organized group, membership in which involved initiation rituals and quasi-military discipline. The Mohist movement flourished for several generations but declined in significance after the early Western Han Period. By then, however, some of its teachings had been incorporated into mainstream Chinese thought.

The book *Mozi*, recording the teachings of Master Mo, was compiled by successive generations of followers in approximately the fourth and third centuries BCE. It was recorded by Han dynasty bibliographers as a work of seventy-one chapters, only fifty-three of which have survived in the text as we know it today; in some cases the titles of the lost chapters have survived but the content is missing. Mohist teachings center on ten key doctrines expounded in what are known as the core chapters of the text, chapters 8–37. These are organized as ten sets of three consecutive essays, each of the three chapters in a set having the same title and denoted as "upper" (*shang*), "middle" (*zhong*), and "lower" (*xia*)—that is, parts A, B, and C. The ten doctrines are: "Elevating the Worthy"; "Conforming to Superiors"; "Impartial Caring"; "Rejecting Aggression"; "Restraint in Consumption"; "Restraint in Funerals"; "Heaven's Will"; "Elucidating Ghosts"; "Rejecting Music"; and "Rejecting Fate."

Several of these core doctrines are distinctively Mohist. For example, the Mohist argument for modest funerals contrasted strongly with the aristocratic provision of lavish funerals for departed elders, a practice seen by Confucians as an expression of filial piety. In rejecting music the Mohists acknowledged its appeal but argued that music tempts people to squander time and resources on a useless pastime. And the Mohist condemnation of aggressive warfare entailed the corollary that defensive warfare was justified; some Mohists pursued careers as specialists in defensive warfare and fortifications. But the most important and distinctive of the core doctrines is "impartial caring" (often translated as "universal love.") This radical idea held that partiality—toward one's family, village, state, or other social unit—inevitably leads to conflict and disorder. This is akin to the Christian injunction to "love thy neighbor as thyself"; only by caring for all humans equally could the negative consequences of partiality be done away with.

Like many Warring States Period intellectuals, the Mohists saw history as a record of devolution from a primitive, harmonious communitarianism to the violence and disorder of the present day. Any historical change was seen as likely to be change for the worse. Their solution to this problem was to propose a highly disciplined meritocracy in which partiality, extravagance, and differences of opinion were eliminated, and in which there would thus be no reason for anyone to resort to war.

Focus: Zhuangzi on death and transformation

The philosopher Zhuangzi taught a radical form of relativism, refusing to concede the validity of individual preferences in the face of the all-encompassing *Dao*. Chapter six of the *Zhuangzi* is entitled "The Great and Venerable Teacher," the teacher being understood as the *Dao* itself. The chapter contains a famous passage on death and transformation that expresses Zhuangzi's outlook clearly and succinctly.

> It happened that Master Lai suddenly fell ill. As he lay gasping and wheezing on the verge of death, his wife and children gathered round, wailing for him. Master Li arrived to see how he was, and said to them, "Shush! Stand back! Do not impede his transformation."
>
> Leaning against the doorway, he said to Master Lai, "How wonderful the Creator is! What do you suppose he will make of you next? A rat's liver, perhaps, or a bug's elbow?"
>
> Master Lai replied, "Wherever the parents may send their child, east or west, north or south, that is where he will go. But yin and yang are far more to a man than his own parents. Now they have brought me to the brink of death. If I were not to heed their command, would I not be intransigent? How are they at fault? The Great Clod has encumbered me with form, belabored me with life, eases me in old age, and will rest me in death. If I have rejoiced in life, should I not rejoice in death as well?
>
> "Now suppose that a smith were about to cast some metal. If the metal should bubble and boil in the crucible and say, 'I demand to be made into nothing less than a legendary sword,' the smith would certainly think that the metal was extremely inauspicious. Just so if I, having once been a man, should insist on taking human form again—the Creator would surely consider me a very inauspicious person. I regard Heaven and Earth as a great furnace, and the Creator as a master smith. How could there be any fault in what they make? In completion I will go to sleep; suddenly I will wake up again."

Focus: Lord Yi of Zeng's tomb

Zeng, a small and almost insignificant polity, was a dependency of the great state of Chu. Its rulers held the relatively high rank of *hou*, and the ruling family claimed descent from the Zhou royal Ji Clan, but any independent power it might once have possessed had vanished by the beginning of the Spring and Autumn Period. Zeng is almost invisible in the early historical record. In modern times a few tombs of Zeng officials have been located and excavated, providing some information about Zeng history. Recently a burial ground dating from the Western Zhou revealed the antiquity of the lineage. But none of those tombs compare to the sumptuous tomb of Lord Yi of Zeng, discovered by construction workers in 1977. Lord Yi of Zeng died around 433 BCE. The tomb, near Leigudun in present-day Sui Prefecture, Hubei Province, had the good fortune to escape almost entirely the attentions of tomb robbers; only one corner of the tomb chamber was breached at some point, and little or nothing was taken. The tomb is as significant for having been carefully and scientifically excavated as for its remarkable contents.

The tomb's four large wooden chambers highlight aspects of a wealthy local lord's life: a boudoir, where the lord slept encased in multi-layered highly decorated lacquered wooden coffins surrounded by the bodies of young women and a private band of stringed instruments very likely for playing popular, rather than ritually orthodox, tunes; an armory filled with personalized weapons; a kitchen full of household goods and preparations for the feast; and a central court for hosting a fabulous banquet. In this central chamber we find the most famous element of the tomb's contents: a full orchestra, including an array of sixty-four double-toned bells and a matching set of chime-stones arrayed around a room set up with low lacquer tables for feasting and an enormous display of bronze vessels for food and alcohol. Bells and chimes had been found in other tombs, but no sets so grand or so complete. These were suspended from lacquered wooden racks, laid out in such a way as to require at least two musicians, wielding wooden mallets, to play each set. The orchestra incorporated a variety of other instruments, including several types of drum, flutes and other wind instrument, and three types of zither-like stringed instrument. Unfortunately, no musical scores exist from early times. We do know from ancient records that music was considered to have a powerful, if not supernatural, influence on living beings and that the type of music played was thought to affect the behavior of people and animals, but we do not know what ancient music sounded like.

Two massive lacquered wooden coffins, nested one inside the other, protected the ruler's corpse. The décor of the inner coffin features humanoid, but distinctly other-worldly, body-guards armed with double-bladed dagger-axes along with a panoply of bird and dragon images (Figure 8.9). Other significant lacquer objects include a box decorated with a depiction of the Big Dipper and the names of the twenty-eight lunar lodges (stars marking out

Figure 8.9 Design of long-necked birds and humanoid figures armed with *ge* dagger-axes from the lacquer coffin of Lord Yi of Zeng, 433 BCE.

stages on the celestial equator), an important document for the history of Chinese astronomy and cosmology. Another lacquer box shows a person in a long-sleeved robe dancing to the beat of a drum, interpreted by many scholars as evidence of shamanistic ritual practices. A standing statue of a long-necked bird crowned with a rack of antlers that may have held a drum hints at the conjoined imagery of flight and music.

The bronzes included a matching set of nine *ding* caldrons and a matching set of *li* sacrificial food containers; these sets of nine may have been a way of reinforcing the Zeng rulers' claim to Zhou royal ancestry. Other bronze goods included several large vessels with heavily encrusted surface decoration that seems typical of a southern regional style and which testifies to the tremendous skill of the local bronze founders and perhaps the use of lost-wax casting methods. The bells were all cast of bronze, including one large *bo* style bell with an inscription explaining that it was a gift from the king of Chu in memory of Lord Yi's mother. The other bells were cast with inscriptions describing their musical tones, thus enabling scholars to reconstruct the ancient scales. Other bronze objects included dagger-axe blades, spearheads, chariot fittings, and heavy bases for the lacquer bell and chime stands.

A final point of interest is that the tomb contained some of the earliest extant documents written on bamboo strips. The principal text in the tomb is a record of the funeral cortege, naming the Zeng nobles and envoys from other states who attended the funeral and describing their chariots and the gifts they donated.

Focus: The death of Shao Tuo

In 316 BCE the family of a middle-aged officer in the Chu court buried him in the family cemetery north of the city. He was a descendant from an earlier Chu ruler, King Zhao (and, indeed, the name Shao could also be read Zhao), so the burial goods placed in the five chambers of his tomb were lavish (over 2,000 items). The tomb had been dug deep into the earth, so the goods were transported from the ancestral shrine in a series of carts down a long ramp to be distributed carefully in each of the five chambers. On top was a large mound composed of different layers of clays representing "five-colored earth." Shao Tuo's body had been dressed and wrapped in multi-layered silk robes, then tightly bound and placed inside two nesting painted wooden coffins.

The coffins were placed in the central chamber, which was surrounded by four other wooden chambers that interlocked in a fly-wheel pattern. The head of the deceased was pointed eastward, as was typical of Chu burials, and the four surrounding compartments each matched one of the four directions, with the smallest being to the west and the biggest to the south and north. The eastern compartment was laid out for a musical banquet. The spirit food, packed and sealed into painted lacquer boxes and jars to be served on lacquer dishes and in bronze vessels, included chestnuts, dates, pears, persimmons, ginger, lotus root, plums, onions, peppers, chickens, piglets, carp, and water buffalo calf, among many other items. The southern compartment included military equipment, tents, and other travel paraphernalia, suggesting that Shao Tuo's afterlife might include a dangerous journey. The western compartment's contents seemed to be an extension of the preparations for travel and included personal items such as a fold-up bed, a lap-lute, fans, hemp shoes, and markers for local resident spirits of the stove, gateway, door, and walkway. The northern compartment also included personal items: some magical ornaments to be worn on his head and sash, a dragon-headed staff, another lap-lute, and all the tools of the writer's trade (bamboo, paring knife, and brush). Besides clothing, combs, and a hairpiece, this chamber also included two texts. One was a record of legal cases he had worked on when he was an official and the other was the last three years of a record written by diviners who tried to cure him of his fatal illness.

Elite Chu men such as Shao Tuo had access to a team of thirteen ritual officers who specialized in different types of divination and sacrifice and could be employed to address concerns by their clients regarding problems in their lives. For elite males, these problems were generally identified as belonging to four realms: military career, government career, family, or residence. Shao Tuo was having problems with his government career and his health, so the diviners alternated shell and stalk divination methods to identify possible spiritual influences that came from the outside environment (perhaps accrued during his business trips), inside his home, and among his family. The ritual officers focused on appeasing with animal sacrifices, or exorcising, different spirits in order to improve Shao Tuo's quality of life. The spirits considered most likely to be causing problems were the recently deceased family members or the local house gods, although the diviners also appealed to ancient kings and sky gods. By the end of the three-year period the diviners became increasingly desperate as Shao's symptoms became more extreme. His *qi* was flowing in the wrong direction (probably evinced by coughing), his "heart and abdomen" area was in pain, and he could barely stand. They gave up on worrying about his career and focused on what unhappy spirits were causing his illness. In the end, nothing could be done, and Shao Tuo died. Survivors packed his tomb with items that would ensure that his ghost would not join the ranks of unhappy revengeful souls, but would instead be a happy and supportive ancestor.

9 The rise and fall of the Qin dynasty

Introduction

At the beginning of the Warring States Period the state of Qin occupied a large territory in the northwest of the East Asian Heartland, "within the passes" where the southward-flowing Yellow River approaches the Qinling Mountains and makes a sharp bend to flow eastwards through the Yellow River Plain. The state's territory included a portion of the Loess Highlands as well as the fertile plain of the Wei River Valley, the old homeland of the Zhou ruling house before and during the Western Zhou Period. Qin's population included substantial numbers of Rong, Qiang, and other non-Sinitic tribal peoples, and the state was regarded as "semi-barbarian" by the old Central States of the Zhou political system. But the Qin rulers adapted themselves to Zhou norms of ancestor worship, cosmology, and ritual, and sought to take Zhou's place in the multi-state world. During the Spring and Autumn Period they focused on diplomatic efforts, but during the Warring States Period they won through military might.

For the first century or so of the Warring States Period Qin's role was limited by succession disputes and other kinds of internal dissention. But, with the implementation of the reforms proposed by the influential prime minister Shang Yang in 358 and 350 BCE, Qin rapidly transformed itself into a power to be reckoned with. Although Lord Shang himself came to a bad end, his reforms lived on. Transformed into a centrally governed state, shorn of outdated aristocratic baggage, the government focused on building economic resources through organizing agriculture with an emphasis on the wealth-generating production of grain and silk. It also mobilized for the training and deployment of large infantry armies. Qin was ready to take on the world.

The Qin capital city, Xianyang, built in 350 BCE on the site of the ancient Zhou capital called Hao, symbolically positioned Qin as the rightful successors of Zhou. In the same vein, in 325 BCE its rulers dropped their old appellation of "lord" (*gong*) and began to call themselves "king" (*wang*). This violated their former tributary relationship to Zhou, setting themselves up as equals to the Zhou Son of Heaven. This upgrade of titles followed a trend among a number of former tributary states; for example, around the same time Lord Hui of Wei (*Wei Hui hou*) renamed himself King Hui of Liang. The late Zhou rulers themselves lacked even vestigial power and, when the last Zhou monarch, King Nan, died in 256 BCE without an heir, the legendary dynasty ended with a whimper. Just previously, in 288 BCE, the king of Qin had proclaimed that in fact he should be called *Di*, adapting the name of the Shang dynasty's High God to a political title meaning something like Supreme Sovereign over all the world. This turned out to be premature, as the still-powerful states of Yan, Wei, Zhao, and others registered their strong disapproval and threatened military action. So the Qin rulers

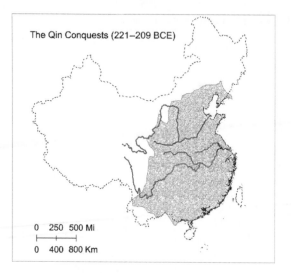

Map 9.1 In 221 BCE the state of Qin succeeded in defeating the last of its rivals, uniting China under one central administration for the first time.

had to be satisfied with the title of "king" until 221 BCE, when they succeeded in conquering all the old states in the former Zhou world. Qin's King Zheng then adopted the newly coined title Qin Shihuangdi, First August Sovereign of Qin.

The struggle of the former Zhou states and their lesser allies, such as the dependencies of Chu in the Yangzi River Valley, against the expansionist efforts of Qin gave the Warring States Period its name. The success of Qin's methodical campaign to conquer and consolidate territory was due to a series of effective rulers and ministers who skillfully mastered the complexities of Warring States diplomacy and alliances. Ultimately their diplomatic machinations, combined with brute military force, resulted in the unification of the territories of the two river valleys, the Yellow and the Yangzi, under a single central government for the first time in history (Map 9.1). This signified the birth of China, and gave the empire its name as well. "China," or some similar derivative of "Qin," subsequently entered the vocabulary of many Eurasian languages.

The campaigns of conquest

The intensification of the military conquest took place during the last half of the Warring States Period, from the late fourth century BCE to 221 BCE. Taking advantage of neighbors weakened through centuries of internal fighting, inter-state warfare, and the trend of larger polities absorbing smaller ones, Qin moved out from its secure position "within the passes" with a highly militarized government that could field vast, well-trained armies. With luck and strategy, it negotiated a series of shifting alliances that allowed it to deploy military force with maximum effect.

First, in 316 BCE, Qin completed the conquest, begun decades earlier, of Shu and part of Ba in the Sichuan Basin and the Yangzi River above the gorges. This was a key link in what might be described as Qin's western strategy to consolidate its power and territorial control. It also gave them access to the resources of the agriculturally rich Sichuan Basin. In the following year Qin inflicted a severe and, for practical purposes, final blow on the Rong tribes within Qin, removing them as a source of domestic concern. With Sichuan firmly in hand, administered from a new Qin-built capital at Chengdu, Qin secured its trade routes to the southwest and its own southwestern flank. The military value of having control of Sichuan was apparent in the Qin campaign against Chu in 312 BCE, when it swept down from "within the passes" and dislodged Chu from its ancestral homeland in the middle Han River Valley and its metropolitan center in Jinancheng, farther south on the north side of the Yangzi. This placed all of western China under Qin control.

The early years of the third century BCE saw a bewilderingly complicated series of alliances that affected the Qin expansion. These alliances were hastily made and quickly broken. A good example is the fall of one of early China's strongest states, Qi, the eastern counter to Qin in the west. Ancient Chinese texts are fond of associating historical events with notorious or legendary figures, and the machinations behind the ultimate fall of Qi are attributed to a famously devious Qi statesman, Tian Wen (also known as the Lord of Mengchang). He forged an alliance of Qi, Hann, and Wei to invade Qin in 298 BCE, leading to a three-year war of attrition. When the invaders penetrated the Wei River Valley, Qin surrendered and agreed to return some previously annexed territory to Hann and Wei. This seeming victory was undermined by political infighting and, in 294 BCE, Tian Wen fled to Wei. Qin, observing the weakness of Hann and Wei without the support of Qi, attacked and regained the disputed territory until an alliance of Qi, Yan, Wei, and Zhao again defeated Qin. But, meanwhile, Tian Wen, still in Wei, organized a coalition of Yan, Wei, Hann, and Zhao to attack Qi while it was occupied with taking over Song, to its south. Qi was devastated in 284 BCE and its army wiped out. Tian Wen stepped back into power in Qi. Qi subsequently recovered some of its territory but never regained its status as a major military power. Qin, meanwhile, took advantage of the situation to continue its encroachment on the Central States from the west.

Next, Qin turned its attention to Chu, in the south. Chu had earlier declared itself an ally of Qi, but did little to aid that beleaguered state. Qin occupied the Chu capital (one of a series of Chu capitals, all called Ying) in 278 BCE. This had the effect of pushing Chu away from the Yangzi River Valley and northeast into the Huai River Plains, where it was hemmed in by Yue to the south and Qi to the north. All three states, Qi, Chu, and Yue, had been weakened by internal political strife and concentrated on mere survival rather than engaging in interstate warfare and diplomacy.

Qin efforts to occupy the Central States incurred some failures, which prompted dynamic internal reforms in response. Zhao strengthened its position by opportunistically forming alliances to expand at the expense of Wei and Qi. In 269 BCE a Qin army was dispatched to put a stop to Zhao's expansionist aggression, but the Qin forces were soundly defeated. This debacle was followed by a shake-up at the Qin court, leading to the rise of the very capable minister Fan Sui and bolstering the position of Fan's political ally, the great general Bo Qi. Under Fan Sui, King Zhaoxiang of Qin centralized the government so that individual commanderies and counties headed by bureaucrats reported directly to him. This undercut a "new aristocracy" that had begun to appear in Qin in the century since Lord Shang's reforms. The aristocracy, consisting of a number of successful military leaders, had been rewarded with huge grants of land. Besides governmental reform, military strategy was also provided with a larger vision beyond opportunistic raiding and annexation of territory. Fan Sui offered instead a policy of deliberate conquest, picking off other states one by one, annihilating their ruling classes and armed forces, and taking total control of their territory by subsuming it into Qin's bureaucratic and more efficient government structure.

The crucial test of this policy came with the Battle of Changping in 260 BCE. Qin tried to annex some territory belonging to Hann (Zhao's ally at the time), but this was resisted by

Zhao. In the battle that followed General Bo Qi lured the Zhao army into an exposed forward position, encircled it, and settled down to starve the Zhao forces into submission. After several weeks the Zhao general, Zhao Kuo, made a desperate but unsuccessful attempt to break out. The Qin forces butchered his entire army, supposedly 400,000 men. But the Qin victory at Changping came at a cost. The Qin army had also suffered substantial casualties in the battle, and Bo Qi advocated resting his armed forces for a while. His advice was rejected, and he committed suicide under duress. When a Qin expeditionary force was slaughtered shortly thereafter while attempting to take the Zhao capital, Fan Sui was cashiered, accused of treason, and executed in 255 BCE.

The late 250s BCE saw an extraordinary sequence of occupants of the throne of Qin. When the long-reigning King Zhaoxiang died in 251 BCE he was succeeded by his son and heir, Lord Anguo, who ascended the throne as King Xiaowen. In the months preceding his coronation, Lord Anguo recalled to the capital his own son, Yiren, who had been a diplomatic hostage in Zhao, and named him as his heir. During his stay in Zhao Yiren had met a rich and influential merchant named Lü Buwei; the two of them seem to have formed a close bond in very short order. Three days after his formal instatement as king Xiaowen died (some say that Lü Buwei had him poisoned), leaving the throne to Yiren, thereafter known as King Zhuangxiang. King Zhuangxiang appointed Lü Buwei as his chancellor and named his own son, Ying Zheng, as heir apparent. King Zhuangxiang's reign was also short; he died in 247 BCE, after only three years on the throne. Ying Zheng, with the dynastic name King Zheng, succeeded him, but, as he was only thirteen years old, Lü Buwei acted as his regent.

King Zheng assumed full powers as an adult in 238 BCE, in the midst of a crisis. An upstart named Lao Ai, who claimed (with little legitimacy) to have connections with the Qin throne, was discovered to be having an affair with the king's mother and plotting with her to alter the line of succession. She had originally been Lü Buwei's concubine, but he had reluctantly given her to Yiren, the future King Zhuangxiang, who admired her beauty. Some people suspected that she was already pregnant at the time, and that Lü Buwei was King Zheng's real father. Regardless of whether or not that was true, her subsequent affair with Lao Ai was a serious scandal. King Zheng's response showed the ruthlessness that would characterize his entire reign. Lao Ai's proven or suspected supporters were all beheaded. Lao Ai himself was torn apart by chariots and his entire family, to three degrees of relationship, was wiped out. Lü Buwei, suspected of disloyalty during these events, was removed from his post as chancellor in 237 BCE; he poisoned himself in 235 BCE on his way to exile in Sichuan. He was succeeded by Li Si, who contributed greatly to the legal framework of the Qin empire.

King Zheng was the future Qin Shihuangdi. Having overcome his internal enemies in the 230s BCE, he resumed Qin's methodical takeover of the remaining warring states. Qin armies marched eastward, overpowering established polities along the Yellow and Yangzi River Valley systems down to the Pacific Ocean. Each was defeated in turn. Hann fell in 230, Zhao in 228, and Wei in 225. In 223 the Chu royal family was slaughtered in Shouchun, Anhui, near the eastern coast; the surviving leaders of Chu surrendered without a fight. Yan fell in 222 after a desperate gamble; in 227 they had dispatched the assassin Jing Ke to the Qin court in an unsuccessful attempt on King Zheng's life. Qi, the last of the great states, surrendered in 221. But the expansion of the empire did not end with the conquest of the old Zhou states. In the decade after 221 Qin armies moved to push back the frontiers in both the north and the south. In the north, troops led by the formidable general Meng Tian engaged the Xiongnu—a multi-ethnic tribal confederation, possibly led by a proto-Turkic elite, that would give the Han dynasty endless trouble—and annexed some of their territory. In the northwest, the Qin empire extended into the Gansu Corridor, incorporated all of the Ordos lands within the great bend of the Yellow River, and reached the fringes of the Gobi. The Great Wall built by the Qin emperor lay considerably to the north of the Ming dynasty wall that we visit today. In the south, Qin armies added to the empire's territory the coastal portions of today's Fujian and Guangdong provinces, and part of Guangxi, as well as occupying some of the southern river valleys formed by north-flowing tributaries of the Yangzi. The Sinitic world had never before extended so far.

Even without these future conquests by the Qin army, by 221 BCE the East Asian Heartland was firmly united under Qin rule. King Zheng claimed the Mandate of Heaven as the First August Sovereign, and an entirely new phase of Chinese history had begun.

Administering the empire

The first order of business, once the conquered Zhou states were pacified, was to initiate a series of reforms. Local aristocrats were disenfranchised (when they survived at all) and relocated to Xianyang, the Qin capital in the Wei River Valley, and their extensive domains were absorbed into a bureaucratically organized central state. All of the land in the empire was newly laid out in commanderies (*jun*) and counties (*xian*). Ultimately there were about forty commanderies, each with a military governor, and nearly a thousand counties, each administered by a magistrate (so there were, on average, about twenty-five counties in a commandery). The counties reported to commanderies, and the commanderies to the capital, thus bypassing any previously existing elite sociopolitical structures within the conquered states and their local systems of administration. This was true even though no systematic way of training and selecting entry-level bureaucrats, such as the exam system of later dynasties, had yet been put in place. Because of the need for literate magistrates and their subordinates, they were often recruited from among the local elites, effectively giving a selection of the disenfranchised aristocracy new but limited access to power. Magistrates maintained their own staffs of secretaries, legal experts, tax assessors, and other trained assistants. The main tasks of government at the county level were to assess and collect taxes, hear criminal and civil legal cases, carry out punishments, maintain roads and other public works, keep registers relating to the performance of corvée labor and military service, and keep the peace. Officials were assessed according to state regulations and could be dismissed or punished for infractions.

The uniformity of this national system was reinforced by elaborate laws concerning what kind of information was to be gathered at the county and commandery levels: records were kept of crops, crop yields, any unusual circumstances such as droughts or floods, household population broken down by gender, age, and occupation, and much more besides. This reporting structure meant that officials in the capital could form reasonable estimates of expected tax revenues or, conversely, the need for relief supplies in stricken areas. The population figures made it possible for the national government to identify areas of surplus population and move people (who had no choice in the matter) to under-populated regions or to unpacified parts of the empire as colonists. For example, in 219 BCE around 30,000 households from various parts of the empire were relocated to an area of Shandong Peninsula previously occupied by less Sinified peoples.

None of these measures could have succeeded without the great explosion in literacy of the Warring States Period and the transformation of the *shi* class from "knights" to "men of service." The ability to read and write became fundamental to any kind of government service above the most menial level. As we will discuss later in this chapter, the Qin state had to walk a fine line between the need for a large corps of literate officials and the undesirable possibility that some of those literate people might begin to think for themselves.

Public works

From his early years on the throne the king of Qin (the future First Emperor) invested heavily in public works projects of various kinds. Two large-scale water-resource projects were begun around 250 BCE and were operational by the time of the Qin unification of the empire. The most famous, and most audacious, of these is the Dujiangyan water-diversion scheme in the Chengdu Plain. Designed and built by the renowned hydraulic engineer Li Bing, it consists of an artificial island that splits the Min River into two channels and a cut made through a rocky cliff that diverts the inner channel into an irrigation system for the Chengdu Plain. A spillway prevents an excessive amount of water from entering the irrigation grid. The finished project provided both flood protection and better irrigation, significantly improving agricultural productivity in the region, and remains in use today.

A second hydrological engineering project was the Zhengguo Canal, completed in 246 BCE, which links two south-flowing tributaries of the Wei River, namely the Jing River and the Luo River. The canal runs parallel to, and north of, the Wei River; straight and deep, compared with the shifting and shallow channels of the Wei, it improved both irrigation and the transportation of goods in the region.

A third great water project begun by the Qin was the Lingqu Canal, in today's Guangxi Province, linking the Xiang River, a northward-flowing tributary of the Yangzi, with the Li River (a tributary of the Gui, which in turn flows into the West River, which joins the Pearl River near present-day Guangzhou). Completed in 214 BCE, this created an integrated canal transport system that enabled barges to travel without interruption on a safe inland waterway from the Yangzi Delta to the Pearl River Delta.

While transport canals were especially suitable for the watery south of the Heartland Region, much of the Northern Heartland depended on land transportation. The Qin greatly extended the existing road system, both by linking older regional roads and by building new ones. The road system served several important purposes: It facilitated the rapid movement of troops; it improved the transport of grain (collected as taxes in the counties and commanderies) to the capital; and it enabled an expansion (highly regulated) of private commerce by merchants. While improving the highway system, the Qin engineers also standardized the width of the roads and the gauge of chariot and cart tracks; previously the lack of uniform standards had impeded efficient travel.

Begun even before the conquest of the empire was completed, the Great Wall is the most famous of Qin's monumental public works projects. Said to have engaged the efforts of 300,000 laborers (including convicts condemned to forced labor, peasants performing corvée service, and some paid workers), it ran from Liaodong in the east to the outer reaches of the Gansu Corridor in the west. Not all of it was new construction; it also linked together existing walls on the northern boundaries of Yan, Wei, Zhao, and Qin itself. (At the same time, existing internal walls were demolished, as were the city walls of former territorial state capitals.) The wall follows the approximate northern boundary of feasible grain agriculture; in effect, it says to China's northern neighbors, "you stay on your side of the wall and be pastoralists, we will stay on our side of the wall and be farmers, and we will be at peace." The effectiveness of the wall as a defensive fortification is a matter of debate. It no doubt had some deterrent effect on small-scale border raiding, but over the course of centuries it was seldom able to stop a determined large-scale invasion (Figure 9.1).

Figure 9.1 Qin-era beacon tower, Shanxi Province. Several states during the Warring States Period built extensive walls and beacon towers.

Feeling secure in his new status as emperor of a united China once the conquest had been completed, Qin Shihuangdi set about building a capital city to match his ambitions. Xianyang was rebuilt and enlarged, and was filled, according to contemporary descriptions, with newly built mansions. Some of these were built for members of the new aristocracy of successful generals who had been rewarded with sumptuous rural territories; after 221 BCE they were expensively bought off and moved to the capital. Likewise, surviving members of the ruling elite of the conquered states were moved to comfortable palaces in Xianyang, where they were supported financially but also kept under surveillance and prevented from intervening in the affairs of their former states.

The construction of the emperor's own grandiose Afang Palace (sometimes spelled Opang or Epang), opposite the capital, on the south bank of the Wei River, was begun in 212 BCE, but the project was still under way when the First Emperor died in 210. If contemporary reports are to be believed, it was designed to be by far the largest palace ever built in the Heartland Region up to that time. The incomplete palace complex was destroyed in 206, when rebel troops occupied the Qin capital, and it was never finished.

The final great public works project of the Qin dynasty was the tomb of the First Emperor himself, now world-famous as the site of the underground army of terra-cotta warriors. Work on the tomb and its associated structures was begun shortly after King Zheng ascended the throne in 247 BCE, and the pace of construction accelerated after 221. An estimated 700,000 workers, mostly criminals sentenced to terms of forced labor, worked on the tomb complex during the years of its construction. The location of the tomb was never a mystery; its huge mound in Lintong, east of Xi'an, was always known to indicate the site of the subterranean tomb. But archaeologists were stunned when in 1974 some farmers digging a well a mile or so east of the tomb came upon an underground army of larger-than-life-size painted terra-cotta warriors (see Focus: The terra-cotta warriors). Arrayed in a huge main pit and two auxiliary pits, the approximately 8,000 figures (including not only soldiers and officers but also chariots and horses) were apparently intended as symbolic guardians, defending the tomb from invaders from the east (the likely source of an invasion of the Wei River Valley). After the discovery of the main pit further investigation located a second large pit, apparently a reserve unit, and a third pit representing the commanding general's post. The general and his staff are depicted as riding in two canopied bronze chariots, modeled in exquisite detail at one-third life-size.

The tomb itself remains unexcavated, and there are no plans to excavate it in the near future. When the tomb is opened it will require vast amounts of money and expertise to excavate, conserve, and display its contents. The Chinese authorities have decided to wait until they are sure the job can be done properly. Treasures await: Sima Qian's account in the *Records of the Grand Historian (Shiji)* describes an elaborate underground palace filled with all sorts of luxury goods and featuring a relief map of China with rivers depicted in liquid mercury. Swivel-mounted crossbows with tripwire triggers and other traps for the unwary guard the interior. Also in the tomb will be the bones of many of the First Emperor's favorite concubines and of workmen killed to prevent them from leaking the secrets of the tomb's defenses. In the center of the tomb, encased in multiple nesting coffins, will be the body of the First Emperor himself. The excavation of this tomb, whenever it happens, will surely be the archaeological event of the century. So far preliminary tests confirm the presence of mercury, lending credence to Sima Qian's description.

Standardization

One of Lord Shang's most important reforms of the mid-fourth century BCE was the standardization of weights and measures. A pint (*sheng*) measure, dated to the year 344 BCE and having a capacity of about 200 cubic centimeters, along with several archaeologically recovered standard weights, gives concrete evidence of the policy of distributing standard measures of weight, capacity, and length to markets throughout the state (see Focus: Weights and measures). These standards were applied to conquered states as they were incorporated into the Qin empire in the 220s BCE.

Another important area of standardization was that of metallic coinage. In the fourth century BCE metal coins came into wide use in the Heartland Region, but there were several different shapes of coins, with different nominal values, associated with several of the powerful states of the time. The Qin issued its first metallic currency, the "half-ounce" (*banliang*) coin, in 336 BCE. Its weight was, of course, derived from the recently introduced standard Qin ounce (*liang*). The shape of the coin—round with a square hole in the middle (for stringing a number of coins together)—remained the standard for Chinese coins until the end of the imperial era in 1911 CE. Each coin was a miniature cosmos: the square earth surrounded by the circle of heaven, a motif that was also common in the design of the backs of bronze mirrors.

A third important area of standardization was the written language. The usual way of writing Chinese characters during the Warring States Period was called the Large Seal Script, which had evolved from the earlier script used in bronze vessel inscriptions. But there were several regional styles of Large Seal Script, and some characters were used in one region but not in others, often with a diverse array of different graphic components to represent the same word. A document on wooden or bamboo slips written in Chu might be difficult for a native of Wei to read, and vice versa. Under Li Si's policy of standardization a single orthography was devised for each character, and many variant or regional characters were dropped. The approved written forms were then promulgated throughout the empire and made mandatory for use in all official documents. It is generally agreed that the uniformity of the written language contributed greatly to the creation and maintenance of a common Chinese culture.

Another reform, perhaps more surprising, established a standard gauge for the spacing of wheels on chariots and other wheeled vehicles; in other words, a standard for the length of axles. This practical measure made for better travel by road. The soil in many parts of northern China is powdery and easily eroded, so that wheeled vehicles quickly make ruts in unpaved roads. Without a standard gauge a road would be worn into several incompatible sets of ruts, making travel rough and slow. With wheels spaced a uniform distance apart, all vehicles rode in the same ruts and travel was smooth and swift. This policy shows the Qin administration at its best: capable of analyzing a situation and coming up with a good policy to deal with it.

Monopolizing knowledge

Chapter 3 of the *Daodejing* says, "The sage, in governing, empties [the people's] minds and fills their bellies, weakens their will and strengthens their bones." And the *Book of Lord Shang*, in chapter 2, concurs: "If the people do not prize learning, they will be stupid; if they are stupid, they will have nothing to do with extraneous matters; if they have nothing to do with extraneous matters they will prize agriculture and not neglect their duties; if the people do not disdain agriculture, the country will be peaceful and safe." The Qin empire subscribed wholeheartedly to those principles. In what was arguably the most totalitarian aspect of Qin's political philosophy, most people were supposed to be ignorant and not think very much at all; those who had access to knowledge were supposed to confine their learning to their assigned duties. Literate officials were indispensible, but thinking independently was discouraged and, in some cases, might incur the death penalty. This view that the government should exercise strict control over knowledge lay behind the most notorious actions of the Qin government: the "burning of books and burial alive of scholars." Those events echoed down the centuries as the worst of the "crimes of Qin."

In 213 BCE Li Si, disturbed that some scholars at court dared to criticize Qin policy and, further, suggested that the Qin regime failed to come up to the standards of the Zhou founders King Wen and King Wu, issued new regulations designed to prevent the expression of such subversive views. All state chronicles taken from the archives of the various states were to be burned, so that history could be narrated exclusively from the Qin point of view. All copies of literary, historical, or philosophical works in private hands were to be turned over to the authorities to be burned for the same reason. Copies of such works might be kept in the Qin imperial library, however, to which access was carefully controlled. Private individuals were allowed to keep only copies of works of practical value on subjects such as medicine, divination, and agriculture. Gathering together to discuss historical or philosophical texts was punishable by death; those who dared to "use the past to criticize the present" were to be killed, along with all members of their families. It is not known how rigorously the destruction of books in private hands was carried out. Probably some individuals dared to hide copies of forbidden books, at great risk to themselves. In any case the imperial library was to be a repository of all books that were otherwise banned. The consolidation of written knowledge in one place had disastrous consequences, however; in the warfare that accompanied the fall of Qin a rebel army burned the imperial library, and many works that existed only in unique copies were lost forever. Early in the succeeding Han dynasty scholars made a concerted effort to restore, from memory, as many lost works as possible.

The "burial alive of scholars" in 212 BCE certainly involved the execution of a large number of people, but whether they were buried alive is uncertain (it depends on how one interprets an unusual word for "execute"), as is whether they were really scholars. The event seems to have involved an alarmist investigation of violations of security regulations. The First Emperor, fearing assassination, divided his time among his many palaces in the strictest secrecy. Revealing, or even discussing, the ruler's whereabouts was punishable by death. The emperor began to suspect that some members of his entourage—a large number of purveyors of elixirs of immortality, alchemists, magicians, fortune tellers, and other practitioners of esoteric arts—were violating this stern prohibition. An investigation turned up many suspects, along with a number of officials with whom they were said to be in contact. All of them were put to death. Horrible as this must have been, later retellings of the story seem to have involved a certain amount of exaggeration with regard to the number of individuals executed and the manner of their death. The description of the executed men as "scholars" misleadingly conjures up an image of individuals heroically dying in defense of ideas; in reality, they seem to have caused breaches of security, or even just indulged in common gossip.

Nevertheless, the principle that unites these two incidents is that of "emptying the people's minds and filling their bellies": especially in the waning years of the Qin dynasty, it was very dangerous to know too much.

Intellectual and religious currents

Despite the First Emperor's penchant for thought control, enacted through Li Si's regulations, it would be a mistake to assume that all intellectual activity came to a halt during the fifteen-year existence of the Qin dynasty. There is no evidence, for example, that the tightly organized Mohist groups were systematically persecuted or forced to disband, or that the Confucian academy at the Kong family mansion in Qufu was forced to cease operations (although presumably it had to surrender or hide its library in 213 BCE and rely on memorized texts instead). In fact, the intellectual atmosphere during the Qin dynasty reveals a continued dialogue over concepts of the Way (*Dao*) and the meaning of humaneness (*ren*), particularly with regard to the value of law and punishment. "Masters of broad learning" were supported by the state and were sometimes consulted by the court or asked to participate in debates on policy. And these scholars were by no means restricted to so-called Legalist thinkers; even followers of Confucius were employed at the court of the First Emperor because of their expertise in rituals. Despite the chilling effect of the state's efforts to restrict what might be said, written, or read, intellectual life under the Qin appears to have remained lively, if perhaps a bit cautious.

The First Emperor presumably carried out the normal ritual duties that had been associated from ancient times with the Zhou kings and, more recently, with the rulers of the territorial states. These included, most importantly, sacrifices to the imperial ancestors on designated occasions, but also rites designed to usher in smoothly the months and the seasons. In 219 BCE Qin Shihuangdi journeyed to the sacred peak of Mt. Tai, at the base of the Shandong Peninsula, to perform what was believed to be an ancient rite called the *feng* sacrifice, announcing to Heaven his acceptance of the Mandate to rule. A problem arose, however, because the rite was performed so seldom (if ever) that no one knew how it should be carried out. In the end, the emperor simply instructed his court ritual officers to come up with an appropriate liturgy.

The Qin worshipped a number of legendary figures. A god of agriculture was invoked in annual harvest rituals. Ancient exorcism and fertility rites were also performed. Mountain deities received sacrifices in exchange for good health. And a female mountain goddess considered as a key to the gates of immortality and worshipped in Han times, Xiwangmu, the Dowager Queen of the West, may already have attracted followers. Other deities of the sky, land, rivers, and lakes were likely selectively worshipped by the Qin.

Like many of his time, the First Emperor was obsessed with achieving long life and even immortality. He patronized many practitioners of esoteric arts. Some promoted macrobiotic diets, sexual arts for the exchange of yin and yang fluids, or regimens of controlled breathing; others claimed to have recipes for elixirs of immortality, which sometimes included dangerous ingredients such as mercury or arsenic. One influential advisor, Xu Fu, claimed to know how to sail to the Penglai Islands in the Eastern Ocean, presided over by the Father-King or Grandpa of the East (Dongwanggong), the eastern counterpart of Xiwangmu. The magical islands were a dwelling-place of immortals and a potential source of elixirs. At his urging, the emperor spent an extravagant amount of money in 219 BCE to build and outfit a fleet of ships, commanded by Xu Fu and crewed by young men and women chosen especially for their beauty, that was sent in search of the islands. The fleet never returned, and another expedition a few years later met the same fate. Interestingly, a Japanese legend claims that the first of these fleets was wrecked on the coast of Japan, and that the survivors remained there. Several temples in Japan commemorate Xu Fu (Japanese: Jofuku) in places that claim to be the site of this (probably mythical) landing.

The Qin court accepted wholeheartedly the cosmological views associated with Zou Yan and others at the Jixia "Academy" in fourth-century BCE Qi. According to Zou Yan's theory, each ruling house ruled through the power of one or another of the Five Phases, which overcome one another in a natural cycle called the Conquest Sequence, Water–Fire–Metal–Wood–Earth (see Table 10.2). Because the Zhou dynasty was believed to have ruled through the power of Fire, its conqueror, the Qin, must rule by the power of Water, because water overcomes fire. Therefore court customs and rituals were to be governed by correlates of Water. Ceremonial robes were to be black, as were chariots, horses, and animal sacrificial victims, because, in Five-Phase theory, black is associated with the Phase Water and the North. The number six, considered a *yin* number (versus nine, a *yang* number) is also a correlate of Water, so the index note of the Qin musical scale was a pitch-pipe six inches long. The fact that the Phase Water was associated with winter, severity, and the carrying out of punishments suited Qin's political philosophy very well.

Imperial progresses

Another ritualistic act hallowed by long custom was the royal progress, a ceremonial trip to far-flung parts of the empire. Shrouded by the mystery of his suite of closed carriages, the First Emperor is known to have made at least five such ceremonial trips in the fifteen years of his imperial reign. We have already noted his journey to Mt. Tai to perform the *feng* sacrifice. Not incidentally, most of his imperial journeys were to the eastern seacoast, where belief in the cult of immortality seems to have been especially strong. These trips echoed the *Daodejing*'s portrayal of the ruler as a hidden but potent source of cosmic power; by traveling throughout the empire he could impress his subjects with his "awesome charisma." He also left behind giant stone-carved inscriptions celebrating his visits to supernaturally charged sites; written in poetic style, they portray him as a sage-emperor. But his last return visit to the eastern seacoast proved to be final.

Ershihuangdi and the collapse of the state

The First Emperor died in 210 BCE. In the course of an imperial visit to the Shandong coast he suddenly became ill and died. His cortege then returned to Xianyang, with the emperor's body in one of the sealed carriages; most of the personnel on this final journey were apparently unaware that the emperor was dead. While he was mortally ill he had written a letter to his eldest son, Fusi, confirming his status as heir apparent and advising him to prepare to take the throne. The letter, however, was intercepted by a high-ranking eunuch, Zhao Gao, who was in charge of imperial communications, and who had formed a plot with one of the emperor's younger sons, Huhai, to snatch the throne away from Fusi. Both Zhao Gao and Huhai had accompanied the emperor on his trip to Shandong and so were well placed to take swift advantage of the ruler's death. Zhao Gao replaced the authentic letter with a forged one ordering Fusi, along with his guardian the great general Meng Tian, to commit suicide, which both of them did. (Imperial orders to commit suicide were usually obeyed, because the alternative would be a far more unpleasant execution.) By the time the First Emperor had been interred in his magnificent underground palace east of Xianyang (along with many of his concubines and dozens of engineers, stonemasons, and laborers who worked on the tomb and who knew its security measures), Huhai had been proclaimed Qin Ershihuangdi, the Second Generation August Sovereign of Qin.

Li Si had reluctantly acquiesced in Zhao Gao's scheme to put Huhai on the throne. But clearly Li Si, left alive, was a threat to Zhao's larger aim of making Huhai his puppet. The axe fell in 208 BCE. Li, by then an elderly man who had devoted his entire career to the state of Qin, was arrested on trumped-up charges of treason. He was severely tortured, and then cut in half at the waist. His family was exterminated.

Huhai's historical reputation is so uniformly negative that it is hard to know anything about his character. Only twenty-one years old when he came to the throne, he seems to have been completely dominated by Zhao Gao, who is remembered in orthodox history as the first of a long line of self-serving eunuchs whose evil machinations precipitated the decline or fall of a dynasty. Huhai may have lacked his father's ruthlessness; he certainly lacked his father's judgment about senior advisors. Nor did he have the personal charisma that had enabled the First Emperor, remote and hidden in his vast palaces and closed carriages, to present himself as a kind of Daoist sage-ruler, attuned to the potent forces of the cosmos itself. The two years of the Second Emperor's rule were a shambles in which Zhao Gao's dominance became increasingly obvious. In early October of 208 BCE Zhao Gao engineered a fake attack on the imperial palace, with his own henchmen playing the role of "bandits." Convinced that he was about to be captured and overthrown, Huhai committed suicide. Zhao Gao's next maneuver was to place Huhai's cousin Wangzi Ying, a grandson of the First Emperor, on the throne, but the eunuch misjudged the situation: one of Ying's first acts was to summon Zhao Gao to the palace, where he had him assassinated. Ying took the throne with the old title "king of Qin," perhaps fearing that his grandfather had offended Heaven by taking the grandiose title of *Huangdi*. The hoped-for thousand-generation dynasty of Qin emperors had come to an end. Ying seems to have been a man of some talent and initiative, but time had run out for the rulers of Qin.

By 209 BCE the first of the rebellions against Qin had already broken out. A minor official named Chen She and his aide Wu Guang were escorting a large group of prisoners to the capital from the Yangzi Valley region to begin their terms of forced labor when they were delayed by heavy rains. Since the penalty for being late was death, Chen and Wu decided to take matters in their own hands. They recruited their convict gang as troops and raised the banner of rebellion, leading a campaign that didn't amount to much more than marauding, but which inspired others to rebel also. This initial rebellion ended badly. In the following year Chen's motley soldiers were routed in a battle with Qin army units, and in the flight from the battlefield Chen and Wu were murdered by their own troops. But by then other rebels had taken the field. One was Liu Bang, a mid-level official in the commandery of Pei, in the eastern section of the old state of Chu. Liu was also in charge of a group of forced laborers and recruited them as a rebel band; one of their first acts was to execute the Qin governor of Pei.

Liu Bang was apparently a good leader and a forceful personality, and he soon drew into his movement several other rebel leaders. Meanwhile, two descendants of Chu royal retainers, Xiang Liang and his nephew Xiang Yu, were leading a large-scale rebellion in the eastern region of the old Chu state. In 208 BCE Liu Bang made common cause with them. The rebel army, gathering momentum, moved northward and finally penetrated the land "within the passes," threatening the Qin capital. The king of Qin, Wangzi Ying, surrendered to Liu Bang in 206 BCE (and was eventually killed by Xiang Yu). Liu Bang then gave himself the title "king of Han," named for a small territory on the upper reaches of the Han River. From that point onwards Liu Bang and Xiang Yu, still nominally allies, competed with one another to complete the overthrow of Qin and establish its successor dynasty. Only one of them, Liu Bang, would survive to claim the Mandate of Heaven.

Qin Shihuangdi in retrospect

It is difficult to form a clear impression of the First Emperor, and not only because he is so distant from us in time and culture. Our view is obscured by more than twenty centuries' worth of negative judgments: Qin Shihuangdi is one of the most reviled figures in all of human history. He has consistently been depicted—beginning with the polemic entitled "The Faults of Qin" by the early Han scholar Jia Yi—as a megalomaniacal, paranoid, cruel, secretive monster. (Conversely, during China's Great Proletarian Cultural Revolution of 1965–76, he was seen instead as a hero of the oppressed masses, largely because of his supposed hostility to Confucianism, which was conflated with the image of traditional or "feudal" pre-1911 society.)

He certainly had an egotistical view of his position and power, reflected in his fondness for raising great monuments to himself. In the course of his five imperial progresses through his realm he had workers carve onto rocky cliffs in huge letters the poems that he wrote (or had written for him) on the occasion. His canals and roads, his extravagant tomb, his never-finished Afang Palace might be taken, according to taste, as evidence of egotism run wild or of large-scale infrastructure building. Perhaps they were some of each. Clearly he tried to do too much, too quickly. In doing so he relied on a level of totalitarianism that was extremely burdensome to the population at large (see Focus: A protest song from the *Book of Odes*).

Han dynasty propagandists made much of the cruelty of the First Emperor's laws, but, so far as we can tell from surviving evidence, the laws of the other states in the Warring States Period were not noticeably more lenient. It is especially telling that the Han dynasty, at its founding, took over the Qin law code unchanged and began to revise it only a couple of decades later. In spite of promises to ease the burden of punishments, Qin law and Han law were very similar. Even before the Qin unification, in polities throughout the Heartland Region the death penalty was imposed for numerous crimes and gruesome forms of execution were sometimes carried out. But while exotic forms of corporal punishment attracted attention, probably the most important punishment from the point of view of the ruling elite was forced labor, an abundant source of manpower for public works projects.

The First Emperor's accomplishments in uniting and administering the empire owed much to his willingness to listen to his talented and dedicated chancellor, Li Si, and to follow the advice of able generals such as Meng Tian. Of all of the accomplishments of the brief Qin dynasty, none was more significant than uniting the country under central rule and bureaucratic control through the institution of commanderies and counties, and using that bureaucratic structure to keep minutely detailed records of crop yields, taxes, corvée and military service, and other such matters to maintain public order. Those measures established a pattern followed by imperial governments of China for over 2,000 years.

Qin's successor, the Han dynasty, was proclaimed in 206 BCE and consolidated in 202 BCE. In the early decades of Han rule officials and intellectuals would spend a great deal of energy trying to understand why Qin fell so quickly and how a similar fate might be avoided. It appeared to many thinkers that the very policies that had led to the Qin conquest—the militarized society, the emphasis on centralized rule, the stringent legal system—contained the seeds of its own destruction. It would turn out not to be an easy task to figure out what elements of Qin centralization and policy to retain and what to discard, and what further innovations were necessary to ensure the stability, prosperity, and longevity of the new regime.

Focus: The terra-cotta warriors

The 8,000 or so slightly larger-than-life-size figures of soldiers and officers that occupy the huge pit complex to the east of Qin Shihuangdi's tomb present an informative case study of the mobilization and management of a large workforce in the creation of monumental structures. The ceramic workers who produced the terra-cotta warriors were just one relatively small and specialized part of a much larger population of workers that created the tomb complex as a whole. The tomb was begun in or shortly after 247 BCE, when King Zheng ascended the throne of Qin—even as a teenager, he began planning a monumental final resting place for himself. Over the years some 700,000 workers, including convicts serving sentences of forced labor, peasants performing corvée duty, and skilled paid workers, were employed in creating the tomb complex. In 231 BCE the area around Lintong, where the tomb complex is located, was made a special administrative district dedicated to tomb construction. In 212 BCE some 30,000 additional families were resettled in Lintong to accelerate work on the tomb. Not all of the features of the tomb complex had been completed when the First Emperor died in 210 BCE, but construction ended when his body was interred.

Because Qin Shihuangdi's capital of Xianyang was greatly expanded with the construction of palaces, ritual buildings, and other structures, the city included a substantial number of skilled workers in the field of architectural ceramics, including bricks, tiles, and drainpipes. Some of those workers were relocated to Lintong to apply their skills to creating terra-cotta warriors. The first order of business was to make molds for the several basic types of figures that, with added features, could make up the individuals of the underground army. These included, among others, heavily armored infantrymen, lightly armored infantrymen, standing archers, kneeling crossbow archers, charioteers, and officers of several different ranks, as well as horses for the chariots. Bodies of all of the human figures were made in molds for lower legs and feet, upper legs, torso, shoulders, hands, and heads. With the exception of hands and heads, the figures were assembled prior to firing, with the separate pieces joined with a slurry of diluted clay that served as cement. Hands were molded in several different configurations, mostly depending on the function of the figure to which they were attached and what kind of weapons they were intended to hold. Heads were made in molds in semi-finished form and were finalized by hand by skilled sculptors who stylized features such as mouths, beards, eyebrows, ears, hairstyles, and so on (Figure 9.2). The assembled figures, weighing some 150–200 kilograms (330–440 pounds) were then taken to kilns for firing at a relatively low temperature (the figures are earthenware, not stoneware or porcelain).

The ceramics workforce seems to have been organized in small work groups, each responsible for turning out completed figures. Each team would have included relatively unskilled workers, who made the simpler molded sections, to more highly skilled workers, who were responsible for heads and hands. After the figures were kiln-fired they became the task of lacquer workers, presumably relocated to Lintong from the main lacquer-producing regions of the Yangzi Valley, who painted the figures in bright colors. Unfortunately the lacquer disintegrates rapidly upon exposure to air when the figures are excavated, so it is

Figure 9.2 Terra-cotta warrior, representing a kneeling crossbowman, from the tomb of Qin Shihuangdi, near Xi'an, Shaanxi Province.

difficult, when viewing the clay army today, to get an impression of how vividly the warriors must have appeared when they were first made. A final step, perhaps performed when the figures were already placed in their appropriate ranks in the underground pits, was to equip them with actual weapons. These were mostly removed within a few years, when the army of a rebel leader, Xiang Yu, looted and burned the pits, taking most of the weapons and causing the wooden roofs of the pits to collapse. (For this reason, all of the terra-cotta warriors that have been excavated were broken into many pieces and required extensive conservation.) Several hundred weapons were overlooked by the rebel forces, including swords, spears, dagger-axes, and arrowheads of several kinds. Equipping the terra-cotta warriors with real weapons is a reminder that the Qin state produced bronze weapons on an industrial scale.

The actual fabrication and finishing of the thousands of figures is impressive enough, but the story does not stop there. Many additional workers would have been needed to quarry and refine hundreds of tons of clay and transport it to the ceramic work area. Still others would have been needed to cut and transport massive amounts of wood to stoke the kilns. Firing ceramics is skilled work, and many kiln workers would have been needed for that. All of these operations would have required well-trained, literate managers to oversee and keep records of the various facets of the work, from maintaining a supply of necessary materials to supervising the production teams. Part of what makes the First Emperor's underground army so impressive today is the realization of the artisanal and managerial expertise that went into its creation.

Focus: Weights and measures

Lord Shang's standardization of weights and measures in the mid-fourth century BCE facilitated taxation and commerce; the same benefits accrued when these standards were applied throughout the empire in 215 BCE. The main units of weight, volume, length, and area are given below, with their approximate value to one decimal place. (Values given are those for the Qin, which continued in use during the Western Han; values changed over long periods of time thereafter.) Common English translations are given where they exist.

Weight

1 *fen* 分: weight of twelve millet grains: ~ 0.05 g
12 *fen* = 1 *shu* 銖: approximately 0.6 g
12 *shu* = 1 *banliang* 半兩: "half ounce" (the weight of a standard Qin coin): approximately 7.5 g, or ¼ oz
2 *ban liang* = 1 *liang* 兩: "ounce": approximately 15 g, or ½ oz
16 *liang* = 1 *jin* 斤 "catty": approximately 245 g, or slightly more than ½ lb
30 *jin* = 1 *jun* 鈞: approximately 7.4 kg, or 16 lb
4 *jun* = 1 *dan* 石 (also pronounced *shi*): approximately 29.5 kg, or 65 lb

Volume

1 *ge* 合: approximately 20 cubic centimeters, or 4 teaspoons
10 *ge* = 1 *sheng* 升 "pint": approximately 200 cubic centimeters, or 7/8 cup
10 *sheng* = 1 *dou* 斗 "peck": approximately 2 liters, or ½ gallon
10 *dou* = 1 *hu* 斛 "bushel": approximately 20 liters, or 5 gallons

Length

1 *fen* 分: approximately 0.23 cm, or 1/10 inch

10 *fen* = 1 *cun* 寸 "inch": approximately 2.3 cm, or 29/32 inch (Note: 1/10, not 1/12, of a "foot" *chi*)

10 *cun* = 1 *chi* 尺 "foot": approximately 23 cm, or 9 inches

6 *chi* = 1 *bu* 步 "double-pace": approximately 1.4 m, or 54 inches

8 *chi* = 1 *xun* 尋 (or *ren* 仞) "fathom": Approximately 1.8 m, or 6 feet

10 *chi* = 1 *zhang* 丈: approximately 2.3 m, or 7½ feet

2 *xun* = 1 *chang* 常 "length": approximately 3.7 m, or 12 feet

4 *zhang* = 1 *pi* 匹 "bolt": approximately 9.2 m, or 30 feet (the length of a standard [2 foot wide] bolt of silk for tax purposes)

1 *li* 里: approximately 0.4 km, or 1/3 mile

Area

1 *mu* (or *mou*) 畝: approximately 67 square meters, or 1/6 acre (7,300 square feet)

100 *mu* = 1 *qing* 頃: approximately 6,700 square meters (6.7 hectares), or 16.7 acres

Focus: A protest song from the *Book of Odes*

In addition to stately hymns celebrating the deeds of long-ago rulers (see Focus: A Zhou ancestral hymn from the *Book of Odes*, in Chapter 6), the *Book of Odes* contains a number of folk songs. These were allegedly heard and written down by officials paying attention to what the common people were saying, and singing, though in fact they might have been composed by members of the elite writing in a folk-song mode. It was widely believed within the ruling class that folk songs provided important evidence of the mood of the people, and that songs of protest or complaint should prompt the ruler to examine his policies and make necessary improvements. The song "Boss Rat" is a famous example of a protest against excessive taxation.

"Boss Rat"

Boss Rat, Boss Rat,
Don't eat our millet.
Three years now we've been dealing with you,
Not that we get a bit of appreciation.
It's time for us to be leaving you,
To go to a happy place—
Happy place, happy place,
Where there will be some place for us.

Boss Rat, Boss Rat,
Don't eat our wheat.
Three years now we've been dealing with you,
Not that you ever give us a thing in return.
It's time for us to be leaving you,
To go to a happy land—
Happy land, happy land,
Where we can get some rest.

Boss Rat, Boss Rat,
Don't eat our seedlings.
Three years now we've been dealing with you,
Not that you ever think how hard we work.
It's time for us to be leaving you,
To go to a happy town—
Happy town, happy town,
Where we won't always have to groan.

The *Book of Odes*, Mao Ode 113

10 The Western Han dynasty through the reign of Emperor Wu

Introduction

Despite the brevity of its existence, the Qin dynasty had an enormous influence on later Chinese dynasties right up to the end of the imperial period. The fifteen years of the Qin served as a kind of prelude to the Han dynasty, which (with a brief interruption) ruled China for over four centuries—a remarkable achievement. Like the Zhou, the Han dynasty is divided into western and eastern phases, and for the same reason: the relocation of the capital from the west (near Xi'an) to the east (near Luoyang). The Western, or Former, Han spans the years from 206 BCE to 7 CE; the Eastern (or Latter) Han ran from 25 CE to 220 CE.

The founder of the Han, Emperor Gao, succeeded in overthrowing the Qin monarchy, but he adopted most of the Qin model of government, which had carried out the reforms of Lord Shang, chancellor Lü Buwei, and chancellor Li Si to such good effect. Emperor Gao also made some significant changes to the Qin model, most notably the re-establishment of regional kingdoms. That proved to be a mistake, though perhaps a necessary one at the time (because Liu Bang's allies expected to be suitably rewarded with kingdoms in return for their loyalty), and the Han government later had to devote significant resources to undo the system of kingdoms and return to the model of Qin centralism.

The Han expanded the territory under its jurisdiction, especially in the south, the northwest, and the northeast. The northern frontier, however, was plagued by the raiding and encroachment of the Xiongnu tribal confederation that controlled the steppelands. For decades, one emperor after another tried to buy peace by the regular (and humiliating) payment of bribes to their northern enemy, but that proved to be insufficient to curb the ambitions of the Xiongnu khans. Finally the fifth Han sovereign, Emperor Wu (the "Martial Emperor"), inflicted a decisive defeat on the Xiongnu, paving the way for the opening of the Silk Road to Central Asia and beyond. An era of domestic peace, new administrative efficiency, good communications networks (inherited from Qin and expanded by Han), and a rising merchant class created spectacular wealth, visible in a number of excavated Han imperial or elite tombs.

The early decades of the Han dynasty were distinguished by a thriving intellectual and literary climate. With great effort, many classic works lost during the Qin Period were restored and commentaries on such works began to be written. Earlier strands of cosmological speculation were augmented with new ideas and woven into a comprehensive and intellectually satisfying explanation of how the world works. Poetry flourished, with poems being composed in new styles and genres by identifiable authors. A number of writers attempted to synthesize philosophical works of the Warring States Period, contributing to debates on what kind of political philosophy was appropriate for the newly constituted empire. And China's first comprehensive work of history, the *Records of the Grand Historian* (*Shiji*), was produced by the father-and-son team of Sima Tan and Sima Qian. That work, along with Ban Gu's *History of the [Former] Han Dynasty* (*Han shu*), completed in the late first century CE, gives us a rich account of the Han era. Along with copious archaeological evidence, including many excavated texts, these works allow scholars to frame a quite detailed picture of Han history. The Western Han dynasty, and especially the reign of Emperor Wu, justifiably persists in historical memory as one of the high points in the long history of the Chinese empire.

The struggle to succeed Qin

In the chaotic years following the death of the First Emperor of Qin, with popular uprisings raging in many parts of the country, two rebel leaders stood out: Liu Bang and Xiang Yu. Both were southerners, from the former state of Chu, but there the resemblance ended. Liu Bang was a commoner who had held a minor official post, roughly akin to a bailiff, in the Qin administration. Xiang Yu, in contrast, was from a distinguished elite Chu family whose members had devoted themselves to military service for several generations. Of all the rebel leaders, Xiang Yu, assisted by his uncle Xiang Liang, seemed the most likely to inherit the mandate of Qin. A number of other rebels joined forces with Xiang Yu, greatly strengthening the military resources available for the battle against Qin's loyalist armed forces. Liu Bang became a formal ally of Xiang Liang and Xiang Yu early in 208 BCE.

One telling feature of the multi-pronged rebellion against Qin was the refounding of several of the old territorial states. In effect, this was returning China back to what most people of the time would have thought of as normal. The bureaucratic centralism of Qin, in long hindsight, strikes us as a natural development because it set the tone for imperial regimes for the next 2,000 years and more, but at the end of the third century BCE it must have seemed radically new, experimental, and not terribly successful. Everyone was used to the pre-Qin multi-state system. The conquered peoples resented being identified as Qin. Accordingly, various rebel leaders set themselves up as lords of Yan, Qi, Hann, Wei, Zhao, and other states. Xiang Liang and Xiang Yu restored the kingdom of Chu in 208 BCE, placing a survivor of that state's old ruling family on the throne as their puppet. Liu Bang took the title king of Han in 206 BCE, and that date is generally regarded as the foundation of the Han dynasty, although four more years of fighting would elapse before he was secure on the throne.

The years 208–206 BCE were marked by fierce battles between rebel armies and Qin imperial troops. Xiang Liang was killed in battle and Xiang Yu's status as leader of the rebel forces was endangered when the main part of his army became bottled up in a town called Julu, besieged by a Qin army under General Zhang Han. With the aid of Xiang Yu's allies the siege was broken and the Qin army suffered heavy casualties. Xiang Yu, who was acquiring a well-deserved reputation for ruthlessness, arranged for the execution of his ally, the Chu general Song Yi, for being ineffective in his efforts to relieve the siege of Julu, thereby removing a potential rival. He then had the puppet king of Chu murdered and took the kingship for himself, reviving the old Spring and Autumn Period title of *ba*, "hegemon," and claiming the allegiance of eighteen territorial states.

Liu Bang, meanwhile, had succeeded in entering the heavily fortified area "within the passes" in late 207 BCE, and occupied the Qin capital at Xianyang, where the hapless king of Qin, the third and last ruler of the Qin empire, surrendered to him. Liu Bang then expected to be recognized as king of Qin, by prior agreement with Xiang Yu. Instead, Xiang Yu arrived in Xianyang with his army, pushing Liu Bang aside. Xiang Yu had the young Qin monarch killed and allowed his troops to loot the city; they also pillaged the underground army of terra-cotta warriors at the tomb of the First Emperor, using the real weapons buried with the clay figures to replenish their own arsenal. The confrontation between Liu Bang and Xiang Yu at Xianyang turned the allies into enemies, and it was clear that one or the other would emerge as the heir to Qin's mandate.

Each side spent the early months of 206 BCE lining up allies and preparing for the showdown to come. Liu Bang gathered his troops and advanced on Pengcheng, Xiang Yu's capital city; Liu succeeded in taking the city, but then found himself trapped in it and besieged in turn as Xiang Yu evacuated his troops. The ensuing battle was a disaster for Liu Bang, who was lucky to escape with a small cavalry escort. Xiang Yu followed up by taking the city of Xingyang, near the last great bend of the Yellow River where it enters the Yellow River Plain. Once again Liu Bang was defeated and was lucky to escape. But Xiang Yu was unable to press on into the stoutly defended area within the passes and, meanwhile, Liu Bang's general Han Xin was winning back substantial territories in the north. (In 203 BCE Han Xin would be rewarded with the title king of Qi.) The two sides then tried to negotiate a peace. Xiang Yu offered to settle matters in single-handed combat with Liu Bang; Liu declined. Then they reached an agreement to divide the empire, with Liu Bang taking the west and Xiang Yu the east. But proposed solution was merely a breathing spell. At the end of 202 BCE the two armies met at Kaixia, in present-day Anhui Province. The ensuing battle went badly for Xiang Yu. He managed to break through Liu Bang's encircling forces, only to commit suicide when he was clear of the battlefield. Liu Bang emerged as the undisputed ruler of China and was known as Han Gaodi, the "High Emperor of Han."

The energy, ambition, leadership skills, bravery, and charisma that led to Liu Bang's victory over his rivals—including the formidable Xiang Yu—continued to guide his steps as emperor. His promises, during the civil wars, to mitigate the hated legal code of Qin turned out to be simply propaganda; the Qin code was maintained almost unchanged during the early Han. He did, however, proclaim a general amnesty, emptying the prisons of convicts in an act of conspicuous benevolence designed to bolster his claim to the Mandate of Heaven. As emperor, Liu Bang also kept his promise to reduce taxes, a ploy to gain popular support. Another legacy of Qin was the identification of the Han dynasty with the Phase Water and its emblems, including the color black. The argument was that Qin never secured its hold on the Mandate, and so was not part of the conquest cycle of the Five Phases. In effect the Mandate was considered to have passed directly from Zhou (Fire, red) to Han. (This question would be reopened several decades later.) In this the emperor sought the advice of Confucian scholars such as Lu Jia, who advised the throne on proper etiquette and the timing and conduct of imperial rituals. The emperor had a reputation for being contemptuous of long-winded and overly ceremonious scholars, but he knew when to solicit, and act upon, learned advice.

Challenges to imperial authority

In the 115 years from the adoption by Liu Bang of the title "emperor" in 202 BCE to the death of Emperor Wu in 87 BCE five rulers occupied the Han imperial throne: Emperor Gao (Liu Bang), 202–195; Emperor Hui, 195–188; Emperor Wen, 180–157; Emperor Jing, 157–141, and Emperor Wu, 141–87. The trajectory of the Han dynasty, from civil war and uncertain prospects to territorial expansion, economic and military strength, and cultural brilliance, was set during the course of these five reigns.

Emperor Gao's death in 195 BCE ushered in fifteen years of instability, when it was by no means certain that the Han dynasty would last much longer than its predecessor, the Qin.

Emperor Gao was succeeded by his fifteen-year-old son Liu Ying, who reigned as Emperor Hui. Completely under the control of his mother, Empress Dowager Lü, the teenaged emperor accomplished nothing of note, although during his reign work progressed on the development and fortification of the new Han capital at Chang'an, not far from the Qin capital at Xianyang. Emperor Hui died in 188, and for the next eight years Empress Dowager Lü acted as regent for two underage heirs to the throne, neither of whom was formally installed as emperor. She came very close to replacing the ruling Liu clan with her own Lü clan before she died in 180 BCE.

The long reigns of Emperor Wen, Emperor Jing, and especially Emperor Wu allowed the dynasty to consolidate and stabilize its rule, laying the foundation for another three centuries of Han rule. Yet turbulence and danger were never far from the surface during the reigns of these early Han emperors. Three serious and, at times, nearly intractable problems repeatedly endangered the empire: the establishment of territorial kingdoms in a large part of the empire and the unruliness of their kings; disputes over succession to the throne; and hostile relations with the Xiongnu tribal confederation on the empire's northern borders.

The Han kingdoms

After his military victory over Xiang Yu Emperor Gao's first task was to stabilize the empire, which had suffered through nearly a decade of warfare. In doing so, Liu Bang seems to have been inspired by the agreement that he had made with Xiang Yu, but which was never implemented: a division of the empire. As that agreement had envisioned, Emperor Gao kept the western part of the former Qin empire for himself as the imperial domain and divided the eastern part into territorial kingdoms that he granted to his surviving senior allies. In some cases this amounted to no more than confirming their title to territory that they already controlled. In fact, the new emperor had little choice in the matter. He had won the empire not as the sole leader of a unified military force but rather as the head of a rather tenuous coalition of rebel leaders. Those leaders now expected to be suitably rewarded.

The division of a major portion of the empire into a collection of semi-independent kingdoms turned out to be inherently unstable, despite the measure of bureaucratic coherence provided by the commandery and county model of administration inherited from the Qin. Emperor Gao was left with the less productive and less populous interior portion of the empire (though the imperial domain did include the strategically crucial area within the passes), while the territorial kings divided up the fertile, heavily populated eastern lands watered by the Yellow, Yangzi, and Huai Rivers. Emperor Gao naturally wanted to exert as much control as possible over the kingdoms and their resources; the kings naturally resisted that control. Some proponents of decentralization hoped that it would bring a return to the idealized government of the Zhou founders King Wen and King Wu—that is, a royal domain surrounded by the territorial polities of loyal nobles who would protect and pay tribute to the central court. Instead, the situation reverted back to the more recent scenario of contending kingdoms.

To deal with this situation Emperor Gao applied steady pressure on the kings, reining them in one by one. Some were demoted from "kings" to the old Zhou rank of "lord" (*hou*) and made to live in the Han capital, following the earlier Qin mode of control. In response, some of the northernmost kingdoms switched their allegiance to the Xiongnu confederation, exacerbating the Xiongnu threat to the Heartland Region. The Xiongnu at that point had already taken advantage of the turmoil of the post-Qin civil wars to encroach on Chinese territory. Still other kings rose in open revolt and were defeated and killed. The upshot was that, by 195 BCE, all but one of Liu Bang's old allies-turned-kings had been ousted and replaced by members of the Liu family, such as the emperor's brothers, sons, nephews, and cousins. An imperial edict specified that henceforth only members of the Liu clan could be invested as territorial kings. In addition, some of the largest kingdoms were also broken up into two or more pieces.

The history of the kingdom of Huainan illustrates the problem of the territorial kingdoms in general. Huainan, a vast tract of territory extending southward from the Huai River in the east, was initially granted to Ying Bu, an old military ally of Liu Bang. Ying Bu rebelled in 196 BCE, igniting a war that would cost Emperor Gao his life. He was shot by an arrow while personally leading his troops to put down Ying Bu's rebellion and the wound became infected. The emperor died soon afterwards, but not before naming one of his numerous sons, Liu Chang, as the new king of Huainan.

It turned out that the eastern kingdoms so strongly valued their independence that even rulers belonging to the Liu clan wanted to be their own bosses. Liu Chang rebelled in 174 BCE, during the reign of Emperor Wen; the rebellion was put down and the erstwhile king died on the road to exile. The kingdom of Huainan was then abolished, only to be restored, much reduced in size, for the late king's son, Liu An, in 164 BCE. He in turn was accused of rebellion in 122 BCE, and committed suicide under duress. The kingdom of Huainan was then permanently abolished and absorbed into the imperial domain.

Emperor Gao's hope that restricting kingship to members of the Liu clan would induce them to act harmoniously and be supportive of the reigning emperor proved futile. The Liu clan territorial kings turned out to be as self-serving and fractious as the original non-Liu kings had been. In response, the central government began to take a harder line in dealing with the territorial kings. The senior advisor Jia Yi (201–169 BCE) was in many respects a proponent of Confucian social and ethical views, but he was also strongly committed to Qin-style centralism and urged Emperor Wen to resist the kings' self-aggrandizement. Chao Cuo (d. 154 BCE), who held high office under Emperor Jing, also forcefully argued for a strong empire. His warnings about the danger posed by the kings proved well founded when in 154 BCE the king of Wu, in concert with several other territorial kings, launched a large-scale rebellion that was serious enough to threaten the continued existence of the Han dynasty. The rebellion was defeated, however, and the rebel kings and their supporters were executed or exiled. That proved to be a turning point in the struggle between the centralizing and frag-menting tendencies in Han China. Although kingdoms continued to exist for the rest of the dynasty's history, by the end of the reign of Emperor Wu in 87 BCE they had been decisively reduced in number and area, and the power of the central imperial regime was never again seriously challenged by the territorial kings (Map 10.1 a–c).

The problem of succession

The death of Emperor Gao and the accession of his teenaged son and heir, Emperor Hui, were attended by a problem that was to vex the Chinese imperial state for centuries to come: a succession dispute. The problem was that the general practice, which held that the eldest son of the ruler's principal wife should be the heir to the throne, was merely a guideline, not a rule. The emperor could name his heir as he chose and rescind that appointment as he pleased. He also had absolute power to promote or demote his wives and concubines. The resulting uncertainty about the identity and status of the heir apparent resulted in a constant, and often literally murderous, competition among wives and concubines to advance the inter-ests of their sons. The accession of Emperor Hui shows this all too well.

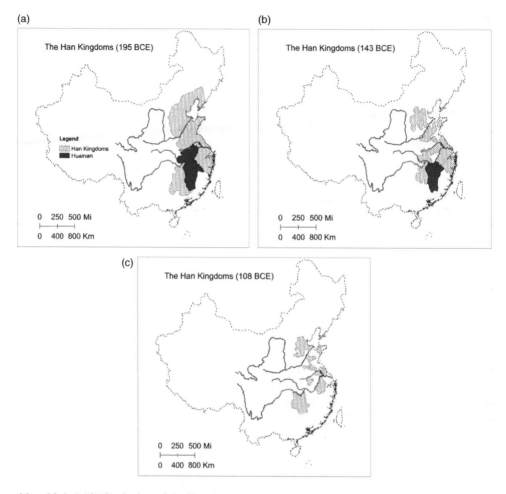

Map 10.1 At the beginning of the Han dynasty Emperor Gao rewarded his military supporters and imperial clansmen with semi-autonomous kingdoms in the eastern part of China. His successors gradually eliminated the kingdoms and annexed their territory to the imperial domain. The kingdom of Huainan, for example, was established in 203 BCE, transferred to one of Emperor Gao's sons in 196, abolished in 174, re-established (with much less territory) in 164, and permanently abolished in 122.

Emperor Gao had named as his heir Liu Ying, the future Emperor Hui, who, following tradition, was the son of Emperor Gao's principal wife, Empress Lü. But the emperor's favorite was actually another son, Liu Ruyi, the child of one of his concubines. Liu Ying is said to have been a delicate and timid child, whereas Ruyi was brave and robust, very much his father's son. A rumor began to circulate that the emperor was planning to demote Liu Ying and name Liu Ruyi as his heir instead, or even that he had already secretly done so. Nevertheless, when Emperor Gao died Liu Ying was installed as emperor, taking the title Emperor Hui. His mother, Empress Dowager Lü, decided to solidify his position (and her own) by eliminating possible rivals to her son. She arranged to have Liu Ruyi poisoned and his mother horribly disfigured and killed. She is also said to have had three other sons of Emperor Gao murdered to forestall any other attempts to challenge her son's grip on the throne. Emperor Hui, according to later accounts, was so horrified by his mother's actions that he sought refuge in alcohol. For whatever reason, he essentially took no part in affairs of state and let his mother rule.

Traditional historical narrative typically portrays politically adept or ambitious women as evil, and the tales about Empress Lü make her seem like a monster. By the time Emperor Hui died of unspecified causes in 188 BCE, at the age of twenty-two, she had almost completely marginalized the imperial Liu clan and named her Lü relatives to key positions in the government and the military. On the emperor's death she assumed the role of regent for first one and then another of the emperor's infant sons, neither of whom was formally installed as emperor, and the first of whom was probably murdered on her orders. While she refrained from taking the title *Huangdi* for herself, she was in all respects the ruler of China during the years 188–180 BCE. Hers was a turbulent reign, marked by Xiongnu incursions in the north and the rebellion of some of the Han kingdoms in the south.

When Empress Lü died in 180 BCE there were three serious candidates for the throne: the kings of Dai and Huainan, who were sons of Emperor Gao, and the king of Qi, who was the founding emperor's grandson. At first the king of Qi took matters in his own hands by leading an army into Chang'an and eliminating all relatives of the late Empress Lü who had been given offices or kingdoms during her reign; the Lü clan was effectively wiped out. After some jostling, which did not rise to the level of outright warfare, it was decided that the successor to Emperor Hui should be Liu Heng, the king of Dai, who took the throne as Emperor Wen. He and his two successors were to take the Han dynasty to a pinnacle of wealth, power, and cultural brilliance. Emperor Wen ruled for twenty-three years, Emperor Jing for sixteen years, and Emperor Wu for fifty-four years, lending much-needed stability to the dynasty's hold on power.

Emperor Wen bequeathed the throne to Liu Qi, his son by Empress Dou. Liu Qi reigned as Emperor Jing, after a transition that was unusually smooth and unmarked by violence. It may be that Emperor Wen heeded the good advice of the statesman/philosopher Jia Yi, who wrote a memorial to the throne emphasizing the importance of avoiding succession disputes. But trouble rose again in the selection of a successor to Emperor Jing. He had named as his heir Liu Rong, a son of Lady Li, a concubine whom Emperor Jing did not bother to promote to the rank of empress (possibly having taken heed of malicious advice). This left her son, the designated heir, in a precarious position. Lady Li was subjected to a vicious campaign of slander and Emperor Jing was forced to remove Liu Rong as heir apparent in 150 BCE. Lady Li is said to have then died of grief (poison seems more likely). Another son, Liu Che, was then named heir and Liu Rong was arrested two years later on trumped-up charges of desecrating the imperial tombs. He was allowed to commit suicide (a more honorable death than being torn apart by chariots).

On the death of Emperor Jing in 141 BCE Liu Che ascended the throne as Emperor Wu. His long reign was punctuated by the murder or suicide of several of his direct descendants. On his death in 87 BCE Emperor Wu was succeeded by a grandson, Emperor Zhao, then aged about seven or eight. He was the first of a series of underage rulers in the first century BCE, a state of affairs that seriously weakened the Han dynasty and indeed led to its temporary downfall.

The Xiongnu threat

The third chronic problem facing the early emperors of Han was the Xiongnu tribal confederation, which controlled a vast territory of steppelands, desert, and mountains north of the

Heartland Region and posed a constant threat to the Han empire's northern frontier. For much of the Han dynasty's first century the Han rulers were in the humiliating position of paying tribute to people whom they considered barbarians.

There has been a great deal of scholarly debate about the ethno-linguistic identity of the Xiongnu, leading to no firm conclusion. The most likely answer is that the term Xiongnu refers broadly to a confederation of culturally and linguistically diverse peoples, including both nomadic pastoralists and settled agriculturalists, who voluntarily or through coercion became part of a grand coalition of northern peoples. The Xiongnu khans and their principal military forces may have spoken a language related to Turkish. As many historical examples show, such confederations have arisen in the vast region of Central Asia either for common defense in response to a threat or in response to an opportunity to prey on weaker neighbors. In the case of the Xiongnu both seem to have been the case; tribes resisted the expansion of the Qin empire and then took advantage of the civil war after the fall of Qin to go on the offensive. Under their great khan Modun (elected to that office in 209 BCE) the Xiongnu recaptured extensive lands, including the Ordos region within the Great Bend of the Yellow River that had been incorporated into the Qin empire by General Meng Tian in 210 BCE. Thereafter, Xiongnu territory extended considerably to the south of the Qin Great Wall.

When Liu Bang proclaimed himself Emperor Gao of Han in 202 BCE he immediately had to consider how to deal with this large, powerful, and aggressive northern neighbor. The northern frontier was vast and difficult to defend; besides, stabilizing the dynasty's control of the Heartland Region necessarily took priority. The upshot was that in 198 BCE Emperor Gao concluded a treaty with Modun specifying that relations between the Han and Xiongnu empires would henceforth be based on the principle of "harmonious kinship" (*heqin*); that is, the Chinese and the Xiongnu rulers should be brothers. But in fact the treaty was unequal; it provided for the payment by the Han emperor of what amounted to a bribe in return for peace. The Han emperor agreed to send an annual embassy that would deliver to the Xiongnu khan tribute including grain, silk, bronze, and various luxury goods. This, for the Chinese, was a shameful reversal of the normal situation in which submissive "barbarians" should offer tribute to the Son of Heaven. A later addition to the treaty specified that a Chinese imperial princess, as a bride for the khan, should be included among the tribute goods. This was, strangely enough, a face-saving measure for the Han ruler; any son that the princess might bear to the khan would be a grandson of the Chinese emperor, and thus obliged to acknowledge the emperor as his superior. But there is no evidence that the Xiongnu were impressed by that argument.

The trouble with the "harmonious kinship" policy, from the Chinese point of view, was that the principle of "peace in return for tribute" did not in fact bring peace. This was not just a matter of small-scale frontier raiding, which might have been a tolerable nuisance; the Xiongnu khans also continued to commit large-scale invasion forces to seize and hold territory. Major invasions in 177, 166, and 158 BCE had to be met with the commitment of tens of thousands of Chinese troops. With every incursion Xiongnu demands for more and better tribute increased. Chao Cuo, who had argued for taking a hard line against the eastern territorial kings, was also a hawk with respect to the Xiongnu. He advocated a reorganization of the Han armed forces, emphasizing cavalry and well-trained, crossbow-equipped infantry, as well as clear-headed strategic thinking. Adopting a more vigorous stance in dealing with the Xiongnu appealed to Emperor Wu, who, shortly after his enthronement in 141 BCE, dispatched a trusted official, Zhang Qian, on a diplomatic mission to the far northwest (see Focus: The travels of Zhang Qian). His mission was to make contact with another pastoral tribe, the Yuezhi, and conclude an anti-Xiongnu alliance with them, thus pressuring the

Xiongnu on two sides. When, after many adventures and difficulties, Zhang Qian succeeded in reaching the Yuezhi, they turned out to have no interest in such an alliance, but the intelligence that Zhang Qian gathered in the course of his travels proved useful in the formulation of foreign policy under Emperor Wu. Meanwhile, the emperor convened two formal court debates, in 135 and 134 BCE, to discuss the question of the Xiongnu, with two prominent statesmen presenting the case for each side of the question. Han Anguo argued in favor of continuing the *heqin* policy, whereas Wang Hui advocated a strong military response to what he portrayed as Xiongnu treachery. The emperor was in favor of military action and, while the first attempt to lure the Xiongnu into a trap ended with the disastrous defeat of the Chinese army in the Battle of Mayi (134 BCE), in the longer term the military option was decisive. Emperor Wu was about to earn his title: the "Martial Emperor."

The 130s BCE saw a number of battles between Han and Xiongnu forces, but no major campaigns. Emperor Wu and his military advisors used those years mainly to strengthen China's military forces along the northern frontier. This involved creating and training larger cavalry units; establishing garrison farms in forward positions along the frontier; augmenting and strengthening fortifications and linking them with beacon fires to permit rapid responses to border raids; creating and stocking granaries to support military operations in the north; and producing weapons in quantity. The disaster at Mayi showed that the Chinese forces still needed improvement before taking on the Xiongnu. Sustained military operations began in 129 BCE and continued for some twenty-five years. Some of the most famous generals in Chinese history, including Huo Qubing, Li Guang, Wei Qing, and Cheng Bushi, came to prominence on northern battlefields. Although the Chinese forces suffered some expensive defeats during the northern campaigns, on the whole the situation went against the Xiongnu. By 119 BCE the northern frontier of the Han empire had been pushed northward toward the old line of Qin control, and the Han court ceased payment of tribute to the Xiongnu khans.

The second decade of the northern campaigns was aimed not only at consolidating these achievements but also at smashing the Xiongnu empire and eliminating its ability to threaten China's northern frontier. Economic reforms, such as the creation of an imperial monopoly on salt and iron in 119 BCE, increased the ability of the Han empire to finance the northern campaigns. With the weakening of the Xiongnu a final series of military actions succeeded in bringing the northwestern Gansu Corridor under Han administration, denying Xiongnu access to the trade routes between Chang'an and the oasis cities of Central Asia. Although the final submission of the Xiongnu would not come until 51 BCE, under the reign of Emperor Xuan, Han power in the northern and northwestern frontiers of the Extended Heartland Region was nearly unchallenged on the eve of the first century BCE. The establishment of regular, imperially sanctioned trade along the Silk Road from about 105 BCE onwards testified to the Han ability to project imperial power far out into Central Asia.

Governing the empire

During the reigns of Emperors Gao and Hui government bureaucracy remained largely unchanged from that of Qin, as the effort to stabilize and consolidate the empire effectively precluded substantial reforms or initiatives. Some of the most extreme forms of capital punishment were abolished, a general amnesty was declared, and the tax on farm produce, collected in grain and silk, was set at one-fifteenth of the value of the crop. These measures seem to have been efforts to portray the Han dynasty as more humane than the Qin. The Han government began to put its own stamp on administrative structures and public policy during the reigns of Emperors Wen and Jing, and Han reforms came to full fruition under Emperor Wu. In 168 BCE the rate of taxation on produce, collected in grain and silk, was cut in half, to one-thirtieth of the value of the crops. Other tax and service obligations remained unchanged; there was a per capita tax of 120 coins on adults (with lesser amounts on children); corvée service of one month per year; and compulsory military service of two years for adult males. Still other taxes were levied on the transport of mercantile goods and on sales of goods in markets. Even with taxes set at fairly modest rates, government revenues soared as domestic peace (disturbed but not seriously disrupted by rebellious kingdoms and aggressive Xiongnu) prevailed. The imperial domain increased in size with the expansion of the empire and the repatriation of territorial kingdoms, and improvements in agricultural practices included the more widespread use of iron tools. Such developments contributed to the growth of government revenue.

Although the state was fairly wealthy the economy was strained by Emperor Wu's expensive military policies—not only the long-term campaign to defeat the Xiongnu but also separate campaigns to expand the empire in the northwest, the southwest, the southeast, and into northern Korea. Measures taken to increase revenue included the creation of government monopolies on the production of salt and iron in 119 BCE and a less successful attempt, in 98 BCE, to monopolize the production of alcoholic beverages (later revised to the levying of an excise tax on them), along with increases in taxes on markets and transport. A new coin, the *wushu*, was introduced in 120 BCE, and soon eclipsed the larger half-ounce (*banliang*) coin that had been introduced during the Qin dynasty. Shortly thereafter, in 113 BCE, the government took over all minting of coinage. At the same time that the government attempted to squeeze more revenue from the populace there was a rise in "banditry" by groups of roving outlaws and malcontents.

The dynamic tension between central and local governments was inherent in the government structure. The senior personnel in the local commanderies and counties were appointed by the high ministers in Chang'an. This was also the case in the territorial kingdoms, especially during the reign of Emperor Jing, who wanted more control over the territorial kings and replaced many of them with his own sons. Although the emperor, the Heaven-ordained ruler, was the center of the government the high officials around him really ran the country. Next in power to the emperor was the chancellor. He, in turn, was aided by a variety of deputies and assistants. There were also military officials and various types of tutor and master, offices that date back to the Western Zhou Period. Then there were nine ministers of state who directly supervised military, civil, and ritual affairs and interfaced with the territorial rulers. Each minister ran a bureaucracy of officers in charge of the nitty-gritty of these affairs, running the legal and tax systems and overseeing other officials in charge of granaries, agricultural work, natural resources, handicrafts, and other supplies. The lowest level of administration, the commanderies and counties, were responsible for the local populations, solving criminal cases, and collecting taxes. They also maintained population registers that provided details on local residents, such as how many males, females, slaves, etc. resided together on which properties. Such data could be used to resolve legal suits as well as to assess the per capita tax and corvée and military service obligations.

The relative wealth that came with the expansion of the empire and its population caused the development of a burgeoning and complex government structure that created a strong demand for literate officials at all levels. The recruitment and training of young elite men became a priority under Emperor Wu. At the very beginning of his reign he issued an edict calling for senior officials to nominate suitable candidates for office. This method of recruitment was renewed several times during his reign. Nominated candidates were supposed to be

questioned in the presence of the emperor to demonstrate their abilities and personal characteristics. In 136 BCE the central government appointed a number of so-called Erudites, official academicians with demonstrated expertise in ancient texts. Very significantly, the texts in
question were those associated with the Confucian tradition, including the *Book of Odes*
(*Shijing*), the *Book of Documents* (*Shujing*), the *Book of Changes* (*Yijing*), the *Ritual Records*
(*Liji*), and the *Springs and Autumns* (*Chunqiu*). The duties of the Erudites included advising
the throne, when so ordered, on issues of ritual, historical precedents, the correct form of
documents, and the like; they also were responsible for training disciples who would be
expected to become members of the official bureaucracy. These measures—the oral examination of candidates in the imperial audience hall, and the establishment of what amounted to
an academy for the training of candidate officials—laid the foundation for the examination
system that was a hallmark of Chinese bureaucratic administration throughout the imperial
period. The fact that the training of candidates was placed in the hands of experts in Confucian texts would shape the ideological stance of Chinese education, and the nature of governments served by academy graduates, for centuries to come.

Imperial rites and religion

Much as the First Emperor of Qin had performed the *feng* sacrifice, which involved cre-
atively reinventing ancient rituals symbolic of former ages, the Han emperors also sought to
express legitimacy through their connection to sacred history and the supernatural. Religious advisors to the emperors would recommend particular rites, including some that, once
performed, are never mentioned in the dynastic histories again. However, certain sacrifices
were regularly performed over many reigns. For example, the "suburban sacrifice" was celebrated in a special area outside the city walls. This rite helped the emperor to establish his
authority with the spirits of Heaven and Earth near the capital. In addition, sacrifices were
performed occasionally on peaks such as Mt. Hua or the more distant Mt. Tai. Other important annual ceremonies involved processions of officials. For example, the public exorcism
ritual called the Nuo included hundreds of officials uttering spells, specially chosen young
eunuchs, twelve of whom were dressed as animals, carrying torches and hand drums, and a
chief exorcist wearing a bear skin with the head fashioned into a mask featuring four golden
eyes. The goal of this event was to sweep the city of ghosts, which would be attracted to the
torches and follow the procession; eventually they would be drowned when the torches were
thrown into a river.

A critical aspect of imperial worship involved sophisticated rounds of sacrifices performed
in memory of one royal ancestor or another. In addition, because of the influence of Confucian advisors, lineages of male and female ancestors would be worshipped as expressions of
filial piety. Of course, the lineages included in the sacrifices, and the particular ancestors
chosen to be remembered, reflected power relationships within the Han court. At times certain ancestors, even past emperors and empresses, were quietly retired to make way for new
lineage priorities.

The imperial ancestral temples at Yong in the Wei River Valley were centers of religious
activity. No doubt reflecting an ancient tradition, liturgies were devised to integrate the worship of nature and cosmic forces with ancestor worship practices at Yong. In 205 BCE
Emperor Gao, while still only king of Han, set up a hall for the worship of the Thearch (*di*)
of the North (linked to the Han by the Phase Water and the color black) to complement existing halls to the Thearchs of the East, South, West, and Center. This allowed the emperors to
integrate abstract and up-to-date cosmology with the traditional worship of royal ancestors,

thus providing an extra layer of legitimacy for their rule. By identifying with the Phase Water and its symbolic connotations and supernatural powers of North and Black, the Han emperors clearly positioned themselves as the rightful heirs of the idealized Zhou dynasty (unlike the discredited Qin). Worship of the Five Thearchs—deifications of the four cardinal directions plus the center—continued throughout most of the Western Han Period, but died out thereafter.

Emperors Hui, Wen, and Jing avoided religious innovations, but Emperor Wu pursued them with enthusiasm. At the instigation of his Confucian advisors (and based on a possibly spurious chapter of the *Book of Documents*), he made preparations to perform the legendary *feng* and *shan* sacrifices on Mt. Tai and other sacred peaks to make contact with the spirits of Heaven and Earth and to serve as proof of his legitimate rule. He succeeded in 110 BCE, and again several times thereafter. Some of these ceremonies were colorful extravaganzas at the base of the mountains and others secret occult sacrifices on a peak with only one or two aides as witnesses. As Qin Shihuangdi had done a century earlier, Emperor Wu relied on his ritual specialists to recreate, as best they could, these long-forgotten rites. Acting on the advice of freelance religious practitioners, during the first two decades of his reign he instituted imperial cults directed at the God of the Soil, the Kitchen God, and the high cosmic power Taiyi, the Great Undifferentiated Unity. These eventually took precedence over the expensive *feng* and *shan* sacrifices, which involved travel, mountain climbing, and the preparation of special costumes and numerous sacrificial animals and jades.

One of the most protracted debates about religious matters during the Western Han concerned the exact nature of the suburban sacrifice, a rite considered important owing to its mention in early texts such as the *Springs and Autumns*. The emperors wished to perform this sacrifice, like many other ancient and barely remembered rites, not only to prove their connection to the past but also to satisfy their contemporary politico-religious needs. Emperor Wen performed the suburban sacrifice in 165 BCE and again in 164; the rites were directed at the Five Thearchs representing deified natural forces rather than at pre-Han ancestors. Emperor Jing performed a similar sacrifice in 144 BCE; Emperor Wu performed the suburban sacrifice in 134 and 123 BCE and on six other occasions during the course of his long reign. In each case there was an unsettled quality to the performance in terms of both its timing and the spirits to be worshipped. Dong Zhongshu (179–104 BCE), a Confucian expert in the *Springs and Autumns*, argued passionately that the suburban sacrifice should be at the start of the New Year and directed towards Heaven. The emperor was to present a sacrifice as if to a patrilineal ancestor, full of filial piety. This would connect the emperor to the ancient Zhou king's role as Son of Heaven. Dong's arguments did not at first succeed in convincing the emperor and his religious officials to define the ritual as he advised them to, but his arguments were later accepted as part of a religious reform in 31 BCE that established the worship of Heaven as the paramount religious obligation of Chinese emperors. That standard continued throughout the rest of the imperial period.

How the sacrifices were performed no doubt incorporated aspects of ancient rituals handed down by Zhou kings and their advisors over the course of generations, but they included many new details added by rulers during the Warring States Period. In general, Han practice seems consistent with what we know of Zhou sacrificial rituals. A key element in the worship of both ancestors and nature deities was the presentation of freshly slaughtered animals to the gods. The type and number of animals, as well as the methods by which they were slaughtered and the types of vessels used to present them at altars, reflected social hierarchy. Sacrifices were displays of wealth and power. Animals included specially raised cattle, horses, and dogs of different colors and ages. Wild animals, such as different types of deer, were also sacrificed.

Animals were usually dismembered and placed in bronze and lacquerware vessels of different shapes on an altar, along with offerings of grain and millet ale. Prayers and songs were chanted; rows of dancers performed particular choreographies to musical sets played on percussion, string, and wind instruments. Officers in charge of the food service, the guests, and the music were on hand as guides to assist the celebrants. These basic contours of the ceremonial performance can be traced back to earlier texts, but subtle details, such as the types of costume, musical set, choreographed dance, sacrificial furniture and other props must have varied over time. Likewise, the ways in which the sacrifices were performed outside the city gates, inside shrines, and on mountaintops must have each been different in significant details.

One clear difference from the early times was a change in how time was understood and recorded. Anciently, the seasons and the endlessly repeating sixty-day cycle were the primary determinants of when to perform sacrifices. By Han times technical advances in astronomy, mathematics, and record keeping led to calls for more detailed calendars. In 104 BCE Emperor Wu promulgated a reformed calendar, the *Taichu* ("Grand Inception") calendar. As a Son of Heaven the emperor had the exclusive right, and also the duty, to publish a calendar, showing that his government was attuned to the rhythms of the cosmos and that he was capable of reading its signs. Even Zhou kings restarted the calendar each time a new king came to the throne. Han officials of the imperial bureau of astronomy devised a calendar that not only kept track of days and months but also predicted lunar and solar eclipses and the positions of the five naked-eye-visible planets with unprecedented accuracy.

In addition to imperial religious observances, local versions of court practices spread with the elite and absorbed regional and local religious networks. Not only did the elite maintain the shrines to local deities and nature spirits but they also commemorated their lineage ancestors, raising them to the status of local deified heroes and marking them with texts carved on stone stelae. The types of god included old categories such as earth (e.g. mountain, river, swamp), astral (e.g. stars, constellations, lunar and calendrical), agricultural (legendary figures such as Shen Nong, the Divine Farmer, Hou Ji (Lord Millet), and Yu the Great), residence (e.g. Gate, Hallway, Earth Altar, Kitchen), and other deities, but increasingly also "immortals"—men (and some women) who were reputed to have achieved states of "no-death."

The cult of immortality, already visible in late Warring States times, became more widespread during the Han as "masters of methods" (*fangshi*) advocated various means of achieving long life or immunity to death. These methods included breathing exercises, calisthenics and other yoga-like practices, elixirs, special diets, and meditation. Emperor Wu was at the forefront of the cult of immortality, and apparently welcomed dozens, or perhaps hundreds, of "masters of methods" to advise him on how to reach that goal. Popular lore of later times portrays Emperor Wu as having made a spirit-journey to the realm of Xiwangmu, the Dowager Queen of the West, a mountain goddess associated with the Kunlun mountains and with methods of attaining immortality. Apparently Emperor Wu had become so adept at the skills of a budding immortal (including flying and the ability to become invisible) that he was invited by the goddess to spend the night with her at the Turquoise Pond. The Kunlun Mountains functioned as a mythical omphalos, an axis of the universe and gateway from earth into Heaven. Imitating Qin Shihuangdi, Emperor Wu also sent a maritime expedition out into the Pacific Ocean in search of the magical realm of Penglai. Likewise, the seekers never returned.

Imperial and elite tombs

The Confucian practice of demonstrating filial piety by giving one's parents a lavish funeral and richly furnished tomb was embraced enthusiastically by members of the Han elite

(Figure 10.1). Phenomenally rich upper-elite tombs—burial places of Han emperors and territorial kings—testify to the wealth of the Western Han empire. Several such tombs have been scientifically excavated, giving a vivid picture of life at the pinnacle of Han society. Outstanding examples are found all over the realm, from the south in Hunan to the north in Shaanxi, the northeast in Hebei, and the southeast in Jiangsu.

Three burials at Mawangdui

Near Changsha in present-day Hunan a family burial ground for a local ruler includes three massive and wealthy tombs. The tombs (numbered in order of their excavation) consist of deep stepped pits furnished with massive wooden chambers containing, in separate spaces, the bodies of the deceased and various tomb offerings. Each tomb was surmounted by a substantial mound. Tomb 2 was that of the Lord of Dai (d. 186 BCE), chancellor to the king of Changsha; that tomb was comprehensively looted at some point and its contents stolen or spoiled. Tomb 1 was that of his widow, the Lady of Dai. Her tomb was astonishingly well preserved, the

Figure 10.1 Wooden tomb figure with silk clothing from a Western Han tomb at Mashan, Jiangling, Hubei Province. Western Han tombs often contain extensive retinues of clay or wooden figures representing officials, soldiers, and servants.

wooden tomb chamber having been surrounded by layers of white clay and charcoal that created an anaerobic environment that inhibited the deterioration of organic material. The body of the Lady of Dai herself was so well preserved that it was possible to conduct a complete autopsy on the corpse. (She apparently suffered from various ailments, including parasitic worms and the chronic effects of an overly rich diet, and had been in ill health for some time before dying in her fifties of a heart attack.) The corpse, heavily wrapped in silk garments, rested in the innermost of three beautifully painted lacquered coffins. In various compartments of the wooden tomb chamber were many lacquerware boxes and trays containing food, medicinal herbs, and cosmetics, along with other grave goods, including small wooden statues of attendants (Figure 10.2). The most remarkable find was a painted silk banner, apparently carried in the funeral procession and then draped over the innermost coffin, depicting the Lady of Dai's after-death journey (see Focus: The Mawangdui funerary banner).

Tomb 3, also well preserved, was the resting place of a fairly young man (d. 168 BCE) thought to be a son of the Lord and Lady of Dai. Although this tomb contained a funerary banner similar to that in Tomb 1 it is best known for its large library of texts written on silk, many of them previously unknown, except for versions of the *Changes* (*Zhouyi*) and the *Laozi Daodejing*. Among the other texts were medical manuscripts describing a variety of healing methods, including magical practices, exercises, breath control, sexual techniques, minor surgery, and adjusting the balance of yin and yang *qi* coursing throughout the body. The young man's tomb also contained three maps depicting rivers, mountains, and trading posts to the south and a chart showing different kinds of comets and how to interpret them as astral omens when contemplating military or other maneuvers. Texts from Tomb 3 at Mawangdui comprised the first of many buried troves of texts that would increasingly shape the field of early China studies (Figure 10.3).

The tomb of Emperor Jing

The mausoleums for the Han emperors are spread over the Wei River Valley, especially to the west of Chang'an (modern Xi'an). At Yangling archaeologists excavated the pits on the

Figure 10.2 A set of five wooden musicians from Mawangdui Tomb 1, some of the many wooden attendants found in the tomb of the Lady of Dai.

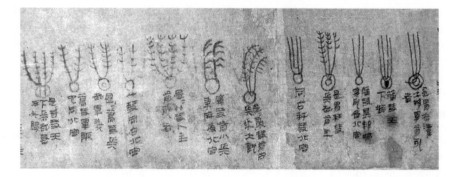

Figure 10.3 Detail of an omen text depicting comets of various kinds and describing how to interpret them, a silk text from Mawangdui Tomb 3, Changsha, Hunan Province, c. 168 BCE.

periphery of the tomb mound for Emperor Jing (157–141 BCE); the main tomb has yet to be opened. But, just as in the case of the First Emperor of Qin's tomb, the tomb's accompanying pits contained a fascinating array of goods: a procession of hundreds of clay models of cattle, pigs, and other animals, depicted at about one-third life-size, and a procession of clay human figures, at the same scale, showing servants, military officers, eunuchs, horsemen, northern warriors (identified by their prominent cheek-bones), and others. The human figures once sported articulated wooden arms and silk robes. The outer pits also contained bronze and clay vessels and a variety of other grave goods. The size, number, and variety of clay human and animal participants in the buried mortuary procession stunningly reflects the prestige of the deceased emperor, the "One Man" at the pinnacle of the Han world.

The tomb of Liu Sheng

Emperor Jing installed his son, Liu Sheng, as king of Zhongshan (d. 113 BCE). Liu Sheng and his wife Dou Wan were buried together in present-day Mancheng County, Hebei Province. Their tomb represents a departure from the traditional style of a vertical pit with nested coffins. Liu Sheng and Dou Wan were buried in a catacomb-style tomb cut out of rock and built with many chambers to imitate a palace. Tombs dug horizontally into mountains or constructed out of brick or stone proved to be more economical and easy to fill than the massive vertical pit tombs of old, and they could easily be reopened as needed to add another body. Their tomb was filled with treasures, including more than 400 bronze objects. Like the tomb itself, some of the objects represented a mix of northern and southern artistic styles, such as a set of bronze leopard-shaped paperweights inlaid with gold and with eyes of red gemstones. Other objects are typical of goods commonly found in rich Han tombs, such as a gilt bronze lamp in the shape of a kneeling servant and an incense burner shaped like Kunlun or Penglai, the legendary mountains of immortals (Figure 10.4). The tomb also contained almost 500 iron tools and weapons, six chariots, more than 500 pottery objects, and lesser amounts of lacquer, gold, and silver. But the tomb is most famous for the full-body jade burial suits worn by both Liu Sheng and Dou Wan. Made of small plaques of jade fastened together with gold wire, the suits were intended to prevent the corpses from decaying (Figure 10.5). In addition, the orifices of the corpses were plugged with jade. Although the belief in the efficacy of jade seems

Figure 10.4 Incense burner of bronze inlaid with gold in the form of a mountain, representing the abode of immortals.

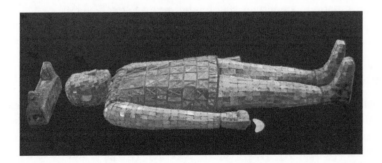

Figure 10.5 Jade burial suit of Dou Wan, Mancheng, Hebei Province, c. 112 BCE. The bodies of Dou Wan and her husband Liu Sheng were completely encased in jade, evidently in an attempt to keep them from decaying.

to have been widespread, the bodies in horizontal tombs did not survive the ravages of time as well as those in hermetically sealed pit tombs, such as have been found in the south.

The influence of this style of tomb—a horizontal stone tomb with the deceased in a jade suit sewn together with silk bands and threads—is seen in the unplundered tomb of Zhao Mo, king of Nanyue (r. 137–122 BCE), far to the south in modern Guangzhou city. The bronzes, pottery, and jade (and sacrificial humans) reveal collections of artifacts and the perpetuation of old traditions from the Heartland area. Even objects from the steppes, often found in northern tombs, were included among the grave goods in this far-southern tomb. Seals written in Chinese testify to the diplomatic relations linking this ancient Viet king with the Chinese empire. But other objects reveal that this king also benefited from trade with peoples in the Persian-speaking western regions and to the south in modern Vietnam.

Methods for trying to ward off decay extended beyond sewing together myriad jade tiles into a suit to carving entire coffins out of jade. Liu Fei, king of Jiangdu (169–128 BCE), was another son of Emperor Jing's who was made a regional king. His tomb, complete with a jade coffin and tons of coins, was recently discovered in present-day Xuyi County, Jiangsu Province. The tomb contained model and life-size chariots, weapons, lamps, and so forth, in quantities befitting a king. He is best known for suppressing rebellions and for his association with one of the Han Period's most famous Confucian scholars, Dong Zhongshu, who was appointed by Emperor Wu to serve as Liu Fei's chancellor in the mid-130s BCE. The emperor may have hoped that Dong's Confucian beliefs would restrain Liu Fei's hawkish views on military matters.

The Western Han focus on mortuary culture reflects the era's strong belief in the afterlife and in the need to appease ghosts. Han people continued the Warring States belief in the power of local ghosts and spirits to affect their health, career, and home. Objects placed in the tombs also protected the tombs from earth and other spirits. Among these protective measures were ceramic dogs and other animals to guard the tombs and legalistic deeds of purchase cementing a contract with the earth gods for the use of the burial space. A fear of the intrusion of underground spirits into the bodies of the deceased may also lie behind the use of protective jade suits and coffins.

Archaeology in China today is often rescue archaeology, with important sites hurriedly excavated when they are threatened by modern development projects. Sometimes it proves impossible to excavate sites with the thorough care that scientific archaeology demands. But, even with these limitations, important Han tombs are discovered and excavated on a fairly regular basis, adding to our picture of the Han as a time of great wealth and cultural brilliance.

Art and literature

The contents of royal tombs such as those described here give a partial but nevertheless impressive picture of the arts in the Western Han Period. Conspicuous in these tombs are utilitarian objects made with fine materials and a superb sense of design that elevate them to the status of works of art. Gilt-bronze oil lamps, jade paperweights, jade jewelry, silver-bronze mirrors, gold- and silver-inlaid chariot fittings, surface-patterned swords and other weapons, incense burners, lacquer tableware and cosmetic boxes, along with dozens of other luxury goods, testify to a thriving artisanal sector designing and producing such objects for the elite.

As almost all such objects that have survived to the present time have been excavated from tombs we have a very imperfect idea of how they would have fit into the domestic décor of the living. It is difficult to visualize what a room in the palace of an elite Han dynasty family would have looked like. However, many Han tombs included miniature collections of multi-storied towers with small walled gardens, fish ponds, pig pens, and even some goods thought to be of use in the afterlife, such as a ceramic toilet. Some things are fairly certain: buildings would have been built in post-and-beam fashion, with large pillars holding up a heavy bracketed roof. The pillars and beams would have been brightly lacquered, perhaps with designs of dragons, phoenixes, and other real or fanciful animals. The textile arts were highly advanced, and both elite persons and their servants would have been dressed in colorful wrapped robes. People in Han times sat on woven reed mats on the floor. Meals were served on low tables (perhaps with chopsticks), and lamps and other decorative objects were probably placed on stands. Some items that would be prominent elements of domestic décor in later times were conspicuous by their absence in Han interiors. Chairs, for example, did not come into common use in China until the Tang dynasty, hundreds of years after the Han. There would be no scroll paintings hanging on the walls, although the walls themselves may have been painted with murals. Cabinets would hold rolls of texts brush-written on silk or on bamboo strips, not string-sewn wood-block printed books in hard cloth binders, as became standard in later times.

Figurative art, in the form of mural paintings, either on silk or on walls, and exorcistic statuary sculpted in relief or in the round, is found almost entirely in the context of tombs. A few very large stone sculptures representing fanciful animals are known from the period, as, for example, near the tomb of the great general Huo Qubing, where they presumably served as spirit guardians. These seem to be precursors of the later practice of lining the approach road to a tomb with sculptures of humans and animals (known most famously today from the "spirit way" lining the avenue to the Ming tombs near Beijing). The painted coffins and funerary banners from Mawangdui give evidence of a lively tradition of figurative art generally featuring processions or religious tableaus of immortals. But, overall, little "fine art" (as opposed to decorative arts) from the Western Han has survived the ravages of the centuries.

The transition of literature from song and historical anecdote into new forms of poetry and narrative prose occurred during the Han. The Western Han saw two notable developments in literary art: the expansion of the Music Bureau (*Yuefu*) as an organ of government and the development of a new literary form called *fu* ("rhyme-prose"). The origins of the Music Bureau are obscure; some of the states of the Warring States Period and later the Qin may have had offices called Music Bureaus. It is clear, however, that Emperor Wu of the Han greatly expanded the staff of the Music Bureau and accorded it new importance. The duties of the Music Bureau embraced both music and poetry, and, indeed, the two were initially inextricably connected: all early Chinese poetry was intended to be sung, chanted, or recited.

Among other duties, the Music Bureau was responsible for composing music suitable for imperial rituals; Emperor Wu's establishment of various new objects of worship necessitated a great deal of appropriate new music. One of the Music Bureau's most important functions was to collect popular songs from all over the empire; these were not just for literary enjoyment but were also a way of taking the political pulse of the populace and staying alert to any signs of discontent or criticism. This tradition is based on a legend of Confucius doing just that to compile the *Book of Odes* (and would continue through into the Communist era as a ritual gesture by those in power to "listen" to the people). These Han-era anonymous songs then led to the development of a new style of "Yuefu poetry," self-consciously literary works written in a deliberately popular mode. Almost all pre-Han poetry, such as that in the *Book of Odes*, was anonymous; in the Han one finds for the first time significant amounts of verse attributed to named poets, including a few poems by Emperor Wu himself.

Fu "rhyme-prose" was a distinctively new genre that emerged in the Han at least in part because of the popularity at that time of the poem "Encountering Sorrow" ("Li sao") and other Chu-style poetry collected in the anthology *Elegies of Chu* (*Chuci*). Perhaps reflecting the southern origins of the ruling Liu clan, there was during the early Han a definite vogue for Chu culture, portrayed as a reflection of the lush, warm, exotic, tantalizingly semi-barbaric milieu (at least as northern elites imagined it) of the Yangzi River Valley and beyond. As the conventional English translation "rhyme-prose" suggests, *fu* occupied a halfway niche between prose and poetry; it was more structured than prose, featuring parallel constructions and shifting rhyme schemes, but freer than the strict regularities of most early Chinese poetry. It also often featured arcane and difficult vocabulary, giving the poet scope to flaunt his control of language and create an emotionally charged, over-the-top work of literary dazzlement. Emperor Wu was a patron of *fu* poetry. The most famous *fu* poet of the Western Han was Sima Xiangru, whose "Rhyme-prose on the Imperial Hunting-Park" ("Shang lin fu") was a lengthy and effusive description of the emperor's private hunting preserve. Sima Xiangru's rival, Yang Xiong (53 BCE–18 CE), criticized the excesses of most *fu* compositions and argued that the popularity of *fu* should be harnessed to convey moral lessons rather than celebrating indulgence. Much of the *fu* rhyme-prose of the Western Han Period features the theme of the frustration of a righteous official whose advice has been rejected by an immoral ruler, a trope tracing back to the Chu poet Qu Yuan. Examples by Han poet-officials include pieces such as Jia Yi's "The Owl" ("Funiao fu"), a philosophical introspection on the meaning of an ill omen; Mei Cheng's (d. 140 BCE) "Seven Stimuli" ("Qi fa") in which study of the Confucian Classics is presented as the ultimate cure for the illness of a dissipated prince; and Yang Xiong's *fu* criticizing the lack of Confucian purity in the performance of state sacrifices and hunts.

In prose literature an important development was the increased use of parallel prose—passages of two or more sentences of identical grammatical structure intended to lend a quasi-poetic gracefulness to prose writing and to enhance the rhetorical force of an argument. Many historical and philosophical works were revised to match this style.

Intellectual life

Intellectual life flourished in the Western Han, picking up the strands of lively debate characteristic of the Warring States Period after the interlude of Qin censorship. Intellectual communities thrived both at the capital and in the courts of regional kings and local officials, as well as in the homes of rich merchants and early industrialists. Many intellectuals were specialists in ritual or magical arts or in philosophical or political discourse. Education, largely the preserve of Confucian scholars, involved a basic curriculum called the Six Arts: ritual (*li*), music (*yue*), archery (*she*), chariot driving (*yu*), writing (*shu*), and techniques (*shu*). Essentially, the Six Arts covered knowledge of the rites to be performed by an elite male in courts and shrines on special dates, basic hunting and military skills for leadership of local militias, literacy in reading and writing, and numeracy in calculating time and keeping accounts. Erudite scholars often traveled to the central court in Chang'an. Ideas developed in one regional court could be tested out in others. The rise of urban centers along trade routes also added to the lively Han marketplace of ideas.

One urgent intellectual task in the early Han Period was the recovery of texts lost as a result of the Qin burning of books. Many texts were associated with oral traditions or linked with physical practices such as musical performances. Experts in various aspects of the arts transcribed them from memory or from fragments of preserved texts. Much as the Music Bureau collected songs, court historians would collect as many texts as possible. Early academies dedicated to the study and teaching of sets of ritual, philosophical, divination, and other texts favored by individual masters arose. As scholars collated the fragments and amalgamated them with what people remembered from oral recitations, they essentially created the Chinese Classics. Texts taught in academies included the *Springs and Autumns*, the *Book of Odes*, the *Book of Documents*, the *Book of Changes*, and the *Ritual Records*. Confucian scholars worked on restoring the *Analects* (the words of Confucius, the *Lunyu*), the *Mengzi* (records of philosophical exchanges between Mencius and local Warring States elites), the *Doctrine of the Mean* (*Zhongyong*, a meditation text on how to incorporate Confucian virtues into one's life), and *The Great Learning* (*Daxue*, a text on the value of higher education; see Focus: *The Great Learning*). We know from their preservation in tombs that the *Book of Changes* and the *Laozi* circulated widely, as did a variety of philosophical texts and technical manuals on such topics as self-cultivation and healing.

In the course of copying the ancient texts the editors updated them into modern script. This introduced errors into the transmitted versions of classics as the scribes sometimes misread the archaic scripts, which were full of regional variants. The Han scholars struggled to make sense of the old texts and wove them together in an order that made sense to them based both on their studies and on the political needs of their academy or local court. As these new copies were themselves copied and handed down they became known as "new script" texts, as opposed to the "old script" texts—post-Qin "discoveries" of hidden caches of old texts that were presented to the courts (often for rewards).

Texts associated with early commentarial traditions, such as the *Zuo Commentary* on the *Springs and Autumns* and the later *Gongyang* and *Guliang* commentaries, were also preserved and copied. Fragments of the *Documents* and various texts associated with the Confucian tradition and written in pre-Qin script were found—so the story went—while workers were repairing a wall at the Kong family mansion in Qufu. The Han histories claim music was heard when they were found. Whether any genuine ancient texts were found or not cannot be verified. Many dismissed the so-called "old text" versions as forgeries, but the recovery of numerous texts from archaeological digs in modern times lends credence to the idea of buried texts, which might have been hidden by Confucian scholars in defiance of the Qin book-burning edict. In any case, during the Han there often appeared both New Text and Old Text versions of the same text, causing great debates among the Erudites as to which one was genuine. Each version attracted partisans who used them to argue different points of view. Han intellectuals working in the tradition of the *Gongyang* and *Guliang* commentaries tended to prefer the New Text versions of the Confucian classics, while those favoring the *Zuo Commentary* were more closely associated with the Old Text versions. Scholars up until modern times debated the authority of the New and Old versions, but the multiple excavated versions found in tombs suggest that is also possible that there was no single or original "mother" version. The process of producing classics likely drew from both types of sources.

Modern scholars also believed until recently that New Script and Old Script texts belonged to particular philosophical schools. The newly discovered texts reveal a tremendous amount of shared vocabulary and ideas among different teachings, and a single tomb was likely to mix together texts representing a range of subjects and viewpoints. On the other hand, the late Western Han intellectual Liu Xin, in his catalog of the contents of the imperial library (the "Yiwen zhi," later included in the *History of the [Former] Han Dynasty* (*Han shu*)), grouped texts as being either philosophical ("intentions," *zhi*) or technical ("methods," *fa*). The scholars associated with particular types of texts were categorized as *jia*, a word that can mean "familial group" and was sometimes mistakenly understood to imply that scholars were organized into schools or guilds. Although private teachers and officially appointed court Erudites often specialized in a single text, the Han elite had wide-ranging interests and there is little evidence that they formed "schools" corresponding to the bibliographical classifications found in Liu Xin's catalogue.

This realization has led modern scholars to re-evaluate the nature of books originally believed to focus on one or another philosophical trend. Instead of a Confucian editing a book to represent only Confucian ideology or the work of a single famous Confucianist, it is apparent that many texts were assembled from many different sources expressing a range of ideas. This was the case, for example, with the work conventionally attributed to the *Springs and Autumns* scholar Dong Zhongshu called the *Luxuriant Gems of the Springs and Autumns* (*Chunqiu fanlu*), which includes groups of chapters on Confucian ethics and social philosophy, others dealing with yin–yang and Five Phase cosmology, and still other chapters on the suburban sacrifice. The lengthy book, though long associated with Dong Zhongshu, turns out not to be entirely his work: recent scholarship has shown that it is a composite work, incorporating the writings of several authors over a period of at least three or four generations, and was compiled into its present form only in the fourth or fifth century CE. Many scholars have argued that Dong was the architect of a "Han Confucian synthesis," weaving together Confucian philosophy with Han cosmology to form a new imperial ideology. But the composite nature of the *Luxuriant Gems* invalidates that theory. Moreover, Dong did not have the official standing or intellectual clout to have created such a synthesis and to have persuaded Emperor Wu to adopt it. Most scholars today have abandoned the long-held notion of a Han Confucian synthesis.

As in the Warring States Period, it was possible for students to study with any number of Han intellectuals who had mastered certain texts and were willing to transmit them to their disciples. The *Shiji* biography of Dong Zhongshu gives us a fascinating account of his method of teaching. Seated behind a curtain, he was invisible to his students and audible only to the most advanced disciples, seated close to him. They were expected to absorb the master's lessons and transmit them to the newer and less-advanced students in return. There is, unfortunately, no way to tell how typical, or not, this teaching method was. But it is certainly true that education, both private and imperially sponsored, flourished during the Western Han Period.

Books on history, philosophy, literature, and technical subjects, such as medicine, astronomy and astrology, physiognomy, and cosmology, circulated among the literate public (which included some women). Increasingly there were also commentaries, and commentaries on commentaries, such as Dong Zhongshu's recorded teachings on the *Gongyang Commentary* on the *Springs and Autumns*. The *History of the [Former] Han Dynasty* preserves several of Dong's memorials to the imperial throne written in response to Emperor Wu's questions on matters of policy. Compendia were an important component of Han literature. Examples include Jia Yi's (201–169 BCE) *New Writings* (*Xin shu*), which contains, among other things, his famous essay on "The Faults of Qin," what appear to be transcripts of lessons to his disciples, and a number of memorials submitted to the imperial throne on a variety of policy issues. *Mr. Han's Supplementary Comments on the Odes* (*Hanshi waizhuan*) is attributed to Han Ying (c. 200–120 BCE), who completed the text during the reign of Emperor Wen. It consists of some 300 anecdotes and aphorisms, each capped with a quotation from the *Book of Odes*, showing how that classic could be used to deepen one's understanding of a wide range of issues. The *Huainanzi* (*Master of Huainan*, 139 BCE) was compiled under the patronage of, and probably with the active participation of, Liu An, the king of Huainan, as a compendium of all the useful knowledge in the world, and was intended for the guidance of a self-cultivated, sagely ruler. Apparently modeled on Lü Buwei's *Lüshi chunqiu* (245 BCE), the *Huainanzi* claims in its final chapter that it has so thoroughly summarized all of the world's useful knowledge that no more books will ever need to be written. Many other works are attributed to Liu An, including a commentary on the Chu lament the "Li sao," but the *Huainanzi* is the only one that survives.

One of the greatest monuments of Han intellectual life is the *Records of the Grand Historian* (*Shiji*), begun by Sima Tan (d. 110 BCE) and completed by his son Sima Qian (c. 145–86 BCE) (for further details, see Focus: The *Shiji*). One of the world's first works of comprehensive historical writing, covering the period from high antiquity to the reign of Emperor Wu, it is comparable to the work of the Greek historian Herodotus. It established the basic model of historical writing that was followed, dynasty after dynasty, down to the end of the imperial era. Like most books during the Han it was carefully created from earlier manuscripts, some of which are still preserved and others not. As such, the Sima father-and-son team wrote the earliest full history of China as a political entity and distinct civilization, although it was one in which there was no obvious attempt to separate mythology from "fact." It was clearly influenced by the Han imperial court's idea of what that history should convey, but the influence of major philosophical trends, Confucianism and Daoism, in the choice of texts and the morals drawn is also clear. Moral authority was defined according to generally accepted cosmological principles combined with the ideological interpretations of old texts.

Cosmology

One of the great achievements of Han intellectuals was the formulation and synthesis of a cosmology that formed the Chinese understanding of how the world works and was influential for many centuries to come. Han cosmology combined a basic level of astronomical science with astrological or religious interpretations of the data. The focus of celestial observation on the celestial north pole and the celestial equator (the projection onto the sky of the earth's equator) went back a millennium or more. Associated with a polar/equatorial orientation was a system for locating the moveable heavenly bodies (the sun, moon, and five naked-eye-visible planets) with reference to stars strung out along the celestial equator (the "lunar lodges"; see below). The ancient understanding of geographical space in terms of five directions (the four cardinal directions plus the center) by the end of the Warring States Period expanded to include eight directions (with equal emphasis on northeast, southeast, southwest, and northwest), and correlations with colors and mythical spirits. During the Han symbolic animals were added: the bluegreen dragon (East); the vermilion bird (South); the white tiger (West); and the "black warrior," a snake entwining a tortoise (North). The motions of celestial bodies and the annual cycle of the seasons were interpreted in terms of these correlations.

Besides astronomical observations, intellectuals pondered the basic principles of life and death, the seen and the unseen. The correlative cosmology was more impersonal and organic than the earlier belief that a pantheon of ancestral spirits and sky gods had to be constantly appeased through sacrifices. Even so, all-embracing Heaven, along with gods, spirits, and ghosts, remained the ultimate motivating forces behind the myriad ceaseless connections and transformations of the visible world. Worship of *Taiyi*, the Great Undifferentiated One, possibly embodied as the Big Dipper, continued well into the Han. At the same time, the Daoist idea of life emerging out of an undifferentiated void through the division of all energy or *qi* into positive and negative forces, yang and yin, was accepted as a fundamental concept. The belief in supernatural beings coexisted, sometimes uncomfortably, with the idea that the world operated in accordance with Dao-driven impersonal forces. A new Han idea, *ganying* ("stimulus and response"), describes how vibrations in the medium of *qi* cause things in the same yin–yang and Five Phase correlative categories (Tables 10.1 and 10.2) to interact with each other. The standard example was that if a string of a musical instrument is plucked the similarly tuned string on another nearby instrument will vibrate. Resonance, in this sense, was how Chinese cosmology explained effective action at a distance.

Harmonizing *qi* in the macrocosm of empire (where the emperor provides the supernatural connection between Earth and Sky) and the microcosm of self was the key goal of all

Table 10.1 Yin–Yang correlates.

Yin	Yang		Yin	Yang
Dark	Light		Black	Red
Cool	Warm		Cold	Hot
Square	Round		Earth	Heaven
Moon	Sun		Water	Fire
Metal	Wood		Female	Male
Damp	Dry		Cloudy	Clear
Rain	Wind		Internal	External
Frost	Dew		Low	High
Autumn	Spring		Winter	Summer
Crawling	Flying		Passivity	Vigor
Valleys	Hills		Recision	Accretion
Punishments	Rewards		Death	Life

Table 10.2 Five Phase correlates.

Phase	Wood	Fire	Earth	Metal	Water
Direction	East	South	Center	West	North
Color	Bluegreen	Red	Yellow	White	Black
Symbol	Bluegreen Dragon	Vermilion Bird	Yellow Dragon	White Tiger	Dark Warrior
Season	Spring	Summer	Midsummer	Autumn	Winter
Planet	Jupiter	Mars	Saturn	Venus	Mercury
Tool	Compass	Balance Beam	Marking Cord	Square	Weight
Musical Note	*Jue*	*Zhi*	*Gong*	*Shang*	*Yu*
Heavenly Stems	*Jia, Yi*	*Bing, Ding*	*Wu, Ji*	*Geng, Xin*	*Ren, Gui*
Number	8	7	5	9	6
Species	Scaly	Feathered	Naked	Hairy	Armored
Flavor	Sour	Bitter	Sweet	Pungent	Salty
Smell	Musty	Burnt	Fragrant	Rank	Putrid
Crop	Wheat	Rice	Millet	Legumes	Grain
Structural System	*Qi* system	Blood System	Skin	Bones	Flesh
Visceral Orb	Splenic	Pulmonary	Hepatic	Choleric	Renal

intellectuals. Proper behavior by the emperor and his court was crucial to the health of the state. An imbalance could lead to bad omens, natural disasters, or rebellions. On occasion, conspicuous acts of benevolence, such as a general amnesty for criminals, were believed to have good concrete results, such as putting an end to a drought. An individual's physical health relied on the correct flow of yin and yang through channels of *qi* inside the body. Bad behavior, ghosts, or improper diet could cause the flow to stagnate in one organ or another, causing illness and death. Human dispositions—anger, sadness, joy—were all processes of *qi* inside the body. Practices for channeling the *qi* to avoid disruption were key steps in a number of different cultivation practices.

The term *Dao* could refer either to a "way" of pursuing some objective (e.g. the *Dao* of the Military) or to The Way, the ultimate cosmic reality of undifferentiated nothingness that existed even prior to the emergence of yin or yang *qi*. While the concept of *Dao*, in both senses, was widely accepted, Han attitudes toward yin and yang varied, particularly as the yin force became more and more associated with female subjectivity and yang with positive male dominance. The classic *Daodejing* text advocated that true strength lay behind perceived weakness, as water, for example, given sufficient time, can erode solid rock. But in that text yin is not obviously female (although the *Dao* was linked to the metaphor of a mother as the portal between non-existence and existence). The *Huainanzi* takes a more neutral stand, seeing yin and yang as essential to one another but implying a preference for yang as associated with new life and growth, in particular with the seasons spring and summer. The yin–yang chapters of the *Luxuriant Gems of the Spring and Autumn* take a powerfully androcentric and misogynistic view of yin and yang, disparaging yin in such chapters as "Yang is Lofty, Yin is Lowly." A similar view is reflected in commentaries on the *Book of Changes*, which, during the Han, combined philosophical speculation with the randomness of divination.

The popular link between personal behavior and natural change is evident in the Han development of the Warring States concept the Five Phases (*wuxing*). Followers of Confucius initially referred to these as five types of "conduct" (*xing*) that could generate internal *de* (a moral power and type of yang *qi*), manifested as humaneness (*ren*), propriety (*yi*), ritual (*li*), knowledge (*zhi*), and sagacity (*sheng*). The term "Five Phases" was borrowed or appropriated by other intellectuals who were in the process of developing the theory of correlative cosmology, so that each type of "conduct" became associated with cyclical natural phenomena. Sometimes translated as "five elements" or "five agents," the Five Phases are strongly associated with the directions and seasons: Wood (East/Spring), Fire (South/Summer), Metal (West/Autumn), Water (North/Winter), and Earth (Center). Han cosmologists understood these cosmic forces to succeed one another in various cycles, the two most important of which were the Production Cycle and the Conquest Cycle. The former applies to natural processes whereby one Phase evolves into the next. For example, Wood burns to produce Fire which then creates Earth (ashes); Earth over time creates Metal (ores) which when smelted produce Water (liquid); Water, in turn, is essential for the growth of Wood. The Conquest cycle emphasizes more aggressive forms of change: Wood is conquered by Metal (chopping), which is conquered by Fire (melting), which is conquered by Water (dousing), which is conquered by Earth (filling or damming), which is conquered by Wood (germination). Han cosmologists integrated yin–yang dualism with Five Phase cyclical changes to create a system for calculating (and thereby gaining some degree of control over) the complex interactions observable in the visible universe.

While mathematical skills were certainly necessary for Han cosmologists, particularly when they used the movements of the stars as the basis for a type of prognostication, numerology also provided philosophical and magical weight to their calculations. Already by the end of the Warring States odd numbers held relative yang weights (1, 3, 5, 7, 9) and even numbers yin (2, 4, 6, 8). Number sets were important, such as those associated with time and the calendar (ten Heavenly Stems, twelve Earthly Branches), with space and the directions (four cardinal directions, eight directions), or with divination (eight trigrams, sixty-four hexagrams). These number sets could be correlated with the Five Phases and yin–yang. For example, Northeast was correlated with Lesser Wood, East with Wood, Southeast with Lesser Fire, South with Fire, and so on.

During the Han Period the ancient sixty-day cycle continued to be maintained in an unbroken sequence stretching back to prehistoric times (see Tables 4.2 and 4.3 in Chapter 4, above.) Beginning in the Warring States Period the sexagenary cycle was also used to keep track of a repeating cycle of sixty years. By the end of the Warring States Period, if not earlier, the twelve "double-hours" by which the Chinese marked daily time were named by the twelve "Earthly Branches." Sometime before the Eastern Han Period the Earthly Branches became linked to a set of twelve symbolic animals, so that the first year of the twelve-year cycle was the "Year of the Rat," the second year was the "Year of the Ox," and so on. The same animal cycle was used to designate the twelve double-hours into which the Chinese divided the day, so that the double-hour from 1 to 3 p.m. was called the "Hour of the Sheep," the double-hour from 3 to 5 p.m. was called the "Hour of the Monkey," and so on.

Han astronomy continued to employ the ancient system of twenty-eight lunar lodges, marked by constellations located along the celestial equator. These were used to describe the location of the sun, the moon, and the five naked-eye-visible planets; the location of a heavenly body in one or another of the lodges had astrological implications for the government that had to be interpreted by experts. The calculation of calendars relied on these experts, and the actions of the government relied on the calendars. In his role as the Son of Heaven the emperor had the exclusive right to create and promulgate calendars; the private calculation of calendars was an act of treason punishable by death. Establishing a calendar was a key element in claiming the Mandate of Heaven.

The fundamental problem for any calendar-maker is that the apparent orbital periods of the sun, moon, and naked-eye-visible planets do not occur in whole numbers of days. In particular, the approximately 29.5 days of the lunar month (thus the approximately 354 days of a lunar year) do not fit neatly into the approximately 365.25 days of the solar year. The result is that any calendar that counts whole numbers of days eventually, and sometimes fairly quickly, loses synchronization with key celestial events such as the summer and winter solstices and the spring and autumn equinoxes. Calendars therefore have to be revised from time to time to make them match more closely the observable phenomena of the sky. The *Taichu* ("Grand Inception") calendar of 104 BCE was an outstanding intellectual achievement. It was based on unprecedentedly accurate observation of the heavenly bodies and calculation of orbital periods; for example, the solar year was defined as 365.2507 days and the lunar month was defined as 29.5309 days, figures more accurate than the old approximations. The *Taichu* calendar, with relatively minor revisions from time to time, set the standard of Chinese calendar-making for several centuries to come.

The *Taichu* calendar also settled (temporarily, as it turned out) a ritual question that had been debated since the early years of the dynasty. Initially Emperor Gao had decided that the Han ruled through the power of Water and that ritual garments should therefore be black, the color associated with Water. This understanding denied the legitimacy of the Qin dynasty, which had also claimed to rule by virtue of Water, and portrayed the Han as using Water to conquer the Zhou dynasty's Fire. The new calendar continued to accept the Conquest Cycle as the appropriate way of thinking about dynastic succession, but (reversing the early Han view) accepted the legitimacy of Qin's claim to have ruled by the power of Water. The Grand Inception calendar therefore established Earth as the ruling Phase of the Han dynasty, because Earth conquers Water (for example, by filling in ponds or damming streams), and Han had conquered Qin. This decision meant that, henceforth, the Han dynasty's ritual garments and other emblems should be yellow, the color of Earth, replacing the black regalia that had been used in the early decades of the dynasty.

In fact, people during the Han era used three kinds of calendars, each appropriate for different purposes. The first was the civil calendar, a soli-lunar calendar designed to harmonize the lunar and solar years. The second calendar was the solar agricultural calendar, which divided the year into twenty-four fifteen-day periods, each named for a natural phenomenon, starting with "Spring Begins" on the forty-sixth day after the winter solstice and continuing with "Rainwater," "Insects Awaken," and so on. These two calendars were very ancient, apparently dating back to the Early Bronze Age, and are described in Chapter 4 above.

The third calendar was a ritual calendar generally known as the "Monthly Ordinances" ("Yue ling"), found in several closely similar versions from the Warring States and Han periods. It is based on correlations on the Five Phases, and thus probably originated no earlier than the mid-Warring States Period. It prescribes the ritual behavior of the ruler for each of the twelve months and the four seasons (some versions add an artificial fifth season of "midsummer" to correlate with the Phase Earth). Thus, in spring, correlated with Wood, ritual garments are green, ceremonies are carried out in the eastern chambers of the "Hall of Light" ("mingtong"), the ruler acts with conspicuous benevolence, and so on with other Wood associations. This calendar portrays an idealized form of royal behavior based on Five Phase theory and it is not clear that it was regularly, or even ever, put into practice, although aspects of its use are evident in popular almanacs regulating daily behavior.

Years were designated in early imperial China by their place in the sixty-year (sexagenary) cycle, and by sequence in a "reign-period," a span of years designated with an auspicious name and subject to change by imperial decree—which might be done, for example, to try to end a period of national misfortune such as a drought. There was no unified system of counting years beyond a single reign. For example, Emperor Wu's thirtieth year as emperor (111 BCE) was year *gengwu*, number seven of the sexagenary cycle, and the sixth year of the Yuanding ("Original *ding*," a reference to sacred bronze vessels of the early Zhou Period) reign-period, which began in 116 BCE. The reign name Yuanding was chosen by the emperor with the help of his ministers, based on calendrical and phase calculations. The later practice of counting consecutive years in an emperor's reign was not yet established in the Han, and none of the calendars in use began with a "year one" marking the beginning of time.

Han cosmography—that is, the shape and structure of the earth—envisioned a square earth under a round heaven. Earth was considered to be flat, symbolically similar to the passenger compartment of a chariot; overhead was the hemispherical dome of heaven, much like an umbrella over the chariot box. Nine as the highest yang number was also the magical number associated with divisions in space. Heaven was divided into nine segments. The earth had been divided by the legendary prehistoric god-king, Yu the Great, into nine contiguous continents surrounded by an ocean. In the sky there was a central disk defined by the circumpolar stars (stars that never, at a given latitude, dip below the horizon) and eight truncated wedges extending in the eight cardinal directions from the central disk to the horizon. The square earth was straightforwardly imagined as a 3 × 3 grid, with a central square and eight outer squares in the eight directions. The 3 × 3 grid figure was an important concept in early Chinese cosmology; one finds it in various contexts, such as Mencius's possibly mythical "well-field" system (named for the shape of the character for "well," 井), in which eight families would each till a square field for themselves and collectively cultivate a central field for the payment of tax grain. The idealized agricultural system of nine reflected in microcosm the divisions of Heaven and Earth. A kind of synchronicity was understood to exist between the matching sections of each layer. According to a doctrine called "field allocation," a celestial event (such as a comet, meteor shower, or nova) in one of the nine segments of heaven was understood to be an ill omen for the corresponding section of the empire.

Celestial omens were also read from the position of the Big Dipper (which the Chinese called the Northern Dipper). Because the stars shift their apparent position relative to the horizon by one degree per day, the "handle" of the Dipper points successively to one or another of the eight outer squares of the earth. This "strike of the Dipper" was also an ill omen for the state concerned. Such calculations were used in military matters, so as to, for example, plan an attack at a time when the target region was cosmologically vulnerable. A model of the cosmos, called a *shi* or *shipan* (commonly translated as "cosmograph"), was widely used to track the handle of the Dipper without having to look at the sky; the cosmograph had a square, fixed "earth plate" inscribed with the names of the twenty-eight lunar lodges, the eight directions, and sometimes other information. The earth plate was surmounted by a round heaven plate that was inscribed with an image of the Dipper and which rotated on a pivot. The heaven plate could be rotated one degree per day to track the movement of the heavens.

Two other conceptual models of the square earth were current in the Warring States, Qin, and Han Periods. One portrayed the earth as a set of nesting boxes. Reading from the innermost box to the outermost one, there were the imperial palace, the imperial domain, the realm of the territorial lords, the zone of pacification (i.e. the frontier), the realm of the submissive barbarians, and the realm of cultureless savagery. This concept is reflected in the *Classic of Mountains and Seas* (*Shanhaijing*), a compendium of real and mythical geography. It is a composite work, the earliest chapters of which might be as old as the late Warring States Period, while the latest perhaps date from the Eastern Han. The first five chapters, "Mountains of the Five Treasuries," describe the mountains of the south, west, north, east, and center of what is recognizably the East Asian Heartland Region, naming and giving the location of what are, for the most part, real places, with their deities, animals, medicinal and other useful plants and minerals, etc. Subsequent chapters, also oriented to the four cardinal directions, describe "Beyond the Seas," "Within the Seas," and "The Great Wilderness," becoming more fanciful and literally outlandish as the distance from the Heartland increases.

The nesting-boxes scheme marks the transition of the term "Zhongguo" from a generic sense of "the central states" of the Zhou multi-state system to a specific designation of "The Middle Kingdom," the center of the world. This model is reflected in the classic called the *Zhouli*, which divided up the entire imperial bureaucracy into nested realms laid out according to the seasons and peopled with numerologically significant numbers of officers. The emperor, in the center, was to practice *wuwei* ("non-action")—that is, to behave completely in tune with cosmic rhythms and take no purposive action. All actions would thus be in complete accord with the cosmic Way (*Dao*), acting spontaneously (*ziran*, "thus of itself") and without the need for human intervention.

The other visualization of the square earth was the game-board of the game "Six Immortals" (*liubo*), which had a central square and subsidiary markings shaped like the letters T, L, and V. Game pieces moved along a set route through the markings, according to the throw of a die, to reach a final goal. The game was used both for gambling and for fortune-telling, and had cosmic implications; it was said to be a favorite game of immortals (and, later, poets). In the very late Western Han Period and into the Eastern Han, bronze mirrors with TLV markings became popular as miniature models of the universe (see Focus: A TLV mirror, in Chapter 11).

Emperor Wu's waning years

The fifty-four-year reign of Emperor Wu brought welcome stability to the Han dynasty and included some notable accomplishments. The fractious regional kings were brought firmly under imperial control, while many kingdoms were absorbed into the imperial realm, others were broken up into smaller pieces, and those that remained were subject to tighter control by the imperial government. Imperial clansmen and heads of powerful regional families were ennobled as lords (*hou*), but found their power and influence tightly restricted. The Xiongnu were decisively defeated and posed little threat to the Heartland Region after the campaigns of 129–119 BCE, even though a lasting diplomatic settlement of relations between Han and the Xiongnu lay some decades in the future. The travels of an intrepid general, Zhang Qian, brought valuable new information about the lands to the west of China and paved the way for regular commerce along the Silk Road. The agricultural and mercantile economies grew, although much wealth was spent on military campaigns to expand the empire. The Grand Inception Calendar of 104 BCE was a major achievement. Emperor Wu's reign is remembered in Chinese history as a golden age, the peak of Han innovation.

In the last few years of Emperor Wu's reign, however, things began to fall apart. In the mid-90s BCE there were outbreaks of unrest among the peasantry in several parts of the empire, seemingly a response to the heavy taxation to which the imperial government had resorted to fund its militant expansionist policies. A more deep-rooted problem was that, despite explicit efforts to prevent relatives of imperial consorts and concubines from achieving positions of political power, several aristocratic families, notably the Li clan and the Wei clan, had insinuated their way to power by marrying members of the imperial Liu family. In 91 BCE what amounted to a private civil war broke out as armed forces recruited by the Li and Wei clans fought in the streets of Chang'an, each clan seeking to oust the other from power. At first the Wei seemed to prevail, but an accusation of witchcraft led to their downfall. (This was not unprecedented; in 130 BCE, accusations that the daughter of Empress Chen was practicing witchcraft led to the dismissal of the empress and the execution of several hundred people supposedly implicated in the case.) The cost of this crisis was enormous. In addition to uncounted deaths in the fighting itself, Empress Wei and her son Liu Qu (who had been appointed heir apparent in 122) were forced to commit suicide and several of her other children were executed. Dozens of other high military and civil officials were implicated in the case and either committed suicide or were executed; the crisis shook the imperial government to its roots, and the dynasty itself came close to collapse. Emperor Wu, growing old and infirm, was fortunate to survive an assassination attempt around the same time.

In 87 BCE the emperor fell seriously ill, and it was evident that he would not live much longer. No heir apparent had been named since the suicide of Liu Qu, and another succession crisis loomed. An ad-hoc coalition of three powerful figures—Huo Guang (brother of the heroic general Huo Qubing), Jin Midi, and Shangguan Jie, supported by other high officials—visited the ailing monarch and persuaded him to name as heir apparent the seven-year-old Liu Fuling, whose mother was neither a Li nor a Wei. Two days later the emperor died and Liu Fuling was enthroned as Emperor Zhao, with the triumvirate serving as his regents. So began nearly a century of generally weak and usually very young emperors of the Western Han, a guarantee of instability that ultimately would lead to the dynasty's temporary demise.

Focus: The travels of Zhang Qian

Zhang Qian (c. 199–113 BCE) was one of the greatest travelers and explorers in human history. In 138 BCE he was sent by Emperor Wu to make contact with the Yuezhi tribal confederation, rivals of the Xiongnu who had begun to migrate westwards into Central Asia under pressure from their more militant neighbors. Traveling with a party of about 100 officials, guards, servants, guides, and interpreters, he was captured by the Xiongnu as he made his way through the Gansu Corridor en route to the western regions. Zhang Qian and his guide, Ganfu, were well treated as captives; Zhang was given a Xiongnu wife and had a child by her.

(The rest of the traveling party disappears from the historical record.) But he did not neglect his duty to the emperor; after ten years of captivity he escaped, with his family and the faithful Ganfu, and resumed his efforts to contact the Yuezhi. When he finally did so he found, to his disappointment, that they had no interest in entering into an anti-Xiongnu alliance with China. To that extent, his mission was a failure.

Zhang Qian, however, used his time in Central Asia wisely, spending nearly a year with the Yuezhi and visiting the Ferghana Valley and the oasis kingdom of Bactria. He came in contact with Sogdian and Parthian merchants from further west, and heard stories about the world of the eastern Mediterranean. He observed the trade between Bactria and India, and surmised that an overland trade route could be established between India and China to supplement the maritime trade between southeastern China and southeast Asia and India, most of which was carried by foreign vessels. His most important intelligence information, from a military viewpoint, was that Central Asia could serve as a reliable supplier of horses for the Chinese cavalry. (Large-scale horse breeding was unfeasible in China itself because of a lack of sufficient grazing land.) Zhang's travels also added immeasurably to China's knowledge of the "western regions."

Zhang and his small party headed back to China in 128 BCE, but they were again captured by the Xiongnu and held prisoner. Two years later they escaped and returned to Chang'an in 125 BCE, to the astonishment of the court. Zhang Qian was richly rewarded for his excellent service, but his traveling days were not yet over. After a couple of failed attempts to organize a second mission to Central Asia, Zhang and his entourage left for the west in 119 BCE, with orders to establish trade relations with another horse-breeding people, the Wusun. This was accomplished successfully and, within a year of Zhang's return to Chang'an in 115 BCE, regular trade caravans were dispatched along what much later came to be called the Silk Road, trading bolts of silk cloth for horses and raw jade, two highly valued commodities in China. These official trading missions, with their military escorts, were joined by private merchants who took advantage of safe travel to the west to engage in private trade. Within a short time Chinese silk was showing up in the trading cities of the eastern Mediterranean and the expanding Roman Empire, prompting a lively discussion there of what silk was made of and where it came from. Meanwhile, China imported glassware, lapis lazuli gemstones, and other luxury goods from Persia, India, and points west. At both ends of the Silk Road conservative commentators railed, with little effect, against the extravagance of imported luxury goods from far away.

Focus: The Mawangdui funerary banner

Both Tomb 1 and Tomb 3 at Mawangdui, the tombs of the Lady of Dai and her son the chancellor (or chancellor-designate) of Changsha, contained T-shaped banners that apparently played important roles in the funeral ceremonies for the tomb occupants (Figure 10.6). Fitted with a loop of ribbon at the top and with tassels at the lower corners, each was apparently carried in the funeral procession of the deceased and then draped over the innermost coffin, in close proximity to the body. Although the Mawangdui banners are, so far, unique in their brightly colored paintings and iconographic complexity, a conceptually similar though much simpler banner from a Han tomb at Wuwei, Gansu Province, suggests that the use of funerary banners was widespread at the time. Scholars speculate that they were carried at the head of the funerary procession and then laid on top of the coffins before the tombs were closed.

The iconography of the Mawangdui banners contains a wealth of information about Han cosmology and religious beliefs. Though some motifs remain unexplained, and there is a

Figure 10.6 The funerary banner from the tomb of the Lady of Dai, Mawangdui Tomb 1, Changsha, Hunan Province, c. 168 BCE.

good deal of scholarly disagreement on some specific points, much of the banners' iconography can be explained with a fair degree of confidence. Here we will concentrate on the banner from Tomb 1, which is closely similar to that of Tomb 3 but in better condition. We will see that a key to understanding the banner's complex decoration is its cosmological dualism, with motifs organized as balancing pairs.

The banner is in two sections: the horizontal bar at the top of the T and the vertical stem below it. Looking first at the vertical portion, we see that its dominant motif is a covered jar of the type called *hu*, commonly found among the offerings in Zhou and Han tombs. In the context of the banner, the *hu*, traditionally a vessel for holding sacred millet ale for consumption during ceremonies, might by Han times be understood to contain an elixir of immortality. The hollow container—a vase or, later, a gourd—was an image also associated with magic mountains, which were envisioned as paradises inhabited by immortals. The Han image of the island of Penghu, the supposed realm of immortals that was the goal of the fleets dispatched by Qin Shihuangdi to find the elixir, resembled a vase-shaped mountain. In the Mawangdui banner the sides of the vessel are outlined by two intertwined dragons; its base is formed by two intertwined sturgeon-like fish, representing the ocean, while its lid is a canopy formed in part by a pair of phoenixes. It is as if the animal décor usually found on the surface of an ancient bronze vessel had come alive.

Near the base of the vessel are two unidentified quadrupeds that probably represent *shen*, sprite-like minor deities; these two are balanced by a pair of similar creatures in the horizontal portion of the banner, depicted as riding on spotted white dragon-like horses. Also near the base are two turtles, symbols of wisdom (because of their shells' ability to give correct answers in oracle bone divination) and of longevity, each surmounted by an owl, a bird whose cry foretells death. Each turtle holds in its mouth what is either a wisp of cloud or a piece of mushroom, also a symbol of longevity. There is also a humanoid figure holding up what turns out to be (as we shall see) the floor of the tomb chamber; this may represent an earth god or the mythical figure of Huntun, a symbol of the cosmic undifferentiation that prevailed before the world began to sort itself into categories of yin and yang. Finally, near the base of the jar, is a red snake; this pairs with an owl in flight just beneath the canopy-lid of the jar. The pairing of a bird of prey and a snake is very common in world mythology; it is a powerful symbol of dualism with connotations of yang–yin, heaven–earth, high–low, flying–creeping, south–north, and so on.

The jar itself is divided into two sections, defined by where the two dragons intertwine through a jade *bi* disk (symbols commonly found at the ends of coffins). The lower section shows the tomb of the occupant. A small group of mourners attends the brightly lacquered coffin, and several sacrificial bronzes, including a *hu* covered jar, are arranged in the tomb. Other, smaller vessels are on a shelf nearby. The ceiling of the tomb chamber is represented by a chime-stone (which pairs with a bronze bell in the upper, horizontal portion of the banner); it is suspended from the *bi* disk by a cord and an elaborate, multi-colored tassel that splits to the left and right above the chime-stone. Perched on the tassel are two composite beings with bird bodies and human heads, wearing official caps. The exact symbolism of this pair is unclear, but winged or bird-bodied figures in Han representational art are understood as depictions of immortals.

In the upper section of the jar, just above the *bi* disk, a pair of leopards hold a square divided by lines into sixteen smaller squares; this seems to represent a ramp leading from the ordinary mundane world down into (or up from) the tomb chamber. Standing near the center of what appears to be a slab of white marble, undoubtedly the floor of a palace room, is the deceased Lady of Dai herself, depicted as in life, wearing a colorfully patterned robe and attended by five servants (which were symbolically represented in the tomb by wooden figurines).

At the junction of the vertical and horizontal registers of the banner is a stone gate, representing Changhe, the gate of Heaven, guarded by a pair of officials wearing voluminous robes, their hands in their sleeves. Just above them is a bronze bell, the balancing element of the chimestone below. To the left and right are two dragons. Above them, on the right, is a red disk with a black crow inside, representing the sun; eight smaller red disks are arrayed in the coils of the right-hand dragon. This possibly represents a constellation; more likely it refers to the myth of Yi the Archer, who, when all ten suns came out on the same day and threatened to burn up the earth, shot down nine of them so that only one sun remained. (Each sun represented one day of the ten-day week; they should only appear one at a time, not all at once.) To the left is the crescent moon, inhabited by a toad bearing in its mouth a large piece of the mushroom of immortality. Riding the left-hand dragon is a young woman; this is Heng'e, wife of the mythical hero Yi the Archer, who has stolen the elixir of immortality and is escaping with it to the moon.

Finally, centered at the top of the banner is the figure of a woman with a long serpentine tail, attended by five cranes (the form which many immortals took in order to fly; note the balance of the five servants in the vertical section with the five cranes of the horizontal section). The identity of this figure has been the source of much controversy. Some scholars believe she represents Xiwangmu, the Dowager Queen of the West, because of her associations with immortality. But Xiwangmu was often shown riding on a tiger and was never pictured with a serpentine tail. In addition, the figure on the banner is not wearing the goddess's distinctive headgear and is not accompanied by her familiars, including a rabbit with a mortar and pestle and a nine-tailed fox. The figure on the banner is very unlikely to represent Xiwangmu. Other scholars have identified her as Nüwa, the sister–spouse of Fuxi, who together laid out the heavens and the earth. But that theory does not fit the case either. Nüwa and Fuxi were depicted in Han murals with intertwined serpentine tales, but as a pair and not alone. Moreover, she is usually shown holding a compass, for laying out round heaven, just as Fuxi holds a carpenter's square to lay out the square earth. In fact, it is most likely that the figure on the banner is the Lady of Dai herself, or rather her *hun* ethereal soul, perhaps in mimesis of Nüwa-like spirits, who became part-dragons to fly through the sky. The subject of the Mawangdui banner is the apotheosis of the Lady of Dai, an allegory of death and immortality that shows her *po* corporeal soul entombed in its coffin and her *hun* soul released to roam the heavens as a newly transformed immortal.

Focus: *The Great Learning*

The Great Learning is a short text (about 1,750 words) composed by an unknown author probably around the end of the third century BCE. It acquired a place of special prominence under the influence of the influential Neo-Confucian philosopher Zhu Xi (1130–1200 CE), who included it as one of the "Four Books" (along with the *Analects*, the *Doctrine of the Mean*, and the *Mencius*) as the basis of a Confucian education. *The Great Learning* relies on chain-reasoning ("If A then B, if B then C . . .") to argue for the close connection between a ruler's cultivation of virtue, *de*, and the successful government of his state, as can be seen in this translation of the first part of the text.

> The Way of the Great Learning consists of shining forth your illustrious virtue, of cherishing the people, and of stopping when you reach the ultimate excellence. If you know when to stop, you will have a definite focus; if you have a definite focus you can achieve quiessence; if you achieve quiessence, you can be tranquil; if you are tranquil, you can have foresight; if you have foresight, you can attain your desired goal.

Things have roots and branches, affairs have endings and beginnings. If you know what comes first and what comes later, you will have come near to the Way.

When the rulers of old wished to shine forth their illustrious virtue throughout the world, they first put their states in order. Wishing to put their states in order, they first regulated their own families. Wishing to regulate their own families, they first cultivated themselves. Wishing to cultivate themselves, they first made their hearts upright. Wishing to make their hearts upright, they first made their intentions sincere. Wishing to make their intentions sincere, they first extended their knowledge to the utmost. Extending one's knowledge to the utmost consists of investigating things. Things being investigated, their knowledge was extended to the utmost. Their knowledge being extended to the utmost, their intentions became sincere. Their intentions having become sincere, their hearts became upright. Their hearts having become upright, their selves became cultivated. Their selves having become cultivated, their families were regulated. Their families being regulated, their states were put in order. Their states having been put in order, the world was at peace.

From the Son of Heaven down to the common people, the first priority is that all must take self-cultivation as the root. If the root is in disorder, it is impossible for the branches to be orderly. Nothing can come of taking important things lightly, and treating trivial things as important.

Focus: The *Shiji*

The *Records of the Grand Historian* (*Shiji*) represents something entirely new in the writing of history in China. Begun by Grand Historian Sima Tan (d. 110 BCE) and completed by his son Sima Qian (d. 86 BCE), this monumental work in 130 chapters attempts to give a history of the known world from antiquity to the author's own lifetime. The book begins with a comprehensive overview of history and then adds additional levels of detail. The work is divided into five groups of chapters: twelve "basic annals," giving a chronological account of the rulers of dynasties from high antiquity to the Western Han; ten "tables," giving genealogies of ruling families and notable members of the high nobility; eight "treatises" on the subjects of ritual, music, mathematical harmonics, the calendar, astronomy and astrology, sacrifices, rivers and waterways, and agriculture and the economy (including taxation and coinage); thirty chapters on "Hereditary Houses," giving accounts of important aristocratic families, mainly of the Zhou Period but including some Qin and Han lineages; and seventy chapters of "Biographies" of prominent people in a wide range of fields, from senior statesmen to wandering knights—some biographies are limited to one individual, while others group several people together.

The *Shiji* has long been subjected to intensive scholarly scrutiny. Most specialists now believe that the text, especially in the chapters dealing with the Western Han Period, was edited and altered by other writers; it is possible that even whole chapters were subsequently rewritten and substituted for Sima Qian's original work. It is seldom clear where Sima Qian got his historical information. He claims to have traveled to the capitals of various Warring States polities to examine their historical records. This is not implausible, but it cannot be verified. In general the *Shiji* is considered the work of a sincere scholar, but it must be read with an awareness of possible error and bias.

Sima Qian has long been a hero of Chinese historians for his dedication to his craft and his personal courage. In 99 BCE a Han general, Li Ling, led a military campaign against the

Xiongnu but was defeated and captured. He was severely criticized by Emperor Wu, and almost all the top officials of the time echoed the emperor's angry response. Sima Qian, however, defended Li Ling, saying that he had acted with bravery and integrity. For his temerity in disagreeing with the emperor he was condemned to death, with the punishment commuted to castration. In a moving letter to his friend Ren An, Sima Qian explained why he did not commit suicide rather than undergo such a humiliating punishment; he chose to live, he said, to fulfill the obligation to finish his father's work, and out of respect to his calling as an historian.

The *Shiji* became the model for the subsequent dynastic histories, beginning with Ban Gu's *History of the [Former]Han Dynasty* (c. 100 CE) and continuing down to a draft history of the Qing dynasty written in the twentieth century, after the collapse of the imperial system. All of those subsequent works dealt with a single dynasty, rather than beginning at the beginning as Sima Qian had done, but their organization into basic annals, tables, treatises, and so on, is closely modeled on the *Records of the Grand Historian*.

One interesting but unanswerable question is how many people, in the Western Han Period, owned or had access to a copy of the *Shiji*. It almost certainly existed in multiple copies or it would not have survived the ravages of time; on the other hand, it would have comprised a heavy, awkward set of hundreds of bundles of bamboo slips or silk rolls, which would have been expensive to reproduce and cumbersome to handle. It eventually became one of the most widely read and studied works in the classical Chinese tradition, but the textual history of its early decades of existence remains obscure.

11 The Later Western Han and the Wang Mang Interregnum

Introduction

The Western Han dynasty lasted for ninety-three years after the death of Emperor Wu in 87 BCE. After a series of mostly young and weak emperors, a high official related to the imperial family through one of the earlier empresses seized the throne, creating a short-lived "New" dynasty. This was the Wang Mang Interregnum. Afterwards the Han royal lineage, the Liu, regained dynastic control, although the restored Han never matched the dynasty's former glory.

Six Han emperors reigned after Emperor Wu and before Wang Mang: Emperors Zhao, Xuan, Yuan, Cheng, Ai, and Ping. Emperor Zhao (87–74 BCE) and Emperor Ping (1 BCE–6 CE) came to the throne as young children; Emperor Zhao died at age twenty-one, Emperor Ping at age fifteen. Emperors Xuan and Cheng were in their late teens when they were enthroned. In addition to these legitimate emperors, Liu He, king of Changyi, was named emperor in 74 BCE on the death of Emperor Zhao, but was deposed four weeks later and was never given a dynastic name. And the infant Liu Ying was named heir apparent in 6 CE, with Wang Mang as his regent; he never became emperor. This succession of young and sometimes short-lived sovereigns, each influenced by regents and other powerful persons close to the throne, led to a general instability in the central court during the final century of the Western Han. Only three emperors with relatively long consecutive reigns provided periods of comparative stability: Emperor Xuan (74–49 BCE), Emperor Yuan (49–33 BCE) and Emperor Cheng (33–7 BCE). Ultimately, however, the forces of long-term decline proved too strong and the dynasty collapsed, being succeeded by Wang Mang's Xin ("New") dynasty (9–23 CE).

Despite the fact that Wang Mang attempted to model his Xin dynasty on an idealized picture of the Zhou government and at the same time enact needed reforms, the Xin dynasty lacked legitimacy in the eyes of China's historians. He had usurped the throne from rightful heirs of a Son of Heaven and his reforms were too ambitious and draconian. Ultimately revolts among the officials and the peasants, combined with border incursions by the Xiongnu and other northern peoples and a devastating flood in the Yellow River Plain, led to his downfall. The demise of the Xin dynasty led to the restoration of the Han and the re-establishment of the Liu clan as the imperial family. The restored Han dynasty moved its capital from Chang'an to Luoyang (just as the Zhou had done in the eighth century BCE), and so is known to history as the Eastern Han (or, alternatively, the Latter Han) dynasty.

Chaos under Emperor Zhao

Emperor Wu, on his death bed, named the seven-year-old Liu Fuling his heir apparent in 87 BCE, and died two days later. The enthronement of the boy-emperor satisfied the political and cosmological necessity of having a member of the imperial clan on the throne as recipient and guardian of the Mandate of Heaven, but there was never a pretense that Emperor Zhao had any role in ruling China. Of course, throughout Chinese imperial history many emperors reigned but did not rule, but Emperor Zhao was a puppet even by that standard, completely dominated by his regents and advisors.

The mutual near-annihilation of the Li and Wei clans in the crisis of 91 BCE, in the waning years of Emperor Wu's long reign, left the Huo clan as the most powerful of the great families of the time. Huo Guang, a much younger brother of the famous (and long deceased) general Huo Qubing, entered into a pact with Jin Midi (who died the next year) and Shangguan Jie, two powerful officials, to serve as a triumvirate of regents for the young Liu emperor; probably it was Huo Guang himself who suggested to the dying Emperor Wu that Liu Fuling be appointed heir apparent. He was an ideal choice, from the point of view of Huo Guang and his allies: not only was he young and malleable but his mother, who had had no ties to the Li or Wei clans, was conveniently dead. The tripartite regency was assisted by the veteran high official Sang Hongyang, known for his mathematical abilities. Sang had held a number of important posts under Emperor Wu and was an acknowledged expert in the agricultural economy.

The enthronement of Emperor Zhao was soon contested. The king of Yan, Liu Dan, a son of Emperor Wu who had his own claim to the throne, formed a plot in 86 BCE to oust the boy-emperor and take his place. The plot failed but Liu Dan adroitly avoided prosecution; being a Liu, he was even allowed to retain his kingdom. But when he tried again in 80 BCE with a scheme that included the planned assassination of Huo Guang, Liu Dan was betrayed and forced to commit suicide. Afterwards the Kingdom of Yan was abolished and absorbed into the imperial domain. Liu Dan no doubt believed he had strong allies, as Shangguan Jie, one of the original triumvirate of regents, was a party to the plot, along with his son Shangguan An and the imperial counselor Sang Hongyang. All were executed. The upshot of these chaotic events was to leave Huo Guang, the sole surviving regent, in a stronger position than ever. The formal structures of government, with its heads of various ministries and other high officials, continued to function, but real, though extra-judicial, power was in the hands of the Huo clan.

The fate of the Huo Clan

Emperor Zhao died in 74 BCE, aged twenty-two, without having named an heir. His widow, aged fifteen (a grand-daughter of Huo Guang) thus became empress dowager, and a message was sent in her name to Liu He, king of Changyi, inviting him to become Emperor Zhao's successor. He responded by racing to the capital at break-neck speed, whereupon he ensconced himself in the palace and immediately began to live a life of riotous excess. Shocked, Huo Guang rescinded the invitation less than four weeks later and deposed Liu He, who never formally became emperor. (His lavish tomb has recently been excavated; the rich funerary offerings included, among many other things, more than ten tons of bronze coins.) The throne was next offered to eighteen-year-old Liu Pingyi, a great-grandson of Emperor Wu, who became Emperor Xuan in 74 BCE.

Emperor Xuan, from the point of view of the Huo clan, had one defect: his consort, Xu Pingjun, who was not related to the Huo clan, had already borne him a son and heir. In 71 BCE, pregnant again, she was murdered on the orders of Huo Guang's wife (apparently without his knowledge) and replaced with one of Huo Guang's daughters. But the end of the family's domination of the throne was near. Huo Guang died, apparently from natural causes, in 68 BCE. His sons and nephews at first retained their positions of power, but the loss of the venerable clan leader left them in a precarious position, while their perceived arrogance alienated other influential clans.

Emperor Xuan, in an act of asserting his authority, affirmed his choice of his son by Xu Pingjun as his heir. This prompted a conspiracy in 66 BCE to overthrow Emperor Xuan and replace him with Huo Guang's son, Huo Yu, but the plot was discovered before it could be implemented. Almost all of the men of the Huo clan were executed or committed suicide and the imperial consort, Huo Guang's grand-daughter, was dismissed from the palace. Emperor Xuan seems to have taken an active interest in public affairs, encouraged debate on policy issues, and resisted any attempts on the part of other powerful families to step into the role vacated by the Huo clan. A significant achievement of his reign was the establishment of a lasting peace with the Xiongnu. A Xiongnu khan (one of two contenders for leadership of the confederation) visited Chang'an in 51 BCE and was accepted not as a tributary or supplicant but as the legitimate ruler of China's northern neighbor. Subsequent emperors failed to follow up on this breakthrough and troubles with the Xiongnu continued, but the northern frontier was relatively pacified and no longer presented a significant problem until Wang Mang's reign. Emperor Xuan died in 49 BCE and was succeeded without turmoil by his son, Emperor Yuan.

Emperor Yuan played no conspicuous role in the government of the empire, but public affairs during his sixteen years on the throne were in the hands of capable officials. They mainly pursued policies of retrenchment, motivated by a desire to regain control over public expenditures that had steadily climbed over the course of time. In the long run Emperor Yuan's most significant action took place before he ascended the throne: he fathered a son, Liu Shi, the future Emperor Cheng, by one of his palace women, Wang Zhengjun. She was from a respectable but not particularly powerful provincial family from Shandong, but her unusual longevity—she died in 13 CE, aged eighty-four—and her own political adroitness enabled her to advance the interests of her family over a period of several decades. Shortly after Emperor Yuan succeeded his father in 49 BCE Wang Zhengjun was elevated to the rank of empress and Liu Shi was named heir apparent.

When Liu Shi was enthroned as Emperor Cheng on the death of his father in 33 BCE, Wang Zhengjun became empress dowager, a position of considerable potential power. A year later her brother Wang Feng became marshal of state, the most powerful office in the imperial administration. He was followed in that office by four other close relatives of the empress dowager, making the office a de facto sinecure of the Wang family. The last of those was Wang Mang, who would play a crucial role in the downfall of the Western Han dynasty.

Emperor Cheng has a mixed historical reputation. He is said to have been well educated and fond of reading the classics; on the other hand, he is criticized for indulging too heavily in carnal pleasures. Like most of the later Eastern Han emperors he showed little interest in the work of government, although he apparently approved of the religious reforms of 31 BCE, which reduced the number, complexity, and expense of the imperially sponsored cults. But Emperor Cheng is best remembered for precipitating yet another succession crisis.

His consort, Empress Xu, did not produce a male heir. Neglecting her, the emperor became infatuated with a talented singer and dancer, Zhao Feiyan ("Flying Swallow Zhao"), who was, of course, of lowly status. Both Flying Swallow and her sister were enrolled in the imperial harem, and Flying Swallow was made empress in 16 BCE. To the emperor's disappointment neither of them produced a son. In a shockingly cold-blooded move, he ordered two sons by other concubines to be murdered at birth; had either boy lived, its mother would almost inevitably have eclipsed the two favored sisters as being the mother of the imperial heir. So he protected Flying Swallow and her sister even at the cost of having no heir apparent. In 8 BCE, at the age of seventeen, Liu Xin (not the scholar and bibliographer with a similar name), a grandson of Emperor Yuan, was named heir apparent and took the throne as Emperor Ai. He was connected on his mother's side to the powerful Fu and Ding clans and was supported by the marshal of state, Wang Gen (Wang Mang's father). His possible rival as heir apparent, Liu Xing (Emperor Cheng's younger brother), died in 8 BCE, having missed his chance for the throne, but his son would become Emperor Ping at age nine a few years later.

Emperor Cheng, who had been plagued with chronic bad health for several years, died in 7 BCE, and Liu Xin was enthroned as Emperor Ai at age twenty, with the approval of his grandmother, Emperor Yuan's widow, Grand Empress Dowager Wang. Around the same time Wang Mang succeeded his uncle as marshal of state, though the Wang clan was to go into temporary eclipse during Emperor Ai's seven-year reign. Emperor Ai soon became the center of a scandal, as he formed what seems to have been a strong homoerotic bond with another young man, Dong Xian. The emperor showered him with honors and wealth, culminating in his appointment in 2 BCE as marshal of state (Wang Mang having been dismissed earlier). All of this incurred the severe disapproval of his conservative government ministers and of powerful extra-governmental clan leaders as well. Not only did Emperor Ai reject the Confucian duty of loyal husband and filial son but his evident desire to play an active role in public affairs disrupted their sense of control. Then, even more shocking, was the emperor's proposal to abdicate, in the manner of the ancient sage-kings Yao and Shun, in favor of Dong Xian, presumably playing the role of worthy minister. This proposal failed.

One notable event early in the reign of Emperor Ai was the promulgation, in 7 BCE, of the Triple Concordance (*san tong*) calendar, a revision of the Grand Inception calendar of 104 BCE with improved calculations. The work of the polymath scholar Liu Xin (not the heir apparent mentioned above), it revisited the question of the dynasty's ruling Phase and proposed that the Production Sequence, not the Conquest Sequence, was most appropriate for understanding the omens associated with the succession of dynasties. Accordingly, new Phase correlates were calculated for all of the rulers of the Heartland Region back to the legendary god-kings of high antiquity, Fu Xi ("Tamer of Beasts," the procreator), Shen Nong (the "Divine Farmer," an agricultural deity), and the Yellow Emperor (first of the mythical sage-emperors). According to the Production scheme, the Phase of the Zhou was Wood, and the Qin was dismissed as illegitimate. This meant that the ruling Phase for the Han was Fire (wood produces fire), and so it was enacted. Fire was associated with the South and the ancient Chu state. It represented life and the peak of yang power. But any hope that the newly revised calendar would usher in an era of greater tranquility proved futile.

Emperor Ai, still only in his mid-twenties, died in 1 BCE without an heir. Grand Empress Dowager Wang, the undisputed leader of the Liu family, immediately stripped Dong Xian of his offices and sinecures; he committed suicide in response. With no designated heir, the nine-year-old Liu Jizi (Liu Xing's son), the last living male descendant of Emperor Yuan and thus a cousin of Emperor Ai, was deemed next in line for the throne. With the Grand Empress Dowager's backing, he mounted the throne as Emperor Ping, with Wang Mang as his regent. A signal accomplishment of Emperor Ping's reign was the census of 2 CE, which gave the population of the Han empire as 12,366,470 households, or 57,671,400 persons. This census, which also enumerated the empire's commanderies, counties, and kingdoms, testifies to the efficient functioning of the imperial bureaucracy, even when the emperor himself played no role in governing the empire. A deeply unfortunate event also took place during Emperor Ping's reign: the Yellow River burst its banks and created a catastrophic flood that inundated much of the river's flood plain, a natural disaster that would be interpreted as a bad omen.

As Emperor Ping's regent, Wang Mang immediately set about restoring the fortunes of the Wang clan. A key move was the appointment of his daughter, about the same age as the young emperor, as the emperor's consort, making Wang Mang the emperor's father-in-law and forcing the emperor into treating him with special respect. It would also result in Wang being the prospective grandfather of the next heir apparent. But there was to be no such heir. Emperor Ping died of unknown causes in 6 CE, leaving Wang Mang as regent to an empty throne.

Emperor Yuan's line of descent was now ended, but among the descendants of Emperor Yuan's father, Emperor Xuan, there were several potential candidates for the throne, some of them adults with potentially valuable political experience. Passing over these candidates, Wang Mang, with the support of the Grand Empress Dowager, chose an infant, Liu Ying, as the heir to the throne. This was a clear and unmistakable signal that Wang Mang intended to continue in power as regent. (He may genuinely have felt that his strong leadership was needed to cope with the disastrous Yellow River flood.) Liu Ying was never enthroned as emperor, however; Wang Mang took the unusual title of Acting Emperor in 7 CE. This naked power grab provoked outrage among powerful members of the Liu clan, and several Liu nobles led armed uprisings against Wang Mang. But Wang Mang controlled the army and all such opposition was defeated; Wang Mang had made certain that his hold on power was secure. At the beginning of 9 CE he abandoned all pretense of ruling on behalf of the Liu clan and announced his receipt of the Mandate of Heaven as first emperor of the Xin (New) dynasty. Accepting the claim of the Triple Concordance calendar that dynastic succession was determined by the Production Cycle of the Five Phases, so that the Han ruled with the power of Fire, Wang Mang proclaimed that his new dynasty therefore ruled with the power of Earth (fire produces earth: ashes). Accordingly, he ordered that all ritual garments be yellow, the color linked with the mythical first emperor and also symbolically associated with the Center. The Han dynasty, seemingly, had come to an end.

A look back: Modernists versus Reformers

Throughout the Western Han Period two visions of government competed for influence and implementation. Modernists and Reformers framed debates on government policies, each finding evidence in different sets of classics aligned either with Legalist or Confucian ideological trends. The former felt that the Zhou model required the additional enforcement of social norms by means of rewards and punishments, and the latter felt that the Zhou model simply had to be adhered to faithfully and made stronger. The Modernists accepted the argument, made forcefully in, for example, the *Huainanzi*, that times change, and policies must change with the times; minimalist rule by inspired sage-kings may have been appropriate for high antiquity, but would not work in the current age. They drew ideas from such texts as the *Book of Lord Shang*, the *Hanfeizi*, and the *Guanzi*, advocated the centralizing tendencies of the Qin dynasty's government, and accepted the need for punitive laws as a device for maintaining public order. The Reformers, on the other hand, did not necessarily dispute the need for change, but found inspiration in works associated with Confucius, such as the *Analects*, the *Odes*, and the *Springs and Autumns*, and argued for the cultivation of model kings and less use of law. Both groups accepted the widespread notion that the Zhou model of government was ideal.

In the early reigns of the Western Han, and particularly during that of Emperor Wu, the Modernists tended to prevail. This was reflected in Emperor Wu's aggressive stance toward the Xiongnu and his expansionist foreign policy more generally; in his efforts to rein in and, in many cases, abolish the territorial kingdoms; in his support for state monopolies on salt, iron, and fermented beverages; and in his founding of a state academy to train potential recruits for the imperial bureaucracy. These policies, and the emperor's generally statist stance, were arguably important contributors to the prosperity and stability of the empire during the early- to mid-Western Han Period—particularly as they continued rather than disrupted what had been put in place by the Qin. Expansion, especially that involving military coercion, was very expensive, however, and strained the state's ability to collect sufficient tax revenue in a fair and relatively non-burdensome way (Figure 11.1). The subsequent financial crisis led to a shift towards the Reformist approach among counselors and ministers of state.

In 81 BCE, in the sixth year of Emperor Zhao's reign, a full-scale court debate was held in the presence of the monarch himself on economic policy, including the question of state monopolies (see Focus: *Debates on Salt and Iron*). The debate had a mixed outcome; although the Reformers prevailed, subsequent efforts to abolish the state monopolies were short-lived and soon rescinded as impractical. The revenue foregone was too high a price to pay for the sake of downsizing government controls. The Reformers, throughout the latter part of the Western Han Period, advocated a traditional reliance on agricultural products remitted to the state as the basis of state revenue, but treasury officials warned of dire consequences if taxes paid in cash were abolished on markets, internal transport, luxury goods, and other such pursuits. One area in which the Reformers did prevail was in a retreat from aggressive action in foreign policy. Once Emperor Wu's expansionist forays into the southwest, northwest, and Korea stopped, and military garrisons were withdrawn from forward positions, Han control over border regions became problematical. The failure to pursue the peace initiative of 51 BCE with the Xiongnu would prove to be a mistake.

Figure 11.1 Mold for casting bronze *wushu* coins, Han dynasty.

One policy issue that vexed Modernists and Reformers alike was the issuance of patents of nobility. As a matter of policy all male descendants of Emperor Gao who were not enthroned as rulers of territorial kingdoms were awarded the title of lord (*hou*), which carried with it a stipend and exemption from certain taxes and duties. There was also constant pressure to confer the same title and privileges on worthy (or just influential) men not of the Liu clan. A rising nouveau riche class made up of merchants or lineages with secondary connections to the royal family put pressure on the throne to relax the old system, modeled on the Zhou, of tightly restricting ennoblement to members of the ruling clan. Repeated attempts by successive emperors to eliminate the burden of these hereditary posts were largely unsuccessful.

On the whole, while the arguments of the Reformists may have seemed to prevail at the policy level, at all other levels of government the Modernists' methods proved more practical. The legal code and tax system were updated but not rescinded. Unfortunately, the dynamic tension between these two groups and the levels of government over which they held sway did not create a stronger and more healthy government. Instead, policy inconsistency fed the unrest and instability characteristic of late Western Han government.

Religious and government reform

Ever since Emperor Gao's construction of a temple to the Thearch of the North in 202 BCE, the number and kinds of temple enjoying imperial patronage, and their associated rituals, grew steadily and haphazardly over the course of the Han Period. Although Reformers generally approved of mortuary worship, the extravagant sums spent on state rituals to nature spirits and unapproved ancestors appalled them. They succeeded in drastically reducing at least three rites to such spirits and their expenditures. The reform of religious practices, announced in an imperial decree in 31 BCE, was largely the work of one of the most influential and highly placed men of the Reform movement, Kuang Heng, who served as chancellor from 36 to 30 BCE (spanning the reigns of Emperors Yuan and Cheng).

By the late decades of the Western Han it was clear that something had to be done about imperial religious observances. Temples to numerous imperial ancestors and to nature deities such as the Earth God, *Taiyi*, and the directional thearchs, in or near Chang'an as well as at distant ritual centers such as Yong, employed tens of thousands of people, ranging from butchers and cooks to ushers and guards to high-ranking temple superintendents. Moreover, some of these cults, while no less expensive, had fallen into semi-disuse. Emperors no longer officiated at most of the ceremonies, especially as so many ritual observances made claims on their time. Under the new policy urged by Kuang Heng, services to *Taiyi* and the directional thearchs were suspended, and the worship of Heaven and Earth, more or less as advocated by Dong Zhongshu in the time of Emperor Wu, was confirmed as the highest imperial ritual obligation, along with sacrifices to the imperial ancestors. New suburban temples were constructed for this purpose and some other cult temples were decommissioned.

One impulse for these religious reforms may have been to invoke Heaven's assistance in giving Emperor Cheng a son and heir. It proved unsuccessful. The decommissioning of temples and the focus on the worship of Heaven and Earth was controversial. The high-born intellectual, official, and member of the royal family Liu Xiang, usually sympathetic to the Reform movement, opposed the discontinuance of worship of any imperial ancestor (see Focus: Liu Xiang and Liu Xin). This may have been due to political concerns over the cutting off of lines of lineage authority, or simply that he feared the possibility that the neglected deities would retaliate against the emperor and his government. Over the next twenty-five years hundreds of temples and shrines were first decommissioned, then restored, then taken out of service again as arguments raged about the scope and expense of imperial cults.

Along with the reform of religious practices and the attempted cut-backs of imperial observances were reforms to the Music Bureau, the operations of which were bound up with the ceremonies at the imperial shrines. By the time of Emperor Cheng the Music Bureau had thousands of employees, including hundreds of musicians, singers, dancers, composers, and lyricists. In 48 and 33 BCE the Bureau was ordered to reduce its payroll, to little effect; finally the Music Bureau was abolished in 7 BCE, and its functions assigned to other parts of the bureaucracy.

One other economic reform mandated reducing the size and contents of imperial tombs. Mortuary display was a key tenet of Confucian practice, one once severely criticized by the Mohists during the Warring States Period. The tombs of the early Han emperors were spectacular constructions, with vast underground chambers and surmounted by huge mounds. The expenses associated with such tombs involved not only their construction and the provision of extravagant grave goods (Figure 11.2) but long-term maintenance as well. The early Han imperial tombs were provided with newly built villages to which tens of thousands of families were forcibly relocated from other parts of the empire to guard and service the tombs. Beginning with Emperor Zhao, regulations were promulgated, apparently at least somewhat effectively, limiting the size of imperial tombs and prohibiting the forced migration of human tomb custodians and guards (and their families).

The Reformists reached their apogee during the New dynasty of Wang Mang, who tried to radically transform the bloated Han government into a utopian Zhou model. The worship of Heaven and Earth was important to his campaign of demonstrating that he was the authorized Son of Heaven, ruling through the Phase of Earth. He even attempted to rebuild a Hall of Light (mingtong), a mandala-like building intended to harness cosmic forces through its geometric design. He tried to reform agriculture and the tax system and continued to weaken

Figure 11.2 Late Western Han lamp in the shape of a bird holding in its beak a circular reservoir for the lamp's oil.

border controls. The policies of his Xin dynasty can be regarded, as we shall see, as an experiment in implementing the Reform agenda. In part for reasons beyond his control, it did not end well.

Han popular religion

The late Western Han Period offers us the first sustained look at popular religion in China. In 3 BCE there was an upsurge in popular enthusiasm, amounting almost to mass hysteria, for the cult of immortality associated with the Dowager Queen of the West (Xiwangmu). As the *Han shu* describes it, thousands of peasants joined a huge procession of devotees who marched across northern China, going as far westward as Chang'an. Carrying straw effigies and banners, chanting, dancing, and singing, they set up camp in the capital and played rounds of *liubo*, the game of immortals. In the capital they obtained lucky talismans of the goddess, after which they dispersed and went home. This event was recorded in the dynastic history because it was unusual and possibly a threat to public order. More generally, however, the official historians had little to say about popular religion. We know almost nothing about the ordinary religious beliefs and practices of Han peasants and workers.

Chinese merchants traveling to Central Asia along the newly opened Silk Road came into contact with Buddhist communities in oasis cities such as Turfan and Bukhara, and may have been responsible for bringing Buddhism back to China. By the end of the Han Period it had clearly been seeded in several urban centers, such as Pengcheng in the Huai River Valley. There were probably some Chinese converts to Buddhism in northern China well before 65 CE, the earliest mention of Buddhism in the official Chinese record. This record was in the *Hou Han shu* (*History of the Latter Han Dynasty*), written by Confucian scholars who objected to anything other than traditional forms of worship and had little interest in publicizing records of unapproved, and especially foreign, religious activities.

The world of ancient China was richly populated with ghosts and spirits and minor deities, all requiring occult activities to service or repel them. Everything was made of *qi*, which could be baleful as well as beneficent. Whirlwinds and dust devils were demonic manifestations that might cause illness. Neglecting the proper sacrifices to the Door God could break up families, cause illness and death, or trigger accidents and disasters such as house-destroying fires. Such matters affected commoners and rulers alike. Ordinary people must have dealt with occult phenomena through local healers and diviners, but at the top of the sociopolitical scale the observation and interpretation of portents and omens was a matter of serious official concern. High ministers in charge of ritual matters interpreted omens on earth and in the sky. Unusual events, such as comets or meteors, might be warnings to the emperor that his conduct was improper and needed to be improved. Events that took place in the sky demanded special attention because they seemed to be warnings from Heaven itself, but terrestrial phenomena could be portentous as well. The unexplained destruction by fire of an imperial ancestral shrine was not just a misfortune, it was a sign that required interpretation and an appropriate imperial response. On the other hand, the sighting—or even better, the alleged capture—of a dragon or a *qilin* was among the best possible omens, as it indicated that a sage ruler was on the throne. ("*Qilin*" is often mistranslated as "unicorn." In the Chinese imagination it was a chimera made up of parts of several different animals. Reports of actual *qilins* may refer to sightings of a saola (*Pseudoryx nghetinhensis*), a very rare wild bovine that superficially appears to have only one horn.) Local officials were responsible for collecting news of strange natural phenomena and passing it up to their superiors for investigation and interpretation. A famous case, dating to the Spring and Autumn Period but still cited in the Han, was of a flock of herons seen flying backwards (presumably fighting a strong headwind) over the state of Song; this was taken as a warning of incipient trouble in that state. A frequent response to omens was the proclamation of an imperial amnesty, emptying the prisons and rescinding or reducing punishments, as a way of generating "virtue" (*de*), by then understood as a kind of beneficent yang *qi*, to counteract the omen's baleful *qi*.

One problem with omens is that they could easily be fabricated. The sighting of mythical animals is an obvious case in point; in the absence of reliable means of documentation, eye-witness testimony could not be confirmed but was too important to ignore. It is certain that some celestial phenomena were faked. Modern astronomers can use computer modeling to show the exact configuration of the sky at any place on earth on any date in the past, and using these methods it is possible to demonstrate that some recorded solar eclipses, for example, could not have occurred or could not have been seen in the Heartland Region as reported. Bogus omens could be used by officials to influence an emperor's conduct.

Omens by definition were random events occurring outside the normal cosmic order. Thus divination, which also relied on randomness for its magical power, was the first tool for determining the nature of the events. Prognostication could not only diagnose the present condition and recommend healing methods but also predict the future. Official diviners examined the shell patterns and movements of a live "spirit" tortoise and also cast milfoil stalks to generate trigrams and hexagrams. The interaction of their yin and yang lines could provide diagnoses and predictions, although texts such as the *Book of Changes*, filled with cryptic sayings for each line, had by then been largely appropriated by court intellectuals as material for philosophical speculation and were less often employed as tools for practical divination. Official astrologers observed the movement of stars and planets, winds from the eight directions, and other phenomena in a procedure called "watching the *qi*." This method relied on physical devices used to ascertain that the *qi* of the eight directions accorded with the annual waxing and waning of yin and yang.

Throughout the Han dynasty there was a proliferation of texts dealing with various topics concerning omens and prognostication. An active metaphor for the cosmos was the image of woven cloth. Texts dealing with divining techniques and omen reading were generally referred to as "weft" (*wei*) texts, to distinguish them from the more fundamental "warp" (*jing*) texts of the established classics. The weft texts cover a very wide range of topics, including physiognomy (the practice of divining a person's character from his or her facial features); geomancy (the practice of finding auspicious locations for buildings or tombs); alchemy; various means for attaining longevity or immortality; the diagnosis and treatment of diseases, including exorcism and sacrificial rituals; and procedures for dealing with droughts and floods, and for bringing or stopping rain. The unifying thread of all of these texts and the procedures they prescribe was the correlative cosmological scheme of yin–yang and the Five Phases. In the Han, because *qi* was the material substance of all reality, an anomaly in anything from the shapes of body parts to irregular trees might be considered a sign. Signs could be positive or negative, but since the people were especially fearful of the supernatural, divination methods had to provide methods for deflecting negative consequences. On the other hand, the expression of *qi* in landscape features might determine the best location for a burial, a site that would keep the deceased happy in his tomb and unlikely to bother anybody. Ironically, despite the connection of occult practices with omenology, even the Reformers could not dismiss it. Wang Mang was particularly fascinated by omens and portents.

Disruption and usurpation: The Xin dynasty

Like all short-lived claimants of the Mandate of Heaven, Wang Mang is vilified in China's official histories, portrayed as a nepotistic conspirator, a rebel, a usurper who deserved his grisly death as he struggled to save his collapsing dynasty. Wang Mang's authority, despite all sorts of good omens, was too fragile to support a new dynasty. It fell without even one imperial succession, undermined by a combination of radical policies and simple bad luck. The historical portrait of Wang Mang is very incomplete; all we know of him is what the court scribes of the restored Han dynasty, the Eastern Han, chose to record.

Reading between the lines of Ban Gu's negative portrait in the *Han shu*, Wang Mang seems to have been well educated, charismatic, ambitious, both devious and ruthless when he felt those qualities were necessary, and sincere in his Reformist beliefs. In his years as regent he promoted a number of useful public works projects, such as new roads and canals. He was also astute enough to pave the way for the establishment of his New dynasty by ensuring that a number of auspicious omens were discovered to legitimize his claim to the Mandate. Claiming that the ruling power of his dynasty was Earth, with its yellow emblems, he employed skilled genealogists to trace his ancestry back to the Yellow Emperor himself, belying his "more recent" and actual origins in the rural gentry. In due course mysterious inscribed stones were discovered and interpreted to mean that the power of Yellow was in the ascendant. This public relations feat helped Wang Mang defeat the opposition. The remaining powerful elite (those he did not crush) were, or pretended to be, convinced by cosmic signs of Wang Mang's legitimacy. Scattered armed uprisings led by various members of the Liu family, each supporting contending Han heirs, were put down without much difficulty.

Wang Mang's formal accession to the throne in 9 CE was followed by a blizzard of new policies and programs, a classic case of trying to do too much too soon. In the first five years of his reign he adjusted the coinage four times, with the overall effect of putting smaller denominations into circulation, thus encouraging the Reformist position of taxes paid in agricultural goods rather than cash. The burden of high taxes paid in grain led to agrarian rebellions. Wang Mang found some Modernist positions useful to his empire building, however, and affirmed the state monopolies on salt, iron, and the minting of coins. In addition, he taxed merchants whenever they transported goods, rented stalls to sell them, or profited from trade. The tax on business profits was China's first income tax. Animals, wood, fish, or mining products caught or produced on public land—Wang Mang followed the Zhou idea that all land belonged to the state—were also taxed. Since many farmers paid in grain and grain was a staple of every meal, he attempted to protect the peasantry from hardship by following a policy associated with the legendary seventh-century BCE economist and political theorist Guanzi (Guan Zhong). This established a system of state granaries and controlled the prices at which grain was bought and sold, supporting the price during years of abundance and lowering it in years of bad harvest. Extra stores also acted as a hedge against the effects of natural disasters, making grain available for famine relief.

As one of his first moves on establishing the new dynasty, Wang Mang demoted to commoner status most of the numerous males of the Liu clan who had been ennobled under the Han dynasty; this had the unwanted side effect of creating a network of resentful ex-aristocrats with vast connections to all key regions of the empire. (Some members of the Liu clan who had convincingly demonstrated their loyalty to Wang Mang were permitted to change their surname to Wang and to keep their titles of nobility.) Wang Mang's obsession with recovering ideal Confucian models of government led him to try to recreate the nine-division well-field system described in the book of *Mencius*. All able-bodied men were assigned plots of farmland of equal size surrounding a central plot of "public" land that they would farm collectively, with the grain so produced being remitted to the state. The rural gentry, facing the prospect of their extensive landholdings being seized and divided up among the peasantry, revolted.

When Wang Mang came to power he sent envoys to the non-Sinitic kingdoms in the northwest, southwest, and northeast. He wanted to avoid the Han plan of paying them to behave submissively, and attempted to force them to acknowledge him as emperor and to pay tribute. Relations with the rulers of these faraway kingdoms deteriorated, and eventually Wang Mang had to resort to force to defend China's frontiers, causing a great financial drain on the imperial treasury. He lost many units of his armies in these battles, further weakening his position in the capital. Even so, Wang Mang might have learned from his mistakes and adjusted his policies to be more effective if two catastrophic floods of the Yellow River, one just preceding his reign and one in the midst of it, had not inundated much of the empire's key agricultural land, made his agricultural tax plan unfeasible, and plunged millions of people into despair.

For most of the first millennium BCE the Yellow River took a northerly path across its vast flood plain, flowing to the Gulf of Bohai with its mouth near the present-day city of Tianjin. The river had a proclivity to silt up its channel, causing the river to spill over its dikes into the surrounding farmland. One breach of the Yellow River dikes during the reign of Han Emperor Wu took over a decade to repair. But the floods of the early first century CE were of a different order of magnitude. The first flood occurred soon after the census of 2 CE, during the reign of the young Emperor Ping; it naturally was seen in some quarters as an omen foretelling the demise of the Han dynasty. The floodwaters are thought to have killed tens of thousands of people outright and to have caused the deaths of as many more from starvation and disease. By the time the waters had drained away the river had split in two, with part of its flow staying in the old northern channel and a new southern branch draining into the Huai River. (Strenuous efforts blocked the southern branch in 70 CE and restored the entire flow of the river to the north. The river would shift its course several more times in the ensuing 2,000 years.)

Floods were bad omens. Just as the one during Emperor Ping's reign portended the end of the Han, the equally catastrophic flood of 11 CE must have been seen as a rebuke of the usurper Wang Mang. Water was overcoming Earth. Thousands died and many more became refugees, often migrating to the relatively sparsely populated southern regions of the empire. When the flood subsided it was found that the northern branch of the river had cut a new channel flowing just to the north of the Shandong Peninsula. The towns along the old, now-dry river bed lost their livelihoods. The effects of the floods lasted for years and, ultimately, doomed the new dynasty.

The restoration of the Han dynasty

As flooding led to famine, especially in Shandong (which was totally cut off from the rest of the Heartland Region by the two branches of the Yellow River), popular indignation at the government's inadequate relief efforts broke out in scattered peasant uprisings and gave rise to bandit gangs of disenfranchised peasants roaming in Shandong and the Yellow River Plain. The gangs preyed on local communities, leading to even more widespread suffering. Some rebel bands evolved into organized uprisings directed against local authorities; county offices were ransacked and officials were murdered or forced to flee. As bands of armed peasants grew into armies and coalesced into a general armed insurrection some rebels began painting their foreheads with red pigment, coming to be known as the "Red Eyebrows." The wearing of red may have been a sign of loyalty to the Han dynasty, whose emblematic color was red according to the Production Cycle of the Five Phases. The red marks also likely functioned as talismans meant to protect the rebels from injury or death.

A first attempt, in 18 CE, to deal with the peasant uprisings as a domestic military emergency was a total failure; an imperial army was unable to make any headway against the rebels. A larger and better-trained army dispatched to Shandong in 22 CE was also unsuccessful; its commanding general was killed and the army retreated in a rout. During that same year Wang Mang's situation became steadily more precarious. The Red Eyebrows movement had numerous members but no effective leadership, so it split into several armies. One controlled Shandong, while others spread out in parts of the Yellow River Plain. Other rebellions, not directly connected with the Red Eyebrows, broke out in the middle and lower reaches of the Yangzi River. One of those armies overran an area known as Nanyang (in today's southern Henan Province), which happened to be the home territory of some minor members of the Han imperial Liu clan, descendants of Emperor Jing several generations removed. Three of them—Liu Yan (also known as Liu Bosheng), his younger brother, Liu Xiu, and their cousin Liu Xuan, worked out a deal with the rebel leaders. Liu Yan would lead their army in exchange for protection for his family. Thus the so-called Xuanshi Army acquired experienced military leadership and became a cause that local elites would support to fight Wang Mang.

Liu Yan proved himself to be a very capable military leader and, by the end of 22 CE, Wang Mang was clearly on the defensive. In March of 23 CE the rebels were ready to proclaim the restoration of the Han dynasty. Contending Liu survivors first enthroned Liu Xuan, and not Liu Yan, as the first emperor of the restored dynasty. Known as the Gengshi (Renewed Beginning) Emperor, he was a feckless leader who feared his more powerful relatives, such as Liu Yan and Liu Xiu. As war continued to rage with Wang Mang's armies, his court failed to be awarded a formal dynastic name, giving later historians the impression that he was not yet the true Han emperor. Large-scale battles between troops loyal to the resurgent Han dynasty and the imperial forces of Wang Mang continued during the summer of 23 CE, with Liu Xiu playing a leading role in inflicting a series of defeats on Wang Mang's forces. Liu Xuan got rid of Liu Yan by accusing him of treason and having him executed.

Meanwhile, in the old capital city, Chang'an, members of a different branch of the Liu family, including the famous scholar Liu Xin, conspired to overthrow Wang Mang. The plot was discovered and all the conspirators were executed or forced to commit suicide. That was not enough, however, to save Wang Mang's crumbling regime. New uprisings continued to break out in many parts of the empire and, crucially, members of the elite began deserting Wang Mang in droves. In the early autumn of 23 CE rebel troops entered Chang'an. Wang Mang died fighting for his life. His body was cut up and his head placed on the city wall in the new Han capital in Luoyang. The Xin dynasty had fallen.

Focus: *Debates on Salt and Iron*

In 81 BCE, when Emperor Zhao was in his mid-teens and the imperial government was effectively in the hands of Huo Guang, a formal debate was held in the presence of the emperor to examine fundamental aspects of government policy. That move was rare but not unprecedented. Formal debates were a recognized means of examining important policy issues, with participants encouraged to speak freely and in some cases to submit written recommendations. The debate of 81 BCE, on the salt and iron monopolies and related issues, was explicitly prompted by reports of hardship and unrest in the countryside, with participants in the debate being asked to explain the causes of popular discontent. This particular debate is unusually well documented because one of the participants, Huan Kuan, wrote a book-length account of the debate several years after the event. Although Huan's book, the *Yan tie lun* (*Debates on Salt and Iron*), is not a transcript of the debate, but a literary reconstruction of it, scholars generally agree that it is a fair representation of the proceedings. The debate featured proponents of what have come to be known as the Modernist and Reformist viewpoints, and Huan Kuan himself was firmly in the Reformist camp, but his summary of the arguments put forward by the leading Modernist, Sang Hongyang, is judicious and even admiring.

The debate itself concentrated on four policy questions: the government monopolies on salt and on iron, the "equitable marketing" system of price controls on markets, and the excise tax on fermented beverages. However, the larger context of the debate was the nature of imperial government itself. Should the imperial government model itself on the early kings of the Zhou dynasty, as the Reformists would prefer, or should it pragmatically employ policies modeled on those of the Qin dynasty and as advocated in such classics as the *Hanfeizi*? The arguments on both sides had value.

The Reformers contended that the government should not engage in business, competing with private merchants. Moreover, the iron agricultural tools produced by government workshops were of inferior quality, causing distress to the peasantry; private artisans produced better products. Further, they asserted, the price of salt set by the government was too high, putting it out of reach of ordinary people; the same was true of the excise tax on ale. As for the equitable management of trade, it would be better to discourage mercantile activity in general, except when it benefited agriculture.

The Modernists replied that the threat of the Xiongnu on the northern frontier was severe and unrelenting. It demanded a military response in the form of garrisons, fortifications, and watchtowers. But those measures were very expensive; the government could not get along without the profits from the salt and iron monopolies and the tax on millet ale (a product indispensable for rituals and banquets). Furthermore, government production of those commodities ensured that they were available to everyone who needed them. Trade should be encouraged but properly regulated. Foreign trade enriched the country; exotic and valuable goods could be acquired in exchange for a few bolts of silk, a commodity plentiful in Han China.

The Reformists countered by saying that most foreign goods were simply unnecessary luxuries. They felt that diplomacy (in practical terms, the payment of bribes in return for peace) was cheaper and more effective than military confrontation, and that government should emphasize virtue, simplicity, and frugality and take agriculture as the basic activity of the populace. Back and forth the arguments ranged, with the debaters resorting to numerous textual citations of precedent and for supporting rhetoric.

Finally, both Modernists and Reformists agreed that government needed to change with the times. But the Reformists insisted that government had to lead people through benevolence and righteousness, while the Modernists scornfully described their opponents as glib debaters with no practical experience in government. In the end, according to the *Yan tie lun*, the Reformists won the debate, if by a narrow margin; but in practical terms the Modernists prevailed. The monopolies on salt and iron, and other Modernist policies, continued unchanged.

Scholars suggest that the Reformist arguments recorded in the *Debates on Salt and Iron* for the first time articulate in detail a Confucian program of government. The book is thus seen as a key work in the development during the Han dynasty of Confucianism as a coherent doctrine. In the bibliographical chapter of the *Han shu* the *Yan tie lun* is shelved with the *Ru* (Confucian) texts.

Focus: Liu Xiang and Liu Xin

Liu Xiang and Liu Xin, father and son, were members of a minor branch of the imperial house of Liu. Liu Xiang (79–8 BCE) was the great-grandson of a younger brother of Emperor Gao. He rose from relative obscurity to become one of the leading writers and intellectuals of the late Western Han Period. His younger son, Liu Xin (46 BCE–23 CE), followed in his father's footsteps.

Liu Xiang showed literary talent from an early age. At around eighteen he presented a large collection of his poems in several styles, including the admired genre of rhyme-prose (*fu*), to Emperor Xuan, who was evidently pleased with them. Liu Xiang's career, and indeed his life, nearly came to an end shortly afterwards, however, when he unwisely vouched for an alchemist who claimed to be able to turn base metals into gold. When the fraudulent alchemist was exposed Liu Xiang was sentenced to death; fortunately, he was ransomed by his elder brother at great expense. Thereafter he held a series of mid-level government jobs but did not make a career in public service. He is best remembered for his scholarly and literary work.

The three main commentaries on the *Springs and Autumns*, the *Gongyang*, *Guliang*, and *Zuo* commentaries, served as a focus of debate among adherents of the Confucian tradition as to the proper interpretation of that classic and its lessons for the present day. The *Gongyang Commentary*, associated with such scholars as Dong Zhongshu and Huan Kuan, was highly favored during the reign of Emperor Wu, but lost ground to the *Guliang Commentary* under his successors. At a court debate in 51 BCE to compare the merits of the two commentaries Liu Xiang took a major role in presenting the *Guliang* case. (His son would later become a champion of the *Zuo Commentary*.) Consistent with the *Guliang Commentary*'s interest in portents and other occult phenomena, Liu Xiang was considered an expert interpreter of omens and played a significant part in explaining the many portents and omens that were reported to the throne in the waning years of the Western Han Period. As a committed Confucian Liu Xiang extolled the virtue of the royal paragons of the past and was vocally critical, at some danger to himself, of the undue influence of great families such as the Wang clan and its matriarch, the Grand Empress Dowager.

As a scholar he brought new intellectual tools to his work on the classics. In particular, he became a recognized expert on the "Hong fan" ("Great Plan") chapter of the *Book of Documents*, which he interpreted in terms of yin–yang and the Five Phases. Of his substantial literary output, only a fraction survives. Most of his poetry has been lost, as has the *Seven Overviews* (*Qi lüe*), a compilation of notes on a wide range of books written jointly with Liu Xin. An abbreviated version of the *Seven Overviews* was incorporated into the bibliographical chapter (chapter 30) of the *Han shu*. His surviving works include the *New Prefaces* (*Xin xu*) and the *Garden of Tales* (*Shuo yuan*), two collections of historical anecdotes and moral stories, the *Stratagems of the Warring States* (*Zhanguo ce*), a collection of historical anecdotes about war and diplomacy, many of which relate to the horizontal and vertical alliances of the Warring States Period, and the *Arrayed Biographies of Women* (*Lie nü zhuan*), a collection of brief lives of women known for their virtue and honor, or the reverse. This may have been written as an implicit criticism of the Grand Empress Dowager or as a lesson book exemplifying proper behavior for the growing number of educated elite women. It has been a durable work, and greatly influenced the education and upbringing of young women for almost 2,000 years.

Liu Xin carried out his father's bibliographical work and completed the *Qi lüe* that his father had begun. Under Emperor Ai he was given the responsibility of collecting and collating the texts preserved in the imperial palace, including supposedly "secret texts" that had been kept in hidden rooms. He thus continued the task of preparing authoritative copies of the books that had been burned by Qin Shihuangdi and recovered orally or from written fragments in the early Han. He studied the *Zuo Commentary* to the *Springs and Autumns*, and urged that book's importance for understanding the annals. As compared with the *Gongyang* and *Guliang* commentaries, it relies less on textual exegesis and more on historical anecdotes that flesh out the brief entries of the *Springs and Autumns*. (His father continued to prefer the *Guliang Commentary*.) Along with his achievement in raising awareness of the *Zuo Commentary* and establishing it as a key Confucian text, Liu Xin's most famous accomplishment was the preparation of the Triple Concordance (*San tong*) calendar of 7 BCE.

In the waning years of the Western Han and into the early years of the Xin dynasty Liu Xin became a loyal advisor of Wang Mang, interpreting portents and giving advice on matters of rituals and ceremonies. Exceptionally, he was allowed to retain the surname Liu, perhaps as a sign of special favor because his daughter had married one of Wang Mang's sons. Amid the chaos of the early 20s CE Liu Xin became disillusioned with Wang Mang and joined a conspiracy to overthrow him and restore the Han dynasty. The plot was discovered and Liu Xin was forced to commit suicide, a few months before Wang Mang's own demise.

Focus: A TLV mirror

Beginning in the late Warring States Period and continuing through the Han and beyond, bronze mirrors were luxury items greatly esteemed by members of the elite. Made of bronze with an unusually high tin content, their flat front surface could be polished to a high degree of reflectivity. Cast into their backs were various pictorial images, as well as prayers and blessings. The magical nature of the mirrors were enhanced by symbolic representations of cosmological ideas (Figure 11.3).

Figure 11.3 A Xin dynasty TLV mirror, early first century CE.

Mirrors from the late Warring States to early Han Periods often feature stylized versions of the character for "mountain" (*shan*, 山), with four such characters marking off a central square; this pattern implies the square earth, the four cardinal directions, and their sacred mountains. Other mirrors from the same period feature stylized tree leaves marking the four, or eight, directions. In the late Western Han and into Wang Mang's New dynasty, a far more elaborate pattern became fashionable; it borrowed the TLV markings of the *liubo* game-board as the key element of a miniature version of the entire cosmos. A TLV mirror enabled its possessor in effect to be able to hold a microcosmic version of the universe in his (or her) hand.

The example shown here is fairly typical. It has a large central knob, pierced, through which a silken cord could be threaded and used to hold the mirror. This central knob represents Mt. Kunlun, the *axis mundi* at the center of the universe, and the abode of the Dowager Queen of the West, goddess of immortality. The knob takes up about half of the space within a large square, representing the square earth. The remaining space is filled with twelve smaller knobs, labeled with the names of the twelve Earthly Branches of the sexagenary cycle. In the context of this miniature cosmography the twelve knobs represent three levels of time: the twelve double-hours of the day, the twelve lunar months of the year, and the twelve years of the orbital period of Jupiter. (The hours and the years were conventionally identified by the twelve animals—rat, ox, etc.—associated with the Earthly Branches.) Attached to the outside of the square earth are four T-shaped figures oriented in the four cardinal directions. These, in conjunction with the V-shaped figures further out toward the edge of the mirror, delineate an imaginary square that may be a reminder that, in the nine-continents cosmology of Zou Yan, the square earth is far more extensive than just the Sinitic Heartland. Each T-shaped figure is flanked by two knobs, eight in all. These represent the eight directions and the eight outer continents of Zou Yan's cosmography, each with its sacred mountain (each of which represents one of the eight pillars holding up the sky at the edges of the earth). They perhaps also recall the eight trigrams of the *Book of Changes*, correlated with the eight directions. Aligned with the straight sides and corners of the square earth are four L-shaped and four V-shaped figures; these attach to the circle further out at twelve points (one for each L, two for each V), again signifying the twelve double-hours of the day, the twelve lunar months of the year, and the twelve years of the Jupiter cycle, with the hours and years bringing to mind their animal symbols (rat, ox, tiger, etc.). In the band containing the Ts, Ls, and Vs, entwined with stylized vines, are the symbolic animals of the four directions, each portrayed at the beginning of its appropriate season: the bluegreen dragon in the northeast, the vermilion bird in the southeast, the white tiger in the southwest, and the dark warrior (a snake entwining a turtle) in the northwest. Other, rather enigmatic, animals fill the remaining space.

Beyond the circle delineated by the Ls and Vs is a band containing an inscription, typical in form and content, which reads: "The New (dynasty) has excellent copper. It comes from Danyang. Smelted with silver and tin, it is pure and bright. On the left the Dragon, and on the right the Tiger, rule the Four Quarters; the Vermilion Bird and the Dark Warrior conform to yin and yang. May your eight sons and nine grandsons govern." Beyond the band containing the inscription is a heavily hatched circle of uncertain significance; just beyond that is a sawtooth band representing the 9,999 points at which the plates of heaven mesh with each other (envisioned as resembling the squiggly lines where the bones of a skull join together). The whole design is surrounded by a wide band filled with waves, representing the great ocean that encircles the world.

It is easy to see how such mirrors, which compressed the entire cosmos onto a bronze disk a few inches in diameter, were treated as marvelous objects associated with immortals.

12 The Han restoration, the Eastern Han dynasty, and the Three Kingdoms Period

The end of ancient China

Introduction

The Xin dynasty came to an end with the death of Wang Mang in 23 CE, but the legitimacy of the restored Han dynasty was by no means assured at that point. Liu Xuan, known as the Gengshi Emperor, claimed the throne but could not unite the country behind him, and is not recognized in the *History of the Latter Han Dynasty* (*Hou Han shu*) as the restored dynasty's first ruler. Liu Xiu, recognized by historians as the founder of the Latter Han and known as Emperor Guangwu, proclaimed himself the Son of Heaven in 25 CE, but another decade of civil war would ensue before he was secure on his throne as the unchallenged ruler of all of China. His dynasty would endure for nearly two centuries, but it never matched the stability and prosperity of the Former Han, despite a fairly promising start. Four rulers—Emperor Guangwu and his three successors—reigned during the first eight decades of the Eastern Han. With the exception of the fourth sovereign, Emperor He, they were adults when they mounted the imperial throne, and their comparatively long reigns ensured the continuity of the dynasty and some measure of stability. But they were followed, for over a century, by a succession of ten child-emperors who were puppets in the hands of one powerful family or another. The second century of the Eastern Han was marred by the rise (and, usually, also the fall) of the great families, the growth of factionalism as inner-palace eunuchs and members of the imperial civil administration vied, sometimes bloodily, for control of the government, and peasant uprisings that morphed into great rebel armies which threatened the dynasty's survival.

The history of the last Latter Han ruler, Emperor Xian, is a sordid tale of bloodshed and betrayal, as powerful men in command of factional armies—Dong Zhuo, Yuan Shu, Cao Cao, and others—maneuvered and fought to control the imperial throne and unite the war-torn empire under their own leadership. When Emperor Xian abdicated in favor of Cao Cao's son, Cao Pi, in 220 CE, it appeared briefly that a new and vigorous dynastic founder might succeed in restoring China's unity. But it was not to be; neither Cao Pi nor his rivals had the strength to accomplish that feat. Instead, for the next forty-five years China had three would-be emperors, rulers of the contending kingdoms of Wei, Wu, and Shu Han. The establishment of the Three Kingdoms represented a mute acknowledgment that China's ancient period had come to an end. When China was finally reunited, after nearly four centuries of disunion, it had entered a new era.

Emperor Guangwu

Liu Xuan, who took the throne as the Gengshi Emperor in 23 CE, had succeeded in outmaneuvering and executing his rival Liu Yan, but he failed to keep Liu Yan's brother, Liu Xiu, on a tight leash. Moving too quickly to organize his dynastic government, he made the mistake of transferring his administration, and the bulk of his loyal armed forces, from Luo-yang to the old capital at Chang'an, allowing his rivals unimpeded access to the rich Yellow River Plain. Perhaps regarding the Red Eyebrows as an unimportant rabble, he declined to reward their leaders as they felt they deserved; they broke with the Gengshi Emperor and went on the march against him. Similarly, he slighted the Nanyang gentry that had played an important role in the defeat of Wang Mang, failing to make them rulers of restored kingdoms. Liu Xiu meanwhile had raised an independent army and took control of the northern reaches of the Yellow River Plain. In the autumn of 25 CE Red Eyebrow forces and Liu Xiu began campaigns to take the Wei River Valley, where the Gengshi Emperor and his dwindling sup-porters were bottled up, realizing too late that, while the area "within the passes" could be a stronghold, once the passes were breeched it became a trap. As the Red Eyebrows entered Chang'an and began to sack the city the emperor fled, but was soon captured and strangled. Liu Xiu, wisely remaining in the northern part of the Yellow River Plain, which was securely under his control, proclaimed himself Son of Heaven.

At that time, however, Liu Xiu as Emperor Guangwu was merely one of about a dozen claimants to the throne. Some, such as candidates pushed forward by different factions of the Red Eyebrows, were members of the old imperial Liu clan, others were not. Liu Xiu was lucky that the various rival claimants were too suspicious of one another to cooperate in trying to defeat him; he also controlled important terrain. He established his capital at Luoyang in late 25 CE and from there began the slow process of pacifying the empire. The Red Eyebrows, having destroyed Chang'an, began to starve there. Evacuating the city, they were ambushed by troops loyal to the independent general Wei Ao and retreated back east of the passes, where they surrendered to Emperor Guangwu and dispersed. Wei Ao, however, was no friend of the Eastern Han emperor; he held onto his stronghold of Gansu, in the far northwest, for years before being defeated. Throughout the decade from 20 to 30 CE one arduous campaign after another was launched to defeat rival claimants and bring their territory into the imperial fold, mostly successfully, as the empire expanded its control eastwards and southwards. One of the most difficult campaigns was against a general named Gongsun Shu, who had proclaimed himself king of Shu (the ancient name for Sichuan) in 24 CE. The long fight against him was notable for including one of China's first naval campaigns. Gongsun Shu had built a pontoon bridge across the Yangzi, blocking access to the Yangzi gorges, but an imperial fleet was able, in the spring of 34 CE, to destroy the bridge and fight its way slowly upriver while other impe-rial forces advanced by land. Progress was painfully slow, but at the end of 36 CE Gongsun Shu himself was killed in a battle with Han troops, and his army surrendered. With that, the long struggle to establish the Eastern Han dynasty had come to a successful end.

Emperor Guangwu was careful to present his regime as a restoration of the Han dynasty, not the founding of a new one. He declared that Wang Mang's New dynasty had been illegit-imate and that its claim to rule by virtue of the Phase Earth and the color Yellow was void. The civil war between Liu Xiu and his various rivals had to a considerable extent involved a war of omens and symbols. Five Phase theory allowed a number of possibilities; Gongsun Shu, to take one example, claimed to rule through the power of Metal (Wang Mang's phase of Earth produces the phase Metal), appropriately for a claimant whose power base was in the west. Emperor Guangwu made the definitive judgment that the Han ruling phase continued to be Fire, as had been decided by his Western Han predecessors in 31 BCE.

Perhaps because of the great expenditure of money, energy, and lives in the course of the post-25 CE civil wars, Emperor Guangwu maintained a generally unaggressive policy on China's borderlands. Although the Xiongnu had been very substantially weakened by the campaigns against them of Emperor Wu and his Western Han successors, the confederation still existed and Xiongnu raids remained a fact of life on China's northern frontier. The possibility of intervening in Xiongnu affairs to China's benefit arose in 51 CE, when rivalry between northern and southern khans divided the nomadic world, but the moment passed without action. For much of the rest of the Eastern Han Xiongnu settlements were allowed to develop unhindered within the Great Wall, to the dismay of the Chinese farming populace. Over the course of the century Xiongnu power declined in the northeast, being replaced by other tribal groups known as the Wuhuan and the Xianbi (or Xianbei). The usual Eastern Han policy toward these hostile peoples was to buy them off with "gifts" of silk, jade, and other luxury goods in return for "tribute" of furs and other northern products. In the far west a reduced Chinese military presence made the Silk Road much more dangerous, as raids from the proto-Tibetan Qiang people went unanswered. A substantial Chinese commitment to protect the Central Asian trade routes was not made until late in the first century CE.

In the far south the extension of Han political administration and the influx of Chinese migrants under the protection of that administration led to resentment and sporadic rebellion among various non-Chinese peoples in that region. One notable example was the revolt of the Yue (i.e. Viet) people in 40 CE, led by two sisters, Trung Trac and Trung Nhi. The rebellion, centered in the Red River delta, reached serious proportions before it was defeated by the great Eastern Han general Ma Yuan in a combined land and naval operation. The Trung sisters were captured and executed in 43 CE; they remain Vietnamese national heroines to this day.

Liu Xiu was thirty years old when he proclaimed himself Son of Heaven; he lived as Emperor Guangwu for another thirty-two years. This long reign was a stroke of good fortune, allowing the emperor and his closest advisors to stabilize the empire and revive its central administration. But, for reasons largely beyond the emperor's control, the imperial throne was never as powerful as it had been under the Western Han. The two intractable problems of the Eastern Han were regionalism and factionalism, and both appeared early in the dynasty's history. As a matter of political necessity Emperor Guangwu distributed kingdoms to all surviving male members of the imperial Liu clan. These kingdoms were deliberately kept small, and their kings had very limited administrative authority in them, but they were nevertheless a disruptive and fissile force. More urgently, Emperor Guangwu had to balance, and keep the goodwill of, three factions that he could not afford to ignore. These were the Nanyang gentry, who had thrown their support to Liu Xiu when it had become clear that the Gengshi Emperor was not going to succeed in establishing himself on the throne, and who expected to be rewarded for their part in aiding Liu Xiu's quest for the emperorship; and the families of Ma Yuan and Dou Rong, two powerful clans with bases in the northwest. Both Ma Yuan and Dou Rong had commanded significant independent military force during the civil wars, and both rather belatedly threw in their lot with Emperor Guangwu when it had become clear that he was going to come out on top.

The results of this factional maneuvering were readily apparent. Emperor Guangwu came under pressure to divorce his principal consort, who was from a relatively unimportant northern family, replacing her with a consort from the Yin clan of Nanyang. This he reluctantly did, and in due course he demoted the former heir apparent and named a new one from his Yin consort. These changes were, however, made without violence, and both the former consort and her children survived.

Meanwhile, Dou Rong had been working diligently to stock the senior ranks of the bureaucracy with Dou family members and their supporters, while Ma Yuan, himself a highly successful general, concentrated on bringing the military under his own control. The Dou clan clearly feared the military power of the Ma clan, however, and set about destroying their rival.

The opportunity came in 48 CE, when a rebellion of non-Chinese people in what is now southern Hunan required urgent attention. Ma Yuan personally led the forces sent to put down the rebellion, and succeeded in doing so, but he died of illness soon thereafter. While he was away on campaign the Dou family launched a calculated attack of slander, accusing Ma Yuan of incompetence, nepotism, embezzlement, and other grievous faults. The slander had its desired effect and, without their patriarch, the Ma clan found it difficult to defend themselves. By the end of Emperor Guangwu's reign the Ma clan was shattered, though not destroyed, and the Nanyang and Dou factions were approaching the peak of their power.

Emperor Guangwu's successors

As a matter of course the factional rivalries of the Eastern Han were played out in a long series of succession disputes. The first two imperial successions of the Eastern Han went smoothly, however. Liu Yang succeeded his father, Emperor Guangwu, on the latter's death in 57 CE; he is known by his dynastic title, Emperor Ming. His mother was Yin Lihua, of the Nanyang Yin clan, and he mounted the throne unopposed. Defying the Dou clan, Emperor Ming chose as his consort a daughter of Ma Yuan, thus reviving to some extent the fortunes of the Ma clan. She, however, was childless, so the child of another palace woman had to be chosen as heir apparent. That was Liu Da, the son of Lady Jia, who was a concubine from a good Nanyang family and a cousin of Empress Ma. Liu Da, ruling as Emperor Zhang, succeeded Emperor Ming on the latter's death in 75 CE, and reigned until 88 CE. This transition also seems to have been amicable and without bloodshed.

The run of well-managed imperial successions came to an end during the reign of Emperor Zhang. His consort was a woman of the Dou clan who had been presented to the palace, along with her younger sister, in a bold move to revive the influence of the Dou. The Dou consort and her sister were both childless, however, creating a dangerous situation. Empress Dowager Ma, widow of Emperor Zhang, then introduced into the harem two sisters of the Song clan, allies of the Ma clan. The elder Song sister gave birth to Liu Qing in 78 CE, and he was duly named heir apparent. Soon afterwards, however, Empress Dowager Ma died, placing her protégé in a dangerous position. At the insistence of Empress Dou, Emperor Zhang's consort, Liu Qing was removed as heir apparent. The Song sisters, placed under arrest, committed suicide.

Liu Zhao, the new heir apparent, was the son of a concubine of the Liang clan, long-time minor allies of the Dou clan. With the heir apparent descended from the Liang lineage, the Liangs seem to have become resentful of their subordinate status and maneuvered to increase their own power at the expense of the Dou clan. The move failed, however; in 83 CE, Empress Dowager Dou struck back. She had Liu Zhao's mother and her sister arrested and they died soon afterwards, whether by murder or suicide is unknown. Their father, the head of the Liang clan, was executed. The Dou family was back in control. Liu Zhao succeeded his father in 88 CE, at the age of twelve; the fourth Eastern Han emperor, he is known as Emperor He. He was the first Eastern Han emperor to succeed to the throne as a child, initiating a pattern that would leave the dynasty weak and vulnerable to factional politics throughout the next century. Empress Dowager Dou became regent for the underage Emperor He and, in turn, empowered her brother, General Dou Xian, to assume practical control of the government on her behalf.

Emperor He had ideas of his own, however. Attaining adult status at the age of fifteen in 91 CE, he removed Dou Xian from office and charged him with conspiring against the throne. Dou Xian and several of his male relatives committed suicide; other family members (with the notable exception of the empress dowager, who was allowed to retire peacefully) were executed or exiled. Among those executed was the historian Ban Gu, who had enjoyed the patronage of Dou Xian. The power of the Dou clan was broken, but the Dou were soon replaced as powers behind the throne by other influential families. Emperor He's first consort was from an influential Nanyang clan, the Yin. Childless, she was accused of witchcraft in 102 CE and died in prison. Her father committed suicide and her principal male relatives were executed or exiled. She was succeeded as empress by a woman of the Deng clan, also from Nanyang. She, too, was childless, but meanwhile Emperor He had had two sons by other palace women. Neither had been named heir apparent. When the emperor died in 106 CE Empress Dowager Deng chose one of those sons, an infant less than a year old, as Emperor Shang. He died a few months later, surely without ever having realized that he was an emperor. Empress Dowager Deng then looked among the large number of possible candidates for the throne to find a suitably underage successor. Her choice fell on a grandson of Liu Qing, who had briefly been heir apparent nearly thirty years previously; Liu You, at age twelve, became Emperor An.

The pattern continued. Emperor An's consort, from the relatively minor but ambitious Yan clan, was childless, but a concubine, Lady Li, had borne a son. She was duly poisoned. The child was named heir apparent but was later demoted under pressure from the Yan clan. Emperor An, who apparently had no stomach for the deadly game of imperial succession, retired to his palace and in 124 CE took the unusual step of appointing a regent to run the government on his behalf. When he died in 125 CE Empress Dowager Yan first selected an infant to succeed him, but the child died within a few months without having been formally installed on the throne. At that point a new element was added to the succession struggle. Since the time of Emperor Guangwu the eunuchs of the inner palace had been developing as a locus of factional power. Now a group of eunuchs declared their support for Emperor An's son by Lady Li and, after a brief armed struggle, they succeeded in staging a coup against the Yan clan. The empress dowager was allowed to retire, her male relatives were wiped out, and Emperor An's son, aged about ten, was enthroned in 126 CE as Emperor Shun.

Emperor Shun occupied the throne for almost nineteen years, an unusual feat for the second century of the Eastern Han, though even he did not reach his thirtieth birthday. His consort, from a revived branch of the Liang clan, was childless. Following the precedent set by Emperor An of appointing a regent for an adult emperor, Empress Liang's father, and subsequently her brother, held that office for Emperor Shun. The emperor's infant son by a concubine had been named heir apparent in 143 CE and when Emperor Shun died in 144 CE the succession proceeded without incident. But the infant Emperor Chong died a few months later, leaving power in the hands of the Liang clan. Empress Dowager Liang chose as the next emperor an eight-year-old descendant of Emperor Zhang, who ascended the throne in 145 CE as Emperor Zhi. He, too, died within a few months, possibly murdered by his regent, Liang Ji. The choice of an heir again fell to Empress Dowager Liang, and she chose another minor, Liu Zhi, who came to the throne in 146 CE as Emperor Huan.

Breaking with the recent past, Emperor Huan managed to live past childhood, and reigned for twenty-two years. Even before he reached his legal majority he was provided with a consort from the Liang clan and was kept firmly under the control of Empress Dowager Liang and her brother, the regent Liang Ji. But Emperor Huan grew up to have a mind of his own. When Empress Liang died in 159 CE the emperor secretly assembled a large force of armed eunuchs and surrounded Liang Ji's palace. He and his wife committed suicide and, in a wave of executions, the Liang clan was comprehensively wiped out. A palace lady from the Deng clan was elevated to the rank of consort in 159 CE, but she, too, proved to be childless. Emperor Huan managed to avoid being totally dominated by the new empress' family, and in 165 CE she was accused of witchcraft and other crimes and ordered to kill herself. The brief revival of the Deng clan had failed, and its leading members were executed.

Emperor Huan's third empress was Dou Miao, from the once-great northwestern family that was making a bid to revive its power. When Emperor Huan died without an heir in 168 CE Empress Dowager Dou again chose a twelve-year-old boy as heir, and he was enthroned as Emperor Ling. Dou Miao's father, Dou Wu, was appointed regent. Dou Wu seems to have been concerned that the steadily rising influence of the palace eunuchs encroached on his own power as regent, and therefore conspired with senior leaders of the imperial civil government, who also had deep concerns about the influence of the inner palace, to round up and slaughter the eunuch leadership. But the plot was discovered and the eunuchs armed themselves to defend the imperial palace. Dou Wu's supporters deserted him and he committed suicide; as usual, the leading males of the Dou clan were executed, along with the imperial grand tutor and other senior members of the bureaucracy who had been part of Dou Wu's plot.

With the demise of Dou Wu the century-long era of great-family domination of the imperial throne came to an end. Great families, as such, certainly did not cease to exist, but now they were mainly local or regional powers, feeding into the Eastern Han's vulnerability to regionalism and disunity. An interesting bit of physical evidence supports the view of the increasing role of local gentry. During the Han grave goods came to include not only clay statuettes of people and animals (symbolic sacrificial victims) but also models of buildings of all kinds, presumably so that the deceased grave occupant could live in comfort. These models included houses, wells, pigsties, sheep pens, granaries, and other domestic structures. As time went on Eastern Han tombs increasingly included models of guarded gatehouses and multi-story watchtowers, good evidence that elite rural families were building fortified houses to protect their own interests (Figure 12.1).

In the capital the eunuchs of the inner palace contended successfully with the professional bureaucracy for control of the dynasty's next emperor. Emperor Ling ascended the throne in

Figure 12.1 Eastern Han clay model of a multi-story watchtower.

168 CE and reigned for twenty-one years, dying in 189 CE. Throughout his reign he was under the domination of the eunuchs. Bureaucratic offices and military rank were, in this reign, no longer filled on the basis of merit, but were sold openly by the chief eunuch and his staff, drastically affecting the ability of the government to administer and protect the country. During his reign serious peasant rebellions broke out, including the large-scale and dangerous Yellow Turbans rebellion of 184 CE. Several claimants of the Mandate of Heaven (including some from the Liu clan itself) arose and were fairly swiftly put down, while increasing numbers of baleful portents, such as comets, unseasonable hailstorms, and women giving birth to deformed children, were reported to the throne. Based on recorded evidence, Emperor Ling seems to have set a new standard of imperial negligence and incompetence, but that judgment is perhaps unfair; it is unlikely that he would have been allowed to pursue any independent initiatives, even if he had been inclined to do so.

Emperor Ling died in 189 CE and was briefly succeeded by his elder son, a boy in his midteens, who was forced to resign the throne a few months later amid the turmoil of a bloody coup by senior civil servants against the eunuchs. He was succeeded by his younger halfbrother, the hapless Emperor Xian, whose sad story is part of the larger tale of the long collapse of the Eastern Han dynasty.

The rise of the eunuchs

At the beginning of the Eastern Han dynasty the number of women in Emperor Guangwu's harem probably did not exceed a dozen or so. That number increased steadily, until by the mid-second century they numbered in the thousands, recruited in batches according to strict criteria of good family, good health, good manners, beauty, and amiability. For the many child-emperors of the Eastern Han the women of the palace must have been simply an additional source of confusion; even adult emperors seem to have paid scant attention to their harems. For the women, giving birth to an imperial son was the ultimate goal, bringing instant promotion to wealth and power (and also landing them in considerable danger); however, for most women the chances of being noticed by an emperor, let alone being chosen to have intercourse with him, were remote. Most of the women ended up being in effect artisans rather than concubines, weaving and doing embroidery to make court robes and regalia. But the chastity of all had to be protected; any child born in the palace had to be unquestionably the emperor's offspring. The role of ensuring that that was so, in China as in many other ancient empires, fell to a corps of eunuchs, who were also recruited on a regular basis as boys, according to strict criteria, subjected to full genital castration, and put to work in the inner palace, where no intact male, save the emperor himself, was permitted to enter.

An inner-palace population of thousands of women needed a staff of thousands to serve them, comprising secretaries, gardeners, guards, cooks, wardrobe masters, and dozens of other occupations. Taken from their families, and with no hope of progeny, the eunuchs were completely dependent on the emperor. Although emperors often assumed (wrongly) that this ensured the eunuchs' complete loyalty, they often abused their power by blocking access to the emperor by high civil servants. The eunuchs were generally despised by government officials. Eunuchs attempted to manipulate rulers; rulers (or in practice, their mother and regents) sometimes encouraged the power of the eunuchs to enhance their leverage with the civil service. The three great loci of factional power—the civil service, the great families, and the eunuchs—engaged in a perpetual dance of shifting influence. Occasionally the situation led to actual violence, as in 168 CE, when the eunuchs foiled Dou Wu's attempted purge of the inner palace and went on to destroy the Dou clan. With Emperor Ling firmly under their control, the eunuchs set about pursuing their own interests; increasing numbers of eunuchs were, contrary to regulations, ennobled as lords (*hou*) and furnished with valuable sinecures. Seizing control of the institutions for staffing the imperial bureaucracy, they sold offices to the highest bidder, while the country outside the capital was increasingly left to its own devices. As these abuses spread and became more blatant, resentment of eunuch power grew.

A partial replay, with different results, of the events of 168 came in 189 CE, during the turmoil surrounding the succession to the throne vacated by the death of Emperor Ling. Having controlled that ruler for twenty-one years, the eunuchs strove to extend their power over his successor and were supported in that by the empress dowager, mother of the newly enthroned emperor. Opposing the eunuchs were He Jin, half-brother of the empress dowager, who tried to promote the interests of the He family as against those of the eunuchs; and two generals, Yuan Shao and Dong Zhuo. After complex maneuvers taking place over several months in 189 CE, during which time He Jin was beheaded in the palace on the orders of the senior eunuchs, the two generals made their move. In late September of that year they blockaded and then invaded the Northern Palace and killed on sight every eunuch they encountered—a death toll of perhaps 2,000 or more. The power of the eunuchs was broken, but at the cost of making the empire nearly ungovernable. The Eastern Han dynasty lurched into its final three decades of existence.

The fall of the Eastern Han

On the night of September 25, 189 CE, amid the massacre of the palace eunuchs, the empress dowager, her son Liu Bian, the recently enthroned emperor, and Liu Bian's younger half-brother Liu Xie, fled the palace, escaping the carnage with a few eunuch supporters. Legend has it that they borrowed a peasant's oxcart as they made their way northwards from the capital. Dong Zhuo, with a small squadron of cavalry, hurried in pursuit, caught up with the fugitives, and brought them back to the palace. There, Liu Bian was forced to abdicate in favor of Liu Xie (who, only about nine years old, seems to have made a good impression on Dong), who was enthroned as Emperor Xian; two days later the empress dowager was put to death to eliminate the possibility that she might become the focus of opposition to the change of boy-emperors. (Liu Bian lasted a bit longer; he was murdered on Dong's orders a few months later.)

Dong Zhuo now controlled the emperor, giving him a big advantage over his rivals, but he realized that he also risked being trapped in Luoyang, which was vulnerable to a siege. He therefore sent Emperor Xian and his large court entourage for safety to Chang'an. Dong then had a freer hand to deal with his opponents. Arrayed against him were several military men acting as more or less independent warlords: Yuan Shao, Cao Cao, Yuan Shu (Yuan Shao's half-brother), Liu Biao, Sun Ci, and Liu Zhang, each controlling large but unstable regions. Sichuan was under the control of the Celestial Masters of the Five Pecks of Rice movement, out of reach of the military leaders. The years that followed were reminiscent of the time of the fall of Qin and the triumph of Han, with shifting coalitions, temporary alliances, and a surfeit of treachery. It was a war for keeps, in which losers did not survive. The difference between the fall of Qin and the last years of the Han is that in the latter case there was still a generally accepted emperor who possessed the Mandate of Heaven. Politically powerless but symbolically powerful, the emperor was the source of legitimacy. The general who had physical guardianship of the emperor was by definition a Han patriot; the others could be portrayed as rebels. It is a measure of the extraordinary power of the concept of the Mandate that this charade could be played out for three decades.

Dong Zhuo was the first to hold the emperor card, but could not sustain that advantage. In 191 CE he was driven out of Luoyang, which he destroyed to deny it to his enemies, and retreated westwards to join the emperor in Chang'an. He was assassinated a year later. With Dong Zhuo dead, the anti-Dong coalition of Yuan Shao, Yuan Shu, and Cao Cao frayed and collapsed. After a number of shifts of power that put the emperor under the control of one or another general, the court made its way back to Luoyang in 196 CE, when the emperor came under the permanent control of Cao Cao. Yuan Shu tried unsuccessfully to establish his own dynasty in 197 CE; he died a fugitive two years later. Sun Ci died in 200 and was succeeded by his son Sun Quan, who maintained control over the southeast. In the climactic battle of this period of dynastic transition, Cao Cao defeated Yuan Shao at Guandu (in present-day Henan Province) in 200 CE, giving him control over all of northern China and the imperial court. Liu Bei, a rising young warlord and erstwhile ally of Yuan Shao, gained control over an independent territory in Sichuan. In the famous 208 CE Battle of the Red Cliffs, in the Yangzi Gorges, Cao Cao tried to drive Liu Bei out of his stronghold, but both his army and his river fleet were decisively defeated. The lines of the future Three Kingdoms were beginning to emerge; Cao Cao in the north, Liu Bei in Sichuan, and Sun Quan in the southeast.

With the court firmly under his control, Cao Cao began acting like a latter-day Wang Mang, heaping offices and honors on himself and his family. Apart from occasional battles to defend the northern frontier against Wusun incursions or to try to wrest territory away from Liu Bei and Sun Quan, northern China was mostly at peace. Cao Cao named himself king of Wei in 217 CE and died early in 220 CE. His son and heir, Cao Pi, inherited his position but then took the step that his father had resisted for years, persuading Emperor Xian to abdicate in his favor. Cao Pi took the title "Emperor Wen of the Wei dynasty," a conscious evocation of long-ago King Wen, founder of the Zhou dynasty. In an unusual act of generosity, the abdicated emperor was left to enjoy a comfortable life in retirement.

But the mantle of Han power could not be shaken off lightly. When word of the emperor's abdication reached Liu Bei in Sichuan he took up the Han banner. He had a very tenuous claim to be related to the Liu imperial family of Han and so proclaimed himself Emperor Zhaolie of Han in 221. He predicted that he and his descendants would continue to hold the Mandate of the Han dynasty forever. However, history was not kind to his legacy. Later historians have generally dismissed the idea that Liu Bei's regime was a legitimate continuation of the Han dynasty, dismissing his "Han" empire as simply Shu Han, "Han in Sichuan" (Shu being the name of the ancient kingdom in Sichuan and a common reference for the region). Meanwhile, to the southeast of the new Wei empire, Sun Quan took advantage of the political turmoil and military stalemate to declare himself Emperor Da of the Wu dynasty in 229. So, with the Wei in the north, Han in the southwest, and Wu in the southeast, the brief but significant era of the Three Kingdoms had begun (Map 12.1).

The Three Kingdoms

The Three Kingdoms Period, an anomalous but relatively stable situation, lasted only a few decades. It was anomalous because it was not a multi-state system with symbolic allegiance to a larger legitimate polity, such as the Zhou, but there were three emperors and three imperial courts. This situation had never arisen before. Theoretically the Mandate of Heaven was not divisible. The idea of the Mandate remained powerful, which is why the emperors of Wei, Shu Han, and Wu clung so persistently to the title. But none of the three could force the unification that the claim of the Mandate implied. The period was stable because there was a rough balance of power among the three "empires." Fighting continued in the 220s and 230s CE,

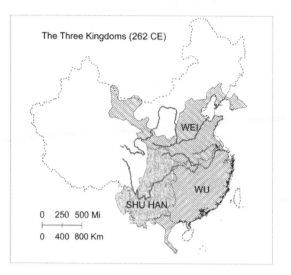

The Three Kingdoms (262 CE)

WEI

WU

SHU HAN

0   250   500 Mi

0   400   800 Km

Map 12.1 The territories of Shu Han, Wei, and Wu during the Three Kingdoms Period.

but the borders remained roughly the same. But, meanwhile, two of the key players passed away. Cao Cao died in 220 CE, after ceding power to his son, and Liu Bei died in 223 CE. The intense personal rivalry combined with a sense of exhaustion after decades of warfare between the two major powers survived only in attenuated form, largely dying down after the 230s.

The roughly fifty years of warfare from the Yellow Turbans revolt in 184 CE to the establishment of the Three Kingdoms in the early 220s had been extremely destructive. It was comparable in its economic and social devastation to the Taiping Rebellion of the mid-nineteenth century or the Sino-Japanese War of 1937–45. The great national census of 2 CE counted a population of some 57 million persons, while a later Eastern Han census, in 156 CE, showed the population essentially stable at 56.5 million. In contrast, a census conducted by the Jin dynasty in 280 CE, when it had conquered the last of the Three Kingdoms, counted a population of slightly over 16 million. That was certainly an undercount, reflecting in part the Jin census takers' inability to reach all parts of the country, but, even allowing for a very considerable downside error, it is clear that the population of China declined dramatically in the turmoil of the end of the Eastern Han and the Three Kingdoms Period. The decline would have been due not only to direct battle casualties and incidental civilian casualties but also epidemics, starvation, or malnutrition brought about by destruction of crops and other means of livelihood, incidental natural disasters, and also, to a very large but incalculable extent, mass migrations of refugees to southern regions.

The three kingdoms or "empires" of Wei, Shu Han, and Wu, weakened by population loss and other aftermaths of decades of warfare, soon collapsed. In 263 CE Sima Zhao invaded and conquered Shu Han on behalf of Wei. Two years later he staged a coup d'état and forced the emperor of Wei to abdicate in his favor, proclaiming himself the first emperor of Jin. In 280 CE he succeeded in conquering Wu, the third of the Three Kingdoms, and succeeded briefly in uniting China once again. A complex series of internal rebellions and invasions by northern nomadic peoples caused the Jin to lose control over much of northern China and in

316 CE the Jin moved their capital to the Huai River region, ceding control of the north to the invaders. With this fragmentation, the three-centuries-long Period of Disunion began.

Intellectual life and the arts

The persistent disfunctionality at the apex of government and society was a key feature of Eastern Han society, but the lack of control also allowed for greater intellectual and artistic freedom. Access to a career in the civil service continued to require knowledge of the classics. Eastern Han intellectuals commented on the classics and taught thousands of students in the national academy. Literacy, though still confined to a small minority of the population, continued to expand, while the increased use of paper made the copying of texts cheaper and more convenient. New trends in religion, notably the introduction of Buddhism and the evolution of Daoism into an organized religion—most likely in response to Buddhism—offered new intellectual perspectives and options for spiritual life. Pictorial art continued to develop, as seen in evolving styles of tomb construction and decoration.

The focus on stabilizing a classical canon continued to occupy Eastern Han scholars. This involved comparing and collating different versions of the classics and deciding which readings to accept or reject, in part through reference to the competing commentarial traditions that had become attached to the transmission of the texts. Of particular concern were the texts of the Five Classics—the *Odes*, the *Springs and Autumns*, the *Documents*, the *Changes*, and the *Rites Records*—which, by then, thanks to the curriculum of the national academy, were firmly identified with Confucius and his followers. In 79 CE Emperor Zhang convened an imperial symposium to debate the meaning of the classics and sort out the various interpretations that were current at the time. The emperor personally took part in the debates. A summary of the proceedings, *The Comprehensive Discussions in the White Tiger Hall (Bohu tong)*, was probably compiled not long after the event itself, though in its present form it shows signs of later editorial changes and textual augmentation. The discussions ranged well beyond the issue of authenticating classical texts to include the integration of yin–yang and Five Phase cosmology with rules of rites and sacrifices and civil law and punishment into the organization of government. The *Bohu tong* serves as an important window into the intellectual life of the Eastern Han.

One of the most important works of scholarship of the Eastern Han Period was the *History of the [Former] Han Dynasty (Han shu)*, by Ban Gu (32–92 CE; see Focus: The Ban family). In a strict sense the *Han shu* was the first of China's official dynastic histories. Whereas Sima Qian's *Records of the Grand Historian (Shiji)* covered the entire history of the world (as it was known to him) from the beginning of civilization up to his own time, the *Han shu* deals exclusively with the Western Han dynasty, from the family background of the founder, Liu Bang, and his establishment of the dynasty in 206 BCE to the death of Wang Mang in 23 CE. Its organization follows that of the *Shiji*, however, comprising imperial annals, genealogical tables, treatises on special subjects ranging from mathematical harmonics to the economy, and biographies. All of the later dynastic histories follow the model set by the *Han shu*, and it came to be accepted that one of the most important duties of any newly established dynasty was to write a history of its immediate predecessor, making it as full and as fair as possible.

One of the most impressive works of public scholarship was the engraving on stone tablets of the entire text of the Five Classics, literally setting in stone the official and authoritative version of those works. The stone-tablet text could function as a giant printing block. Scholars and students could make manuscript copies or ink rubbings (using the newly developed medium of paper). This represented the imperial court's ongoing commitment to propagate an authoritative version of the Confucian classics as the basis of official scholarship. Cai Yong (132–192 CE), a renowned scholar famous for his expertise in rituals and music as well as in astronomy and mathematics, supervised the work from its beginning in 175 CE to its completion in 183 CE.

While the *Bohu tong*, the *Han shu*, and the stone classics represent outstanding works of public scholarship, private scholarly work also flourished in the Eastern Han. One noted scholar was Wang Chong (c. 27–100 CE), who held minor offices in the civil service but neglected his official career to devote himself to his own research and writing. His major work, *Discourses Weighed in the Balance* (*Lun heng*) was the first Chinese book to make skeptical rationalism a philosophical principle. He explicitly denied that Heaven was conscious of human interests and had the ability to intervene in human affairs. He questioned accounts of ghosts and spirits, arguing that encounters with supernatural beings were often delusions, representing misunderstandings of natural phenomena. He was similarly skeptical of omens and portents. He advocated a critical reading of the classics and denied that the rulers of antiquity had superhuman sage-like abilities. Wang was interested in natural philosophy and cosmology, investigating the physical properties of matter and observing the habits of animals. He questioned the standard cosmography of his time, which envisioned the earth as square and flat (or slightly convex) and covered by the hemispherical dome of heaven; the corners, he said, would not fit. Wang may have been influenced by a view of the universe that was gaining acceptance during his lifetime, of the earth as a sphere located in the center of a spherical universe around which the sun, moon, and planets moved in their orbits. That view is especially associated with the polymath Zhang Heng (78–139 CE; see Focus: Zhang Heng), who, among many other achievements, made improvements in the armillary sphere (a nest of rings indicating the horizon, meridian, equator, and other significant celestial great circles).

Private scholars were also responsible for a growing body of commentaries on classical works that were not part of the Confucian canonical tradition. One such commentator was Gao You (c. 168–212 CE), who wrote extensive commentaries to the *Lüshi chunqiu* and the *Huainanzi*, laying the foundation for subsequent study of those important works of the third and second centuries BCE. Ma Rong (79–166 CE) also wrote commentaries on the *Laozi* and the *Huainanzi*. Wang Fu (c. 87–165 CE), who never held public office, was known as the author of *Discourses of a Hermit* (*Qianfu lun*), a work that touches upon many topics in an attempt to synthesize the best features of classical texts of several traditions.

One of the most significant private intellectuals of the Eastern Han was Xu Shen (c. 55–c. 147 CE), whose *Explaining Words and Analyzing Characters* (*Shuowen jiezi*) was the first analytical dictionary of the Chinese language (see Focus: What is Chinese writing? in Chapter 5); it laid the foundation for all subsequent philological work on the Chinese language. In addition, he wrote an influential commentary, *Variant Meanings in the Five Classics* (*Wujing yiyi*).

In the visual arts representational painting and sculpture continued to flourish and are preserved in tomb settings. Tombs of local elites testify to the importance of regionalism as a factor in Eastern Han society. They come in several varieties—stone-built tombs with interiors covered with relief sculpture in the eastern Yellow River Plain and Shandong; tombs lined with large bricks depicting in low relief scenes ranging from mythology to the leisure pursuits of the wealthy, particularly in the Sichuan Basin; and tombs lined with small painted bricks depicting scenes from daily life in the northwest (Figures 12.2–12.4). Though far more modest than the extravagant tombs of members of the imperial lineage or prominent figures

Figure 12.2 Plowing with oxen. Stone relief from an Eastern Han tomb in Shaanxi Province.

Figure 12.3 Rubbing of a scene of a musician playing tuned bells, from a carved stone tomb at Yinan, Shandong Province.

at court, and very different in style and visual impact from each other, they have in common the claims they make of the local importance and continuity of lineage of the rural gentry and reflect the rise of local cultic practices around shrines.

The development of stylized calligraphy as a mode of individual expression rather than for display in public works of art, such as on bronze vessels, certain bamboo and silk manuals, and stone stele began during the Eastern Han. Artistic achievement became one of

Figure 12.4 Banquet scene on a pictorial tomb brick from Sichuan Province. Note the absence of chairs.

many talents necessary for a truly accomplished scholar. For example, one of the many accomplishments attributed to the great polymath Zhang Heng is that he was a skilled painter and calligrapher. Besides the rise of individual fame outside of the court setting signifying the Han dynasty generally, there were a number of influential technical changes. One was the increased availability of paper, which provided a cheap and convenient medium on which to practice calligraphy. Another was a change in the standard script style and the awareness of script evolution made possible by Xu Shen's *Explaining Words and Analyzing Characters.*

The invention of paper has traditionally been credited to the eunuch official Cai Lun (c. 50–121 CE), who was for some time a superintendent of the imperial workshops, but archaeological evidence shows clearly that paper was known in China at least by the early Western Han Period. Cai Lun may have improved the manufacturing process, making paper more widely available. Paper was convenient for artists and bureaucrats alike. During the Eastern Han the *kaishu* script replaced the earlier *lishu* style; the *kaishu* script was less ornate, involving clear angles and parallel lines of white and black space. Calligraphy as an art form developed rapidly in the post-Han era, and China's most famous calligrapher, Wang Xizhi (303–361 CE), lived only slightly more than a century after the fall of Han. Calligraphy has continued up to modern times to be a litmus test of refinement.

In tandem with the rise of the art of calligraphy was the rise of poetry, incorporating the old classical forms with new concepts borrowed from Daosim and Buddhism that expressed the disengagement of local literati from the political process. This was epitomized in the Three Kingdoms Period by an infamous group known as the Seven Sages of the Bamboo Grove, whose drunken antics are chronicled in a fifth-century CE book of fictional tales called *A New Account of Tales of the World* (*Shi shuo xinyu*). Including such figures as Xi Kang and Ruan Ji, these educated men of aristocratic Han families rejected government service, pursued the search for immortality in rural retreats away from urban centers, and wrote poetry in the style popular during the time of the last Han emperor, Emperor Xian (the Jian'an Era, 196–220 CE). The great military figure of the late Eastern Han, Cao Cao, and his son Cao Zhi were both known for their poetry in the *jian'an* style. The poetry of the anti-government recluse rose out of the imitation of earlier *Odes* and Music Bureau (*yuefu*) styles and the prominent use of *fu* rhyme-prose in the Western Han Period to criticize corruption and waste. This form of poetic protest continued into the Eastern Han. Elaborate and allegory-filled descriptions of capitals and royal processions were designed to entertain the imperial court, but also to overwhelm the reader to the point of revulsion; the intended result was to stimulate a desire for the pure and unsullied life. The theme of describing regional capitals in this way was mastered by scholar–officials and aristocrats such as the historian Ban Gu (32–92 CE), the scientist Zhang Heng (78–139 CE), and the writer Zuo Si (c. 250–c. 305 CE). Han poets, although generally trained in the Confucian classics, also studied texts linked to the occult, such as commentaries on the *Book of Changes*, Daoist texts, and "mysteries." A fascination with the idea of a retreat from official life into the countryside was associated with the pursuit of immortality and ultimately intertwined with the Buddhist view of "reality" as an illusion. This continued into the Three Kingdoms Period.

While the political sphere was full of turmoil, scholars continued to consolidate Confucian and Daoist canons. Wang Bi (226–249 CE), despite the brevity of his lifetime, produced important commentaries to both the *Changes* (*Yijing* or *Zhouyi*) and the *Laozi*. Guo Xiang (d. 312 CE) wrote the first important commentary on the *Zhuangzi*. Wang and Guo were known as early exponents of the literary and rhetorical style known as Abstruse Learning (*xuanxue*), devoted to the study of arcane meanings in the Daoist classics. A related movement was "Pure Speech" (*qingtan*), a kind of Daoist-flavored, self-consciously literary and metaphysical dialogue meant to interrogate life's mysteries. The Seven Sages of the Bamboo Grove were masters of "Pure Speech." Poets were multi-talented, excelling in the Six Arts linked to "cultivation" (*wen*), such as music (especially of the *qin* lap-lute) and writing.

Science and medicine continued to advance. The hydraulic engineer and inventor Ma Jun (220–265 CE), often seen as the intellectual successor to Zhang Heng, made a long-term contribution to the development of Chinese agriculture by inventing the square-pallet chain pump for use in irrigating fields of grain. Han mathematicians developed theories, many focusing on factors of nine, as seen in early treatises used in the Han, such as *Writings on Calculation and Numbers* (*Suanshu shu*), the *Classic for the Calculation of [Celestial] Circuits and Gnomen [Measurements]* (*Zhou Bi suanjing*), which contains the oldest Chinese proof of the Pythagorean Theorem, and *Nine Chapters on Calculation Techniques* (*Jiuzhang suanshu*). The late Han physician Hua Tuo (140–208 CE) was an expert in surgical techniques, drugs (including anesthetics and novel medicines possibly imported from outside China), and occult techniques, some of which he may have learned from Buddhists. He was one of Cao Cao's doctors. Han healing methods at first focused on heat treatments of blocked *qi* points, but acupuncture is attested as early as the first century. Physicians monitored as many as twelve channels of *qi* moving throughout different regions of the body, a method that would evolve into pulse diagnostic methods (commonly applied even today). Poets and others believed that proper exercise of the body and control over the *qi* would lead to metamorphoses of their bodies from mortal flesh into immortal jade. They practiced different methods, such as diet, exercise, breath, and sexual techniques. Discussions about medical theory, healing methods, and cosmology are seen in the *Inner Canon of the Yellow Emperor* (*Huangdi neijing*) and the *Classic of Great Peace* (*Taiping jing*).

Buddhism and Daoism

Buddhism entered China during the Han possibly as a result of Silk Road contacts, travelers' accounts, and an influx of foreign practitioners and teachers into the cities. Buddhists in Chang'an, Luoyang, and other major cities very likely established "house temples" or other designated spaces for community worship. The first official notice of Buddhism in China comes in 65 CE, when Liu Ying, king of Chu and a younger brother of Emperor Ming, is described in the *History of the Latter Han Dynasty* (*Hou Han shu*) as having performed Buddhist rituals in his capital city of Pengcheng. The same passage notes that he offered sacrifices to Huang-Lao—that is, the Yellow Emperor (*Huangdi*)—and Laozi, two legendary figures that had merged into a single Daoist deity. Emperor Ming sent a delegation, a few years later, to Central Asia to find out more about Buddhism. The delegation returned with two Buddhist monks, for whom the emperor built the White Horse Temple in Luoyang—which still stands, though none of its original buildings has survived; it is the oldest continuously active Buddhist temple in China.

The acceptance of a foreign religion into China relied on borrowing Daoist terms and concepts. During the Eastern Han and Three Kingdoms Periods Buddhism was very incompletely and incorrectly understood in China. The Buddhist scriptures contain many words and concepts that had no equivalents in the Chinese language, and the early Buddhist teachers and translators in China resorted to two methods to deal with this problem of vocabulary. One was to use Chinese characters to make a syllable-by-syllable phonetic transcription of the Buddhist terms; this rendered the terms pronounceable but often incomprehensible. The other method was to use extant Chinese words, often drawn from Daoism, to translate Buddhist concepts; so, for example, *yoga* became "Dao," and *nirvana* became "wuwei"; this made the terms seem familiar but at the cost of twisting the Buddhist concepts. It was difficult to distinguish the differences in Buddhist works of the two principal forms of Buddhism, Theravada (the Teachings of the Elders, in which enlightenment is limited to a few) and Mahayana (the Greater Vehicle, in which enlightenment is available to everyone).

Mahayana Buddhism spread rapidly in China during the later decades of the Eastern Han Period and the subsequent Three Kingdoms Period. Buddhism added new dimensions into the theological and metaphysical discussions concerning cosmic mysteries, particularly as it focused on the role of the individual and the shortness of life. The concept of reincarnation into a physical living form after death rather than simply recycling back to Nothingness as in Daoism became popular. Buddhism also recognized that inherent in life is suffering and tragedy. To transcend the cycle of birth a person must adhere to a pattern of good deeds and approved behaviors so as to avoid negative karma, the sum total of one's actions in all past lives as expressed in the events of one's present life. The Four Noble Truths of Buddhism explain: all life entails suffering; suffering stems from attachment to the illusory world; attachment can be overcome; the method to overcome attachment is to follow the Noble Eightfold Path. The Noble Eightfold Path consists of right understanding, right thinking, right speech, right action, right livelihood, right effort, right mindfulness, and right enlightenment. Complete enlightenment and attaining nirvana (a state of no-birth and immortality) required submerging one's illusory ego into the universal consciousness, a concept appealing to those who practiced Daoist methods for attaining the jade body.

Both Buddhism and Daoism urged disengagement and a retreat from political life, whether through highly disciplined monasticism or eccentric and sometimes outlandish behavior. Many aristocrats, despite their training in Confucian classics, were attracted to these alternative philosophies. The ultimate conquest, after the end of the Three King-doms Period, of parts of northern and northwestern China by Inner Asian peoples who in some cases practiced both shamanism and Buddhism helped to institute Buddhism as an accepted religion in China. Nevertheless, Buddhism in China during the first three centu-ries CE was hampered by theological misunderstandings, faultily translated scriptures, organizational confusion, and other problems. Not until the fifth century CE, with the translations of scriptures by the great scholar Kumarajiva and his associates, did Bud-dhism become fully integrated into China's philosophical and spiritual life (Figure 12.5). Meanwhile, China's own major religious movement, Daoism, was also evolving, in part under Buddhist influence.

Archaeological discoveries of fragments of ancient Daoist texts reveal that, at the same time that Buddhist texts and practices became known, a Daoist canon was formed. Laozi (and the Huang-Lao variation) was deified and worshipped like Buddha. Laozi's "mother" became the focus of a method of self-cultivation that involved identifying with the mother and developing within oneself an embryo symbolic of embodying the *Dao*. It was during this time period that the "education of the fetus" also became a Confucian technique that pregnant elite women were encouraged to follow.

Early in the Eastern Han Period several variants of the *Classic of Great Peace* (*Taiping jing*) began to circulate and to attract the attention of the imperial court. In 165 CE Emperor

Figure 12.5 The oldest dated Buddha image in China (420 CE), from the Bingling Temple, Gansu Province.

Huan sent an official party to offer sacrifices and conduct ceremonials at the supposed birth-place of Laozi, east of Luoyang. He may have been influenced by his consort, Empress Dou, who seems to have been interested in Daoist ideas. The notion of Great Peace (*Taiping*) was associated with a utopian politico-religious vision of a new form of government and society that would replace the existing order. That concept lay at the heart of the two great insurrections, closely associated with the development of Daoism as an organized religion, that took place during the late second century CE: the Yellow Turbans and the Five Pecks of Rice movement.

The Yellow Turban rebellion of 184 CE took its name from the head-scarves worn by its members. This was a clear dynastic challenge to the Eastern Han, which ruled by the power of Fire and used red regalia in ceremonies; in Five Phase theory, Fire produces Earth, whose color is yellow. Great Peace was the explicit goal of the movement, which worshipped Laozi and the Yellow Emperor in the form of Huang-Lao. The Yellow Turbans, based in Shandong and the eastern Yellow River Plain, was recognized as a threat by the imperial government and suppressed with military force in 185 CE. (General Dong Zhuo, who would become an important figure in the machinations surrounding the demise of the Eastern Han, won imperial favor for his successful campaign against the Yellow Turbans.) But the movement, fragmented but not exterminated, would survive to influence the future course of organized Daoist religion.

The Five Pecks of Rice movement, named for the initiation fee required of those who wished to join, arose in Sichuan, also in the mid-180s CE. There is speculation, but little evidence, that the Yellow Turbans and the Five Pecks of Rice movements were somehow linked; it seems to be the case that they simply coincided in time, perhaps both in response to Daoist utopian ideas that had entered into general circulation by that time. The western movement was led by a charismatic preacher named Zhang Daoling, along with his son Zhang Heng (not the scholar and inventor with a similar name) and his grandson Zhang Lu. The Zhangs referred to themselves as Celestial Masters and founded a lineage of hereditary Daoist supreme masters that continues to the present day. Their main object of worship was Laozi, known as Lord Lao Most High (*Shangqing Laojun*).

The Celestial Masters sect increased its power and influence by developing a hierarchy of clergy, with suitable ordination rituals, and by enrolling in the movement popular temples dedicated to folk religious practices of various kinds and imposing on them the movement's orthodox divinities, sacred texts, and standards of worship. In doing so they were probably influenced by Buddhism, which was busily building temples, ordaining priests and enrolling monks, and translating the sacred scriptures.

The Five Pecks of Rice movement played a political role in the waning years of the Eastern Han, but the main development of Daoism as an organized religion came in the centuries after the Three Kingdoms. Wei Huacun (251–334 CE) left the Celestial Masters sect to establish the Highest Purity (*Shang qing*) sect, based on Mt. Mao (*Mao shan*), near present-day Nanjing. Many new texts were "revealed" by disciples after sexual relationships with female divinities (a liaison depicted as a yearning in *fu* and other Chu-style poems and interpreted as a metaphor for the attention of the emperor by the scholar–official). Tao Hongjing (456–536 CE) built on Wei Huacun's work and edited the sect's new scriptures, including *Declarations of the Perfected* (*Zhengao*). He also worked on standardizing and documenting Daoist meditation, dietary, and alchemical practices, as well as the use of charms and amulets. These ideas would be further developed by Ge Hong (283–343 CE) in the famous work *Master Who Embraces Simplicity* (*Baopu zi*). Over the centuries that followed many commentaries and new texts would be added to the Daoist and Buddhist canons and collected by one emperor or another, depending on their preferences.

The legacy of the Three Kingdoms

The last decades of the Eastern Han and the early years of the Three Kingdoms Period were a time of relentless bloodshed, treachery, and cruelty, a time when conscript soldiers were slaughtered by the thousands and ordinary people died or became refugees by the millions. But the Three Kingdoms Period is not generally remembered in that way. Quite the reverse is true: it is remembered as a time of gallantry and heroism, of loyal friends and honorable enemies, of colorful personalities and clever ingenuity. For centuries the Three Kingdoms Period has been remembered, in China's popular imagination, with admiration and pride.

The principal source for Three Kingdoms history is the *Chronicle of the Three Kingdoms* (*Sanguo zhi*), a sober official account in the tradition of China's official dynastic histories. It recognizes Cao Cao's Wei dynasty as the legitimate successor to the Eastern Han and treats Liu Bei and Sun Quan as unsuccessful would-be claimants of the Mandate. A large number of folkloric tales grew up, however, that gradually changed the way the period was viewed. Heroic figures dominated the imaginations of later writers. The Tang poet Du Fu (712–770 CE) seems to have been sympathetic to Liu Bei's cause and especially fascinated by the figure of Zhuge Liang. The Song dynasty historian Sima Guang (1019–1086 CE) continued to see Wei as the legitimate successor dynasty, but Zhu Xi (1130–1200 CE), not long afterwards, was sympathetic to Liu Bei's claim of legitimacy. The new perception of Liu Bei as the tragic hero of the tale is evident in the dozens of plays and operas of the Yuan dynasty (1271–1368 CE) on Three Kingdoms themes; Zhuge Liang is portrayed as a sage and a master strategist, while Cao Cao and Cao Pi, father-and-son founders of the Wei dynasty, are invariably villains, clad in voluminous black robes and wearing ferocious make-up.

These popular tales and theatrical pieces were turned by the fourteenth century into one of China's most famous premodern novels, the *Romance of the Three Kingdoms* (*Sanguo yanyi*), by Luo Guanzhong. The novel features the heroes Liu Bei, Zhang Fei, and Guan Yu as pledging undying friendship and loyalty. Liu Bei, straightforwardly viewed as the legitimate heir of the Han, is upright but not capable of taking on Cao Cao and Sun Quan by himself; he needs his friends. Zhang Fei is the epitome of courage, while Guan Yu is fearless in battle and a paragon of loyalty and righteousness. (Guan Yu was deified during the Sui dynasty, 589–618 CE, and is still worshipped in Daoist temples as the God of War.) A latecomer to the cause is Zhuge Liang, who becomes a key protector of Liu Bei and his son and heir, Liu Shan. Zhuge Liang is portrayed as a great general and statesman, but, further, is given attributes of the archetypal trickster of folklore, using supernatural abilities to read the stars to escape from threatening circumstances.

The *Romance of the Three Kingdoms* continues to be a source of inspiration to modern Chinese leaders and is the font of a steady stream of movies and television programs featuring scenes from the novel. The noble hero fighting foreign or immoral rulers (for what was in essence the Mandate of Heaven) who threaten the integrity of an imagined Chinese utopia is a persistent political and cultural theme. The ancient world continues to be important in modern China, as leaders and ordinary citizens search the past as the possible source of an ideal model for dealing with the ambiguous, morally complicated present.

Focus: The Ban family

Ban Biao, some of his relatives, and his immediate descendants formed one of the most illustrious families of the first century CE. Several members of the family played diverse and important roles in the history of the Eastern Han dynasty.

The Ban family's roots were in the southern state of Chu, but during the Western Han Period some of its members migrated to the northwestern frontier region, where they became prosperous cattle dealers and gained a close familiarity with the commerce and culture of the Silk Road. The family's fortunes got a boost when one of its young women, known as Lady Ban (c. 48–c. 6 BCE) became one of Emperor Cheng's concubines and was known for her skill as a poet. Her great-nephew, Ban Biao (3–54 CE), a scholar and intellectual, established a reputation as an amateur historian, writing essays commenting upon and proposing corrections to Sima Qian's *Shiji*. He died in 54 CE, and his son Ban Gu (32–92 CE) took up the challenge of completing his father's project of a new history of the Western Han Period. Word of Ban Gu's private historical research reached the court of Emperor Ming in around 60 CE, and Ban Gu was accused of subversion and usurping the prerogatives of the emperor. Ban Gu was arrested, but his twin brother Ban Chao, who was already making himself a favorable reputation as a military man, successfully pleaded for his release. Ban Gu was assigned to work in the imperial library, and in 66 CE was commissioned to write a history of the Western Han dynasty; the private project had become an official undertaking. He devoted the rest of his life to that work, but his life was cut short; he had become a protégé of Dou Xian and, when the latter was removed from office by Emperor He in 91 CE, Ban Gu was among the many members of Dou Xian's entourage to fall with him. He was executed in 92 CE.

Another branch of the family was associated with a growing interest in the classics of Daoism. Ban You (d. 2 BCE), a cousin of Ban Biao, was a scholar in the imperial library during the reign of Emperor Cheng. He acquired a copy of the *Zhuangzi*, which in due time he bequeathed to his son Ban Si. Ban Si became known as an expert in the *Zhuangzi* and a skeptic about the claims made for Confucianism as the basis of a well-ordered society.

Ban Gu's twin brother, Ban Chao (32–102 CE), avoided being swept up in the purge of the Dou clan. He was a military man who spent much of his career on the northwestern frontier and in the oasis cities of Central Asia. An acknowledged expert in what the Chinese called the "western regions," he won a notable victory over the Xiongnu in 91 CE, permanently dislodging them from the Turfan basin area and restoring Chinese influence there. His youngest son, Ban Yong (?–128 CE), inherited his father's position as Superintendent of the Western Regions and further extended Chinese control there, persuading local rulers to make tribute missions to Luoyang and encouraging Chinese settlers to move to garrison farms in the frontier region.

Ban Zhao (49–140 CE), the younger sister of the Ban twins, became one of the most famous female scholars in Chinese history. A poet, writer, astronomer, and mathematician, she completed the *History of the [Former] Han Dynasty* after her brother's death, finishing some of the genealogical tables and writing the treatise on astronomy. Widowed at an early age, she devoted herself to scholarship, writing a number of other works, mostly now lost. She is most widely remembered as the author of *Admonitions for Women* (*Nüjie*), a book that has remained influential down to the present day. Despite her own relative independence as a highly educated female intellectual, in *Admonitions for Women* she advocates a very conservative view of the role of women in society, urging them to be modest, quiet, chaste, and submissive to their husbands. However, she did criticize physical punishment of wives as counterproductive and advocated education for women (to benefit their sons). Living to a very great age, she carried the prestige of the Ban family well into the second century CE.

Focus: Zhang Heng

Zhang Heng (78–139 CE) was a man of extraordinarily broad and fertile interests and accomplishments, the sort of "Renaissance man" that appears only rarely in human history. A mathematician, astronomer, inventor, cartographer, poet, painter, calligrapher, and civil servant, he is regarded in today's China as one of that country's great cultural heroes, a figure who can justifiably be compared to Leonardo da Vinci. He was from a prominent family in the Nanyang region that had played a significant role in the restoration of the Han dynasty and that maintained a rich tradition of scholarship and public service. He studied in Chang'an, and then in the imperial academy at Luoyang, where his mathematical and literary skills attracted attention. After serving in a series of relatively minor official positions he was appointed Chief Astronomer to the imperial court, serving in that position under emperors An and Shun. His duties in that office, which fell under the administration of the Ministry of Rites, were mainly astrological and omenological, involving the interpretation of portents and the selection of auspicious days for imperial activities. He successfully argued against a proposed reform of the calendar in 123 CE; but, although the calendar was not altered, Zhang's strongly stated views may have offended important officials at court. This may explain why he was never promoted to the office of Grand Historian. He thus had a distinguished but somewhat truncated official career, but in any case is better known for his work as an astronomer, inventor, and writer.

As an astronomer Zhang argued correctly that moonlight is reflected sunlight; the moon is dark when its own shadow blocks the sunlight, and brightly lit when it is exposed to the light of the sun. In propounding this view he may have been aided conceptually by the armillary sphere, which modeled a geocentric cosmos in which the earth is orbited by the moon, the sun, and the planets. The armillary sphere had been introduced in China during the Western Han Period, possibly reflecting Greek influence via Central Asia, and would have been well known to Zhang Heng. Zhang is said to have used water-driven gears to turn the armillary sphere into a mechanical model of the cosmos. The details of that device are unclear, however, and it is not certain that it could have accurately imitated the movements of celestial bodies. It is indisputable, however, that Zhang was familiar with water-powered devices and understood the need for constant water pressure to yield accurate results. His addition of an extra outflow vessel to the standard clepsydra (water clock) dramatically improved the device's time-telling accuracy.

Zhang Heng's most famous invention was a seismograph. It consisted of a bronze vessel with eight dragon heads equally spaced around its shoulder, each dragon holding in its mouth a metal ball that could be released to fall into a frog-shaped bell. Inside, it had a bottom-pivoted pendulum and eight spring-loaded triggers, one for each dragon. In the event of a distant earthquake the dragon in the direction of the quake would release its ball to ring the bell, whereupon relief supplies could be dispatched even before word of the quake reached the court. Modern reconstructions of this seismograph have been shown to work satisfactorily.

While Zhang is famed for his inventions, it must be conceded that most of them fall into the category of "ingenious devices" with few practical applications. Later biographers of Zhang rightly lamented that he had never been appointed Minister of Works, a position in which his fertile inventive mind could have achieved more concrete results. One field in which Zhang made an important practical contribution was cartography; he was one of the originators of the grid system of mapping.

In his own lifetime Zhang Heng was famous for his rhyme-prose (*fu*) compositions; he was one of the last masters of that genre. Only a few of his compositions have been preserved. He was also said to have been an artist and calligrapher, although none of his artistic work survives, even in copies, and so it is impossible to know what it looked like. But enough of Zhang's life's work in several different fields is known from contemporary descriptions to be able with confidence to rank him with history's greatest polymath geniuses.

Suggestions for further reading

Chapter 1: Introduction to Ancient China

K. C. Chang and Pingfang Xu, *The Formation of Chinese Civilization: An Archaeological Perspective*. New edition, ed. Sarah Allan. New Haven and London: Yale University Press, 2005.

Rowan K. Flad and Pochan Chen, *Ancient Central China: Centers and Peripheries Along the Yangzi River*. Cambridge and New York: Cambridge University Press, 2013.

James Legge, trans., *The Chinese Classics*. 5 vols in 4. Oxford: Oxford University Press, 1893; reprinted, Hong Kong: Hong Kong University Press, 1960.

Feng Li, *Early China: A Social and Cultural History*. Cambridge and New York: Cambridge University Press, 2013.

Li Liu and Xingcan Chen, *The Archaeology of China: From the Paleolithic to the Early Bronze Age*. Cambridge World Archaeology. Cambridge and New York: Cambridge University Press, 2012.

Michael Loewe and Edward L. Shaughnessy, eds, *The Cambridge History of Ancient China: From the Origins of Civilization to 221 B.C.* Cambridge and New York: Cambridge University Press, 1999.

Gideon Shelach-Lavi, *The Archaeology of Early China: From Prehistory to the Han Dynasty*. Cambridge and New York: Cambridge University Press, 2015.

Denis Twitchett and Michael Loewe, eds, *The Cambridge History of China, Volume One: The Ch'in and Han Empires, 221 B.C.–A.D. 220*. Cambridge and New York: Cambridge University Press, 1986.

Chapter 2: Geography, climate, and the physical setting of Chinese history

Mark Elvin, *The Retreat of the Elephants: An Environmental History of China*. New Haven: Yale University Press, 2006.

Feng Li and David Branner, eds, *Writing & Literacy in Early China*. Seattle: University of Washington Press, 2011.

Katheryn M. Linduff and Yan Sun, eds, *Gender and Chinese Archaeology*. Walnut Creek: Altamira Press, 2004.

J. E. Spencer and William L. Thomas, *Asia East by South: A Cultural Geography*. 2nd edition. New York: John Wiley & Sons, 1971.

Chapter 3: The Neolithic Era and the Jade Age

K. C. Chang, *Early Chinese Civilization: Anthropological Perspectives*. Cambridge, MA: Harvard University Press, 1976.

Elizabeth Childs-Johnson with Gu Fang, *The Jade Age: Early Chinese Jades in American Museums*. Beijing: Science Press, 2009.

Richard C. Francis, *Domesticated: Evolution in a Man-Made World*. New York: W. W. Norton, 2015.

David N. Keightley, ed., *The Origins of Chinese Civilization*. Berkeley: University of California Press, 1983.
Anne P. Underhill, *Craft Production and Social Change in Northern China*. New York and London: Kluwer Academic/Plenum Publishers, 2002.

Chapter 4: The Early Bronze Age

Sarah Allan, *The Heir and the Sage*. San Francisco: Chinese Materials Center, 1981.
Roderick B. Campbell, *Archaeology of the Chinese Bronze Age: From Erlitou to Anyang*. Los Angeles: The Cotsen Institute of Archaeology Press, 2014.
Li Liu and Xingcan Chen, *State Formation in Early China*. London: Duckworth, 2003.
David W. Pankenier, *Astrology and Cosmology in Early China: Conforming Earth to Heaven*. Cambridge and New York: Cambridge University Press, 1913.

Chapter 5: The Shang dynasty

Sarah Allan, *The Shape of the Turtle: Myth, Art, and Cosmos in Early China*. Albany: SUNY Press, 1991.
K. C. Chang, *Shang Civilization*. New Haven and London: Yale University Press, 1980.
David N. Keightley, *The Ancestral Landscape: Time, Space, and Community in Late Shang China, ca. 1200–1045 BC*. Berkeley: Institute for East Asian Studies, 2000.
David N. Keightley, *Sources of Shang History: The Oracle-Bone Inscriptions of Bronze Age China*. Berkeley: University of California Press, 1978.
John Lagerway and Marc Kalinowski, eds, *Early Chinese Religion: Part One: Shang through Han (1250 BC–220 AD)*. 2 vols. Leiden: Brill, 2009.
Ralph D. Sawyer, *Ancient Chinese Warfare*. New York: Basic Books, 2011.
Robert L. Thorp, *China in the Early Bronze Age: Shang Civilization*. Philadelphia: University of Pennsylvania Press, 2006.

Chapter 6: The Western Zhou Period

Constance A. Cook, *Ancestors, Kings, and the Dao*. Cambridge, MA: Harvard University Asia Center, 2017.
Constance A. Cook and Paul R. Goldin, eds, *A Sourcebook of Ancient Chinese Bronze Inscriptions*. Early China Special Monograph Series, Number 7, Berkley: Society for the Study of Early China, 2016.
H. G. Creel, *The Origins of Statecraft in China*. Vol. 1. Chicago: University of Chicago Press, 1970.
Cho-yun Hsu and Kathryn M. Linduff, *Western Chou Civilization*. New Haven: Yale University Press, 1988.
Feng Li, *Bureaucracy and the State in Early China: Governing the Western Zhou*. Cambridge and New York: Cambridge University Press, 2012.
Feng Li, *Landscape and Power in Early China: The Crisis and Fall of the Western Zhou, 1045–771 BC*. Cambridge and New York: Cambridge University Press, 2009.
Edward Shaughnessy, *Sources of Western Zhou History: Inscribed Bronze Vessels*. Berkeley: University of California Press, 1991.

Chapter 7: The Spring and Autumn Period

Lothar von Falkenhausen, *Chinese Society in the Age of Confucius (1000–250 BC): The Archaeological Evidence*. Los Angeles: The Cotsen Institute of Archaeology Press, University of California, Los Angeles Press, 2006.
Cho-yun Hsu, *Ancient China in Transition: An Analysis of Social Mobility, 722–222 BC*. Stanford: Stanford University Press, 1965.

Mark Edward Lewis, *Sanctioned Violence in Early China*. Albany: SUNY Press, 1990.

Yuri Pines, *Foundations of Confucian Thought: Intellectual Life in the Chuniqu Period, 722–453 B.C.E.* Honolulu: University of Hawai'i Press, 2002.

Edward L. Shaughnessy, *Before Confucius: Studies in the Creation of the Chinese Classics*. Albany: SUNY Press, 1997.

Newell Ann Van Auken, *The Commentarial Transformation of the Spring and Autumn*. Albany: SUNY Press, forthcoming.

Arthur Waley, trans., *The Analects of Confucius*. New York: Vintage, 1989.

Arthur Waley, trans., *The Book of Songs: The Ancient Chinese Classic of Poetry*. Edited with additional translations by Joseph R. Allen. New York: Grove Press, 1996.

Burton Watson, trans., *The Tso chuan: Selections from China's Oldest Narrative History*. New York: Columbia, 1989.

Chapter 8: The Warring States Period

Sarah Allan, *Buried Ideas: Legends of Abdication and Ideal Government in Early Chinese Bamboo-Slip Manuscripts*. Albany: SUNY Press, 2015.

Roger T. Ames, *Dao De Jing: A Philosophical Translation*. New York: Ballantine Books, 2003.

Roger T. Ames and Henry Rosemont, Jr., *The Analects of Confucius: A Philosophical Translation*. New York: Ballantine Books, 1999.

Erica Fox Brindley, *Ancient China and the Yue: Perceptions and Identities on the Southern Frontier, c. 400 BCE–50 CE*. Cambridge: Cambridge University Press, 2015.

Erica Fox Brindley, *Music, Cosmology, and the Politics of Harmony in Early China*. Albany: SUNY Press, 2013.

Annping Chin, trans., *Confucius: The Analects*. New York: Penguin Books, 2014.

Constance A. Cook, *Death in Ancient China: The Tale of One Man's Journey*. Leiden: Brill, 2006.

Constance A. Cook and John S. Major, eds, *Defining Chu: Image and Reality in Ancient China*. Honolulu: University of Hawai'i Press, 1999.

Scott Cook, trans., *The Bamboo Texts of Guodian: A Study & Complete Translation*. 2 vols. Ithaca: Cornel University Press, 2012.

James I. Crump, Jr., trans., *Chan kuo ts'e*. Oxford: Clarendon Press, 1970.

A. C. Graham, trans., *Chuang Tzu: The Inner Chapters*. London: George Allen & Unwin, 1981.

A. C. Graham, *Disputers of the Tao: Philosophical Argument in Ancient China*. La Salle, II: Open Court, 1989.

A. C. Graham, *Studies in Chinese Philosophy and Philosophical Literature*. Albany: SUNY Press, 1990.

Eric L. Hutton, trans., *Xunzi: The Complete Text*. Princeton: Princeton University Press, 2014.

Philip J. Ivanhoe and Bryan W. Van Norden, *Readings in Classical Chinese Philosophy*. New York and London: Seven Bridges Press, 2001.

Ian Johnston, trans., *The Mozi: A Complete Translation*. New York: Columbia University Press, 2010.

John Knoblock, trans., *Xunzi: A Translation and Study of the Complete Works*. 3 vols. Stanford: Stanford University Press, 1988.

John Knoblock and Jeffrey Riegel, trans., *Mozi: A Study and Translation of the Ethical and Political Writings*. Chinese Research Monograph 68. University of California, Berkeley: Institute of East Asian Studies, 2013.

Guolong Lai, *Excavating the Afterlife: The Archaeology of Early Chinese Religion*. Seattle: University of Washington Press, 2014.

D. C. Lau, trans., *Mencius*. Harmondsworth: Penguin, 1970.

D. C. Lau, trans., *Tao Te Ching*. Harmondsworth: Penguin, 1963.

D. C. Lau and Roger T. Ames, trans., *Sun Bin: The Art of Warfare: A Translation of the Classic Chinese Work of Philosophy and Strategy*. Albany: SUNY Press, 2003.

Mark Edward Lewis, *Writing and Authority in Early China*. Albany: SUNY Press, 1999.

Margaret J. Pearson, *The Original I Ching: An Authentic Translation of the "Book of Changes" Based on Recent Discoveries*. Tokyo and Rutland: Tuttle, 2011.

Michael J. Puett, *To Become a God: Cosmology, Sacrifice, and Self-Divinization in Early China*. Cambridge, MA: Harvard University Asia Center, 2002.

W. Allyn Rickett, trans., *Guanzi: Political, Economic, and Philosophical Essays from Early China*. 2 vols. Princeton: Princeton University Press, 1985, 1998.

Henry Rosemont, Jr., *A Reader's Companion to the Confucian Analects*. Honolulu: University of Hawai'i Press, 2014.

Harold D. Roth, *Original Tao: Inward Training (Nei-yeh) and the Foundations of Taoist Mysticism*. New York: Columbia University Press, 1999.

Edward L. Shaughnessy, *Unearthing the Changes: Recently Discovered Manuscripts of the Yi Jing (I Ching) and Related Texts*. New York: Columbia University Press, 2014.

Richard J. Smith, *Fathoming the Cosmos and Ordering the World: The Yijing (I Ching, or Classic of Changes) and its Evolution in China*. Charlottesville: University of Virginia Press, 2008.

Richard J. Smith, *The I Ching: A Biography*. Princeton: Princeton University Press, 2012.

Lillian Lan-ying Tseng, *Picturing Heaven in Early China*. Cambridge, MA: Harvard University Press, 2011.

Arthur Waley, *The Analects of Confucius*. New York: Vintage Books, 1989.

Burton Watson, trans., *The Complete Works of Chuang-tzu*. 3rd edition. New York: Columbia University Press, 2003.

Chapter 9: The rise and fall of the Qin dynasty

Anthony J. Barberi-Low and Robin D. S. Yates, *Law, State, and Society in Early Imperial China, A Study with Critical Edition and Translation of the Legal Texts from Zhangjiashan Tomb 247*. 2 vols. Leiden: Brill, 2015.

Derk Bodde, *China's First Unifier: A Study of the Ch'in Dynasty as Seen in the Life of Li Ssû 280?–208 B.C.* Leiden: E. J. Brill, 1938.

J. J. L. Duyvendak, trans., *The Book of Lord Shang: A Classic of the Chinese School of Law*. London: Arthur Probsthain, 1928; reprinted, Chicago: University of Chicago Press, 1963.

Martin Kern, *The Stele Inscriptions of Ch'in Shih-huang: Text and Ritual in Early Imperial Chinese Representation*. New Haven: American Oriental Society, 2000.

John Knoblock and Jeffrey Riegel, trans., *The Annals of Lü Buwei: A Complete Translation and Study [Lüshi chunqiu]*. Stanford: Stanford University Press, 1999.

Lothar Lederhose, *Ten Thousand Things: Module and Mass Production in Chinese Art*. Princeton: Princeton University Press, 2000.

Mark Edward Lewis, *The Early Chinese Empires: Qin and Han*. Cambridge, MA: Belknap Press, 2010.

Yang Liu, ed., *Beyond the First Emperor's Mausoleum: New Perspectives on Qin Art*. Minneapolis: Minneapolis Institute of Arts, 2012.

Yuri Pines, Lothar von Falkenhausen, Gideon Shelach, and Robin D. S. Yates, eds, *Birth of an Empire: The State of Qin Revisited*. New Perspectives on Chinese Culture and Society. Berkeley, University of California Press, Global, Area, and International Archive, 2013.

Ralph D. Sawyer, trans., *The Seven Military Classics of Ancient China*. Boulder, CO: Westview Press, 1993.

Chapter 10: The Western Han dynasty through the reign of Emperor Wu

K. E. Brashier, *Ancestral Memory in Early China*. Cambridge, MA: Harvard University Asia Center, 2011.

Mark Csikszentmihalyi, *Material Virtue: Ethics and the Body in Early China*. Leiden: Brill Press, 2004.

Nicola Di Cosmo, *Ancient China and Its Enemies: The Rise of Nomadic Power in East Asian History*. Cambridge and New York: Cambridge University Press, 2002.

Stephen W. Durrant, *The Cloudy Mirror: Tension and Conflict in the Writings of Sima Qian*. Albany: SUNY Press, 1995.

A. C. Graham, trans., *The Book of Lieh-tzu: A Classic of Tao*. New York: Columbia University Press, 1960.

Donald Harper, trans., *Early Chinese Medical Literature: The Mawangdui Medical Manuscripts*. London and New York: Kegan Paul International Press, 1998.

John B. Henderson, *The Development and Decline of Chinese Cosmology*. New York: Columbia University Press, 1984.

James R. Hightower, trans., *Han Shih Wai Chuan: Han Ying's Illustrations of the Didactic Application of the* Classic of Songs. Harvard-Yenching Institute Monograph Series, Vol. 11. Cambridge, MA: Harvard University Press, 1952.

Bernard Karlgren, *The Book of Documents. Bulletin of the Museum of Far Eastern Antiquities* 22 (1950): 1–81. Reprinted, Göteborg: Elanders, 1950.

David R. Knechtges, *The Han Rhapsody: A Study of the Fu of Yang Hsiung (53 B.C.–A.D. 18)*. Cambridge and New York: Cambridge University Press, 1976.

David R. Knechtges, trans., *Wen Xuan or Selections of Refined Literature*. Vol. 1: *Rhapsodies on Metropolises and Capitals*; Vol. 2: *Rhapsodies on Sacrifices, Hunts, Travel, Palaces and Halls, Rivers and Seas*. Vol. 3: *Rhapsodies on Natural Phenomena, Birds and Animals, Aspirations and Feelings, Sorrowful Laments, Literature, Music, and Passions*. Princeton: Princeton University Press, 1982, 1987, 1996.

Michael Loewe, *Crisis and Conflict in Han China*. London: Allen and Unwin, 1974.

Michael Loewe, *The Government of the Qin and Han Empires, 221 BCE–220 CE*. Indianapolis: Hackett, 2006.

Michael Loewe, *Ways to Paradise: The Chinese Quest for Immortality*. London: Allen and Unwin, 1979.

John S. Major, Sarah A. Queen, Andrew Seth Meyer, and Harold D. Roth, trans., *The Huainanzi: A Guide to the Theory and Practice of Government in Early Han China*. New York: Columbia University Press, 2010.

William J. Nienhauser, ed. and trans., *The Grand Scribe's Records [Shiji]*. 9 vols to date. Bloomington: Indiana University Press, 1994–.

Michael Nylan, *The Five "Confucian" Classics*. New Haven: Yale University Press, 2001.

R. P. Peerenboom, *Law and Morality in Ancient China: The Silk Manuscripts of Huang-Lao*. Albany: SUNY, 1993.

Michèle Pirazzoli-t'Serstevens, *The Han Dynasty*. New York: Rizzoli, 1982.

Sarah A. Queen and John S. Major, trans., *Luxuriant Gems of the Spring and Autumn [Chunqiu fanlu]*. New York: Columbia University Press, 2015.

Clae Waltham, *Shu ching: Book of History. A Modernized Edition of the Translation of James Legge*. Chicago: Henry Regnery, 1971.

Aihe Wang, *Cosmology and Political Culture in Early China*. Cambridge and New York: Cambridge University Press, 2000.

Chapter 11: The Later Western Han and the Wang Mang Interregnum

Anthony J. Barbieri-Low, *Artisans in Early Imperial China*. Seattle: University of Washington Press, 2007.

Essen M. Gale, trans., *Discourses on Salt and Iron: A Debate on State Control of Commerce and Industry in Ancient China*. Leiden: E. J. Brill, 1931.

Anne Behnke Kinney, ed. and trans., *Exemplary Women of Early China: The Lienü zhuan of Liu Xiang*. New York: Columbia University Press, 2014.

Yingshi Yu, *Trade and Expansion in Han China: A Study in the Structure of Sino-Barbarian Economic Relations*. Berkeley: University of California Press, 1967.

Chapter 12: The Han restoration, the Eastern Han dynasty, and the Three Kingdoms Period

Kimberly Besio and Constantine Tung, eds, *Three Kingdoms and Chinese Culture*. Albany: SUNY Press, 2007.

Hans Bielenstein, "The Restoration of the Han Dynasty, with Prolegomena on the Historiography of the *Hou Han Shu.*" *Bulletin of the Museum of Far Eastern Antiquities (Stockholm)*. 4 vols. *BMFEA* 26: 1–209, 1954; 31: 1–287, 1959; 39: 1–198, 1967; 51: 1–300, 1979.

Miranda Brown, *The Politics of Mourning in Early China*. Albany: SUNY, 2007.

Carine Defoort, *The Pheasant Cap Master (He guan zi): A Rhetorical Reading*. Albany: SUNY Press, 1997.

T. J. Hinrichs and Linda L. Barnes, eds, *Chinese Medicine and Healing*. Cambridge, MA: Harvard University Press, 2013.

Terry F. Kleeman, *Celestial Masters: History and Ritual in Early Daoist Communities*. Cambridge, MA: Harvard University Asia Center, 2016.

Martin J. Powers, *Art and Political Expression in Early China*. New Haven: Yale University Press, 1991.

Moss Roberts, trans., *The Romance of the Three Kingdoms*. Berkeley: University of California Press, 1999.

Isabelle Robinet, *Taoist Meditation: The Maoshan Tradition of Great Purity*. Albany: SUNY, 1993.

Erik Zürcher, *The Buddhist Conquest of China*. 3rd edition. Leiden: Brill, 2007.

Index